D0012108

The History of the English Language

The History of the English Language

A source book

David Burnley

Longman
London and New York

Longman Group UK Limited,
Longman House, Burnt Mill, Harlow,
Essex CM20 2JE, England
and Associated Companies throughout the world.

Published in the United States of America
by Longman Publishing, New York

© Longman Group UK Limited 1992

All rights reserved; no part of this publication may be
reproduced, stored in a retrieval system, or transmitted
in any form or by any means, electronic, mechanical,
photocopying, recording, or otherwise without either the
prior written permission of the Publishers or a licence
permitting restricted copying in the United Kingdom issued
by the Copyright Licensing Agency Ltd, 33–34 Alfred Place,
London, WC1E 7DP.

First published 1992

British Library Cataloguing-in-Publication Data
Burnley, David
    The history of the English language: A source book.
    I. Title
    420.9

    ISBN 0–582–02522–2
    ISBN 0–582–02521–4 pbk

Library of Congress Cataloging-in-Publication Data
Burnley, J. D.
    The history of the English language: a source book / David
Burnley.
    p.   cm.
    Includes bibliographical references and index.
    ISBN 0–582–02522–2 — ISBN 0–582–02521–4 (pbk.)
    1. English language—History—Sources. 2. English language—Old
English, ca. 450–1100—Texts. 3. English language—Middle English,
1100–1500—Texts. 4. English language—Early modern, 1500–1700-
-Texts. 5. English language—Dialects—Texts. I. Title.
PE1075.5.B87   1992
420.9—dc20
                                                                    91–2521
                                                                       CIP

Set in 10/12pt Times Roman

Produced by Longman Singapore Publishers (Pte) Ltd.
Printed in Singapore

Contents

List of Plates

Acknowledgements

We are indebted to the following for permission to reproduce copyright material: Oxford and Cambridge University Presses for extracts from *New English Bible*, Second Edition © 1970; the Bodleian Library, University of Oxford for MS. Junius 1, fol. 70v (The *Ormulum*) and MS. Hatton 20, fol. 1v (*Cura Pastoralis*); the Master and Fellows of Corpus Christi College, Cambridge for MS. 61, fol. 27r (*Troilus and Criseyde*); The John Rylands University Library of Manchester for Caxton's *The Fayt of Arms and of Chyvalrye*, fols. 141r and 141v; The University of Sheffield Library for the first two pages from the first edition of Milton's *Paradise Lost* Book IX.

Preface

A source book does not try to usurp the role of a fully
explanatory and discursive history of the language, nor replace
the information and advice which can be offered to the student
by a teacher. It seeks only to make conveniently available to
students and teachers alike a resource which can be used to
illustrate the development, and something of the variety, of the
English language used in Britain through nearly thirteen
centuries.

A variety of purposes and levels of competence among the
users of this book is foreseen. Some very early dialect texts and
classics of philological investigation (such as the *Ormulum* or
Ancrene Wisse) are included, and the provision of a proportion of
rhymed verse permits rhyme analysis. But the translation of
earlier texts, and some marginal glossing, is intended to make
analysis of the linguistic features of these texts more practicable
for those whose purposes do not demand a reading knowledge of
the earliest stages of the language.

The overall structure of the book sustains the consensus view
of the development of the language through successive historical
periods towards the goal of present-day standard English. Thus,
apart from one letter from King James VI of Scotland, Scottish
texts have not been included, since they are considered to belong
to a distinct and specialised development. The progress of
English is outlined in brief introductions to the texts of each
period, as well as illustrated in chronologically contrasted and
parallel passages from the Bible, situated in the final section of
the book. Despite this arrangement, the main collection of texts
facilitates an alternative view, which emphasises the stylistic and
dialectal complexity of English and acknowledges the importance
of variation in linguistic change. Among the possible topics which
might be developed in using this collection are the relationship

between dialect speech and the standard at various periods, and its social implications; the influence upon English of foreign languages; the occurrence of colloquial expression in writing; or the characteristics of Latin-based prose. The selection of particular types of writing from a range of periods permits the exploration of certain pathways through the history of English: scientific writings, from Ælfric to Darwin; the continuing art of letter writing; or the development of the language of a particular region. Attitudes to, and the understanding of, language from the fourteenth to the nineteenth centuries forms a connected theme, which emerges in the later selections in scholarly discussion of the study of language in general, and of English in particular. Lexicography, from an anonymous fourteenth-century concordance to Johnson and the editors of the *Oxford English Dictionary*, is particularly well represented.

Unless otherwise stated in the introduction to the text, excerpts of medieval origin have modern capitalisation and punctuation, and apart from æ, þ, and ð in Old English, and these with the addition of ʒ in Middle English, modern letter-forms are used. Abbreviations have been silently expanded. Later texts reproduce the spelling and punctuation of the originals, but with modern letter-forms. Facsimiles of some texts, manuscript and printed, are provided in order to demonstrate features of orthography and text presentation which cannot be appreciated from printed versions.

I gratefully acknowledge the assistance I have received from the staff of the British Library, the Lambeth Palace Library, and the Imperial War Museum. My thanks are due in particular to the Keeper of Western Manuscripts, the Bodleian Library, for permission to reproduce MSS Junius 1 and Hatton 20; to the Librarian and Fellows of Corpus Christi College, Cambridge, for MS 61; the Librarian, the John Rylands University Library, Manchester, for the facsimile of Caxton's *Fayttes of Armes*; and the Librarian, Sheffield University Library, for the facsimile of Milton's *Paradise Lost*. I am grateful also to Mrs D.J. Finch for permission to print the letter of Private D.J. Sweeney and to Mrs Katherine Cleasby-Thompson for those of Captain Ainslie Douglas Talbot.

Without the willingness of colleagues in Sheffield to offer helpful advice and to cover during a term's study leave, of my students cheerfully to adopt the role of guinea pigs for some of the texts incorporated, and my wife and children to deliver coffee to the keyboard, the preparation of this book would have been much less pleasurable and much longer delayed. I should like to record my appreciation of them all.

JDB
University of Sheffield
September 1990

Abbreviations

AN	Anglo-Norman
BL	British Library
EDD	*English Dialect Dictionary*
EM	East Midland
EModE	Early Modern English
Fr.	French
CUL	Cambridge University Library
ME	Middle English
MED	Middle English Dictionary
Lat.	Latin
MDu	Middle Dutch
MLG	Middle Low German
MS	Manuscript
MSS	Manuscripts
OE	Old English
OED	*Oxford English Dictionary*
OF	Old French
ON	Old Norse
WM	West Midland
OSc	Old Scandinavian
Sp.	Spanish
WS	West Saxon

Chronology

Ruler		Historical events	Literary events
	400	Withdrawal of Roman forces (410)	
		Anglo-Saxon Settlement commences	
Legendary King Arthur	500	Last Roman Emperor deposed (476)	
	600	Conversion of Kent to Christianity (597)	
Edwin, King of Northumbria (616–33)		Conversion of Northumbria (625)	
Penda, King of Mercia (626–55)		Sutton Hoo ship burial (635)	
	700		Cædmon's Hymn
Offa, King of Mercia (757–96)	800	Danish raids commence (787)	
Alfred the Great, of Wessex (871–99)	900	Dane-law established (886)	Anglo-Saxon Chronicle begun
		Unification of England	
Æthelstan (924–40)			*Brunanburh*

Rulers	Events	Literary Works
Ethelred the Unready (978–1016)		West Saxon Gospels
		Battle of Maldon
	1000 Death of Ælfric (1010)	
Cnut (1017–35)		
Danish Rule (1017–42)		
Edward the Confessor (1042–66)		
William I (1066–87)		
William II (1087–1100)	**1100** Norman Conquest (1066)	
Henry I (1100–1135)		
		Peterborough Chronicle ends
Stephen (1135–54)	Oxford University established (1167)	*Ormulum*
Henry II (1154–89)		
Richard I (1189–99)	**1200** Loss of Normandy (1204)	
John (1199–1216)		
Henry III (1216–72)	Arrival of the Friars (1221)	*Ancrene Wisse*
Edward I (1272–1307)	**1300** Annexation of Wales (1277)	
Edward II (1307–27)		
Edward III (1327–77)	Statute of Pleading (1362)	
Richard II (1377–99)	**1400**	Wycliffite Bible
Henry IV (1399–1413)		*Canterbury Tales*
Henry V (1413–22)	Loss of Gascony (1453)	
Henry VI (1422–61)		

Monarchs	Events	Literature
Edward IV (1461–83)	Wars of the Roses (1455–85)	Skelton
Edward V (1483)/Richard III (1483–85)	Introduction of printing (1476)	Tyndale's Bible
Henry VII (1485–1509)	Discovery of America (1492)	
Henry VIII (1509–47)	**1500**	
Edward VI (1547–53)/Mary (1553–58)	Dissolution of the Monasteries (1536–9)	
Elizabeth I (1558–1603)	Loss of Calais (1558)	
James I (1603–25)	East India Co founded (1600)	A. V. of Bible (1611)
	Union with Scotland (1603)	Shakespeare First Folio (1623)
	First American colonies	
	1600	
Charles I (1625–49)		*Paradise Lost* (1667)
The Commonwealth (1649–60)		
Charles II (1660–85)		
James II (1685–88)		
William (1689–1702) and Mary (1689–94)		
Anne (1702–14)	**1700**	*Newton's Opticks* (1704)
George I (1714–27)		*Rape of the Lock* (1714)
George II (1727–60)		
George III (1760–1820)		*Johnson's Dictionary* (1755)
	American Declaration of Independence (1776)	
	First Australian colonies	
	1800	
George IV (1820–30)	First passenger railway (1830)	
William IV (1830–37)		*Pickwick Papers*
Victoria (1837–1901)	India under Crown rule (1858)	
	Primary Education Act (1870)	
		New English Dictionary (1884)

D. H. Lawrence

New English Bible

1900   First petrol-driven car (1885)
Earliest aircraft (1903)
First public radio broadcast (1906)
First World War (1914–18)

Edward VII (1901–10)
George V (1910–37)

George VI (1937–53)
Elizabeth II

Old English (700–1100)

Old English, and Anglo-Saxon, are names used by modern scholars for the written version of a language used in England from the departure of the Romans until some time after the Norman Conquest. Its speakers referred to it as *Englisc*, the language of the Angles, who were the major ethnic group consistently identified among the Germanic settlers of Britain in early sources. These people must have spoken a language closely similar to that used by other Germanic peoples along the North Sea coast from Denmark to the Rhine, but in a period of some seven centuries following the earliest settlement their language underwent major developments. Direct written evidence of these is available only from the last four hundred years of this evolution, and indeed the vast majority of our information about Old English is preserved in manuscripts written in the tenth and eleventh centuries. Apart from the runic alphabet, which had been used in earlier Germanic society for inscriptions on all kinds of objects, from weapons to standing stones, the earliest speakers of English, despite artistic skills evident in archaeological discoveries like those at Sutton Hoo and from Kentish cemeteries, were both pagan and illiterate. The coming of Christianity in AD 597 introduced Latin literacy to England, which was followed by attempts to render the English language in the letters of the Latin alphabet – those which survive to the present day. Old English forms of the Latin letters in the Hiberno-Saxon script were very different from modern printed forms, as can be seen in the case of the ‹s› and ‹r› in the facsimile (p. 18), and in addition Old English used some letters no longer found in English: 'eth' ‹ð› and 'yogh' ‹ȝ› (the latter printed as g in modern editions) were derived from Irish Latin, 'thorn' ‹þ› and 'wynn' were runes (the latter printed as w in modern editions), and the Latin digraph 'ash' ‹æ›. Thorn and eth are equivalent to ‹th› in the modern spelling system, and indeed ‹th› is not unknown in early Old English. The letters ‹v› and ‹z› were not normally used in Old English texts, and their roles were filled respectively by ‹f› and ‹s›.

The scribes who wrote the manuscripts which are our only source of information about Old English lived in various parts of England and wrote a version of the language which they spoke every day. Consequently OE manuscripts, especially from the earlier period, preserve evidence of dialectal variation in the pronunciation and grammar of the language. Modern scholars (Campbell 1969:1–22) have distinguished several groupings: West Saxon (the language of King Alfred and England south of the Thames but excluding Kent) is distinct from non-West Saxon, which includes both Kentish and Anglian. Anglian is in turn divided into Northumbrian (spoken from the Humber to the Forth) and Mercian in the Midlands. No distinct evidence survives for the languages of Sussex, Essex or East Anglia, and an unrelated Celtic language, closer to Welsh, was spoken until quite late in the Lake District, the Welsh marches, and the British kingdom of Elmet close to Leeds in the old West Riding of Yorkshire. After about AD 975, as the result of West Saxon domination of the rest of the country, a degree of standardisation emanating from Winchester is to be found in Old English documents. This means that the vast majority of surviving Old English literature, which post-dates this standardisation, is written in Late West Saxon. The excerpts in this book illustrate something of both the variety of dialects and the West Saxon standard.

By comparison with Modern English, Old English was written relatively 'phonetically'. Consequently, when reading, each letter is individually sounded, even double consonants and those occurring in initial consonant clusters, as in ‹hring›, ‹hlaford›, ‹writan›, ‹gnornian› and ‹cniht›. Vowels, because of the origins of the spelling system, had a similar value to that in Latin or modern European languages. The group ‹sc› was pronounced as modern ‹sh›, ‹cg› as the consonantal sounds in *judge*, and ‹c› in the environment of a front vowel (*æ, e, i, y*) as modern ‹ch›. Following a front vowel ‹h› was pronounced very much as the ‹ch› in German *nicht*, and following a back vowel like the ‹ch› in Scots *loch*. The ‹ʒ› (usually written g in modern editions) was pronounced as modern ‹g›, except initially before most front vowels, where its pronunciation was like modern ‹y-›. In medial or final position, it had the value of the ‹g› in modern German ‹sagen›.

Like German, Old English possessed a complex inflexional grammar. The Nominal Group exhibited concord (agreement) between the article, modifier and head for number, gender and case. There were four cases (nominative, accusative, genitive and dative) and three genders (masculine, feminine and neuter). Traces of dual number and of instrumental case existed in the personal pronouns and definite article respectively. Nouns possessed distinct sets of inflexional endings, by which they can be classified as Strong or Weak nouns. In addition, according to the syntactical environment, any adjective could adopt a set of either Indefinite or Definite (Strong or Weak) inflexions. The declension of three characteristic Strong nouns together with the appropriate forms of the definite article and the Definite form of the adjective is given here.

Masculine noun ('the long day')

	Singular	*Plural*
Nom.	se langa dæg	þā langan dagas
Acc.	þone langan dæg	þā langan dagas
Gen.	þæs langan dæges	þāra langena daga
Dat.	þæm langan dæge	þæm langum dagum

Neuter noun ('the distant land')

	Singular	*Plural*
Nom.	þæt feorre land	þā feorran land
Acc.	þæt feorre land	þā feorran land
Gen.	þæs feorran landes	þāra feorrena landa
Dat.	þæm feorran lande	þæm feorrum landum

Feminine noun ('the old learning')

	Singular	*Plural*
Nom.	sēo ealde lār	þā ealdan lāra/e
Acc.	þā ealdan lāre	þā ealdan lāra/e
Gen.	þære ealdan lāre	þāra ealdena lāra
Dat.	þære ealdan lāre	þæm ealdum lārum

Similar paradigms for Weak nouns preceded by an Indefinite adjective after the indefinite article are these:

Masculine noun ('a bold warrior')

	Singular	Plural
Nom.	ān beald wiga	bealde wigan
Acc.	ānne bealdne wigan	bealde wigan
Gen.	ānes bealdes wigan	bealdra wigena
Dat.	ānum bealdum wigan	bealdum wigum

Neuter noun ('a blind eye')

	Singular	Plural
Nom.	an blind ēage	blind ēagan
Acc.	an blind ēage	blind ēagan
Gen.	anes blindes ēagan	blindra ēagena
Dat.	anum blindum ēagan	blindum ēagum

Feminine noun ('a young lady')

	Singular	Plural
Nom.	ān geong hlǣfdige	geonga/e hlǣfdigan
Acc.	āne geonge hlǣfdigan	geonga/e hlǣfdigan
Gen.	ānre geongre hlǣfdigan	geongra hlǣfdigena
Dat.	ānre geongre hlǣfdigan	geongum hlǣfdigum.

Verbs also fell into Strong or Weak types. The former indicated their preterite tense by a change in the root vowel, the latter by the addition of a dental suffix to the stem, thus *scinan, scan*, 'shine, shone' and *lufian, lufode*, 'love, loved'. New verbs were formed only on the pattern of the Weak conjugation, joining Weak Class 2 verbs, which are distinguished by an infinitive in *-ian* rather than *-an*, a present participle in *-iende* rather than *-ende*, and preterite and past participle forms with *-od-* rather than *-ed-*. All verbs marked their past participle by the use of a prefix *ge-*.

Like other languages, Old English expanded its vocabulary by means of external borrowing. Some of its wordstock can be traced to ancient borrowing from Latin in the centuries before the migration of the Germanic tribes to England: *strǣt* ‹strata via, 'paved road'; *weall* ‹vallum, 'stockade'; *win* ‹vinum, 'wine'; *gimm* ‹gemma, 'gem'; *dihte* ‹dictare, 'to order'; *mynster* ‹monasterium. Other words derive from the later Latin of the Church and of learning: *æstel* ‹?hastula, 'little spear'; *fers* ‹versus, 'verse-line';

stær ‹Irish *stoir* from Latin *historia*. More important than its borrowing, Old English, like German, made much use of compounding and derivation in the creation of new wordforms. Thus the word *ealdorbiscop*, literally 'chief-bishop', is used by the translator of Bede's *Ecclesiastical History* to render the Latin *primus pontificum*, and Ælfric uses the form *leorningcniht*, 'learning-servant/boy', for 'disciple', and *hēahfæder*, literally 'high-father', for 'patriarch'. Full use was also made of derivational affixes, so that the Latin *trinitas* is rendered *þrȳnes*, *ascensio*, *ūpāstignes*, and *incarnatio*, *menniscnes*.

Anglo-Saxon literature, which flourished largely under religious auspices but which still preserved a strong interest in heroic values, made fullest use of creative compounding. Poetic compounds for 'sea' include *swanrād*, 'swanroad' and *hwælrād*, 'whaleroad' as well as the quasi-compounds *ȳða ful*, 'cup of the waves' and *ganetes bæð*, 'gannet's bath'. Metaphoric and metonymic expressions, which congregate around certain familiar themes of Old English poetry, such as seafaring, warfare and weapons, are matched by groups of synonyms related to the same themes. Thus the words *beorn*, *scealc*, *freca*, *guma*, *wiga*, *hæleþ*, *eorl*, *gar·berend*, *hyse*, and *rinc* may all be translated as 'warrior'. Groups of synonyms and ready compounding could function together to suggest fresh compounds; thus the unparalleled *wælfeld*, 'slaughter-field, battle field', in *Brunanburh* must have been suggested by one of the seventy or so other compounds with the same first element, probably by its synonym, *wælstōw*. In poetry, compounds are often formed for connotational rather than denotational effect; thus compounds with *morgen*, 'morning', and with *ceald*, 'cold', tend to carry connotations of doom only loosely connected with their everyday meanings, and both *eald*, 'old', and *ær*, 'before', may have strongly approbatory associations. Both groups of synonyms and lexical creativity were encouraged by the nature of the verse, which consisted of two half-lines (a and b) connected by an alliterative pattern.

Frequently, the meaning of a word or phrase in the first pair of half-lines would be summed up in variant wording by a half of the succeeding line. Both the existence of a stock of synonyms commencing with different letters, and the possibility of creating new ones by compounding and derivation are obviously of great convenience to this feature of the discourse structure of Old English verse.

Đā þǣr Byrhtnoð ongan   beornas trymian,
rād and rǣdde,   rincum tǣhte.

Then Byrhtnoth began to draw up the warriors there, rode about and instructed, directed the warriors.

Approximately 30,000 lines of verse are still extant, but this quantity is greatly exceeded by extant prose. This includes legal and administrative texts such as charters, wills, writs and codes of law, religious writings such as sermons and devotional works, both translated from the Latin and original, histories and annals, and works intended to be of a practical instructional nature in secular as well as religious matters. The excerpts included in this collection can give no more than a taste of the richness which survives.

1 *Dialect texts*

These two texts are included in order to give more advanced students the opportunity to investigate something of the regional variety of the language preserved in Old English sources. Both are also illustrative of the origins of later linguistic developments. The Lindisfarne Gospel gloss in particular demonstrates inflectional changes associated with Middle English already in progress; the Vespasian Psalter gloss demonstrates continuity within dialects, showing affinities with the language of the Middle English *Ancrene Wisse*.

Dictionaries were uncommon in an age when books had to be copied by hand, and English–Latin dictionaries of any size were not available until the fifteenth century. Consequently, readers tended to ease the demands made upon their linguistic competence by inserting the English equivalents above the Latin words of the text. This practice is called 'glossing' (‹Lat. *glosa*; cf. *OED gloze*), a word whose semantic development is instructive. In the following excerpts, for convenience, the relative positions of Latin texts and Anglo-Saxon glosses have been reversed.

A   The Vespasian Psalter gloss

The Vespasian Psalter (British Library MS Cotton Vespasian A.I) contains the psalms in a Latin version (known as the Roman version) which preceded Jerome's Vulgate Bible, nine canticles and three hymns as well as prayers and some liturgical material. It is a luxury work produced on good-quality vellum with considerable richness of decoration. Whoever ordered its production intended it for the altar or cathedral treasury rather than the library, but exact details of its origin are unknown. Its modern history begins with a reference by Matthew Parker in 1566 and its acquisition by Sir Robert Cotton in 1599. Beyond this, there has been some scholarly controversy, but an early fifteenth-century account of its ancient treasures by a monk of the abbey of St Augustine's, Canterbury, contains the description of a book, alleged to have been brought by St Augustine, which has been identified as the Vespasian Psalter. The current consensus is that the Latin manuscript was produced in Canterbury in the first half of the eighth century. At some time in the ninth century an English interlinear gloss was added to the Latin text of the original, not apparently by a local man but by someone who had received training in a Mercian scriptorium and so wrote consistently in a Mercian dialect. Parallels with the language of the ME *Ancrene Wisse* are taken to suggest a West Mercian origin.

Excerpt (i) is the apocryphal Psalm 151, added in the MS as an afterthought to the original total; excerpt (ii) is one of the nine canticles.

These excerpts share with the Lindisfarne Gospel gloss many features common to Anglian texts, for example: the failure of breaking before l-groups (*befalden*; *swalwan*; *alle*); smoothing of diphthongs before sounds written *c*, *g* or *h* either alone or with *r* or *l* intervening (*betwih*; *smēgu*; *ēgan*); the writing of the *i*-mutation of ō as ōē (*fōedde*) and -*ad* rather than -*od* in the past participles of Weak Class 2 verbs (*welgelīcad*; *gehefeldad*). Some features, however, are more characteristic of Mercian alone, for example: forms lacking diphthongisation by preceding palatal consonants (*scēp*, *gēra*), and above all the Mercian 'second fronting' of short *æ* to *e* and short *a* to *æ* (the preceding two and *wes*; *segde*; *cweð*; *daega*).

(i)

Pusillus   eram   inter   frater   meos   et   adolescentior
Lytel   ic   wes   betwih   brōður   mīne   ond   iu[n]gra

in domo patris mei pascebam oves patris mei manus meae
in hūse feadur mīnes ic fōēdde scēp feadur mīnes. Honda mīne

fecerunt   organum;   digiti   mei   aptaverunt   psalterium   et
dydun   organan;   fingras   mīne   wysctun   hearpan.   Ond

quis adnuntiavit Domino meo? ipse Dominus, ipse omnium
hwelc   segde   Dryhtne   mīnum?   Hē   Dryhten,   hē   allra

exaudivit me; ipse misit angelum suum, et tulit me de ovibus
5   gehērde mec; hē sende engel his, ond nōm mec of scēpum

patris   mei,   et   unxit   me   in   misericordia   unctionis
feadur mīnes, ond smirede mec in mildheartnisse smirenisse

suae fratres mei boni et magni, et non fuit beneplacitum in
his brōur mīne gōde ond micle, ond ne wes welgelīcad in

eis   Domino.   exivi   obviam   alienigenae,   et
him Dryhtne. Ic ūtēode ongegn fremes cynnes men, ond

maledixit   me   in   simulacris   suis;   ego   autem
wergcweodelade mec in hergum heara; ic sōðlīce

evaginato   ab   eo   ipsius   gladio   amputavi   caput   ejus,
10 gebrogdnum from him his āgnum sweorde ic ācearf hēafud his

et   abstuli   obprobrium   de   filiis   Israhel.
ond onweg āfirde edwīt of bearnum Israēla.

(ii)

Ego dixi in dimedio dierum meorum: vadam ad portas
Ic cweð in midum daega mīnra: ic fearu tō gete

inferi quaesivi residuum annorum meorum; dixi: non videbo
helle. Ic sōhte lāfe gēra mīnra; ic cweð: ic ne gesīo

Dominum Deum in terra viventium non aspiciam hominem
ultra
Dryhten God in eoran lifgendra. Ne gelōciu ic mon
māē

et habitatorem quievit generatio mea; ablata est, et
15 ond eardiend. Gestilde cnēoris mīn; wilāēded is, ond

convoluta est a me quasi tabernaculum pastorum praecisa
befalden is from mē swē swē geteld heorda. Forcorfen

est velut a texente vita mea; dum adhuc
is swē swē from ðǣm weofendan līf mīn; mit te nū gēt

ordirer succidit me de mane usque ad vesperam finies
gehefeldad ācearf mec. Of marne oð ēfen geendas

me; a vespere usque ad mane quasi leo sic contrivit
mec; from ēfenne oð margen swē swē lēa swē fordrǣste

omnia ossa mea; de mane usque ad vesperam finies me sicut
20 all bān mīn; of marne ot ēfen geendas mec. Swē swē

pullus hirundinis sic clamabo; meditabor ut columba
brid swalwan swē ic cleopiu; ic smēgu swē swē culfre.

adtenuati sunt oculi mei aspicientes in excelso Domine, vim
Geðynnade sind ēgan mīn gelōcende in heanis. Dryhten, nēd

patior; responde pro me, quid dicam, aut quid
ic ðrōwiu ondsweora fore mē hwet ic cweðe oððe hwet

respondebit mihi quod ipse fecerim recogitabo omnes annos
ondsweora🖝 mē ðæt ic seo[l]fa dōa. Ic ðencu all gēr

meos in amaritudine animae meae. Domine, si sic vivitur,
25 mīn in bitternisse sāwle mīnre. Dryhten, gif swē bi lifd,

aut in talibus vita spiritus mei, corripies me, et
oððe in weolerum līf gāstes mīnes, geðrēas mec, ond

vivicabis me. ecce in pace amaritudo mea amarissima;
gelīffestes mec. Sehðe, in sibbe bitternis mīn sīe bittreste;

tu autem eruisti animam meam, ut non perirem et
ðū sōðlīce generedes sāwle mīne, ðet ic ne forwurde. Ond

projectisti post tergum tuum omnia peccata mea, quia
āwurpe on bec ðīnne alle synne mīne, forðon

non infernus confitebitur tibi, neque mors laudabit te.
30 nales hel ondette ē, ne dēa here ec.

non expectabunt qui descendunt in lacum veritatem tuam;
Ne bīdað ðā ofdūne steogun in sēað sōðfestnisse ðīne;

vivens vivens ipse confitebitur tibi, sicut et ego hodie.
lifgende, lifgende hē onddetteð ðē, swē ond ic tō dege.

pater filiis notam faciet veritatem tuam. Domine salvos
Feder bearnum cūðe dōð sōðfestnisse ðīne. Dryhten, hāle

nos fac; et psalmus nostros cantabimus cunctis diebus vitae
ūs dōa; ond salmas ūre wē singað allum degum līfes

nostrae in domo Domini.
35 ūres in hūse Dryhtnes.

Notes

6 **smirede mec** 'anointed me'　The verb (WS *smierwan*) exhibits
the lack of breaking characteristic of Anglian texts (also *afirde* in line
11. The pronoun form (WS *mē*) is characteristically Anglian and
archaic, but is found in WS verse and inscriptions such as that on the
Alfred Jewel, which reads 'Ælfred mec hēht gewyrcan'.

9 **wergcweodelade** 'cursed' (WS **weargcwedolian*)　Anglian dialectal features are evident in almost every syllable. *Werg-*, like
hergum in the same line, shows Anglian smoothing of the diphthong
ea. The preterite formed with *-ad* rather than *-od* is characteristic of

Anglian Weak Class 2 verbs. The form *cweodel* has a diphthong derived from the back mutation of *e* by an earlier back vowel in the second syllable. Back mutation of *e* occurred in West Saxon only when labial or lateral consonants intervened.

heara (WS *hiera*)   A form created by analogy with the second-fronted then back-mutated demonstrative form *þeara*, also found in *VP*. Compare the *ha* forms of the plural pronoun in the *Ancrene Wisse*.

12 **dæga** (WS *daga*)   Second fronting of short *æ* to *e* and of short *a* to *æ* is a phenomenon peculiar among the Anglian dialects to the language of the Vespasian Psalter gloss. It is called 'second' by counting the similar development of Germanic short *a* to OE short *æ* as the first example of such fronting. It did not take place before *l*. Other examples are: *cweð* (12); *hwet* (23); *bec* (29). The forms *gete* (WS *geate*) and *gēr* (WS *gēar*, lines 12, 13) are derived from the second fronting of an *æ* surviving by the lack of diphthongisation by the preceding palatal *g* characteristic of the Mercian dialect.

14 **gelōciu ic**   The first-person present tense form of the Weak Class 2 verb *gelōcian*. The *-u* inflexional ending is characteristic of earlier Anglian texts.

21 **ic cleopiu**   A back-mutated form with the Anglian *-u* ending. Notice the use of the present tense to render the Latin future, as also *ic ðencu* (24) and *hereð* (30).

34 **degum**   The expected form would be *dægum*, with second fronting of the *a* restored before back vowels in all dialects. This form must be an analogical development from the regular singular *deg*.

B The Lindisfarne Gospel gloss

With the possible exception of the Bewcastle Cross, the Lindisfarne Gospels (BL Cotton Nero D IV) are the most imposing physical monument of pre-Conquest Northumbrian culture. A tenth-century note on folio 259 records that the book was written by Eadfrith, bishop of Lindisfarne from 698 to 721. Since the monastery of Lindisfarne had been founded by Aidan, a member of the Celtic Church, the manuscript shows many points of contact with the Irish artistic tradition. In its decoration and writing it closely resembles the Irish Book of Kells, but there are also similarities in effect between its pages of carpet-like decoration and the Anglo-Saxon garnet and gold jewellery from Sutton Hoo.

The monastery on Lindisfarne was vulnerable to attack and in 875 the monks were forced to desert their home under the pressure of Danish raids. They carried with them the relics of St

Cuthbert, and their famous Gospels. From 883 until their settlement in Durham in 995 the Lindisfarne community lived in Chester-le-Street, a few miles away, and it was probably here that one of their number inserted an interlinear English gloss above the Latin text. This gloss furnishes one of the most important sources extant for the study of the Northumbrian dialect in Old English.

This late Northumbrian text already exhibits significant divergence in its inflexional system from the more familiar WS forms. Loss of final *-n* is common in verb infinitives (*efneglæda*; *sealla*; *dōa*) (see Early ME, p. 63) and Weak adjectives (*seista*), and the second-person singular and third-person singular and plural of present-tense verbs is frequently written *-es* or *-as* (*stondes gē*; *ðū efnes*; *hēa gebiddas*; *hīa wōenas*). Other characteristically Northumbrian features are: ‹a› written before *r* where WS has *ea* (*arð*); confusion of *ea* and *eo* (*feolo*, *geade*); frequent use of *-o* to represent a final unstressed vowel (*oðero*; *idlo*; *willo*); and the writing of ‹oe› where WS has *e* by *i*-mutation of *o* (*fōerde*; *cuoe*; *gedōenendo*) and between *w* and *r* (*woercmenn*).

(i)

Simile   est   enim   regnum   caelorum   homini   patrifamilias
Gelīc is forðon rīc heofna ðæm menn fador hīerodes

qui   exiit   primo   mane   conducere   operarios   in
sē ðe fōerde ærist *vel* ār in merne efneglæda ðā woercmenn in

vineam   suam.   Conventione   autem   facta   cum
wīngeard his. Gesomnung uutetlice gewearð mið ðæm

operariis   ex denario diurno   misit
wyrcendum *vel* woercmonnum of penning dæghuæmlīce, sende
eos
his

in vineam.   Et egressus circa horam tertiam vidit alios
5 in wīngeard. And gefōerde ymb tīd ðȳ ðirdda gesæh ōðero

stantes   in   foro   otiosus.   Et   illis   dixit:
standende in sprēc *vel* in ðingstōw idlo. And ðæm cueð:

Ite et vos in vineam et quod iustum fuerit dabo vobis.
Gāað and gīe in wīngeard and þætte reht bið ic selo īuh.

Illi autem abierunt. Iterum autem exiit circa sextam
Ðā uutetlice geēodon. Eftsōna sōðlice geēode ymb ðā seista

et nonam horam et fecit similiter. Circa undecimam vero
and nōn tīd and dyde gelīc. Ymb ðā ellefta ēc

exiit et invenit alios stantes et dicit illis: Quid
10 geēade and gemōette ōðero stondende and cuoeð him: Hwæt

hic statis tota die otiosi. Dicunt ei: Quia nemo
hēr stondes gē allen dæge idlo. Cuōēdun him: forðon nænig

nos conduxit. Dicit illis: Ite et vos in vineam.
monn ūsig efne gelæde. Cuoeð him: Gāað and gīe in wīngeard.

Cum sero autem factum esset dicit
Mið ðȳ efern *vel* ic sædi uutetlice geworden wēre cuoeð

dominus vineae procuratori suo: Voca operarios et
hlāfard ðære wīngearde girōēfæ his: Cēig ðā wercmenn and

redde illis mercedem incipiens a novissimis usque ad
15 geld him meard ongann from ðæm lætmēstum wið ðæm

primos. Cum venissent ergo qui circa undecimam
forðmēstum. Mið ðȳ gecuōmun uutetlice ðā ðe ymb ðā ællefta

horam venerant acceperunt singulos denarios. Venientes
tīd gecuōmon onfengon suindrigo penningas. Cymende

autem et primi arbitrati sunt quod plus essent
uutetlice and forðmēsto gedōēmendo wēron þæt forðor wēron

accepturi acceperunt autem et ipsi singulos
onfengendo onfengon uutetlice *vel* ēc and ðā ilco syndrige

denarios et accipientes murmurabant
20 penningas and mið ðȳ gefengon hīa huæstredon *vel* deglice

adversus patremfamilias dicentes: Hi novissimi
yfle sprēcon wið ðæm hīorodes cuoðendo: ðās hlætmēsto

una hora fecerunt et pares
ān tīd *vel* huīl dydon *vel* worohton and ðū efnes *vel* gelīco

illos nobis fecisti qui portavimus pondus
ðā ūs ðū dydest wē ðā ðe bēron hefegnise *vel* byrðen

diei et aestus. At ille respondens uni eorum
ðæs ðæges and hæto *vel* byrn. Sōð hē onduearde ānum hiora

dixit: Amice non facio tibi injuriam
25 cueð: Lā frēond *vel* lā mēg ne dōm ic ðē laæðo *vel*

nonne   ex   denario   convenisti   mecum.   tolle   quod
baeligniso āhne for pennig ðū cuōme mec mið. Nim þætte

tuum   est   et   vade   volo   autem   et   huic
ðīn is and gāa *vel* geong. Ic willo uutetlice and ðissum

novissimo dare sicut et tibi. aut non licet mihi quod
hlætmēsto sealla swā and ðē; *vel* ne is rehtlīc mē þæt

volo facere an oculus tuus nequam est quia ego bonus
ic willo dōa *vel* ēgo ðīn wōhgfull is forðon ic gōd

sum.   Sic   erunt   novissimi   primi   et   primi
30 am. Suæ bīðon ðā hlætmēsto forðmēst and ðā forðmēst

novissimi.   multi   sunt   enim   vocati   pauci   autem
hlætmēst. Monige sint forðon gecēigdo lythwon uutetlice

electi.
gecoren

(ii)

Orantes   *autem nolite*
Hēa gebiddas *vel* ðon gīe gebiddas uutetlice nallas gē

multum   *loqui   sicut   ethnici   faciunt   putant*
feolo *vel* monigful gesprēca suæ esuico dōas; hē wōēnas

enim   quod   in   multiloquio   suo   exaudiantur.
35 forðon ðā ðe in monigfald sprēc his bīðon gehēred.

Nolite   ergo   assimilari   eis   scit   enim   Pater   vester
Nallas gē ðonne wosa gelīc him wāt forðon fader īurre

quibus   opus   sit   vobis   ante   quam   petatis   eum.
of ðǣm ðearf sīe *vel* is īuh ǣr ðon gīe bidde hine.

Sic ergo   vos orabitis:
Suē ðonne īuih gīe bidde:

Pater   noster   qui   es   in   caelis
fader ūsær ðū arð *vel* ðū bist in heofnum *vel* in

sanctificetur nomen tuum. Adveniat regnum tuum.
40 heofnas, sīe gehālgad noma ðīn. Tōcȳmeð rīc ðīn.

Fiat voluntas tua sicut in caelo et in terra. Panem
Sīe willo ðīn suæ is in heofne and in eorðo. Hlāf

nostrum super substantiale da nobis hodie. Et demitte
ūserne ofer pīstlic sel ūs todæg, and forgef

nobis debita nostra sicut nos dimittimus debitoribus
ūs scylda ūsra, suǣ uōē forgefon scyldgum

nostris. Et ne inducas nos in temtationem. Sed libera
ūsum. And ne inlǣd ūsih in costunge, ah gefrīg

nos a malo.
45 ūsich from yfle.

Si enim dimiseritis hominibus peccata eorum
Gif forðon gīe forgēafas monnum synna hiara,

dimittet et vobis Pater vester caelestis delicta vestra.
forgefes and oc īuh fader īuer heofonlic synna īuerra.

Si autem non dimiseritis hominibus nec Pater
Gif sōðlice gīe nalles forgeafa monnum, ne fader

vester dimittet peccata vestra.
īuerre forgefes synna īuerre.

Notes

2 **in merne** (WS *in morgne*) This late form exhibits *i*-mutation of *o* and simplification of the following consonant group.

5 **gesǣh** (WS *gesēah*) An example of Anglian smoothing.

6 **sprēc** (WS *sprǣc*) WS *ǣ*[1] is represented in Anglian texts by *e*.
   in ðingstow Final -*e* is omitted in this dative form.

7 **þætte** A contracted form of the relative *þæt þe*.
   ic selo The present tense form is used to render a Latin future, as is usual in OE.

11 **allen dæge** (WS *eallum dæge*) The Northumbrian spelling suggests uncertainty in the form of the inflection.

14 **hlāfard ðǣre wīngearde girōēfæ his** This phrase is a good example of the inflectional confusion already apparent in tenth-century Northumbrian. A WS version would read *hlāford ðǣs wīngeardes gerēfan his*, 'the lord of the vineyard to his reeve'. Here *wīngeard* is a Strong and *gerēfa* a Weak masculine noun. In this text, *wingeard* seems to be considered Strong feminine, and *gerēfa*, having lost its final -*n*, is treated as though it were also a Strong noun. Final -*æ* is found in inflections in early Northumbrian texts, but here probably represents orthographical confusion between *æ* and *e*.

20 **hīa** Northumbrian form of the WS *hīe*, 'they'. As also *hēa* (33).

35 **bīðon** (WS *beōð* – *bið* sing.) The Northumbrian plural is evidently formed by analogy with the plural *sindon* of the verb *wesan*.

36 **wosa** (WS *wesan*) This form, with back mutation by *a* and rounding after *w*, is characteristically Northumbrian.

39 **ūsǣr** (WS *ūre*)   The Northumbrian form is restricted to verse in WS. Other characteristically Northumbrian personal pronoun forms are *ūsih/ūsich* (44/45) and *īuh* (7). The form *mec* (26) is used more widely in Anglian texts, but is restricted to verse in WS.

in heofnum *vel* **in heofnas**   The glossator offers a choice of dative or accusative forms to render the Latin ablative.

47 **oc**   The use of *oc*, apparently without the sense 'but', and simply as an additive conjunction, is extremely rare in OE and may imply the influence of Scandinavian *ok*.

2 Alfred's Preface to the Pastoral Care

King Alfred the Great succeeded to the throne of Wessex at a time of acute danger from Danish invasion, but by a combination of military tactics and diplomacy related in the *Anglo-Saxon Chronicle* and Asser's *Life of Alfred*, he succeeded in making his kingdom sufficiently secure to devote time during his last decade to his own education and that of his people. He himself learned to read at the age of thirty-eight, and with the aid of scholars assembled from both home and abroad, he sought to make available in English those Latin texts which he judged to be of greatest educational advantage. Six major Latin works were translated into English in the course of this educational initiative, including Bede's *Ecclesiastical History of the English People* and Boethius's *Consolation of Philosophy*, later translated also by Chaucer and Queen Elizabeth I.

The *Cura Pastoralis* of Gregory the Great, a work of guidance for holders of ecclesiastical office, was one of those books which King Alfred judged it 'most necessary' for the clergy of his kingdom to know. It had the additional attraction that its author had been the pope who had, in 597, sent St Augustine to bring Christianity to England. At the beginning of his translation Alfred placed a prefatory letter in which he explains the circumstances in which his decision was made and canvasses the collaboration of the reader in his educational plans. There is general agreement that this preface represents Alfred's own composition.

The translation of the *Pastoral Care* was produced in multiple copies for distribution to the various dioceses, and survives today in half a dozen manuscripts, two of which date from the king's lifetime. The excerpt is based on the better preserved of these, Bodleian Lib Hatton 20, a manuscript which Alfred sent to his old friend Bishop Wærferð of Worcester. That it remained in Worcester after the Anglo-Saxon period is proved by the early thirteenth-century glosses, largely in Latin, added by a Worcester scribe whose work is recognisable by his characteristically tremulous handwriting. The manuscript was introduced to scholarship by Joscelyn and Parker in the late sixteenth-century.

This excerpt represents the WS language of the last decade of the ninth-century: Early West Saxon of the kind found also in the Parker MS of the *Anglo-Saxon Chronicle* from its beginning until

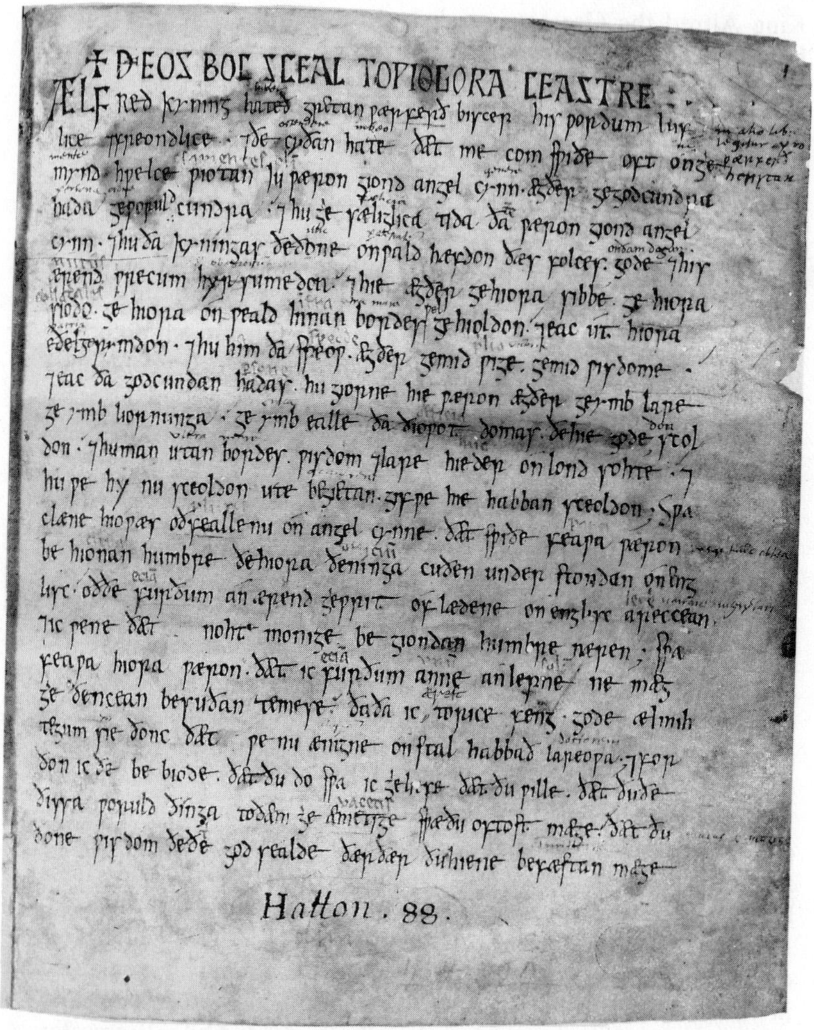

Plate 1 *Cura Pastoralis*, fol. 1v

the entry for 924. The most striking indicator of the early state of the language in this text is its use of ‹io› alongside ‹eo› spellings and its full and correct use of grammatical inflexions.

The facsimile illustrates the opening page of the text, with the direction to Worcester written in insular half-uncials at the head. Half-uncials are a display script derived on the continent from the uncial script (cf Latin *uncia* 'an inch') favoured for legal and schoolbooks. The main text is a rather untidy Hiberno-Saxon script, whose character set, although based on the Latin alphabet, has been adapted for use in England. Note the use of long *s*, and of long *r* and long *f*, as well as the rune 'wynn' for *w* in *wærferð*. The Irish Latin form of *g* (yogh) is used and the derivation of *ð* 'eth' from insular *d* is apparent. The digraph *æ* is also used. Capitalisation is not used for punctuation purposes, except for capital short *s* forms to commence clauses. Nevertheless, a fairly complex punctuation system marks three degrees of pause between clauses. There are no abbreviations except for the use of the Tironian sign for 'and', and an acute accent is sometimes used (especially over the vowel in *on*) perhaps to indicate that the pronunciation should receive some degree of stress. In line 5, the form *woruld*, originally lacked its *d*, and was marked for correction by a triangle of three dots. The word *furðum* in lines 16 and 18 has the Latin gloss *etiam* added in the tremulous hand of the thirteenth-century Worcester annotator.

Ælfred kyning hāteð grētan Wǣrferð biscep his wordum luflīce
ond frēondlīce; ond ðē cȳðan hāte ðæt mē cōm swīðe oft on
gemynd, hwelce wiotan iū wǣron giond Angelcynn, ǣgðer ge
godcundra hāda ge woruldcundra; ond hū gesǣliglica tīda ðā
5 wǣron giond Angelcynn; ond hū ðā kyningas ðe ðone onwald
hæfdon ðæs folces Gode ond his ǣrendwrecum hīersumedon;
ond hīe ǣgðer ge hiora sibbe ge hiora siodu ge hiora onweald
innanbordes gehīoldon, ond ēac ūt hiora ēðel rȳmdon; ond hū
him ðā spēow ǣgðer ge mid wīge ge mid wīsdōme; ond ēac ðā
10 godcundan hādas, hū giorne hīe wǣron ǣgðer ge ymb lāre ge
ymb liornunga, ge ymb ealle ðā ðīowotdōmas ðe hīe Gode
dōn scoldon; ond hū man ūtanbordes wīsdōm ond lāre hieder
on lond sōhte; ond hū wē hīe nū sceoldon ūte begietan, gif wē
hīe habban sceoldon. Swǣ clǣne hīo wæs oðfeallenu on
15 Angelcynne ðæt swīðe fēawa wǣron behionan Humbre ðe
hiora ðēninga cūðen understondan on Englisc oððe furðum
ān ǣrendgewrit of Lǣdene on Englisc āreccean; ond ic wēne
ðætte nōht monige begiondan Humbre nǣren. Swǣ fēawa
hiora wǣron ðæt ic furðum ānne ānlēpne ne mæg geðencean
20 be sūðan Temese ðā ðā ic tō rīce fēng. Gode ælmihtegum sīe
ðonc ðætte wē nū ǣnigne onstal habbað lārēowa. Ond for ðon
ic ðē bebīode ðæt ðū dō swǣ ic gelīefe ðæt ðū wille, ðæt ðū ðē
ðissa woruldðinga tō ðǣm geǣmetige, swǣ ðū oftost mæge,
ðæt ðū ðone wīsdōm ðe ðē God sealde ðǣr ðǣr ðū hiene
25 befæstan mæge, befæste. Geðenc hwelc wītu ūs ðā becōmon for
ðisse worulde, ðā ðā wē hit nōhwæðer ne selfe ne lufodon, ne ēac
ōðrum monnum ne lēfdon; ðone naman ǣnne wē lufodon ðætte
wē Crīstne wǣren, ond swīðe fēawa ðā ðēawas.
Ðā ic ðā ðis eall gemunde, ðā gemunde ic ēac hū ic geseah, ǣr
30 ðǣm ðe hit eall forhergod wǣre ond forbærned, hū ðā ciricean
giond eall Angelcynn stōdon māðma ond bōca gefylda, ond ēac
micel mengeo Godes ðīowa; ond ðā swīðe lȳtle fiorme ðāra bōca
wiston, for ðǣm ðe hīe hiora nānwuht ongietan ne meahton,
for ðǣm ðe hīe nǣron on hiora āgen geðīode āwritene. Swelce
35 hīe cwǣden: 'Ūre ieldran, ðā ðe ðās stōwa ǣr hīoldon, hīe
lufodon wīsdōm, ond ðurh ðone hīe begēaton welan ond ūs
lǣfdon. Hēr mon mæg gīet gesīon hiora swæð, ac wē him ne
cunnon æfter spyrigean. Ond for ðǣm wē habbað nū ǣgðer
forlǣten ge ðone welan ge ðone wīsdōm, for ðǣm ðe wē
40 noldon tō ðǣm spore mid ūre mōde onlūtan.'
Ðā ic ðā ðis eall gemunde, ðā wundrade ic swīðe swīðe ðāra
gōdena wiotena ðe giū wǣron giond Angelcynn, ond ðā bēc
ealla be fullan geliornod hæfdon, ðæt hīe hiora ðā nǣnne dǣl
noldon on hiora āgen geðīode wendan. Ac ic ðā sōna eft mē

King Alfred sends in cordial and amicable style greeting to his bishop Wærferð; and I cause you to know that it often comes into my mind what learned men there once were throughout England, both religious and laymen; and how blessed a time it was then throughout England; and how the kings who had rule over the people obeyed God and his messengers; and how they maintained both their peace, morality and control within, and also expanded their realm externally; and how they were successful then in both war and counsel; and also the religious people, how zealous they were in both teaching and learning, and concerning all the services that they had to render to God; and how from abroad they came here into this land seeking wisdom and instruction, and how we now have to get them from abroad, if we must have them. So completely was learning fallen away in England that there were very few on this side of the Humber who could understand their divine services in English or translate even a letter from Latin into English; and I think that there were not many beyond the Humber. There were so few of them that I cannot think of even a single one south of the Thames when I succeeded to the kingdom. Thanks be to almighty God that we now have any supply of teachers. And therefore I command that you do as I believe you wish, that you disengage yourself as often as you can from worldly affairs to the end that you apply the wisdom that God gave you wherever you can apply it. Think what punishments then came upon us on account of this world, when we neither loved it for itself nor passed it on to other men; we loved alone the name that we were Christians, and very few [of us loved] the practices.

When I remembered all this, then I remembered too how I saw, before it was all ravaged and burned, how the churches throughout the whole of England were full of books and of treasures, and also a great host of God's servants; but they had very little benefit from the books because they could not understand anything of them because they were not written in their own language. It is as if they had said 'Our forefathers who had these places before us loved wisdom, and through it they acquired riches and bequeathed them to us. Their track may still be seen here, but we do not know how to follow it. And so now we have relinquished both the wealth and the wisdom, because we did not wish to bend with our mind to that trail.'

When I remembered all this then I wondered very greatly at the good scholars who were once throughout England, and who had entirely learned all those books, that they had not

45 selfum andwyrde, ond cwæð: 'Hīe ne wēndon ðætte ǣfre
menn sceolden swǣ reccelēase weorðan ond sīo lār oðfeallan:
for ðǣre wilnunga hīe hit forlēton, ond woldon ðæt hēr ðȳ
māra wīsdōm on londe wǣre ðȳ wē mā geðēoda cūðon.'

Ðā gemunde ic hū sīo ǣ wæs ǣrest on Ebriscgeðīode funden,
50 ond eft, ðā hīe Crēacas geliornodon, ðā wendon hīe hīe on heora
āgen geðīode ealle, ond ēac ealle ōðre bēc. Ond eft Lǣdenware
swǣ same, siððan hīe hīe geliornodon, hīe hīe wendon ealla
ðurh wīse wealhstodas on hiora āgen geðīode. Ond ēac ealla
ōðra Crīstna ðīoda sumne dæl hiora on hiora āgen geðīode
55 wendon. Forðȳ mē ðyncð betre, gif īow swǣ ðyncð, ðæt wē ēac
sume bēc, ðā ðe nīedbeðearfosta sīen eallum monnum tō
wiotonne, ðæt wē ðā on ðæt geðīode wenden ðe wē ealle
gecnāwan mǣgen, ond gedōn, swǣ wē swīðe ēaðe magon mid
Godes fultume, gif wē ðā stilnesse habbað, ðætte eall sīo gioguð
60 ðe nū is on Angelcynne frīora monna, ðāra ðe ðā spēda hæbben
ðæt hīe ðǣm befēolan mǣgen, sīen tō liornunga oðfæste, ðā
hwīle ðe hīe tō nānre ōðerre note ne mǣgen, oð ðone first ðe hīe
wel cunnen Englisc gewrit ārǣdan. Lǣre mon siððan furður on
Lǣdengeðīode ðā ðe mon furðor lǣren wille ond tō hīerran hāde
65 dōn wille.

Ðā ic ðā gemunde hū sīo lār Lǣdengeðīodes ǣr ðissum āfeallen
wæs giond Angelcynn, ond ðēah monige cūðon Englisc gewrit
ārǣdan, ðā ongan ic ongemang ōðrum mislicum ond manig-
fealdum bisgum ðisses kynerīces ðā bōc wendan on Englisc ðe is
70 genemned on Lǣden *Pastoralis*, ond on Englisc 'Hierdebōc',
hwīlum word be worde, hwīlum andgit of andgiete, swǣ swǣ ic
hīe geliornode æt Plegmunde mīnum ærcebiscepe, ond æt
Assere mīnum biscepe, ond æt Grimbolde mīnum mæsseprīoste,
ond æt Iōhanne mīnum mæsseprēoste. Siððan ic hīe ðā geliornod
75 hæfde, swǣ swǣ ic hīe forstōd, ond swǣ ic hīe andgitfullīcost
āreccean meahte, ic hīe on Englisc āwende; ond tō ælcum
biscepstōle on mīnum rīce wille āne onsendan; ond on ælcre bið
ān æstel, se bið on fiftegum mancessa. Ond ic bebīode on Godes
naman ðæt nān mon ðone æstel from ðǣre bēc ne dō, ne ðā bōc
80 from ðǣm mynstre uncūð hū longe ðǣr swǣ gelǣrede biscepas
sīen, swǣ swǣ nū, Gode ðonc, welhwǣr siendon. Forðȳ ic wolde
ðætte hīe ealneg æt ðǣre stōwe wǣren, būton se biscep hīe mid
him habban wille, oððe hīo hwǣr tō lǣne sīe, oððe hwā ōðre bī
wrīte.

wished to translate any part of them into their own language. But then I soon answered myself and said: 'They did not believe that ever men should be so careless and teaching fall away so: they neglected it deliberately, intending that there should be the more wisdom in the land the more languages that we knew.'

Then I remembered how the Law was first found in the Hebrew language, and afterwards, when the Greeks learned it, they turned it all into their own language, and also all the other books. And similarly the Romans, after they had learned it, turned it all through skilled translators into their own tongue. And also all other Christian people have changed some part of it into their own language. Therefore it seems to me better, if it seems so to you, that we also turn some books – those that are most necessary for all men to know – into that language which we all may understand, and cause, as we very easily may with God's help [and] if we have peace, that all the free-born young people that are now in England, among those who have the means to apply themselves, should be set to learning, as long as they are competent for no other employment, until they know well how to read English writing. Let a man afterwards learn deeper in the Latin language when he desires to learn more and to achieve a higher office.

When I remembered how before this the teaching of the Latin language had so fallen away throughout England, although many knew how to read English writing, then, among the other various and manifold concerns of this kingdom, I began to translate into English the book which is called *Pastoralis* in Latin, and in English 'Shepherd-book', at times word for word, at times sense for sense, as I learned it from Plegmund my archbishop, and from Asser my bishop, and from Grimbold my priest, and from John my priest. After I had learned it, and as I understood it, and most meaningfully might interpret it, I turned it into English; and I intend to send one to each diocese in my kingdom; and in each will be a pointer which will be worth fifty mancuses. And I command in God's name that no man should take the pointer from the book, nor the book from the monastery – [it is] unknown how long there may be such learned bishops as now, thanks to God, there are everywhere. Therefore I have desired that they always remain at that place, unless the bishop wishes to have them with him, or it [the book] is on loan somewhere, or someone is making a copy of it.

Notes

1–2 **hāte grētan Wǣrfer biscep** ... **ond ē cȳan hāte** 'commands Bishop Wærferð to be greeted and I order you to be informed'   This greetings formula is close to that found in contemporary writs.

12–13 **man** ... **sōhte** 'people ... sought'   *Man* is frequently used in OE as an indefinite pronoun, and may often be translated 'they' or rendered by a passive construction.

18 **nǣren**   A contracted negative form of the subjunctive (*ne* + *wǣren*). The subjunctive is required by the implicit hypothesis in the verb *wēnan*. Cf. *cwǣden* (35) and *sceolden* (46).

24 **ðone wīsdōm** ... **hiene**   The noun *wīsdōm* is masculine, and therefore requires the masculine accusative *hiene*. In line 26, however, natural gender asserts itself, and the neuter accusative *hit* refers to *wīsdōm*.

25 **hwelc wītu us ða becōmon** 'what punishments then came upon us'   The reference is probably to the Scandinavian invasions. Medieval commentators habitually regard national misfortune as divine retribution.

30 **eall forhergod** ... **ond forbærned**   The *for-* prefix, which is etymologically related to Latin *per-*, carries an implication of intensification and often of ruination. Compare its use in the excerpt from the *Peterborough Chronicle*.

47–48 **ðȳ māra wīsdōm** ... **ðȳ wē mā**   This correlative construction employing the instrumental case of the definite article is quite common. Literally 'by that much more wisdom . . . by that much we knew more about languages'.

55–63 The construction of this sentence is somewhat tortuous, involving many embedded and dependent clauses. Its structure can best be indicated by a table.

```
FORÐȲ mē ðyncð [gif īow swǣ ðyncð]
        ðæt wē ēac sume bēc [ðā ðe niedbeðearfosta . . .]
        ðæt wē ðā on ðæt geðīode wenden . . . . . .
OND gedōn [swǣ wē swīðe ēaðe magon . . . . . . . . .]
        ðætte eall sīo gioguð [ðāra ðe ðā spēda . . .]
                sīen tō liornunga oðfæste
            ðā hwīle ðe . . . . . .
            oð ðone first . . . .
```

Note the quasi-causative use of *gedōn* and the use of inflected forms of the demonstrative pronoun as a clause connective: *frīora manna . . . ðāra ðe.*

72–74 **Plegmunde** ... **Assere** ... **Grimbolde** ... **Iohanne**   All are scholars whom Alfred attracted to Wessex to aid in his work of cultural reconstruction. Plegmund was of Mercian origin and became Archbishop of Canterbury in 890; Asser was a Welshman who wrote a Latin biography of Alfred; Grimbold came from France; John was from Saxony and became abbot of Athelney, Somerset.

78 **æstel**   The word has been derived from Latin *hastula*, 'little spear', and is thought on the evidence of glosses to mean a pointer to be used in reading. Its value is great. Fifty mancuses was the legal value of fifty oxen or three hundred sheep. It has been suggested that the 'Alfred Jewel', discovered at Athelney but now in the Ashmolean Museum, Oxford, once adorned an *æstel*. The word *mancus* is a rare Arabic borrowing into OE.

3   Cædmon

The account of how a cow-herd received poetic skills through divine intervention is given in Bede's *Historia Ecclesiastica*, where Bede asserts that Cædmon was the first to write religious poetry in English, and quotes the sense of this first poem 'but not the order of the words', since this cannot be rendered in Latin. Many manuscripts, however, quote the English version of what has become known as Cædmon's Hymn. The verbal ordering to which Bede referred is worth noticing, for it is generally characteristic of OE verse style. The line is divided syntactically and metrically into two halves, linked by alliteration. There is no rhyme. Within the structure of the line, a sense of balance arises from the two half-lines, and the subject matter unfolds in a partially repetitive way. Semantically related words and phrases are balanced against one another creating the characteristic effect of parallelism of sense and structure with variation in expression. This results in a solemn and portentous manner appropriate to the subject matter.

Both Bede (673–735) and Cædmon were Northumbrians. The former spent his entire life after the age of seven in the monastery at Jarrow on Tyne, but achieved scholarly eminence throughout Western Europe. Cædmon's biography is unknown, but he was attached as a lay brother to the the monastery of Abbess Hild in Whitby, so that the miraculous events described in the excerpt must have taken place during her abbacy, that is, between 657 and 680.

As a scholar, Bede wrote exclusively in Latin, and the earliest texts of his *Ecclesiastical History* are Latin ones. The version of Cædmon's Hymn given in the earliest Latin manuscript (CUL MS Kk. 5. 16) is written in the Northumbrian dialect and dates from a very few years after Bede's death. It reads as follows.

Nu scylun hergan   hefænricæs uard
metudæs maecti   end his modgidanc
uerc uuldurfadur   sue he uundra gihuaes
eci dryctin   or astelidæ
he aerist scop   aelda barnum
heben til hrofe   haleg scepen
tha middungeard   moncynnæs uard
eci dryctin   æfter tiadæ
firum foldu   frea allmectig

The version in the excerpt below differs considerably from this, both because it is much later and because it is written in West Saxon rather than the original Northumbrian. Bede's work, like Gregory's *Pastoral Care*, was one of those selected for translation into English as part of King Alfred's educational initiatives at the close of the ninth century. The work was in fact done by Mercian translators employed by the king, but in the manuscript upon which the following text is based (Bodleian Library MS Tanner 10) considerable West Saxonisation has taken place. Nevertheless, the pairing of near synonyms (*gemæred ond geweorðad*; *halette ond grette*) and some Anglian forms – *-ad(e)* preterite and past participle inflections; *neten* (70); *gehwerfde* (71); *wreoton* (73) *gemde* (84) – may still testify to their work.

In ðeosse abbudissan mynstre wæs sum brōðor syndriglīce mid godcundre gife gemæred ond geweorðad, for þon hē gewunade gerisenlice lēoð wyrcan, þā ðe tō æfæstnisse ond tō ārfæstnisse belumpen, swā ðætte, swā hwæt swā hē of
5 godcundum stafum þurh bōceras geleornode, þæt hē æfter medmiclum fæce in scopgereorde mid þā mæstan swētnisse ond inbryrdnisse geglængde ond in Engliscgereorde wel geworht forþbrōhte. Ond for his lēoþsongum monigra monna mōd oft tō worulde forhogdnisse ond tō geþēodnisse þæs heofonlican līfes
10 onbærnde wæron. Ond ēac swelce monige ōðre æfter him in Ongelþēode ongunnon æfæste lēoð wyrcan; ac nænig hwæðre him þæt gelīce dōn meahte, for þon hē nales from monnum ne þurh mon gelæred wæs, þæt hē þone lēoðcræft leornade, ac hē wæs godcundlīce gefultumed ond þurh Godes gife þone
15 songcræft onfēng. Ond hē for ðon næfre nōht lēasunge ne īdles lēoþes wyrcan meahte, ac efne þā ān þā ðe tō æfæstnesse belumpon, ond his þā æfestan tungan gedafenode singan.
    Wæs hē se mon in weoruldhāde geseted oð þā tīde þe hē wæs gelȳfdre ylde, ond hē næfre nænig lēoð geleornade. Ond hē for
20 þon oft in gebēorscipe, þonne þær wæs blisse intinga gedēmed, þæt hēo ealle sceolden þurh endebyrdnesse be hearpan singan, þonne hē geseah þā hearpan him nēalēcan, þonne ārās hē for scome from þæm symble ond hām ēode tō his hūse. Þā hē þæt þā sumre tīde dyde, þæt hē forlēt þæt hūs þæs gebēorscipes ond ūt
25 wæs gongende tō nēata scipene, þāra heord him wæs þære neahte beboden, þā hē ðā þær in gelimplicre tīde his leomu on reste gesette ond onslēpte, þā stōd him sum mon æt þurh swefn ond hine hālette ond grētte ond hine be his noman nemnde:

In this abbess's monastery was a certain brother outstandingly honoured and made famous by divine grace, because he was accustomed to compose suitable songs such as pertained to religion and piety, so that, whatever he learned of religious literature from scholars, after a short space of time he brought that forth well wrought in the English tongue and in poetic language adorned with the greatest sweetness and inspiration. And through his songs the spirits of many men were often kindled with contempt for the world and desire for association with the heavenly life. And also many like him among the English nation afterwards began to compose religious poetry; but none could do it like him, because he was not instructed by a man nor through men, so that he learned that poetic skill, but he was divinely aided and through the grace of God received the power of poetry. And therefore he could never make a fictional or unprofitable poem, but those alone which pertained to religion, and which befitted that pious tongue of his to sing.

He was, this man, settled in the worldly estate until the time when he was of advanced age, and he had never learned any poetry. And because of that, often at a party, when there was considered to be an occasion for celebration, so that they all in order had to sing to the harp, whenever he saw the harp draw near him, he got up in embarrassment from the feast and went home to his house. When he did that on one particular occasion, left the house with the party and went out to the cattle shed (whose care was entrusted to him that night) and at the appointed time he laid down his limbs in

'Cedmon, sing mē hwæthwugu.' Þā ondswarede hē ond cwæð:
30 'Ne con ic nōht singan; ond ic for þon of þeossum gebēorscipe ūt
ēode, ond hider gewāt, for þon ic nāht singan ne cūðe.' Eft hē
cwæð, se ðe mid hine sprecende wæs: 'Hwæðre þū meaht mē
singan.' Þā cwæð hē: 'Hwæt sceal ic singan?' Cwæð hē: 'Sing mē
frumsceaft.' Þā hē ðā þās andsware onfēng, þā ongon hē sōna
35 singan in herenesse Godes Scyppendes þā fers ond þā word þe
hē næfre gehȳrde, þāra endebyrdnes þis is:

Nū wē sculon herigean   heofonrīces Weard,
Meotodes meahte   ond his mōdgeþanc,
weorc Wuldorfæder,   swā hē wundra gehwæs,
40 ēce Drihten,   ōr onstealde.
Hē ærest sceōp   eoran bearnum
heofon tō hrōfe,   hālig Scyppend.
ā middangeard   monncynnes Weard,
ēce Drihten,   æfter tēode
45 firum foldan,   Frēa ælmihtig.

Þā ārās hē from þæm slæpe, ond eal þā þe hē slæpende song
fæste in gemynde hæfde, ond þæm wordum sōna monig word in
þæt ilce gemet Gode wyrðes songes tōgeþēodde. Þā cōm hē on
morgenne tō þæm tūngerēfan, þe his ealdormon wæs; sægde him
50 hwylce gife hē onfēng. Ond hē hine sōna tō þære abbudissan
gelædde ond hire þā cȳðde ond sægde. Þā hēht hēo gesomnian
ealle þā gelæredestan men ond þā leorneras, ond him
ondweardum hēt secgan þæt swefn ond þæt lēoð singan, þæt
ealra heora dōme gecoren wære, hwæt oððe hwonon þæt
55 cuman wære. Þā wæs him eallum gesegen, swā swā hit wæs,
þæt him wære from Drihtne sylfum heofonlic gifu forgifen. Þā
rehton hēo him ond sægdon sum hālig spell ond godcundre lāre
word; bebudon him þā, gif hē meahte, þæt hē in swinsunge
lēoþsonges þæt gehwyrfde. Þā hē ðā hæfde þā wīsan onfongen,
60 þā ēode hē hām tō his hūse, and cwōm eft on morgenne, ond
þȳ betstan lēoðe geglenged him āsong ond āgeaf þæt
him beboden wæs.

Þā ongan sēo abbudisse clyppan ond lufigean þā
Godes gife in þæm men; ond hēo hine þā monade ond lærde
65 þæt hē woruldhād ānforlēte ond munuchād onfēnge; ond hē
þæt wel þafode. Ond hēo hine in þæt mynster onfēng mid his
gōdum, ond hine geþēodde tō gesomnunge þāra Godes þēowa,
ond hēht hine læran þæt getæl þæs hālgan stæres ond spelles.
Ond hē eal þā hē in gehȳrnesse geleornian meahte mid hine
70 gemyndgade, ond swā swā clæne nēten eodorcende in þæt
swēteste lēoð gehwerfde. Ond his song ond his lēoð wæron

rest and fell asleep, then there stood before him a certain man in a dream and he hailed him and greeted him and called him by his name: 'Cedmon, sing me something.' And he answered and said: 'I don't know how to sing; and that's why I went out from this party, and came away here, because I didn't know how to sing.' Again, he who was speaking with him said: 'Nevertheless you can sing for me.' Then he said: 'What have I to sing?' He said 'Sing to me about the creation.' When he had received this reply, he began to sing at once lines and words in praise of God the Creator which he had never heard before, their order is this:

> Now we have to praise the guardian of the heavenly kingdom, the power and the conception of the creator, the deeds of the father of glory, as he, the eternal lord, established the beginning of every wonder. He, the holy creator, first shaped heaven as a roof for men on earth. Then mankind's guardian, almighty and eternal lord, afterwards adorned the fields for men.

Then he arose from that sleep and all those things that he had sung in his sleep he had fixed in memory, and quickly he added to those words many words in the same metre of song dear to God. Then in the morning he came to the estate overseer, who was his superior; he told him what a gift he had received. And he immediately led him to the abbess and told and revealed those things to her. Then she commanded all the most learned men and scholars to be gathered and ordered him to tell the dream and sing the verse before them, so that it might be discerned by the opinion of all of them, what that gift was and where it had come from. Then it was apparent to them all, just as was indeed the case, that the heavenly gift had been bestowed on him by the Lord himself. Then they told and recounted to him a holy story and words of religious teaching; they instructed him then, if he could, that he should turn it into the harmony of poetry. When he had received it in that manner, he went home to his house, and came back in the morning, and sang to them, giving back what had been dictated to him adorned with the finest poetry.

Then the abbess embraced and esteemed the grace of God in the man; and she admonished him and advised him that he should give up the secular world and take up the monastic life; and he readily consented to that. And she received him into the monastery with his goods, and affiliated him to the congregation of the servants of God, and instructed him to

swā wynsumu tō gehȳranne þætte þā seolfan his lārēowas æt
his mūðe wreoton ond leornodon. Song hē ǣrest be middan-
geardes gesceape ond bī fruman moncynnes ond eal þæt stǣr
75 Genesis (þæt is sēo ǣreste Moyses booc); ond eft bī ūtgonge
Israhēla folces of Ǣgypta londe ond bī ingonge þæs gehātlandes
ond bi ōðrum monegum spellum þæs hālgan gewrites canōnes
bōca, ond bī Crīstes menniscnesse ond bī his þrōwunge ond bī
his ūpāstīgnesse in heofonas ond bī þæs Hālgan Ḡastes cyme
80 ond þāra apostola lāre; ond eft bī þǣm dæge þæs tōweardan
dōmes ond bī fyrhtu þæs tintreglican wiites ond bī swētnesse þæs
heofonlecan rīces hē monig lēoð geworhte. Ond swelce ēac ōðer
monig be þǣm godcundan fremsumnessum ond dōmum hē
geworhte. In eallum þǣm hē geornlīce gēmde þæt hē men ātuge
85 from synna lufan ond māndǣda, ond tō lufan ond tō geornful-
nesse āwehte gōdra dǣda; for þon hē wæs se mon swīþe ǣfæst
ond regollecum þēodscipum ēaðmōdlīce underþēoded. Ond
wið þǣm þā ðe in ōðre wīsan dōn woldon, hē wæs mid welme
micelre ellenwōdnisse onbærned; ond hē for ðon fǣgre ænde his
90 līf betȳnde ond geendade.

For þon þā ðǣre tīde nēalǣcte his gewitenesse ond forðfōre,
þā wæs hē, fēowrtȳnum dagum ǣr, þæt hē wæs līchomlicre
untrymnesse þrycced ond hefgad, hwæðre tō þon gemetlīce
þæt hē ealle þā tid meahte ge sprecan ge gongan. Wæs þǣr in
95 nēaweste untrumra monna hūs, in þǣm heora þēaw wæs þæt
hēo þā untrumran ond þā ðe æt forðfōre wǣron inlǣdan
sceoldon, ond him þǣr ætsomne þegnian. Þā bæd hē his þegn
on æfenne þǣre neahte þe hē of worulde gongende wæs þæt hē
in þǣm hūse him stōwe gegearwode þæt hē gerestan meahte.
100 Þā wundrode se þegn for hwon hē ðæs bǣde, for þon him þūhte
þæt his forðfōr swā nēah ne wǣre; dyde hwæðre swā swā hē
cwæð ond bibēad. Ond mid þȳ hē ðā þǣr on reste ēode, ond hē
gefēonde mōde sumu þing mid him sprecende ætgædere ond
glēowiende wæs, þe þǣr ǣr inne wǣron, þā wæs ofer
105 middeneaht þæt hē frægn hwæðer hēo ǣnig hūsl inne hæfdon.
Þā ondswarodon hēo ond cwǣdon: 'Hwylc þærf is ðē hūsles?
Ne þīnre forþfōre swā nēah is, nū þū þus rōtlīce ond þus
glædlīce tō ūs sprecende eart.' Cwæð hē eft: 'Berað mē hūsl
tō.' Þā hē hit þā on honda hæfde, þā frægn hē hwæþer hēo ealle
110 smolt mōd ond būton eallum incan blīðe tō him hæfdon. Þā
ondswaredon hȳ ealle ond cwǣdon þæt hēo nǣnigne incan tō
him wiston, ac hēo ealle him swīðe blīðemōde wǣron; ond hēo
wrixendlīce hine bǣdon þæt hē him eallum blīðe wǣre. Þā
ondswarade hē ond cwæð: 'Mīne brōðor, mīne þā lēofan, ic
115 eom swīðe blīðemōd tō ēow ond tō eallum Godes monnum.'

learn the narrative of the holy history and message. And he assimilated all those things which he could learn by hearing, and just like a clean beast chewing its cud, turned them into the sweetest song. And his song and his poetry were so appealing to hear that his teachers themselves learned and wrote from his mouth. He sang first about the creation of the world and the origin of mankind and all the history of Genesis (that is the first book of Moses); and after about the exodus of the Israelites from the land of Egypt and their entrance into the promised land, and about many other stories from the text of the canonical books, and about Christ's incarnation and his passion and about his ascension into heaven and about the advent of the Holy Ghost and the teaching of the apostles; and after that about the day of approaching judgement and about the horror of excruciating punishment; and he made many poems about the sweetness of the heavenly kingdom. And he made many others like them about divine graciousness and justice. In them all he zealously took heed to draw men away from the love of sins and evil deeds, and awakened them to love and desire for good deeds; because the man was very pious and humbly committed to monastic discipline. And he was incensed with the fervour of great anger against those who wished to act in any other way; and therefore he closed and ended his life in a becoming way.

So when the time of his departure and death drew near, he was for fourteen days before oppressed and burdened by physical infirmity, yet so moderately that all the time he could both speak and walk about. There was in the vicinity an infirmary, in which it was their custom to put the sick and those that were on the point of death, and look after them all together. Then on the evening of the night that he was to depart the world he told his attendant to prepare a place for him in the infirmary so that he may rest. Then the attendant marvelled why he told him this because it seemed to him that that his death was not so near; nevertheless he did as he said and instructed. And then he went there to his resting place, and rejoicing in spirit, he was chatting and joking somewhat together with those who were already in there. It was past midnight when he asked whether they had any Eucharist inside. Then they answered him and said: 'What need have you for Eucharist? Your passing is not so near, now you are speaking to us so cheerily and merrily.' He said again: 'Bring the Eucharist to me.' When he had it in his hands, he asked

Ond swā wæs hine getrymmende mid þȳ heofonlecan wegneste
ond him ōðres līfes ingong gegearwode. Þā gȳt hē frægn, hū
nēah þǣre tīde wǣre þætte þā brōðor ārīsan scolden ond
Godes lof rǣran ond heora ūhtsong singan. Þā ondswaredon
120 hēo: 'Nis hit feor tō þon.' Cwæð hē: 'Teala: wuton wē wel þǣre
tīde bīdan.' Ond þā him gebæd ond hine gesegnode mid
Crīstes rōdetācne, ond his hēafod onhylde tō þām bolstre, ond
medmicel fæc onslēpte, ond swā mid stilnesse his līf geendade.
Ond swā wæs geworden þætte swā swā hē hlūttre mōde ond
125 bilwitre ond smyltre wilsumnesse Drihtne þēode, þæt hē ēac
swylce swā smylte dēaðe middangeard wæs forlǣtende, ond tō
his gesihðe becwōm. Ond sēo tunge, þe swā monig hālwende
word in þæs Scyppendes lof gesette, hē ðā swelce ēac þā
ȳtmǣstan word in his herenisse, hine seolfne segniende ond his
130 gāst in his honda bebēodende, betȳnde. Ēac swelce þæt is
gesegen þæt hē wǣre gewis his seolfes forfōre, of þǣm wē nū
secgan hȳrdon.

Notes

8 **lēoþsongum . . . (lēoðcræft . . . songcræft)**   The words *lēoð* and
song are used interchangeably. No distinction is made between
poetry and song. The first of these words is therefore tautologous,
and probably compounded for decorative purposes.

12–13 **from monnum ne þurh mon**   OE *from* has an agentive significance.
The translators also exploited the ambiguity of OE *mon*, in its senses
respectively of 'man' and 'mankind'. Thus, he was not taught by men
nor through the agency of mankind. The phrase *þurh mon* is thus
parallel and in contrast with *þurh Godes gife* in the following *ac*-
clause.

15 **nǣfre nōht lēasunge**   Double negation is normal in OE. However,
the accumulation of heavy negators – he *nales* . . . *ne* (12); *nǣfre
nǣnig lēoð* (19) – and the front shifting of *ne* – *ne con ic nōht singan*
(30) – may be taken to be emphatic.

16 **þā ān þā ðe**   Literally, 'those alone those that'.

20 **gebēorscipe**   The base of this derived form is *bēor*, 'beer'; the
prefix *ge-* has a collectivising meaning; and the suffix *-scipe* forms
abstract from concrete nouns.

whether they all had a tranquil and friendly spirit without any rancour towards him. Then they all answered and said that they felt no rancour towards him, but they were all very well disposed to him; and they in turn bade him that he should be well disposed to them all. Then he answered and said: 'My brothers, my dear friends, I am well disposed to you and to all God's men.' And so he was strengthened by the heavenly viaticum [Eucharist administered to the dying] and prepared for entry into the next life. But still he asked how close to the hour it was when the brothers should arise and raise up praise to God, singing their matins. Then they answered: 'It is not long till then.' He said: 'Well: let us await that hour.' And then he prayed and crossed himself with the sign of Christ's cross, and lowered his head to the pillow, and slept for a little while, and so in tranquillity he ended his life. And so it came about that in just as pure and innocent a spirit and serene devotion as he had served God, so with a similarly tranquil death he was relinquishing the world, and came into his sight. And that tongue, that had set so many salutary words in praise of the Creator, then ended in the same way with final words in his praise, as he crossed himself and commended his spirit into his hands. So also it is apparent from what we have just heard tell that he was aware of his own departure.

25 **wæs gongende** *egressus esset*   The expanded form, consisting of the verb 'to be' and the present participle, is particularly common in this excerpt (cf. 32; 98; 103–4; 108). It usually translates the Latin imperfect or imperfect subjunctive, but in 98 renders a construction with the future participle *erat exiturus*.

27 **ā stōd him sum mon æt**   Literally, 'then stood to him a certain man by'. The idiom exhibits the usual SV inversion after an adverbial (*þā*) and the preposition occurs as usual at the end of the group.

29 **Cedmon**   The more familiar spelling *Cædmon* is a West Saxonisation of this, the original Northumbrian form of the name.

46 **eal þā þe hē slǣpende song**   The demonstrative *þā* must be interpreted as neuter plural 'those things'. *Slǣpende* is the present participle functioning as qualifier of *hē*.

68 **hēht**   The older, poetic and Anglian form (used also on the Alfred Jewel inscription) of the preterite, *hēt*, of the verb *hātan*.

91 **forfōre**   Literally 'journey forth', but so common a euphemism in OE that it is best translated as 'death'.

129–30 **hine seolfne segniende ond his gāst in his honda bebēodende, betÿnde**   Imitates the Latin *signando sese et spiritum suum in manus commendando, clauderet*.

4 A Homily of Ælfric

Ælfric (c.955–c.1010) is one of a handful of Anglo-Saxon authors whose name is known to us. He was a priest and a monk who lived all his life in Wessex and was influenced by the monastic and intellectual revival presided over by Æthelwold. After teaching in the monastic school in Winchester, he proceeded to the monastery at Cerne Abbas, Dorset, where his Catholic Homilies were written between about 986 and 992. In 1005 he became abbot of the new monastery at Eynsham in Oxfordshire. His purpose in writing the Homilies, he explains, is to make the essential teachings of the Church available in simple terms to those incapable of understanding Latin. About two-thirds of Ælfric's collection are, like this excerpt, homilies in the stricter sense of the word: that is, sermon discourses in which a scriptural narrative is followed by a spiritual or moral interpretation of the text. Here, after relating the scriptural account of the workers in the vineyard, Ælfric states his authority for making a traditional equation between the vineyard and the kingdom of heaven, going on from there to a more detailed allegorical and moral interpretation of the narrative.

As Alfred noted in his Preface to the translation of *Cura Pastoralis* (Excerpt 2), monastic culture had sadly declined since the great days of Bede's Northumbria. But Ælfric lived in a time of reconstruction, for which Alfred's military and cultural efforts and Æthelstan's victory at Brunanburh (Excerpt 6) had provided the foundation. Wessex had gained dominance and imposed some unity upon England, and with the support of King Edgar, Archbishop Dunstan and Bishops Oswald and Æthelwold worked to reconstitute monastic life, modelling their practices on those of northern France. Æthelwold, to whose school Ælfric belonged, had a particular interest in literacy, and his Winchester school developed certain characteristic verbal choices which are exemplified in Ælfric's writings. More significantly, a relatively consistent way of writing West Saxon was developed, which, through its adoption by royal clerks, became used beyond the West Saxon dialect area by others writing in English. This excerpt is written in this standard West Saxon, which is the language of most extant Old English literature.

Drihten sǣde þis bigspel his leorningcnihtum, ðus cweðende: *Simile est regnum cęlorum homini patrifamilias, qui exiit primo mane conducere operarios; et reliqua.* Se Hǣlend cwæð þæt heofenan rīce wǣre gelīc sumum hīredes ealdre, sē ðe fērde on 5 ǣrnemerigen, and wolde hȳrian wyrhtan intō his wīngearde. þā gewearð þām hlāforde and ðām hȳrigmannum wið ānum peninge, and hī ēodon intō ðām wīngearde. Eft, ymbe undern dæges, ēode þæs wīngeardes hlāford ūt, and gemētte ōðre hȳrmenn standende ȳdele on ðǣre strǣt; and hē cwæð him 10 tō: 'Gāð intō mīnum wīngearde, and ic sylle ēow þæt riht bið.' Hī ðā ēodon tō his weorce be ðām behāte. Ymbe midne dæg and nōntīde ēode se hīredes ealdor ūt, and dyde hand swā gelīce. Æt nēxtan, twā tīda ofer nōne ēode se hlāford and gemētte mā wyrhtan standan, and him tō cwæð: 'Hwī stande 15 gē hēr ealne dæg ǣmtige?' Hī andwyrdon: 'For ðan þe ūs nān mann ne hȳrde.' Se hlāford cwæð: 'Gāð into mīnum wīngearde.' Witodlīce on ǣfnunge cwæð se hlāford tō his wīcnere: 'Clypa ðās wyrhtan and āgyld him heora mēde. Fōh on ðām endenēxtan, oð þæt þū cume tō ðām fyrmestan.' Þā cōmon ðā endenēx- 20 tan þe on ǣfnunge wǣron gehȳrede, and heora ǣlc underfēng ǣnne pening. Hwæt, ðā fyrmestan þe on ǣrnemerigen cōmon wēndon þā þæt hī māran mēde onfōn sceoldon. Ðā underfēn- gon hī ǣnlīpige penegas, swā swā ðā ōðre. Þā ongunnon hī tō ceorigenne ongēan ðone hīredes ealdor and cwǣdon: 'Ðās 25 endenēxtan menn worhton āne tīde, and þū dydest hī ūs gelīce æt ðǣre hȳre, wē ðe bǣron byrðene ðises dæges and hǣtan.' Þā andwyrde se hlāford and cwæð tō heora ānum: 'Þū frēond, ne dō ic ðē nǣnne tēonan. Hū lā, ne gewearð unc tō ānum peninge? Nim þæt ðīn is and gā ðē forð. Ic wille sōðlīce syllan 30 þisum latestan swā micel swā ðē. Hū ne mōt ic dōn þæt ic wylle? Oððe ðīn ēage is yfel, for ðan ðe ic eom good?' Þus wǣron þā latestan fyrmeste and þā fyrmestan endenēxte. Fela sind gecīgede and fēawa gecorene.

Grēgōrius se trahtnere cwæð þæt þis godspel hæfð langne 35 tige on his trahtnunge, ðā hē wile mid sceortre race befōn, þæt hit tō hefigtȳme ne ðince þām heorcnigendum.

Mīne gebrōðra, gelōme ic ēow sǣde þæt heofonan rīce getācnað þās andwerdan gelaðunge, for ðan þe rihtwīsra manna gegaderung is gecweden heofenan rīce. Se hīredes ealdor is 40 ūre Scyppend, sē ðe gewylt ðā ðe hē gesceōp, and his gecorenan on þisum middanearde geāgnað, swā swā hlāford his hīred on his healle. He hæfð þone wīngeard gewislīce ealle ðā gelēafful- lan gelaðunge, swā swā se wītega cwæð Isaias: 'Sōðlīce Godes wīngeard is Israhēla hīwrǣden.' Mid þām naman is geswutelod

The Lord told this parable, saying thus to his disciples: *Simile est regnum celorum homini patrifamilias qui exiit primo mane conducere operarios et reliqua.* The Saviour said that the kingdom of heaven was like a certain master of a household who went in the early morning and wished to hire labourers in his vineyard. Then the lord and the hired men settled on one penny, and they went into the vineyard. About the third hour of the day the owner of the vineyard went out again and met some other labourers standing unemployed in the street, and he said to them: 'Go into my vineyard, and I will give you what is just.' They then went to his work according to that promise. Around midday and the ninth hour the master of the household went out and made similar bargains. Next, two hours after the ninth hour, the master went out and met more workmen standing and said to them: 'Why are you standing here all day unoccupied?' They replied: 'Because no one hired us.' The master said: 'Go into my vineyard.'

Truly in the evening the master said to his steward: 'Call those workmen and pay them their wages; begin from the last until you come to the first.' Then the last ones who were hired in the evening came, and each of them received one penny. Well, the first ones who came in the early morning expected then that they should receive a greater reward. When they received a single penny just like the others, they began to complain against the master of the household, and said: 'Those last men worked for one hour and you treated them like us in payment, we who bore the burden and heat of this day.' Then the lord replied and said to one of them: 'Friend, I do you no injury; look, did we not agree between us on one penny? Take what is yours and go. I truly intend to give to this last as much as to you. What, may I not do what I wish? Or are you resentful because I am generous?' Thus were the last first, and the first last. Many are called and few chosen.

Gregory the commentator said in his commentary that this gospel has a long significance which he will relate with a short account, so that it may not seem too burdensome to those hearing it. My brothers, repeatedly I have told you that the kingdom of heaven represents this present congregation, because a gathering of righteous people is called the kingdom of heaven. The master of the household is our Creator, he who has power over those whom he created, and claims his chosen on this earth just as a lord his retinue in his hall. He owns the vineyard; that is, the whole congregation of the

45 eal Godes folc. Be ðām wīngearde cwæð Drihten tō Iūdēiscre
ðēode: 'Ic secge ēow, þæt Godes rīce bið ēow ætbrōden, and
bið forgyfen ðære ðēode þe his wæstmas wyrcað.' Þes wīngeard
sprytte Godes gecorenan, fram ðām rihtwīsan Ābel oð ðām
endenēxtan hālgan ðe on ende þyssere worulde ācenned bið,
50 swilce hē swā fela wīnbōga getȳddrode. Witodlīce ðæs hīredes
ealdor gehȳrde wyrhtan intō his wīngearde on ærnemerigen,
eft on undern, and on midne dæg, on nōntīde, and on ðære
endlyftan tīde; for ðan þe hē fram frymðe middaneardes oð
his geendunge ne āblinð tō āsendenne bydelas and lārēowas
55 tō lærenne his folc, þæt hī symle þā misweaxendan bōgas of
āscrēadian, þæt ðā tōweardan ðēonde bēon. Witodlīce gif se
wīngeard næfð þone ymbhwyrft, and ne bið on riht gescrēadod,
ne bið hē wæstmbære, ac forhraðe āwildað. Swā ēac Godes
folc, būton ðā lārēowas scrēadian symle ðā leahtras þurh
60 heora lāre āweg, ne bið þæt læwede folc wæstmbære on
gōdum weorcum.

faithful, just as the prophet Isaiah said: 'Truly God's vineyard is the tribe of the Israelites.' By that name is indicated all God's people. Concerning the vineyard, God spoke to the Jewish people: I tell you that the kingdom of God shall be snatched away from you and be granted to that people which labours for its increase.

This vineyard grows with God's elect from the righteous Abel until the last saints who will be born at the end of this world. Just as he propagated so many vine-shoots, certainly the master of the house hired labourers into his vineyard in the early morning. Again at the third hour, and at midday, the ninth hour, and at the final hour because he from the beginning of the world until its end does not cease from sending preachers and instructors to teach his people so that they may continuously prune out the badly growing shoots so that the future ones may be thriving. Indeed, if the vineyard does not have that cultivation, and is not properly pruned, it is not productive, but very quickly goes wild. So, too, God's people without instructors continuously to prune away sins through their teaching. An ignorant population is not productive in good works.

Notes

1 **his leorningcnihtum** 'his disciples' The word *cniht* in OE means 'servant' or 'boy'. This compound and the word *gelaðung* (38), meaning the Church as congregation, are considered to represent verbal choices characteristic of the Winchester school.

8 **ēode þæs wīngēardes hlāford ūt** Note the tendency of the preposition to appear at the end of the clause separated from its associated verb. Like modern German, Old English has some verbs with separable prefixes: *ūt-gān* occurs as well as *gān . . . ūt*.

10 **ic sylle** The present tense is normally used in OE for future reference.

12 **dyde hand** The idiom refers to the custom of striking hands on a bargain.

14–15 **Hwī stande gē** The form with final -e replaces the usual plural inflexion, -að, when the subject pronoun immediately follows the verb.

22 **hī māran mēde onfōn sceoldon** The usage here admirably illustrates the sense of inevitability, rather than simple futurity, borne by OE *sculan*.

28 **ne gewearð unc tō ānum peninge** Literally, 'did it not agree (happen) to us two for one penny'. The construction is impersonal, but the use of the dual form *unc* serves to emphasise the contract.

40 **gewylt** This form of *gewieldeð* exhibits the syncope of inflexional

-*e*- and the subsequent assimilation of stem and inflexional consonant which is typical of WS. Anglian preserves the ending -*eð*.

his gecorenan   The past participle, *ge-coren*, of *ceosan*, 'to choose' (which is a kind of verbal adjective), is converted to a Weak noun and used substantively.

54 **bydelas and lāreowas**   Ælfric goes on to explain that these are, in the different ages, the patriarchs (which he renders *hēahfæderas*), the prophets, and apostles.

58 **wæstmbǣre**   A transparent compound, meaning literally 'fruit-bearing'.

5 Ælfric's Cosmology

This excerpt contains the account of creation given in Ælfric's *De Temporibus Anni*, a work completed around 993 when he was at Cerne Abbas, and which survives in eight manuscripts. The earliest, CUL MS Gg. 3. 28, on which the present text is based, is nearly contemporary with the work's composition. The major sources used are the scriptural account given in Genesis and two Latin works of Bede, *De temporum ratione* and *De natura rerum*. Knowledge of cosmology was introductory to an understanding of astronomy, and this was of importance in medieval monasteries since the computation of the calendar was based upon it, which in turn made possible the certain identification of religious feast days. Characteristically, Ælfric appends an allegorical and moral interpretation to the natural science he recounts. This piece of scientific writing illustrates quite well some of the features of Ælfric's earlier prose style: a simple and non-Latinate vocabulary, phrasal repetition and sequences, and phrases syntactically and semantically balanced and contrasted. Balance may depend simply on semantic opposition (*on dæg bufon eorðan and on niht under ðysse eorðan*); or semantic opposition within a correlative syntactic structure (*Ælc ðing swā hit ðē fyrr bið swā hit ðē læsse ðincð*); or the semantic opposition may be constructed around the alliteration of a common word-pair (*Sēo is weaxende þurh āccennedum cildum and wānigende þurh fordfārendum*). Ælfric's artistry, in keeping with his concern to write in the simple style which he thought appropriate for instruction, seeks to be unobtrusive. His work is none the less constructed with considerable skill.

As explained in the previous excerpt, Ælfric's training in Winchester ensured that he wrote in standard West Saxon, which is the language of this excerpt also. Note the third person singular present-tense verbs *scīnð* (20), *onlīht* (49), *oferswīð* (50), and *ārīst* (55). All exhibit the syncope of inflexional -*e*- characteristic of WS and later Kentish OE. In the latter two there is also assimilation to the consonantal sound of the stem. The sequence of sound changes in the development of *onlīht* was: *onlīhteð* > *onlīhtð* > *onlīhtt* > *onlīht*.

On ðam ðriddan dæge gesceōp se ælmihtiga God sæ and eorðan and ealle eorðlice spryttinga. Ðās ðrȳ dagas wǣron būton sunnan and mōnan and steorran and eallum tīdum gelīcere wǣgan mid lēohte and þeostrum aðenede. On ðām fēorðan

5 dæge gesceōp God twā miccle lēoht þæt is sunne and mōna and betǣhte þæt māre lēoht þæt is sēo sunne tō ðām dæge and þæt lǣsse lēoht þæt is se mōna tō ðǣre nihte. On ðām ylcan dæge hē geworhte ealle steorran and tīda gesette. On ðām fīftan dæge hē gesceōp eal wyrmcynn and ðā micclan

10 hwalas and eal fisccynn on mislicum and menigfealdum hīwum. On ðām sixtan dæge hē gesceōp eal dēorcynn and ealle nȳtenu þe on fēower fōtum gāð and þā twēgen men Adam and Ēuan. On ðām seofoðan dæge hē geendode his weorc and sēo wucu wæs ðā agān.

15 Nū is ǣlc dæg on ðysum middanearde of ðǣre sunnan līhtinge. Sōðlice sēo sunne gǣð be Godes dihte betwux heofenan and eorðan on dæg bufon eorðan and on niht under ðysse eorðan eal swā feorr adūne on nihtlicere tīde under þǣre eorðan swā hēo on dæg bufon ūpāstīhð. Æfre

20 hēo bið yrnende ymbe ðās eorðan and eal swā lēohte scīnð under ðǣre eorðan on nihtlicere tīde swā swā hēo on dæg dēð bufon ūrum hēafdum. On ðā healfe ðe hēo scīnð þǣr bið dæg and on ðā healfe ðe hēo ne scīnð ðǣr bið niht. Æfre bið on sumere sīdan þǣre eorðan dæg and æfre on sumere sīdan

25 niht. Ðæt lēoht ðe wē hātað dægerēd cymð of ðǣre sunnan þonne hēo ūpweard bið and hēo ðonne tōdrǣfð þā nihtlican ðēostru ðurh hire micclan lēohte. Eal swā ðicce is sēo heofen mid steorrum āfylled on dæg swā on niht ac hī nabbað nāne līhtinge for ðǣre sunnan andwerdnysse. Wē hātað ænne dæg

30 fram sunnan ūpgange oð æfen ac swā ðēah on bōcum is geteald to ānum dæge fram ðǣre sunnan ūpgange oð þæt hēo eft becume þǣr hēo ǣr ūppstāh: on ðām fæce sind getealde fēower and twenti tīda. Sēo sunne is swīðe micel – eal swā brād hēo is þæs ðe bēc secgað swā eal eorðan ymbhwyrft – ac

35 hēo ðincð ūs swīðe unbrād forðan ðe hēo is swīðe feor fram ūrum gesihðum. Ælc ðing swā hit ðē fyrr bið swā hit ðē læsse ðincð. Wē magon hwæðere tōcnāwan be hire lēoman þæt hēo unlȳtel is. Swā hraðe swā hēo ūpāstīhð hēo scīnð geond ealle eorðan gelīce and ealre eorðan brādnysse endemes oferwrīhð.

40 Ēac swilce ðā steorran ðe ūs lȳtle ðincað sind swīðe brāde ac for ðām micclum fæce þe ūs betwēonan is hī sind geðūhte ūrum gesihðum swīðe gehwǣde. Hī ne mihton swā ðēah nān lēoht tō eorðan āsendan fram ðǣre hēalican heofenan gif hī swā gehwǣde wǣron swā swā ūrum ēagum ðincð. Sōðlice se

On the third day the Almighty God created sea and earth and all the vegetation in the world. Those three days were lacking sun and moon and stars, and all times were overspread in equal measure by light and dark. On the fourth day God created two great lights, that is the sun and the moon, and assigned the greater light, that is the sun, to the day and the lesser light, that is the moon, to the night. In the same day he made all the stars and established the seasons. On the fifth day he created the race of creeping things and the great whales and the race of fish in many and various forms. On the sixth day he created all kinds of animals and all beasts that walk on four feet, and the two humans Adam and Eve. On the seventh day he completed his task and the week was then past.

Now, each day in this world results from the sun's light. Indeed, by God's arrangement, the sun moves between the heaven and earth: during the day above the earth and by night beneath this earth, just as far down below the earth at night-time as it ascends above during the day. Constantly it is running around this earth, and shines just as brightly beneath the earth at night-time as it does during the day above our heads. On that side where it shines there is day, and on that side where it does not shine there is night. Always there is on one particular side of the earth day, and always on the other side night. The light which we call dawn comes from the sun rising, and it then drives away the night-time darkness with its great light. The sky is just as thickly filled with stars in the day-time as at night, but they have no brightness because of the sun's presence. From sunrise until evening we call one day, however in books it is reckoned as one day from the sun's rising until it comes again [to that point] where it earlier arose: in that space of time are counted twenty-four hours. The sun is very large – as books say, it is just as wide as the entire circumference of the earth – but it seems very small to us because it is very distant from our sight. The further anything is the smaller it seems. We may discern however that it is large on account of its great light. As soon as it rises, it shines alike over the whole earth and covers equally the entire breadth of the earth. Similarly, the stars which seem small to us are very broad, but because of the great space that is between us, they seem very small to our sight. But they could not thus send any light from their exalted heaven if they were as small as they appear to our eyes. Truly the moon and all stars receive light from the great sun and none

45 mōna and ealle steorran underfōð lēoht of ðǣre micclan
sunnan and heora nān nǣfð nǣnne lēoman būton of ðǣre
sunnan lēoman; and ðēah ðe sēo sunne under eorðan on
nihtlicere tīde scīne þēah āstīhð hire lēoht on sumere sīdan
þǣre eorðan þe ðā steorran bufon ūs onlīht and ðonne hēo
50 ūpagǣð hēo oferswīð ealra ðǣra steorrena and ēac þæs mōnan
lēoht mid hire ormǣtan lēohte.

Sēo sunne getācnað ūrne hǣlend Crīst se ðe is rihtwīsnysse
sunne swā swā se wītega cwæð: *Timentibus autem nomen
domini orietur sol iustitie et sanitas in pennis eius* 'Ðām
55 mannum þe him ondrǣdað Godes naman ðām ārīst rihtwīsnysse
sunne and hǣlð is on hire fiðerum.' Se mōna ðe weaxð and
wānað getācnað þās andwerdan gelaðunge ðe wē on sind.
Sēo is weaxende þurh ācennedum cildum and wānigende
þurh fordfarendum. Þa beorhtan steorran getācniað ðā
60 gelēaffullan on Godes gelaðunge ðe on goddre drohtnunge
scīnað. Crīst sōðlice onlīht hī ealle þurh his gife swā swā se
godspellere Iohannes cwæð: *Erat lux uera que inluminat
omnem hominem uenientem in hunc mundum* 'Ðæt sōðe lēoht
cōm þe onlīht ælcne mannan cumendne to ðisum middanearde.'
65 Nǣfð ūre nān nān lēoht ǣnigre gōdnysse būton of Crīstes
gife. Se ðe is sōðre rihtwīsnysse sunne gehāten.

Notes

5 **twā miccle lēoht þæt is sunne and mōna**   The phrase *þæt is*
concords with neither *lēoht* (as it does by chance in the next line) nor
sunne or *mōna*. It is rather an independent explanatory clause
equivalent to Latin *videlicet* or *scilicet*.

9–10 **wyrmcynn . . . hwalas . . . fisccynn**   We have here an attempt at
scientific classification of types of creatures, and it is probably more
than coincidental that the word *cynn* is both etymologically
connected with, and has the sense of, Latin *genus*, which had already
been used in such contexts by Latin authors. More widely in OE
usage *wyrm* may include many types of worm, snake and insect.
Hwæl is used of walruses as well as whales, and in *Physiologus*, the
whale is classed as a fish. Seals may even be considered *fisccynn*.

11–12 **dēorcynn . . . nȳtenu**   The apparent distinction between wild and
domesticated animals suggested by Bede's Latin is not made in wider
OE usage, where *nȳten* is used of a badger, and both explicitly tame
reindeer and a wild panther are equally referred to as *dēor*.

12–13 **þā twēgen men Adam and Ēuan**   The concept of *man* as the name
of a species is sufficiently distinct from its reference to the male to
permit what sounds in modern English an extraordinary statement.

of them has any brightness except from the sun's brightness, and although the sun may shine beneath the earth at night-time yet its light goes to one side of the earth and lights the stars above us, and when it comes up it overwhelms the light of all the stars and of the moon with its intense brightness.

The sun symbolises our saviour Christ, he who is the sun of righteousness, as the prophet says: *Timentibus autem nomen domini orietur sol iustitiae sanitas in pennis eius*, 'To those men who fear God's name shall arise the sun of righteousness and healing is in his wings.' The moon which waxes and wanes signifies this present congregation which we are in. It is growing through children born and dwindling through deaths. The bright stars signify the faithful in God's congregation who shine in virtuous living. Christ truly illuminates them all through his grace just as the evangelist John says: *Erat lux vera que inluminat omnem hominem venientem in hunc mundum*, 'The true light came that enlightens each man coming into this world.' None of us has the light of any goodness except by God's grace. He that is called the sun of true righteousness.

20 **lēohte** 'lightly'   Adverbs are readily formed from nouns by the addition of -*e* to the stem.

26 **tōdrǣfð**   The prefix *to-* is etymologically related to the word *two*, and carries the force of separation or splitting. In combination with some agentive verbs it therefore acts as an intensifier.

30–33 **ēah on bōcum is geteald . . . fēower and twenti tīda**   *Byhrtferð's Manual* refers to the period from sun-up to sundown as the *ceorlisc* day. The twenty-four-hour day is described in Bede's Latin as *dies . . . artificialis*. Cf. Chaucer, 'Man of Law's Tale', 2, and 'Squire's Tale', 116, where the artificial day is from sunrise to sunset, and the natural day is twenty-four hours.

35 **hēo ðincð ūs swiðe unbrād**   An impersonal construction, 'it seems to us. . .'. The verb *ðyncan* is usually used impersonally, *ðencan* personally, i.e. meaning 'to think'. Note the passive construction (41–42).

36–37 **swā hit ðē fyrr bið swā hit ðē lǣsse ðincð**   The impersonal verb is here contained in a correlative construction using *swā . . . swā* and the repeated instrumental form of the demonstrative *ðe*.

56 **hire fiðerum**   *Hire* refers to *sunne*, which is feminine. *Fiðer* is used for both 'feather' and 'wing' in OE. The latter word is a Scandinavian borrowing.

65 **Næfð ure nān nān lēoht**   Literally, 'None of us has no light.'

6 The Battle of Brunanburh

The *Anglo-Saxon Chronicle* in four different manuscripts contains as the entry for the year 937 a brief heroic poem, telling of a crushing defeat inflicted on a coalition of Picts and Scots, Strathclyde Welsh, and Norse Vikings by the West Saxons. The victory at Brunanburh was important in establishing national unity under West Saxon dominion, and contemporary awareness of this fact may lie behind the triumphalistic tone of the poem. Despite its historical importance, the site of the conflict has been forgotten. All that can be said with certainty is that Brunanburh was somewhere in northern England or southern Scotland, and that the flight of the Scandinavians to their ships indicates a site not far from the sea or some large estuary. Despite the opinion of the early twelfth-century chronicler Florence of Worcester that the Vikings approached the battlefield from the Humber, it is probable that the battle took place on the western side of the country.

The *Battle of Brunanburh* was written to commemorate the great deeds of Æthelstan and for an elite who would appreciate the expression of the heroic ideals of the past in a very correct and formal verse. The metre is very regular, and copious use is made of synonyms, compounds, and the parallelism and variation characteristic of correct OE verse. The technique has been seen as artificial, the conscious re-creation of standards developed in much earlier poetry. The poetic language is highly conventional, and more than twenty half-lines are recorded elsewhere. Nevertheless, a large number of compounds are unknown from other sources and may be original, *ealdorlang, heaþolind, scipflota, hereflēma, bilgesleht, wælfeld, hasupād, gārmitting, gūðhafoc* among them. Variant readings in some manuscripts are of a kind which suggest that the scribe was unfamiliar with the phrasing of poetic language, and that it gave him difficulty. See the notes for some examples.

The text below, based on MS A of the *Anglo-Saxon Chronicle*, was written in Winchester about 955. It is predominantly in West Saxon but contains a number of words of an archaic or dialectal kind, apparently added by the poet to his composition for the sake of ornament. There are also a number of late inflexional forms: *-an* for *-on* (5, 23, 52, 53, 70, 71, 72, 73); *-an* for *-um* (6, 24), *-un* for *-um* (43). *-Un* for *-on* (10, 22, 27, 28, 47, 48) is probably the survival of an archaic and poetic spelling.

Hēr Æþelstān cyning,   eorla dryhten,
beorna bēahgifa,   and his brōþor ēac,
Ēadmund æþeling,   ealdorlangne tīr
geslōgon æt sæcce   sweorda ecgum
5 ymbe Brunanburh;   bordweal clufan,
hēowan heaþolinde   hamora lāfan
afaran Ēadweardes;   swā him geæþele wæs
from cnēomǣgum,   þæt hī æt campe oft
wiþ lāþra gehwæne   land ealgodon,
10 hord and hāmas.   Hettend crungun,
Sceotta lēoda   and scipflotan
fǣge fēollan.   Feld dunnade
secga swāte,   siðþan sunne ūp
on morgentīd,   mǣre tungol,
15 glād ofer grundas,   Godes condel beorht,
ēces Drihtnes,   oð sīo æþele gesceaft
sāh tō setle.   Þær læg secg mænig
gārum āgēted,   guma norþerna
ofer scild scoten,   swilce Scittisc ēac
20 wērig, wīges sæd.   Wesseaxe forð
ondlongne dæg   ēorodcistum
on lāst legdun   lāþum þēodum,
hēowan hereflēman   hindan þearle
mēcum mylenscearpan.   Myrce ne wyrndon
25 heardes hondplegan   hæleþa nānum
þæra þe mid Anlafe   ofer ēargebland
on lides bōsme   land gesōhtun
fǣge tō gefeohte.   Fīfe lǣgun
on þām campstede   cyningas giunge
30 sweordum āswefede,   swilce seofene ēac
eorlas Anlāfes,   unrīm heriges,
flotena and Sceotta.   Þǣr geflēmed wearð
Norðmanna bregu,   nēde gebēded
tō lides stefne   lītle weorode;
35 crēad cnear on flot,   cyning ūt gewāt
on fealene flōd,   feorh generede.
Swilce þǣr ēac se frōda   mid flēame cōm
on his cȳþþe norð,   Costontinus,
hār hildering;   hrēman ne þorfte
40 mēcga gemanan: hē wæs his mǣga sceard,
frēonda befylled   on folcstede,
beslagen æt sæcce,   and hīs sunu forlēt
on wælstōwe wundun   forgrunden,
giungne æt gūðe.   Gelpan ne þorfte

In this year King Æthelstan, the lord of warriors, giver of rings to men, and also his brother, Prince Eadmund, won eternal glory in battle with the edges of swords around Brunanburh; they, the sons of Eadweard, split the shield-wall, hacked the battle-shields with swords; as it was inborn in them from their ancestors that they should often in battle defend land, treasure and homes against every foe. The enemy perished, the men of the Scots and the sailors fell doomed. The field streamed with the blood of men, from when the sun in the morning, the glorious day-star, bright candle of God the eternal lord, glided up over the plains, until when that noble creation sank to rest. There lay many a warrior destroyed by spears, many a Northman shot above his shield, so also Scots exhausted, satiated with battle. Through the entire day the West Saxons pressed forward in troops on the track of the hostile people, hewed the fugitives cruelly from the rear with stone-sharpened blades. Neither did the Mercians refuse fierce hand-play to any of the heroes among those who with Anlaf, over the stirring sea in the bosom of the ship, had come to land, as doomed men to the fight. Five young kings lay on the battlefield, laid to rest by swords, and also likewise seven of Anlaf's earls, and countless of the Scottish and Viking army. There the chief of the Northmen, compelled by necessity, was driven to the prow of his ship with a scanty band; the king launched his ship on the water, departed on the tawny flood, and saved his life. So also there did the wise Constantine go north in flight to his home, the grey-headed warrior had no cause to rejoice in the company of kinsmen. He was deprived of kin and of friends killed on the field of battle, struck down in the strife, and he left his son in the place of slaughter, destroyed by wounds, young in battle. The grey-haired warrior, the old dissembler, had no need to boast about the clash of swords; no more had Anlaf. With the remnants of their armies they need not laugh and say that they were better in warlike deeds on the battlefield, in the clash of standards, the meeting of spears, the encounter of men, the exchange of weapons, in which they competed on the field of slaughter against the sons of Eadweard. The Northmen, a sad remnant left by the javelins, departed humiliated in their nailed boats upon Dingesmere seeking Dublin, back to Ireland across the deep water. Likewise the brothers, both together, king and prince, made for home, the West Saxon land, exultant from battle. They left behind them to share the corpses the dark-coated

45 beorn blandenfeax   bilgeslehtes,
eald inwidda,   ne Anlāf þȳ mā;
mid heora herelāfum   hlehhan ne þorftun,
þæt hēo beaduweorca   beteran wurdun
on campstede,   cumbolgehnāstes,
50 gārmittinge,   gumena gemōtes,
wǣpengewrixles,   þæs hī on wælfelda
wiþ Ēadweardes   afaran plegodan.
Gewitan him þā Norþmen   nægledcnearrum,
drēorig daraða lāf,   on Dingesmere,
55 ofer dēop wæter   Difelin sēcan,
eft Īra land,   ǣwiscmōde.
Swilce þā gebrōþer   bēgen ætsamne,
cyning and æþeling,   cȳþþe sōhton,
Wesseaxena land,   wiges hrēmge.
60 Lētan him behindan   hrǣ bryttian
saluwigpādan,   þone sweartan hræfn,
hyrnednebban,   and þane hasupādan,
earn æftan hwīt,   ǣses brūcan
grǣdigne gūðhafoc   and þæt grǣge dēor,
65 wulf on wealde.   Ne wearð wæl māre
on þis ēiglande   ǣfre gīeta
folces gefylled   beforan þissum
sweordes ecgum,   þæs þe ūs secgað bēc,
ealde ūðwitan,   siþþan ēastan hider
70 Engle and Seaxe   ūp becōman,
ofer brād brimu   Brytene sōhtan,
wlance wīgsmiþas,   Wēalas ofercōman,
eorlas ārhwate,   eard begēatan.

one, the black, horny-beaked raven, and the dun-coated one, the white-tailed eagle, to enjoy the carrion, the greedy war-hawk, and that grey beast, the forest wolf. According to what books and old scholars tell us, there was never yet in this island before this time a greater slaughter of people killed by the edge of the sword since the Angles and Saxons, coming from the east across the broad ocean, landed here, and, proud war-smiths, they sought out Britain, overcame the Welsh, and eager for glory took possession of a homeland.

Notes

1 **Hēr**   Not strictly speaking a part of the poem, but the usual device for marking the place of an entry in the annals.

6 **hamora lāfan**   A poetic phrase referring to swords: 'the leavings of hammers'.

14–16 **mǣre tungol . . . condel beohrt . . . sīo æþele gesceaft; Godes . . . ēces Drihtnes**   Two interlocked strands of a common OE poetic device, semantic parallelism with variation in wording.

18 **āgēted**   Along with *geflēmed* (32), *nēde* (33), *hlehhan* (47) and *ēiglande* (66), this represents an Anglian form, where WS would have *ie/y* as the result of the *i*-mutation of *ea*.

24 **mēcum mylenscearpan**   This interesting phrase contains an Anglian form restricted in WS to verse, *mēce*, 'sword, blade', an otherwise unrecorded poetic compound *mylenscearp*, 'sharpened on a grindstone', and a confusion of the inflexional endings *-an*/*-um* characteristic of Late WS.

49 **cumbolgehnāstes** 'clash of standards'   The word, which is unrecorded elsewhere, was not immediately understood by the copyist of A, who at first wrote the nonsensical *culbodgehnades*.

53 **Norþmen nægledcnearrum**   MS D (datable to about 1016) here reads *norðmen dæg gled on garum*, which sounds like an attempt to make sense of matter dictated but not understood. The compound *nægledcnearrum* is not recorded elsewhere, nor is the word *cnear* (35), which is used of Scandinavian ships and may be borrowed from that source; cf. Old Norse *knörr*, gen. *knarrar*.

7   The Battle of Maldon

In the year 991 the Essex militia commanded by their *ealdorman*, Byrhtnoth, confronted an invading force of Vikings near Maldon. The latter had landed on the island of Northey in the Blackwater estuary, which was joined to the mainland by a narrow causeway uncovered at low tide. In order to break the stalemate and commence battle, Byrhtnoth allowed the enemy to cross the causeway, an evidently risky tactic which is not unparalleled in medieval warfare (Oman 1953). With hindsight, however, the poet sees that Byrhtnoth's decision cost him the victory and his life, yet he presents the facts in no spirit of disapproval.

The *Anglo-Saxon Chronicle* mentions the incident only briefly, but probably not more than a decade after the event a poem was composed, which in contrast to *Brunanburh*, which rejoices in military strength, sought to emphasise the loyalty and heroism of Byrhtnoth's retainers in defeat. A more reflective and idealistic work which values virtues more than might, *The Battle of Maldon* is metrically looser and less metaphorically ornamented than more formal OE poetry but uses considerable rhetorical skill in the composition of speeches. The poem employs much traditional diction: the synonym group *beorn, rinc, lēod, man, hæleð, wiga, guma* for 'man, warrior', poetic compounds such as *gārræs*, 'spear-onslaught' (32), *gūðplega*, 'battle-play' (61), and *wīhaga*, 'battle-hedge' (102), and fixed formulae such as *wordum mælan* (26). The compound *bricgweard*, 'bridge-guard' (85), seems to have been the poet's own creation.

The only manuscript of the *Battle of Maldon* was destroyed in the Cotton fire of 1731, but a transcription had been made by David Casley, deputy keeper of the Cottonian collection, and it is upon this that all modern editions are based. The text is written in standard West Saxon, and its lateness is suggested by signs of spelling confusion in representing inflexions consisting of a vowel followed by a nasal consonant: *handon* (7), *folman* (21, 108), *lēodon* (23).

brocen wurde.
Hēt þā hyssa hwǣne   hors forlǣtan,
feor āfȳsan,   and forð gangan,
hicgan tō handum   and tō hige gōdum.
5 Þā þæt Offan mǣg   ǣrest onfunde,
þæt se eorl nolde   yrhðo geþolian,
hē lēt him þā of handon   lēofne flēogan
hafoc wið þæs holtes,   and tō þǣre hilde stōp;
be þām man mihte oncnāwan   þæt se cniht nolde
10 wācian æt þām wīge,   þā hē tō wǣpnum fēng.
Ēac him wolde Ēadrīc   his ealdre gelǣstan,
frēan tō gefeohte,   ongan þā forð beran
gār tō gūþe.   Hē hæfde gōd geþanc
þā hwīle þe hē mid handum   healdan mihte
15 bord and brād swurd;   bēot hē gelǣste
þā hē ætforan his frēan   feohtan sceolde.
    Ðā þǣr Byrhtnōð ongan   beornas trymian,
rād and rǣdde,   rincum tǣhte
hū hī sceoldon standan   and þone stede healdan,
20 and bæd þæt hyra randas   rihte hēoldon
fæste mid folman,   and ne forhtedon nā.
Þā hē hæfde þæt folc   fægere getrymmed,
hē līhte þā mid lēodon   þǣr him lēofost wæs,
þǣr hē his heorðwerod   holdost wiste.
25 Þā stōd on stæðe,   stīðlīce clypode
wīcinga ār,   wordum mǣlde,
se on bēot ābēad   brimlīþendra
ǣrænde tō þām eorle,   þǣr hē on ōfre stōd:
'Mē sendon tō þē   sǣmen snelle,
30 hēton ðē secgan   þæt þū mōst sendan raðe
bēagas wið gebeorge;   and ēow betere is
þæt gē þisne gārrǣs   mid gafole forgyldon,
þon wē swā hearde   hilde dǣlon.
Ne þurfe wē ūs spillan,   gif gē spēdaþ tō þām;
35 wē willað wið þam golde   grið fæstnian.
Gyf þū þat gerǣdest,   þe hēr rīcost eart,
þæt þū þīne lēoda   lȳsan wille,
syllan sǣmannum   on hyra sylfra dōm
feoh wið frēode,   and niman frið æt ūs,
40 wē willaþ mid þām sceattum   ūs tō scype gangan,
on flot fēran,   and ēow friþes healdan.'
    Byrhtnōð maþelode,   bord hafenode,
wand wācne æsc,   wordum mǣlde,
yrre and ānrǣd   āgēaf him andsware:

. . . was broken. Then he ordered each of the young men to abandon his horse, drive it far away, and go forward concentrating on his strength and fighting spirit. As soon as Offa's kinsman discovered that the earl would not tolerate slackness he let his beloved hawk fly from his hands towards the wood, and stepped towards the battle. That way it might be understood that the boy did not intend to weaken in the fight when he took up weapons. In addition to him, Eadric too wished to serve his leader, his lord, in the fight; he then began to carry his spear forward into combat. He maintained a valiant spirit as long as he could hold his shield and broadsword with his hands; he fulfilled his proud boast when he had to fight before his lord.

Then Byrhtnoth began to draw up the warriors there, rode about and instructed them, directed how they had to stand and hold the position, and ordered that they should hold their round shields properly, firmly in their fists, and that they should have no fear. When he had suitably arranged the army, he dismounted among the men where it was most pleasing to him, where he knew his personal guard to be most loyal. Then a Viking messenger stood on the bank and loudly called, spoke in words; he arrogantly delivered the seafarers' message to the earl, where he stood on the shore: 'Bold seamen have sent me to you, ordered me to tell you that you may quickly send rings in exchange for security; and it is better for you that you buy off this onslaught with tribute than we should share such cruel battle. We need not destroy each other, if you are sufficiently wealthy; we are willing to establish a truce in exchange for the gold. If you who are most influential take the view that you wish to ransom your people, give to the seamen on their own assessment money for friendship and accept peace from us. We intend to embark with the payment, go to sea, and keep the peace with you.'

Byrhtnoth spoke, raised his shield, brandished his slender spear, and spoke in words, angered and resolute, gave him an answer: 'Do you hear, seafarer, what this army says? They will give you spears as a tribute, the deadly spear-point and the ancient sword, equipment that will not avail you in battle. Messenger of the seamen, report back again, say to your people the much more unwelcome news that here stands with his troop a noble earl who will defend this country, Ethelred, my lord's, home, its people and its land. The heathen shall fall in the battle. It seems to me too shameful that with

45 'Gehȳrst þū, sælida,　hwæt þis folc segeð?
Hī willað ēow tō gafole　gāras syllan,
ættrynne ord　and ealde swurd,
þā heregeatu　þe ēow æt hilde ne dēah.
Brimmanna boda,　ābēod eft ongēan,
50 sege þīnum lēodum　miccle lāþre spell,
þæt hēr stynt unforcūð　eorl mid his werode,
þe wile gealgean　ēþel þysne,
Æþelrēdes eard,　ealdres mīnes,
folc and foldan.　Feallan sceolon
55 hǣþene æt hilde.　Tō hēanlic mē þinceð
þæt gē mid ūrum sceattum　tō scype gangon
unbefohtene,　nū gē þus feor hider
on ūrne eard　in becōmon.
Ne sceole gē swā sōfte sinc　gegangan;
60 ūs sceal ord and ecg　ǣr gesēman,
grim gūðplega,　ǣr wē gofol syllon.'
Hēt þā bord beran,　beornas gangan,
þæt hī on þām ēasteðe　ealle stōdon.
Ne mihte þǣr for wætere　werod tō þām ōðrum;
65 þǣr cōm flōwende　flōd æfter ebban,
lucon lagustrēamas.　Tō lang hit him þūhte,
hwænne hī tōgædere　gāras bēron.
Hī þǣr Pantan strēam　mid prasse bestōdon,
Ēastseaxena ord　and se æschere.
70 Ne mihte hyra ǣnig　ōþrum derian,
būton hwā þurh flānes flyht　fyl genāme.
Se flōd ūt gewāt;　þā flotan stōdon gearowe,
wīcinga fela,　wīges georne.
Hēt þā hæleða hlēo　healdan þā bricge
75 wigan wīgheardne,　se wæs hāten Wulfstān,
cāfne mid his cynne,　þæt wæs Cēolan sunu,
þe ðone forman man　mid his francan ofscēat
þe þǣr baldlīcost　on þā bricge stōp.
Þǣr stōdon mid Wulfstāne　wigan unforhte,
80 Ælfere and Maccus,　mōdige twēgen,
þā noldon æt þām forda　flēam gewyrcan,
ac hī fæstlīce　wið ðā fȳnd weredon,
þā hwīle þe hī wǣpna　wealdan mōston.
Þā hī þæt ongēaton　and georne gesāwon
85 þæt hī þǣr bricgweardas　bitere fundon,
ongunnon lytegian þā　lāðe gystas,
bǣdon þæt hī ūpgangan　āgan mōston,

our money you should embark uncontested now you have penetrated thus far into our homeland. Nor shall you so easily carry off treasure: point and edge shall bring us together, grim war-play, before we give tribute.' He then commanded the warriors to go bearing shields so that they all stood on the river bank. Nor might the warband get at the other because of the water; there high tide came flowing after the ebb, the waters enclosed them. Too long it seemed to them till they bore spears together. There they stood in force alongside the river Blackwater, the East Saxon vanguard and the ship army. Neither might any of them injure the other unless someone through an arrow's flight received his death. The tide went out; then the sailors stood ready, many Vikings eager for combat. Then the protector of men ordered a battle-hardened warrior called Wulfstan to hold the bridge; it was Ceola's son, brave like all his people, who with his javelin killed the first man who most boldly there stepped on to the bridge. There stood with Wulfstan unafraid warriors, Ælfhere and Maccus – a valiant pair – those would not flee at the ford, but they unflinchingly defended against the enemy as long as they could handle weapons. When they realised and clearly saw that they found fierce bridge-guards there, the wretched strangers began to use cunning. They asked that they might have a landing place to go over the ford, bringing foot-soldiers.

Then the earl, on account of his overconfidence, allowed too much land to a more hateful people. Byrhthelm's son called across the cold water (the warriors listened): 'Now room is made for you, come quickly to us, warriors to the battle; God alone knows who may control the battlefield.' The slaughterous wolves advanced (they did not care about the water), the Viking band, west across the Blackwater bore shields over the bright water, seamen bearing lime-wood shields to land. There Byrhtnoth with his warriors stood ready against the enemy. He ordered the battle-line to be formed with shields and that the war-band hold firm against the enemy. The fight was near, glory in battle. That time was come when there doomed men should perish. There a shout was raised up, the ravens circled, the eagle greedy for carrion; there was uproar on the ground. Then they let fly from their hands file-hard spears, cruelly sharpened javelins; bows were busy, shield received point.

ofer þone ford faran,   fēþan lǣdan.
Ðā se eorl ongan   for his ofermōde
90 ālȳfan landes tō fela   lāþere ðēode.
Ongan ceallian þā   ofer cald wæter
Byrhtelmes bearn   (beornas gehlyston):
'Nū ēow is gerȳmed,   gāð ricene tō ūs,
guman tō gūþe;   God āna wāt
95 hwā þǣre wælstōwe   wealdan mōte.'
Wōdon þā wælwulfas   (for wætere ne murnon),
wīcinga werod,   west ofer Pantan,
ofer scīr wæter   scyldas wēgon,
lidmen tō lande   linde bǣron.
100 Þǣr ongēan gramum   gearowe stōdon
Byrhtnōð mid beornum;   hē mid bordum hēt
wyrcan þone wīhagan,   and þæt werod healdan
fæste wið fēondum.   Þā wæs feohte nēh,
tīr æt getohte.   Wæs sēo tīd cumen
105 þæt þǣr fǣge men   feallan sceoldon.
Þǣr wearð hrēam āhafen,   hremmas wundon,
earn ǣses georn;   wæs on eorþan cyrm.
Hī lēton þā of folman   fēolhearde speru,
grimme gegrundene   gāras flēogan;
110 bogan wǣron bysige,   bord ord onfēng.

Notes

1 **brocen wurde**   The beginning of the poem is missing, but not many lines can have been lost.

2–4 **hēt . . . forlǣtan . . . āfȳsan . . . gangan . . . hicgan**   All are infinitives dependent on *hēt*, the later preterite form of *hātan* (see excerpt 3, line 68).

6 **se eorl**   In early verse this means 'man, warrior', but here is a title equivalent to *ealdorman*. Influence by Scandinavian *jarlr* has been suggested.

9 **oncnāwan**   The prefix *on-* has ingressive aspect – that is, it directs attention to the beginning, the bringing about, of the state denoted by the verbal base.

se cniht   The word is about to undergo important semantic changes. In OE it develops from 'boy, servant' to 'retainer'. The modern sense 'knight' appears in the twelfth century.

24 **heorðwerod**   Literally 'hearth-troop'. The compound implies those troops closest to the leader, the household retainers who shared his hall.

35–39 **grið fæstnian . . . niman frið**   The word *grið* is a Scandinavian borrowing. The collocation with *frið* is a formula of legal origin found also in the *Ormulum*.

42 **Byrhtnōð maþelode** A formulaic phrase for introducing a formal speech. Uses a verb restricted to verse (cf. *wordum mǣlde*). A similar formula is employed in the eighth-century south German epic, the *Hildebrandeslied*.

47 **ǣttrynne ord and ealde swurd** The word *ǣttryne* literally means 'poisoned', but there is no evidence for the use of poisoned weapons in Anglo-Saxon England; therefore translate as 'deadly'. *Ealde* is approving. Weapons and ornaments handed down from previous generations were greatly valued, since the pace of technological change was not such as to render them obsolete, and they were seen as having proved their worth.

52 **þe wile gealgan** The force of the verb *willan* is here clearly that of intention. Compare the sense of inevitability in *sceoldon* (105).

75–8 **se wæs hāten . . . þæt wæs Cēolan sunu . . . þe . . . þe** A sequence of quasi-relative clauses. Note the use of the masculine form of the demonstrative followed by what is properly the neuter form (here used indefinitely without concord) and then the two uses of the relative particle *þe*.

89 **for his ofermōde** The sense of this word is disputed. Although it can mean 'pride' in religious contexts, the implicit moral criticism of that interpretation seems inappropriate to the qualities of a heroic leader. Nevertheless, it is undeniable that the poet questions Byrhtnoth's judgement in the light of events by his words *landes tō fela*.

91 **Ongan ceallian þā ofer cald wæter** The phrase is paralleled in Scandinavian literature, and the suggestion that it is a literary formula is supported by the use of the Anglian form rather than the WS *ceald*. On the gloomy associations of the word in Old and Middle English literature, see Salmon 1968.

110 **bord ord onfēng** The use of the singular to describe an action envisaged to be repeated many times throughout the battlefield is a characteristic feature of OE (and also of ME alliterative) epic style.

Early Middle English (1100–1300)

The beginnings of Middle English might plausibly be associated with the invasion of 1066, after which England found itself host to a second language, Norman French, alongside the English used by the majority. But to equate the beginning of Middle English with the Norman Conquest would be only partly true, and to understand why this is the case it is necessary to outline some of the major differences between the stages of the language which modern scholars have called Old and Middle English.

Changes in the progression from Old to Middle English are traceable at every level of analysis. Phonologically, Middle English is distinguished by the progressive monophthongisation of the OE diphthongs spelt ‹ea› and ‹eo› and the emergence of new diphthongs through the vocalisation of the sequence vowel + final [j] in words like *way* and *lay*. More importantly, the grammar of English underwent striking changes. The OE inflexional system distinguishing case, gender and number in nouns and adjectives was greatly simplified as the vowels in unstressed inflexional endings ceased to be differentiated in pronunciation. The OE dative plural *-um* was already spelt ‹an› and ‹on›, indicating indistinct pronunciation, in Late West Saxon (see Excerpt 7), and the wealth of OE noun and adjective inflexions was gradually reduced to *-es*, *-en*, *-ene* and the ubiquitous *-e*. In the North the loss also of final *-n* produced a situation anticipating Modern English at a very early date (see Excerpt 1). As inflexions became less important in indicating the syntactical function of nouns, the role of prepositions increased, and word order became more fixed within clauses. The definite article was steadily reduced to the simple form *þe*. Verbs were also affected so that in both the South and the North the third person ceased to distinguish adequately between singular and plural (NorthOE *-es*; *-as* > NME *-es*; *-es* and WS *-eþ*; *-aþ* > SME

-eþ; *-eþ*). The personal pronouns also became indistinct as the result of phonetic change, and new forms began to appear: *scæ*, 'she', is found first in the *Peterborough Chronicle* (1154), and *þe33*, 'they', is first recorded in the *Ormulum* (*c*. 1180) (see Excerpt 9).

This last is notable apart from its function in the grammar since it is a wordform borrowed from a Scandinavian language: Early Middle English is distinct from OE also by the relatively high number of recent foreign lexical borrowings. Many of these are, of course, from Norman French, but a substantial number, especially in the North and East, are from Danish and Norwegian. These are words borrowed into English from settlers in the Danelaw in the two hundred years preceding the Conquest but, as a result of the cultural status of the West Saxon written standard, not recorded in writing until after the Norman Conquest, when the English language itself lost prestige by comparison with French. This incidental effect of the Norman Conquest is the final major differentiating feature between Old and Middle English which will find a place here. From being a language of high status, relatively standardised in written form by scribal training, English fell into lower esteem beneath both Latin and French as written languages. Lacking any centralised authority to legislate its writing in standard form, English began to be written individually by scribes in their own local dialects employing the skills they had learned for rendering Latin and French. This brought about changes to the spelling system, so that in the course of the thirteenth century ‹æ› and ‹ð› gradually disappeared and ‹sc›, ‹c + front vowel› and ‹cg› came to be written ‹sh›, ‹ch› and ‹gg› respectively. Above all, Middle English emerged as a language of variety. The diversity of the spoken language, which in modern times has once again been hidden by a written standard, is ever present in written Middle English.

Clearly, the changes described above did not happen at once. They took place over many centuries and at a different pace in the various dialect areas. Generally speaking, inflexional loss was more rapid in the areas settled by Scandinavians, so that the South and South-West, which had remained under continuous West Saxon control, preserved the grammar of the Anglo-Saxon language longest. The following features are characteristic.

> OE ‹y› is written ‹u› (western part only);
> OE ‹eo› continued to be written as late as the four-teenth century in the West;

Initial [s] and [f] had been voiced, and were written ‹z› and ‹v›;

-*en* plurals survive in nouns in considerable numbers;

Feminine and plural third person pronouns are still restricted to forms beginning with *h*- (*ha, he, heo*);

i/y survives as a verbal past participle prefix;

Weak Class 2 verbs are still distinguished from other Weak and Strong verbs by the presence of an -*i*- in the infinitive, the third-person plural present tense, and the present participle (*luuien, luuie, luuiende/luuinde*).

In a few respects, however, the South diverged from earlier OE more markedly than the North. Thus the long *ā* of OE in words like *stān, hām* or *hlāford* was rounded to *ō* in the South but remained unchanged in the North. The plural dative inflexion -*um*, which had been reduced to a sound represented by the spellings ‹-an› and ‹-on› in late West Saxon, seems to have survived longer in the Danelaw, where it was preserved by identification with the same inflexion in Danish. Furthermore, the Old English of Kent had been distinct from that of Wessex, so that Middle English there still preserved the distinction by which:

West Saxon ‹y› was written ‹e›;

the reflex of West Saxon *ēo* was written ‹ie› (from earlier *īo*).

Both of these spellings reflect changes which had taken place long before the Conquest. In the North, too, OE dialect divergences re-emerged in Middle English. In the tenth century, the Lindisfarne Gospel gloss already exhibits the loss of final -*n* in verb infinitives and provides evidence of third-person present-tense forms in -*es* and -*as* (see Excerpt 1B p. 12). These latter both appear in Middle English as -*es*, the ancestor of the form of the modern third-person present singular. Two further distinguishing features of the northern dialect in Middle English are the present participle form ending in -*ande* and the spelling of OE ‹hw› and ‹cw› with ‹qu› or ‹quh›. The participle ending derives from Scandinavian influence upon this dialect, the spelling from the influence of French-trained scribes.

It is evident from this brief discussion – which can do no more than give an impression of the variety of Middle English – that the emergence of the language changes associated with the beginning of Middle English were only loosely connected with the Norman Conquest. In many cases, the dialect writing that the Conquest initiated simply revealed changes which had been in progress for more than two centuries, or diversity which had already been part of pre-Conquest Old English. It revealed also the extent of lexical, syntactical and grammatical influence upon Old English which had come from the extensive Scandinavian settlement of the preceding two hundred years. Scandinavian influence was now apparent not only in hundreds of lexical borrowings, but also among grammatical words such as pronouns (*they*, *their*, *them* and probably *she*), prepositions (*til* and *fro*), derivational affixes (*um-*, *-leik*), and even the inflexional ending *-ande*. Yet, far-reaching as the influence of Scandinavian upon Old English was, it was not the sole contributory factor in the emergence of Middle English. Rather, we should look to a coalition of contributing factors implicit within Old English, accelerated by contact with Scandinavian, and completed by the Norman Conquest. The major contribution of this last was to suppress standardised English before setting it free in infinite new variety, and subsequently enriching its vocabulary by copious loanwords and phrases.

8 The Peterborough Chronicle

The *Peterborough Chronicle*, preserved in Bodleian Library MS Laud Misc. 636, is a descendant of the *Anglo-Saxon Chronicle*, instituted during the reign of King Alfred and maintained at various monastic sites throughout Anglo-Saxon England. In Peterborough, the compilation of the *Chronicle* survived the Conquest, and continued longer than elsewhere. In 1116 it was destroyed by fire but re-established by copying a version borrowed from a southern source. From 1121 to 1132 the renewed record was kept by a Peterborough monk, writing on six different occasions. His work is followed by a single continuous account which covers the remaining years until 1154, when the *Chronicle* was discontinued.

The perspective of the Continuations differs from what went before, exhibiting the foreshortening effect of parochialism. Events around Peterborough loom larger than those of national importance, and the warmth of feeling that proximity generates contributes to greater vigour in the narrative. Personal experience and close acquaintance are drawn upon as testimony, and indignation enlivens rhetorical structures. In the excerpts given below, the accounts of the career of Henry d'Angély and of the anarchy of Stephen's reign are both highly coloured presentations of an affronted Peterborough viewpoint. It is as well to remember that in the annal for 1123 the annalist speaks with approval of Henry, but he changed his mind on further acquaintance. Although the atrocities described in the 1137 annal have general truth, the Peterborough area seems to have been particularly unfortunate in suffering the tyranny of Geoffrey de Mandeville, who fortified the abbey of Ramsey.

The language of the two Peterborough Continuations is distinct from that of the borrowed annals, since elements of the local language and features associated with Early Middle English supersede an essentially standard West Saxon original. This is very clear from the morphology. Already in the First Continuation the simplification of inflexions is well advanced: in the definite article, accusative forms appear for dative (*tofor þone weofede*; *fram þa selua tune*), and among the nouns, plurals of whatever case frequently end in -*es* (*þurh his micele wrences*, 40). Weak nouns have adopted the -*es* plurals proper to Strong masculine nouns (*huntes*, 67; *bucces*, 70), and Weak Class 2 verbs are no longer distinguishable by their inflexional -*i*- from other weak verbs (ð*olen*, 50; *hunten*, 67). The characteristically northern and east Midland loss of the prefix has already occurred in past participles (*numen*, 19; *gifen*, 56). East Midland developments, as well as continuity from Anglian OE, are evident also in the spelling and phonology (see Notes). French borrowing is absent in the first excerpt, except as personal or place names, but a few words of probable Scandinavian origin are found (*oc, toc, baðe*).

A   First Continuation (1127)

Mcxxvii Ðis gear heald se kyng Heanri his hird æt Cristes-
mæsse on Windlesoure. Þær wæs se Scotte kyng Dauid and
eall ða heaued, læred and læuued, þet wæs on Engleland.
And þær he let sweren ercebiscopes and biscopes and abbotes
5 and eorles and ealle þa ðeines ða þær wæron his dohter
Æðelic Englaland and Normandi to hande æfter his dæi, þe
ær wæs ðes Caseres wif of Sexlande; and sende hire siððen to
Normandi, and mid hire ferde hire broðer Rotbert eorl of
Gleucestre and Brian þes eorles sunu Alein Fergan, and lett
10 hire beweddan þes eorles sunu of Angeow, Gosfreið Martæl
wæs gehaten: hit ofþuhte naþema ealle frencisc and englisc,
oc se kyng hit dide for to hauene sibbe of se eorl of Angeow
and for helpe to hauene togænes his neue Willelm. Ðes ilces
gæres on þone lententide wæs se eorl Karle of Flandres
15 ofslagen on ane circe þær he læi and bæd hine to Gode tofor
þone weofede amang þane messe fram his agene manne. And
se kyng of France brohte þone eorles sunu Willelm of
Normandi, and iæf hine þone eorldom, and þet landfolc him
wið toc. Þes ilce Willelm hæfde æror numen ðes eorles dohtor
20 of Angeow to wife, oc hi wæron siððen totweamde for
sibreden: þet wes eall ðurh þone kyng Heanri of Engleland.
Siððen þa nam he þes kynges wifes swuster of France to wife;
and forþi iæf se kyng him þone eorldom of Flandres.
    Ðes ilce gæres he gæf þone abbotrice of Burch an abbot,
25 Henri wæs gehaten, of Peitowe, se hæfde his abbotrice Sancte
Iohannis of Angeli on hande. And ealle þa ærcebiscopes and
biscopes seidon þet hit wæs togeanes riht, and þet he ne
mihte hafen twa abbotrices on hande. Oc se ilce Heanri dide
þone king to understandene þet he hæfde læten his abbotrice
30 for þet micele unsibbe þet wæs on þet land, and þet he dide
ðurh þes Papes ræd and leue of Rome and ðurh þes abbotes

1127   At Christmas in this year King Henry held his court in Windsor. King David of Scots was there and all the chief men, both learned and laymen, who were in England. And there he got the archbishops, bishops, abbots, earls and all the noblemen who were there to swear that his daughter, Æthelic, who had previously been the Emperor of Germany's wife, [should have] England and Normandy after his time; and afterwards he sent her to Normandy, and her brother Robert, Earl of Gloucester, and Brian, son of the earl Alein Fergan, travelled with her, and he had her married to the son of the Earl of Anjou, [who] was called Geoffrey Martel: all the French and English were never more affronted, but the king did it in order to have friendly relations with the Earl of Anjou and to get help against his nephew, William. In this same year during Lent, Charles, Earl of Flanders, was slain by his own men as he lay in church and prayed to God before the altar, during the mass. And the King of France brought the earl's son, William, from Normandy, and gave the earldom to him, and the people of that land accepted him. This same William had previously taken as wife the Earl of Anjou's daughter, but they were afterwards separated on grounds of consanguinity: that was all by the agency of King Henry of England. After that he took as a wife the sister of the king of France's wife; and that is why the king gave him the earldom of Flanders.

In this same year he gave the abbacy of Peterborough to an abbot from Poitou, called Henry, who possessed the abbacy of St Jean d'Angély. And all the archbishops and bishops said that it was improper, and that he could not possess two abbacies. But the same Henry gave the king to understand that he had given up his abbacy on account of the great

of Clunni and þurh þæt he wæs legat of ðone Romescott: oc
hit ne wæs naðema eallswa, oc he wolde hauen baðe on
hande, and swa hafde swa lange swa Godes wille wæs. He
35 wæs on his clærchade biscop on Scesscuns; siððan warð he
munec on Clunni, and siððon prior on þone seolue minstre;
and siððon he wærð prior on Sauenni. Þaræftor, þurh þet he
wæs ðes kynges mæi of Engleland and þes eorles of Peitowe,
þa geaf se eorl him þone abbotrice of Sancte Iohannis minstre
40 of Angeli. Siððon, þurh his micele wrences, ða beiæt he þone
ærcebiscoprice of Besencun, and hæfde hit þa on hande þre
dagas; þa forlæs he þet mid rihte, forþi þet he hit hæfde æror
beieten mid unrihte. Siððon þa beiet he þone biscoprice of
Seintes, þet wæs fif mile fram his abbotrice; þet he hæfde
45 fulneah seoueniht on hande; þenon brohte se abbot him of
Clunni, swa swa he æror dide of Besencun. Þa beþohte he
him þet gif he mihte ben rotfest on Engleland þet he mihte
habben eal his wille. Besohte þa þone kyng and sæide him þet
he wæs eald man and forbroken man, and þet he ne mihte
50 ðolen þa micele unrihte and þa micele unsibbe ða wæron on
here land, and iærnde þa þurh him and ðurh ealle his freond
namcuðlice þone abbotrice of Burhc. And se kyng hit him
iætte, forði þet he wæs his mæi and forþi þet he wæs an hæfod
ða að to swerene and witnesse to berene þær ða eorles sunu of
55 Normandi and þes eorles dohter of Angeow wæron totwemde
for sibreden. Þus earmlice wæs þone abbotrice gifen betwix
Cristesmesse and Candelmesse at Lundene. And swa he ferde
mid þe cyng to Wincestre. And þanon he come to Burch.
And þær he wunede eallriht swa drane doð on hiue: eall þet
60 þa beon dragen toward, swa frett þa drane and dragað
fraward – swa dide he: eall þet he mihte tacen, wiðinnen and
wiðuten, of læred and of læwed, swa he sende ouer sæ; and
na god þær ne dide ne na god ðær ne læuede. Ne þince man
na sellice þet we soð seggen; for hit wæs ful cuð ofer eall land
65 þet swa radlice swa he þær com – þet wæs þes Sunendæies þet
man singað 'Exurge, quare obdormis, Domine?' – þa son
þæræfter þa sægon and herdon fela men feole huntes hunten.
Ða huntes wæron swarte and micele and ladlice, and here
hundes ealle swarte and bradegede and ladlice, and hi ridone
70 on swarte hors and swarte bucces. Þis wæs segon on þe selue
derfald in þa tune on Burch and on ealle þa wudes ða wæron
fram þa selua tune to Stanforde; and þa muneces herdon ða
horn blawen þet hi blewen on nihtes. Soðfæste men heom
kepten on nihtes; sæidon, þes þe heom þuhte, þet þær mihte
75 wel ben abuton twenti oðer þritti horn–blaweres. Þis wæs

unrest that was in that land, and that he did that by the advice and permission of the pope of Rome, and the abbot of Cluny, and because he was the agent of papal taxation: but it was not at all so, and he wished to possess both, and so he did as long as God's will allowed it. In his clerical career he was bishop in Soissons; afterwards he became a monk in Cluny, and after a prior in the same monastery; and afterwards he became prior at Souvigny. After that, because he was kinsman to the king of England and the Earl of Poitou, the earl then gave him the abbacy of the monastery of St Jean d'Angély. Afterwards, through his great cunning and trickery, he obtained the archbishopric of Besançon, and had it for three days; then, justly, he relinquished that which he had previously unjustly obtained. Then he got the bishopric of Saintes, which was five miles from his abbacy; that he possessed for very nearly a week; the abbot of Cluny brought him from there, just as earlier he did from Besançon. Then he thought to himself that if he might take root in England that he could have all his own way. He implored the king and told him that he was an old and broken man and that he could not suffer the great injustice and disturbance that were in their land, and he desired through him and through all his important friends the abbacy of Peterborough. And the king obtained it for him, because he was his kinsman and because he was prominent in swearing the oath and bearing witness when the son of the Earl of Normandy and the Earl of Anjou's daughter were separated for consanguinity. Thus the abbey was wretchedly bestowed in London between Christmas and Candlemass. And so he went with the king to Winchester, and from there he came to Peterborough. There he lived just as the drone does in the hive: all that the bees bring in the drone devours and takes away – as he did: all that he could take, from inside and out, from clerks and common people, he sent across the sea; he contributed nothing and left nothing. Nor should any man think it marvellous that we state the truth; for it was well known throughout the land as soon as he came there – it was on the Sunday when '*Exurge* [etc.]' is sung – then immediately after many men saw and heard many hunters hunt. The hunters were dark and huge and ugly, and their hounds all dark and wide-eyed and ugly and they rode on dark horses and dark goats. This was seen in the same deer-park in the township of Peterborough and in all the woods from the same town to Stamford. And the monks heard the horns blown that they

sægon and herd fram þet he þider com eall þet lententid onan
to Eastren. Þis was his ingang: of his utgang ne cunne we iett
noht seggon. God scawe fore!

Notes

1 **Ðis gear** 'this year'   Annals frequently begin with some version of
this phrase, but in earlier entries the dative case is clearly indicated.

3 **heaued**   The spelling ‹u› of the voiced fricative consonant between
vowels, normally spelt ‹f› in OE, is owing to French influence, cf.
hauene (12), *læuede* (63), but also *hæfod* (53).

5 **ðeines**   The spelling (cf. OE *ðegn*) suggests the emergence of a
new diphthong /ei/, as also in *seidon* (27), *dæi* (6) and *læi* (15).

6 **Æðelic**   Better known as Matilda. She had been married to the
Emperor Henry V, who died in 1125.

9 **Alein Fergan**   Count of Brittany. *Brian* and *sunu* are in apposition. Although in apposition with *þes eorles*, the name *Alein Fergan*
is not inflected.

12 **dide**   The ‹i› spelling in words where OE has ‹y› represents an
unrounding of the OE vowel characteristic of the east Midlands in
ME. Cf. *þince* (63).

13 **Willelm**   William Clito, son of Robert Curthose, Duke of
Normandy.

16 **fram his agene manne** 'by his own men'   In OE *fram* takes the
dative, whose plural was *mannum*. The dative form here is modelled
on that of the singular of masculine nouns, but in correct OE *man*
has a mutated dative singular, *men*. The writer's failure to
understand this inflexional system is apparent.

22 **þes kynges . . . to wife**   The head of the noun phrase is *swuster*,
which is preceded by two genitive modifiers in the OE manner, and
succeeded by a dative qualifier. The phrase *to wife* is also a dative
idiom meaning 'as a wife'. A dative *-e* is often used in such phrases,
but may be omitted: *of Engleland* (21).

34 **swa Godes wille wæs**   This phrase suggests that the passage was
written after Henry had ceased to hold St Jean d'Angély in 1131, but
the closing words of the excerpt imply composition before his
departure from England in 1132.

blew at night. Sensible men stayed in at night; they said, as it seemed to them, that there might well be about twenty or thirty hornblowers. This was seen and heard from [the time] that he came all that Lent up to Easter. This was his arrival: of his departure we cannot yet speak. May God provide!

41–42 **þre dagas** The monophthongisation of OE *ēo*, which is found at an early date in the east Midlands, is suggested by other spellings in this text: *ben* (47), *blewen* (73).

43 **beieten** WS *begieten*. In WS the palatal consonant (written *g*) diphthongised the following *e*. The spelling here is descended from an Anglian antecedent.

65 **þes Sunendæies** Sexagesima Sunday, 6 February 1127.

68 **Ða huntes** The allusion is probably to the 'Wild Hunt', a legend of ghostly hunters riding on stormy nights led by the Devil. Analogous hunts are found in Celtic and Scandinavian myth, where the leader is the god Odin.

69 **bradegede** 'broad-eyed' The form *egede* suggests an OE antecedent spelt *ēge* rather than WS *ēage*, the product of Anglian smoothing.

71 **derfald** WS *dēorfeald*. The spelling exemplifies both the east Midland monophthongisation of *ēo* and the failure of the breaking of *æ* before *l*-groups characteristic of Anglian OE. Cf., however, the spelling *eald* (49).

72 **herdon** WS *hīerdon*. The *i*-mutation of *ēa* produced *īe* in West Saxon, but *ē* in Anglian dialects.

B Final Continuation (1154)

Mcxxxvii Ðis gære for þe king Stephne ofer sæ to Normandi, and ther wes underfangen forþi ðat hi uuenden ðat he sculde ben alsuic alse the eom wes, and for he hadde get his tresor; ac he todeld it and scatered sotlice. Micel hadde Henri king
5 gadered gold and syluer, and na god ne dide me for his saule tharof.

Þa þe king Stephne to Englalande com, þa macod he his gadering æt Oxeneford; and þar he nam þe biscop Roger of Serebyri, and Alexander biscop of Lincol, and te canceler
10 Roger, hise neues, and dide ælle in prisun til hi iafen up here castles. Þa the suikes undergæton ðat he milde man was, and softe and god, and na iustise ne dide, þa diden hi alle wunder. Hi hadden him manred maked and athes suoren, ac hi nan treuthe ne heolden. Alle he wæron forsworen and here treothes
15 forloren, for æuric rice man his castles makede and agænes him heolden; and fylden þe land ful of castles. Hi suencten suyðe þe uurecce men of þe land mid castel-weorces. Þa þe castles uuaren maked, þa fylden hi mid deoules and yuele men. Þa namen hi þa men þe hi wenden ðat ani god hefden,
20 bathe be nihtes and be dæies, carlmen and wimmen, and diden heom in prisun, and pined heom efter gold and syluer untellendlice pining: for ne uuæren næure nan martyrs swa pined alse hi wæron. Me henged up bi the fet and smoked heom mid ful smoke. Me henged bi the þumbes other bi the
25 hefed, and hengen bryniges on her fet. Me dide cnotted strenges abuton here hæued, and uurythen it ðat it gæde to þe hærnes. Hi diden heom in quarterne þar nadres and snakes and pades wæron inne, and drapen heom swa. Sume hi diden in crucethur, ðat is, in an ceste þat was scort and nareu and
30 undep; and dide scærpe stanes þerinne, and þrengde þe man þærinne ðat him bræcon alle þe limes. In mani of þe castles wæron lof and grin: ðat wæron rachenteges ðat twa oþer thre men hadden onoh to bæron onne. Þat was sua maced ðat is fæstned to an beom, and diden an scærp iren abuton þa
35 mannes throte and his hals, ðat he ne myhte nowiderwardes, ne sitten ne lien ne slepen, oc bæron al ðat iren. Mani þusen hi drapen mid hungær. I ne can ne I ne mai tellen alle þe wunder ne alle þe pines ðat hi diden wrecce men on þis land; and ðat lastede þa xix wintre wile Stephne was king, and
40 æure it was uuerse and uuerse. Hi læiden gæildes on the tunes æure umwile, and clepeden it 'tenserie'. Þa þe uurecce men ne hadden nammore to gyuen, þa ræueden hi and brendon alle

1137 In this year King Stephen went over the sea to Normandy; and was received there because they thought that he would be just like his uncle was, and because he still had his treasure; but he divided and scattered it foolishly. King Henry had gathered much gold and silver, and no good for his soul was done with it. When King Stephen came to England, he held a parliament at Oxford, and there he took Roger, bishop of Salisbury, and Alexander, bishop of Lincoln, the chancellor Roger, his nephews, and imprisoned them until they surrendered their castles. When the traitors realised that he was a gentle man and soft and good and did not exact [harsh] justice, they all perpetrated atrocities. They had done him homage and sworn oaths, but they did not keep any faith. They were all perjured and their oaths abandoned, for every powerful man made his castles and held [them] against him; and filled the land full of castles. They greatly oppressed the poor men of the land with the building of castles; when the castles were made, they filled them with devils and wicked men. Then they took those people that they thought had any property, both by day and by night, men and women, and put them in prison and tortured them for their gold and silver with unspeakable torture; for never were martyrs tortured as they were. They were hung up by the feet and smoked with foul smoke. They were hung by the thumbs or by the head and coats of mail hung on their feet. Knotted strings were placed around their head and were twisted until they went to the brain. They put them in a dungeon where there were adders and snakes and toads, and they killed them in that way. Some they put in a torture-box: that is, in a chest that was short, narrow and shallow. And they put sharp stones in it and pressed the man in there so that they broke all his limbs. In many of the castles there were headband and halter: those were chains such that two or three men had difficulty in carrying one. It was made thus, that is, fastened to a beam. And they put a sharp iron [blade] around the man's throat and neck, so that he could not [move] in any direction, nor sit, nor lie, nor sleep, but had to support all that iron. They killed many thousands by starvation. I do not know nor can I tell all the atrocities nor all the torments that they did to poor men in this land; and that lasted for the nineteen years that Stephen was king, and continuously it got worse and worse. They imposed taxes on

the tunes, ðat wel þu myhtes faren al a dæis fare, sculdest thu
neure finden man in tune sittende, ne land tiled. Þa was corn
45 dære, and flec and cæse and butere, for nan ne wæs o þe land.
Wrecce men sturuen of hungær. Sume ieden on ælmes þe
waren sum wile rice men; sume flugen ut of lande. Wes næure
gæt mare wreccehed on land, ne næure hethen men werse ne
diden þan hi diden. For ouersithon ne forbaren hi nouther
50 circe ne cyrceiærd, oc namen al þe god ðat þarinne was, and
brenden sythen þe cyrce and al tegædere. Ne hi ne forbaren
biscopes land ne abbotes ne preostes, ac ræueden munekes and
clerekes, and æuric man other þe ouermyhte. Gif twa men oþer
iii coman ridend to an tun, al þe tunscipe flugæn for heom,
55 wenden ðat hi wæron ræueres. Þe biscopes and lered men heom
cursede æure, oc was heom naht þarof, for hi uueron al for-
cursæd and forsuoren and forloren. War sæ me tilede, þe erthe
ne bar nan corn, for þe land was al fordon mid suilce dædes,
and hi sæden openlice ðat Crist slep, and his halechen. Suilc,
60 and mare þanne we cunnen sæin, we þoleden xix wintre for
ure sinnes.

Notes

1 **þe king Stephne**   The word order of the title is not that of OE
(*Ælfred cyning*), and although it may imitate Latin, the presence of
the definite articles suggests that it is modelled on Norman French.
French loanwords include: *tresor, canceler, prisun, castles, iustise,
tenserie.*

3 **get** 'yet, still'   Compare note to First Continuation (43).

5 **na god ne dide me**   An impersonal construction. *Me* is an
unstressed form of *man*. For *dide* see First Continuation, note on
line 12. Note here *king* (1); *sinnes* (61).

10 **dide ælle in prisun**   The phrase is perhaps modelled on French,
faire en prison. Cf. *iustise ne dide, faire justice* (12).
   iafen up   Verbs with a following prepositional element (phrasal
verbs) emerged under Scandinavian influence. Cf. *him wið toc* (ON
taka við), First Continuation (19).

12 **wunder** 'atrocities'   The noun is a neuter plural and therefore
correctly endingless. Most nouns in the excerpt have the *-es* plural
derived from the nominative and accusative plural of OE strong
masculines. A weak plural is preserved in *halechen* (59).

the villages again and again, and called it 'protection-money'. When the poor folk had no more to give, they robbed them and burned all the villages, so that you might well travel a whole day's journey and you would not find anyone settled in a village nor the land cultivated. Then corn was expensive, and meat, and cheese, and butter, for there was none in the country. Poor people died of starvation. Some survived on charity who were once rich men; some fled from the land. There was never more misery in the land, and neither did heathens do worse than they did; for too often they spared neither the church nor the churchyard, but they took everything of value that was inside and afterwards burned the church and everything together. Neither did they spare the bishops', abbots' or priests' land, but robbed monks and clerics, and every man robbed any other whom he could overpower. If two or three men came riding into a village, all the villagers fled because of them; they thought that they were robbers. The bishops and learned men continually cursed them, but that was nothing to them, for they were all excommunicated, perjured and damned. Wherever the earth was tilled, it bore no corn, for the land was all ruined by such deeds. And they said openly that Christ and his saints slept. Such, and more than we can say, we suffered for nineteen years for our sins.

15 **rice man**   Here probably derived from OE *rīce*, 'powerful', but in line 47 the context suggests semantic association with French *riche*.

20 **carlmen**   ON *karlmenn*. There is substantial lexical influence from Scandinavian sources in the excerpt: *bathe, syluer* (OE form is *seolfor*), *bryniges, hærnes, drapen, þrengde*. The prefix in *umwile* (41) is of Scandinavian origin.

29 **crucethur** 'torture-box'   Probably derived from the Latin *cruciator*.

46 **sturuen of hungær**   The verb still has the more general sense of OE *steorfan*, 'to die'.

53 **æuric man other þe ouermyhte**   The verb is in the subjunctive, and its subject is the relative particle *þe*, dependent on *æuric man*. The direct object is *other*.

9 The Ormulum

The *Ormulum* is a collection of metrical homilies (sermons or religious discourses containing an illustrative story) based on gospel stories, each followed by an interpretation for 'your souls' need'. The twenty thousand lines of the extant text represent only a fraction of the initial plan, which may be considered merciful, since its author's literary skills are not of a high standard. Orderliness of presentation and zeal for instruction are his major characteristics: his verse is rigidly regular, and his faith in the rhetorical device of *inculcatio* (the repetition of an instructional point) is wearying. The essential interest of this text lies in its role as a linguistic witness.

The author gives his name as Orm in an opening address to his brother, Walter, a fellow Augustinian canon. The name is of Scandinavian origin, and recent research (Parkes 1983) suggests that the text may have been written in an area of relatively heavy Scandinavian settlement, at Bourne in Lincolnshire, the home at a later date of Robert Mannyng (see Excerpt 16). The composition can be dated on palaeographic evidence at about 1180.

The value of the *Ormulum* for linguistic analysis arises from the fact that it is written in the author's own hand, and is therefore free from copying errors, but it has particular significance through the author's personality and purpose. Unlike most medieval authors, Orm takes extreme pains to preserve the form as well as the content of his text. Regularity of metre is matched by remarkable consistency in spelling. Further details are given in the notes, but one peculiar aspect of this may be discussed here. Firstly, a definition: an open syllable is one with the structure CV-, and a closed syllable has the structure -VC (where V = vowel or diphthong, and C = consonant). In two-syllable words, like *faderr*, the medial consonant (*d*) begins the second syllable, so that the first syllable is open (CV-). Orm's spelling system takes account of these syllable types. After a short vowel or diphthong in closed syllables, Orm doubles the final consonant (*þatt, wass, menn*), but in open syllables, the consonant beginning the next syllable is not doubled (*sune, faderr, hafenn*). Consequently, a single consonant in a closed syllable shows that the preceding vowel is long, and so the *Ormulum* contains valuable evidence about lengthening before consonant groups (*land*, 3; *halden*, 134; but *lanng*, 6). Moreover, a distinction in metrical distribution between OE short vowels in open syllables and the other possible combinations can be used to show that ME open syllable lengthening had not yet occurred in words like *faderr* and *sune*.

Orm was greatly concerned for his spelling system and in his Dedication begs any copyist neither to omit words nor harm the metre, and that:

> . . . he loke wel þatt he
> An bocstaff wríte twiȝȝess
> Eȝȝwhær þær itt uppo þiss boc
> Iss writenn o þatt wise.
>
> (*Dedication*, 103–6)

Otherwise, he says, English cannot be written correctly. The fallacy in this, in a land where English was spoken so variously, seems to have escaped him. There is, however, no evidence that anyone attempted to copy his work, and it survives only in Bodleian Library MS Junius I.

The facsimile illustrates Orm's awkward and unprofessional hand. His manuscript is written in two tall columns, but in order to ensure that the interpretation of his exemplary story begins at the head of the second column, he has been forced to write the close of the Bible story across two column-widths at the foot of the page, and use uncharacteristic abbreviations in the formulaic phrase *Off ure sawle nede* (104). Although the letters *f* and superscript *r* have their continental form, the descent of Orm's writing from Anglo-Saxon practice is evident in the use of *æ*, *þ*, *ȝ*, the rune 'wynn' for *w*, and the insular forms of the letters: *a*, *r*, and *s*. The special form of *g*, by which he denotes the stop [g] is clear in *ḡodd*, and the digraph *ȝh* can be seen in *ȝho*. The type in which the *h* is written superscript, and which represents the velar fricative occurs in *serrȝhen* (72). Doubling of consonants to indicate a preceding short vowel is accomplished in a variety of ways: by the use of superscripts, and by doubling the abbreviation marks for *n* or *m* as well as in the usual manner. Note, too, the special form of doubled *þ* in *kiþeþþ*.

Plate 2   *Ormulum*, fol. 70v (*opposite*)

Secundum Lucam XV: Cum factus esset Ihesus Christus annorum xii ascendentibus illis

Affterr þatt tatt te Laferrd Crist
Wass cumenn off Egyppte
Inntill þe land off Ḡalile,
Till Nazaræþess chesstre,
5 Þæraffterr seȝȝþ þe ḡoddspell boc
Bilæf he þær well lannḡe
Wiþþ hise frend, tatt haffdenn himm
To ȝemenn annd to ḡætenn,
Wiþþ Marȝe þatt hiss moderr wass
10 Annd maȝȝdenn þwerrt ūt clene,
Annd wiþþ Josæp þatt wass himm sett
To fedenn annd to fosstrenn.
Annd illke Lenntenn forenn þeȝȝ
Till ȝerrsalæmess chesstre
15 Aȝȝ att te Passkemesnedaȝȝ,
Swa summ þe boc hemm tahhte,
To frellsenn þær þatt heȝhe tid
O þatt Judisskenn wise,
Forr þatt teȝȝ wærenn ḡode menn,
20 Annd ḡodess laȝhess heldenn.
Annd siþþenn, o þatt ȝer þatt Crist
Wass off twellf winnterr elde,
Þeȝȝ comenn in till ȝerrsalæm
Att teȝȝre Passkemesse,
25 Annd heldenn þær þatt hallȝhe tid
O þatt Judissken wise.
Annd Jesu Crist wass þær wiþþ hemm,
Swa summ þe ḡoddspell kiþeþþ.
Annd affterr þatt te tid wass ḡan
30 Þeȝȝ wenndenn fra þe temmple
Annd ferrdenn towarrd Nazaræþ
An daȝȝess ḡanḡ till efenn,
Annd wenndenn þatt te Laferrd Crist
Wiþþ hemm þatt ḡate come,
35 Annd he wass þa bihinndenn hemm
Bilefedd att te temmple;
Annd tatt ne wisste nohht hiss kinn,
Acc wennde þatt he come,
Annd ȝedenn heore weȝȝe forþ
40 Till þatt itt comm till efenn,
Annd ta þeȝȝ misstenn þeȝȝre child,

After the Lord Christ was come from Egypt into the land of Galilee, to the city of Nazareth, the Gospel says he remained there after that for a very long time with his friends who took care of him and protected him, with Mary who was his mother and a virgin utterly pure, and with Joseph who was appointed to support and nurture him. And each Lent they went to the city of Jerusalem always at the festival of the Passover just as the book instructed them, to observe there that important feast in the Jewish manner, because they were good people and maintained God's laws. And afterwards, in that year that Christ was twelve years of age, they came to Jerusalem at their Passover and kept that holy festival in the Jewish manner. And Jesus was there with them, as the Gospel reveals. And after the festival was past, they went from the temple and journeyed towards Nazareth one day's march till evening, and [they] thought that the Lord Christ came that way with them; and he was left behind them at the temple; and his kinsfolk did not know that, but thought that he had come and they went on their way forward until it came to evening, and then they missed their child and it worried them, and they went and looked for him among relatives and acquaintances, and they found no trace of him because he was at the temple. And then they went back again to search for that dear child and came back to Jerusalem to look for him within. And they found him there on the third day in the temple among the group of Jews who were informed about the Bible. And there he sat questioning them about their book's teaching. And it seemed to all there who heard him a great marvel that he was so profound and so wise in answering and in asking. And Saint Mary came to him and spoke thus to him: 'Dear son, why did you treat us like this, causing us such trouble? The two of us have searched for you everywhere, both I and your father with grieving heart and heavy spirit. Why did you do this deed?' And then Jesus Christ said to them both thus: 'Why were you so concerned to seek me? Why did you grieve? Did you not know that I ought to advance my father's will? Nor that I ought to be concerned about his affairs?' And at that time they could not fully understand that speech; and he then went off with them and complied with their wishes, and came with them to Nazareth, as the Gospel makes clear. And he submitted himself and

Annd itt hemm offerrþuhhte,
Annd ȝedenn till, annd sohhtenn himm,
Bitwenenn sibbe annd cuþe,
45 Annd teȝȝ ne fundenn nohht off himm,
Forr he wass att te temmple.
Annd teȝȝ þa wenndenn efft onnȝæn
Þatt dere child to sekenn,
Annd comenn efft till ȝerrsalæm,
50 To sekenn himm þær binnenn.
Annd teȝȝ himm o þe þridde daȝȝ
Þær fundenn i þe temmple,
Bitwenenn þatt Judissken flocc
Þatt læredd wass o boke;
55 Annd tære he satt to fraȝȝnenn hemm
Off þeȝȝre bokess lare;
Annd alle þatt himm herrden þær,
Hemm þuhhte mikell wunnderr
Off þatt he wass full ȝæp annd wis
60 To swarenn annd to fraȝȝnenn.
Annd Sannte Marȝe comm till himm
Annd seȝȝde himm þuss wiþþ worde,
'Whi didesst tu, lef sune, þuss
Wiþþ uss, forr uss to swennkenn?
65 Witt hafenn sohht te widewhar
Icc annd ti faderr baþe
Wiþþ serrhfull herrte annd sariȝ mod,
Whi didesst tu þiss dede?'
Annd tanne seȝȝde Jesu Crist
70 Till baþe þuss wiþþ worde,
'Whatt wass ȝuw swa to sekenn me?
Whatt wass ȝuw swa to serrȝhen?
Ne wisste ȝe nohht tatt me birrþ
Min faderr will forþenn?
75 Ne þatt me birrþ beon hoȝhefull
Abutenn hise þingess?'
Annd teȝȝ ne mihhtenn nohht tatt word
Ȝet ta wel unnderrstanndenn;
Annd he þa ȝede forþ wiþþ hemm
80 Annd dide hemm heore wille,
Annd comm wiþþ hemm till Nazaræþ,
Swa summ þe ḡoddspell kiþeþþ,
Annd till hemm baþe he lutte annd bæh
Þurrh soþfasst herrsummnesse,
85 Annd wass wiþþ hemm till þatt he wass

bowed to them both through firm obedience, and remained with them until he was thirty years of age. And our lady Mary took all that she saw and heard of her son Jesus Christ, and concerning his divinity, and held it all in her thought, just as the Gospel makes known, and she laid it all together for ever in the treasure chest of her thought. And her son grew and thrived both in wisdom and in age, and he was beloved and dear to God and good people; and that was just, for he was God, and good in every way. Here, this way, this Gospel ends, and it behoves us to search through it to see what it teaches us about the needs of our soul.

Off þrittiʒ winnterr elde.
Annd ure laffdiʒ Marʒe toc
All þatt ʒho sahh annd herrde
Off hire sune Jesu Crist,
90 Annd off hiss ḡoddcunndnesse,
Annd all ʒhŏt held inn hire þohht,
Swa summ þe ḡoddspell kiþeþþ,
Annd leʒʒde itt all tosamenn aʒʒ
Inn hire þohhtess arrke.
95 Annd hire sune wex annd þraf
I wissdom annd in elde,
Annd he wass Ḡodd annd ḡode menn
Well swiþe lef annd dere;
Annd tatt wass rihht, forr he wass Ḡodd,
100 Annd ḡod onn alle wise.
Her endeþþ nu þiss ḡoddspell þuss
Annd uss birþ itt þurrhsekenn,
To lokenn whatt itt læreþþ uss
Off ure sawle nede.

Notes

2 **cumenn**   As in the *Peterborough Chronicle*, written thirty years
earlier and sixteen miles to the south, past participles no longer
possess the OE prefix: *sett* (11); *ḡan* (29).

5 **seʒʒþ**   The third-person singular present tense ends in (*e*)*þ*. Orm
uses the ʒ graph for the palatal [j] and his own version of Carolingian
g for the velar plosive [g].

7 **frend**   The OE mutated plural was endingless; the form with *e* is
of Anglian origin, since in that dialect *īo* was not *i*-mutated (WS
friend) and developed to *ēo*. Orm's text provides striking evidence of
the EM monophthongisation of *eo* to *e*, since, to about line 13,000,
he wrote ‹eo› but then changed his practice, writing ‹e› and
systematically correcting his earlier work.

10 **þwerrt ŭt** 'utterly' (ON *þvert* + *ut*)   The passage contains ample
evidence of the influence of Scandinavian languages: *till* (used in the
sense of motion towards); the pronoun *þeʒʒ*, *þeʒʒre*; *ḡætenn* (8);
summ (16); *laʒhess* (20); *aʒʒ* (15); *fra* (30); *ḡate* (34); *mikell* (58);
baþe (70), etc. The use of the acute accents and the breve elsewhere

can be explained in some cases by a desire to distinguish homographs, but in the case of monosyllables such as the examples in the excerpt, the accents may be intended to emphasise that the syllable is long, despite the expectations of Latin readers.

22 **winnterr**   The usual noun plural in the *Ormulum* is *-es*, which is extended to OE neuters (*þingess*) and one mutated form (*bokess*), but a few common expressions have other endings or are without ending: *wiþþ worde* (62) and genitive plural *sawle* (104).

28 **kiþeþþ**   OE *cȳþan*. The *i*-spelling of OE *y* is characteristic of east Midland texts: *kinn* (37); *didesst* (68).

41 **þeʒʒ** , **þeʒʒre**   Although not all exemplified in the excerpt, the *Ormulum* is the earliest ME text to exhibit the modern, Scandinavian-derived set of third-person plural pronouns. In unstressed positions within the sentence, the OE *h-* forms are still used for the oblique cases: *heore, hemm*.

56 **lare**   The rounding of /a:/ to /ɔ:/, which commenced in the South, is not found in this early text: *sariʒ* (67); *swa* (71).

60 **swarenn and fraʒʒnenn**   Weak Class 2 verbs no longer possess a distinct inflexional *-i-*. Indeed, the reduction of all inflexional vowels to an invariable *-e* is further advanced here than in the *Peterborough Chronicle*.

65 **Witt hafenn** 'We two have'   Dual number survives in the personal pronouns, in increasingly formulaic use, until the mid thirteenth century. The verb 'have' (OE *habbað*) here shows the analogical extension of the fricative from the second- and third-person singular forms (*hæfst, hæfð*). The inflexional *-en* of the plural present is characteristic of east Midland ME, and is derived from the OE subjunctive. Comparison of the spelling *hafenn* with that of the preterite *haffdenn* – (7) is a good illustration of Orm's spelling consistency, in which the addition of the preterite suffix causes the first syllable to become closed, requiring a doubling of the consonant before the short *a*.

71 **Whatt wass ʒuw**   *ʒuw* is dative, and the construction is an impersonal idiom, as also *me birrþ* (73).

88 **ʒho**   This form, together with the form *scæ* in the *Peterborough Chronicle* annal for 1140, are among the earliest evidence for the ancestor of the modern form *she*. The sequence of the graphs ‹ʒ› and ‹h› is used by Orm in two distinct ways, presumably with distinct significance: with superscript *h*, ‹ʒʰ› represents the voiced velar fricative in words like *heʒhe* (17) and *laʒhes* (20); its voiceless equivalent Orm writes ‹hh› (*mihhtenn, sahh, nohht*). The graph ‹ʒh› is written with normal *h* only in the word *ʒho*. In view of Orm's phonetic care, this may imply that a unique sound is involved here.
    sahh and herrde   The verb *sahh* exhibits Anglian smoothing of the long *ēa* diphthong found preserved in WS. The form *herrde*, too, is Anglian, since the *i*-mutation of *ēa* which produced *hīerde* in WS resulted in *hērde* in Anglian areas.

91 **ʒhŏt**   An elision of *ʒho* and *itt*.

Having lost its opening pages, the text now called *Vices and Virtues* survives, without any indication of its author's title, only in British Library MS Stowe 34. Its content is an exchange between a soul, who confesses its sins, and allegorised Reason, who then expounds the virtues. The exchange is not conceived in a dramatic spirit, however, and no true dialogue develops. Rather, the work constantly shows traces of thematic compilation, both in minor stylistic choices (for example the introductory formulae *hier . . . cumþ*) and in the organisation of its material according to well-established schema such as the five wits, the seven gifts of the Holy Ghost, the three Christian virtues, the four cardinal virtues, and the four daughters of God. Following such inherited schema rather than developing his own theme sometimes leads the author into repetition. Although lacking some of the stylistic vigour and attractive humanity of the *Ancrene Wisse*, its near contemporary, *Vices and Virtues* is not without literary accomplishment, and as a representative of very early religious prose from the eastern half of England, it is an important witness.

Its origins are obscure. The Stowe manuscript may be dated on palaeographical grounds to about 1200, and is known to have belonged in the sixteenth century to William Fleetwood, Recorder of London. Nothing is known of the author of the work, but as a lettered man he is likely to have been associated with some religious order. He does not, however, direct his work towards a monastic audience, and indeed he refers to 'these monks' rather distantly as an example to his audience. Other statements suggest that, although associated with some order, he was not himself a monk (*Þa ðe bieð on religiun, hie bieð under scrifte, swa bihoueð us alswa*). It is possible that the 'us' to whom he refers was a college of secular canons.

The London associations of the manuscript are largely borne out by the language in which it is written. It is copied by two scribes, the first of whom tended to preserve more fully the older spellings of his exemplar, but the evidence of both suggests an early text from the East Saxon area. Generally southern and early features are the well-preserved inflexional system, the use of prefixes to indicate the past participle, the preservation of final *n* in the infinitive, *h*-forms of the personal pronouns, and the distinct Weak Class 2 forms: *luuieð* (77) and *luuien* (95). More specific indications of a south-eastern origin are signs of rounding of OE *ā* at a very early date, ‹a› spellings for WS *ǣ* and the writing of the reflex of WS *y* as ‹e› and ‹u›: *euele* (4), *kenne* (17), *wurse* (15). Further details are given in the notes.

Of witte. Hier after cumþ an oðer Godes ȝiue þe is icleped *sciencia*, þat is, inȝehied oðer witt. Ðurh hire ðu miht witen alle craftes ðe on boche bieð ȝewriten. Hie ðe takð gode þeawes and god lif to leden, hu ðu scalt fram ðan euele buȝen and hu ðu
5 scalt gode werkes don. Ac hit bieð sume ðe bieð swiðe wise ihealden ðurh ðessere Godes ȝiue, and want hem seluen and iec sumen oðre te michele hearme, þat ðe Godd hem ȝaf for here michele gode. Herof sade ðe apostel: *Scientia inflat, karitas edificat.* He seið þat ðis scarpe iwitt swelð ðane mann ðe hes
10 haueð wiðuten charite. On swilche wise hie swelð ðat he latt wel of him seluen, and forhoweð oðre ðe swo ne cunnen; and on swilche wise he forliest ðat him betst scolde helpen, þat is, Godes luue and mannes. For ðan þat wite ðu te fulle soðe, ðanne ðu forliest mannes luue for ði modinesse, þe þingð ðat þu naust
15 naht to wurðin ne te luuen ane wurse mann ðane ðu art, oðer ðat he nis alswa wis alse ðu, oðer he nis na swa riche se ðu, oðer of swa heiȝe kenne swa ðu, oðer naht alswa wurðed mann swa ðu on ðare lease woreld; and for ðelliche þing hine forhowest and forlatst ðat tu ne wilt to him clepiȝen, ne to his niede him
20 helpen. Fulȝewis ðu forliest hier rihtes Godes luue and his grace, and nem ðis to forbisne! Bute ðu habbe Godes luue and alre manne, ðu ne miht don non god ðe æure Gode bie ȝecweme. Ðarof sade ðe apostele: 'Gif ic deale all ðat ic habbe for Godes luùe, and ȝiet on-uuen ðan ȝiue mine likame to
25 barnin al to duste for Godes luue, and ic hatie on-lepi mann, ðanne ne habbe ic naht kariteð, and swa ic habbe all forloren.' Nu seið sum mann: 'Scal ic luuiȝe ðane euele mann?' Hlest hwat se heiȝeste ðe seið: *Diliges proximum sicut te ipsum*, 'Luue ðine nexte alswa ðe seluen, hwat manne swo he æure bie.' Ne bie he
30 næure swa swiðe forȝelt, æure he is ðin nexte after ȝekynde. Luue ða ȝekynde, and hate his euel. ȝif ðu miht hit bieten, biet hit alswo ðu woldest ðat me bette þin, ȝif ðu wære swo forȝilt also he, and þenc ðat ðe writt seið þat æure bie ðe mildce ouer ðe rihte dome. For ðelliche þinge maniȝe of ðe wel wise
35 menn forlieseð Godes luue and his grace, forði ðat hie ne habbeð, ne reccheð to habben, here emcristenes luue, ac

Here, after this, comes another gift of God, which is called *scientia*, that is understanding or knowledge. Through it you may know all the skills that are written in books. It teaches you good behaviour and to lead a good life, how you ought to turn away from evil, and how you ought to do good deeds. But there are some who, through this gift of God, are considered very wise, but turn to great harm to themselves and also to some others that which God gave them for their great benefit. The apostle said this about it: *Scientia inflat, caritas aedificat.* He says that 'This keen understanding puffs up the man who has it without charity.' It puffs him up in such a way that he thinks well of himself, and despises others who are not so aware; and in this manner he loses what ought to help him best, that is the love of God and man. Therefore know the whole truth, when you relinquish men's love through your pride, it seems to you that you do not have to esteem or love any man inferior to yourelf: either because he is not so wise as you, or he is not so rich as you, or from so noble a family as you, or not such a respected person as you in the deceptive world; and for such things you despise him, and neglect to call on him, nor help him in need. Certainly, here you justly lose God's love and his grace, and take this as an example! Unless you have the love of God and of all men, you can do no good deed that may ever be pleasing to God. The apostle said this: *Si distribuero omnes facultates meas, etc.*, 'If, for God's love, I share out all that I have, and yet further than that, give my body to be burned to dust for God's love, but I hate a single person, then I do not possess love, and so I have lost everything.' Now someone will say: 'Ought I to love the wicked man?' Listen to what the Most High tells you: *Diliges proximum sicut te ipsum*, 'Love your neighbour as yourself, whatever kind of man he may be.' Be he never so guilty, he is always your neighbour in nature. Love the shared nature, and hate his wickedness. If you might reprove it, reprove it as you would wish someone to reprove yours, if you were as guilty as he, and remember that

hopieð to here michele wisdome, and ofte bieð beswikene.
Wolden hie hlesten ðane hali apostel, swa hie ne ðorften! *Si
quis uidetur inter nos sapiens esse, stultus fiat ut sit sapiens*,
40 '3if 3eure ani,' he seið, 'is ihealden for wis on ðare woreld,
becume sott, and swa he mai bien wis.'
Ðe wise woreld-mann, he halt michel sothade ðat mann
forlate, for Godes luue, hus and ham, wif and child, and gold
and seluer, and alle worldes wele, and becume swo michel
45 wrecche alswo he ðe naht ne hadde; seið ðat him is betere to
sitten on his a3en, and 3iuen almessen and herber3in sæli
menn, ðanne he scolde al ðat laten, and libben bi oðre
mannes almesse. Hleste we herof Cristes a3ene dom, and
swa we mu3en bien ðe sikerere of ðese iflite. Hit seið on ða
50 hali goddspelle þat an riche iungman cam to Crist be ðo
dai3en ðe he hier lichamliche was wuniende, and seide: *Quid
faciam, domine, ut habeam vitam eternam?* 'Hlauerd,' cwað
he, 'hwat mai ic don ðat ic mihte hauen ðat eche lif?' Vre
drihten him andswerede, and seide: *Mandata nosti,*
55 '3ecnoust þu Godes bebodes. Ne sleih, ne ne stell, ne
reaue, ne forli3e ðe on hordomes, ne oðre Godes forbodes
ne tebrec.' 'A, hlaueerd,' cwað he, 'alle ðese bebodes ic
habbe ihealde fram childhade, swa ðat ic nabbe nan
tebrocen.' Ðe 3iet him andswerede Crist: 'God man ðu art
60 al swo he ðe non heued-senne ne haueð idon.' *Si uis
perfectus esse, vade et uende omnia que habes, et cetera*,
'Gif ðu wilt,' he seide, bien ðurhut god mann, 'ga and sell
all ðat tu hafst, and 3if hit Godes wrecchen, and swa fol3e
me.' Ðies 3unge mann 3iede awei sari. Hier we habbeð
65 ilierned ðat it is betere to læten all ðat te mann awh, mid
gode wille, þanne he abide allhwat deað hit him beneme,
his unþankes. Hlest nu hwat Crist sade be ða riche manne
ðe 3iede awei sari, and his ræd nolde lesten: 'Ne mai na
more,' cwað he, 'ðe riche mann cumen in to heuene riche,
70 ðanne mai ðe oluende cumen ðurh ðe nædle ei3en.' *Ve
uobis diuitibus, qui habetis consolationem uestram*, 'Wa
3eu,' cwað he, '3ie riche menn, ðe habbeð swa michele
blisse of 3euer michele richeise, þat 3ie Godd for3eten and
3eure saule hæle!' For ði ne mai wexen non god sad of
75 Godes wordes on 3eure herte molde, for ðan michele
embeðanc ðe 3ie habbeð on 3eure michele wele, ðe 3ie
michel 3itsið, and luuieð, and likeð, and dradeð to
forliesen. Amang alle ðese embeðankes is ðe wrecche
hierte swa iheue3ed, þat non Godes word upp ne mai
80 springen, ne of Godd þenken, ne of his riche, ne of his

Scripture says that mercy should always be above strict justice. On account of such things, many very wise men lose God's love and his grace, because they do not have, nor care to have, their fellow Christian's love, but put their trust in their great wisdom, and are often deceived. If they would [only] listen to the apostle, they would not stand in this need! *Si quis videtur inter vos sapiens esse, stultus fiat, ut sit sapiens*, 'If any of you,' he says, 'is considered wise in worldly things, let him become a fool, and thus he may be wise.'

The worldly wise man considers it great foolishness that, for God's love, a man should give up house and home, wife and child, and gold and silver, and all worldly prosperity, and become so much a poor man as he who had nothing; he says that it is better to stay put with his own things, and give charity and lodging to blessed men, than that he should leave all that, and live on other people's charity. Let us listen to Christ's own judgement on this, and thus we may be surer in this dispute. It says in the holy Gospel that a rich young man came to Christ in the days when he was dwelling incarnate here, and he said: *Quid faciam, Domine, ut habeam vitam aeternam?* 'Lord,' he said, 'what should I do so that I may have eternal life?' Our Lord answered him and said: *Mandata nosti*, 'You know God's commandments. Thou shalt not slay, nor steal, nor rob, nor commit adultery, not break any other of God's commandments.' 'Ah, Lord,' he said, 'I have kept all these commandments from childhood, so that I have not broken any.' Then again Christ answered him: 'You are a good man to the extent that you have not committed any capital sin.' *Si vis perfectus esse, vade et vende omnia quae habes etc*, 'If you wish,' he said, 'to be a thoroughly good man, go and sell all that you have and give it to God's poor people, and thus follow me.' This young man went away downcast. Here we have learned that it is better to give up all that one owns voluntarily than to wait until death takes it away against one's will. Listen now to what Christ said about the rich man who went away downcast, and would not heed his advice: 'The rich man,' said he, 'may no more come into the kingdom of heaven than may the camel come through the eye of a needle.' *Vae vobis divitibus, qui habetis consolationem vestram*, 'Woe to you,' he said, 'you rich men who get so much pleasure from your great wealth that you forget God and the well-being of your souls!' Therefore no good seed may grow in the soil of your heart for the great concern you have with your great wealth, that you covet so much, and

saule hale. Ac gleues and skentinges, and hundes and
hauekes, and alle ðo þing ðe ȝeu hier gladien mai, þat ȝe
willen bliðeliche isien and ȝehieren; and all ðis ȝe mihten
hauen, ȝif ȝe Godd luueden mare ðanne all ðis ðe we
85 embe hauen ispeken. Maniȝe of ȝeu bien swiðe beswikene.
Weneð ðat ȝe luuen more Godd ðanne ȝe don ȝeure eihte;
ac læt him seggen ðat soðeste, ðe is mid rihte Soð icleped:
Vbi est tesaurus, ibi est et cor tuum, 'Ðar ðe ðin hord is, þær
is þin herte,' he sæde. Ðar is ðin herte ðarof ðe ðu mæst
90 þenkst, and ðar is ðin mæste luue. Vnderstand nu wel ðe
seluen, and loke hwaðer ðu þenke more of Godd ðe of ðin
eihte, and wite ðu te soþe: hwarof ðu mare þenkst, ðat tu
luuest mare.

Walewa ðas siðes, þat ani mann ðat Godd hafð iȝiuen
95 witt and wisdom, scall luuien more ðe scaftes ðe Godd
ȝescop ðanne he do his sceppend, ðe him and alle þing
ȝescop! Lieue saule, ic ðe warni and ȝierne bidde ðat tu,
mid ðessere Godes ȝiue ðe *scientia* hatte, understande and
lierne fastliche ða ȝekyndes of sennes, hwannen and
100 hwanne hie cumen, þat ðu muȝe bien war wið hem; and
ðar ðu art ðurh hem ȝewunded, ðat ðu cunne hes halen;
and eft, of ðese hali mihtes, ðat tu hes kunne wel
ȝecnawen, and mid Godes fultume wiðhealden.

Notes

1 **Hier**   In the manner of the *Anglo-Saxon Chronicle*, the author
uses the word to situate his treatment of a particular virtue in a
sequence probably imposed by his source. The spelling ‹ie› is
problematic. It is the usual spelling in this text for WS *ēo*, Kentish *īo*,
the latter of which was spelt ‹ie› in south-eastern Middle English.
The scribe sometimes first writes ‹eo› ‹e›, then corrects to ‹ie›,
suggesting that he is following a spelling tradition not his own. Use
here of ‹ie› for OE *ē* (also in *ȝie*, 73 and *bieten*, 31) and perhaps
ȝehieren (83) is a natural confusion in a man whose own language did
not preserve a distinction between OE *ēo* and *ē*.

3 **takð**   The WS word *tǣcan* has *ǣ²* (derived from the *i*-mutation of
ā). The ‹a› spelling of the WS *ǣ¹* and *ǣ²* was restricted to Essex and
Middlesex. Elsewhere, spellings were ‹æ, e, ea›.

love, and like, and dread to lose. Amid all these concerns the poor heart is made so heavy that no word of God may spring up, nor remembrance of God, nor of his kingdom, nor of the salvation of one's soul. But entertainment and amusement, and hounds and hawks, and all those things that may delight you here, which you eagerly desire to see and hear; and you could have all this, if you loved God more than all this that we have spoken about. Many of you are greatly deceived. You think that you love God more than your possessions; but let him say what is most true, who is justly called Truth: *Ubi est thesaurus, ibi est et cor tuum*, 'Where your treasure is, there is your heart,' he said. Your heart is in that place you think of most, and there is your greatest love. Now, understand yourself well, and consider whether you think more about God than about your belongings; and know the truth: whatever you think about more, that you love more.

Alas for the ways of any man to whom God has given understanding and wisdom and who loves more greatly things that God has created than he does his creator, who made him and all things. Dear soul, I warn and earnestly entreat you that you, with this gift of God which is called *scientia*, understand and securely learn the natures of sins, whence and when they may come, so that you may be on your guard against them; and when you are wounded by them, that you may know how to cure them; and further, about these holy virtues, that you may know well how to recognise them, and with God's help keep them.

6 **want**   The Anglian form would have been *wendeð*, and the syncope and assimilation of the inflexion suggests West Saxon. However, the spelling of the reflex of Germanic short *a* + *i*-mutation as an ‹a› rather than ‹e› before *n* is found only in Essex and London.

8 **sade**   The loss of /j/ before a following *d* is characteristic of non-Anglian areas, but Kentish has the form *sede*, since OE short *æ* appeared as *e* in Kentish OE.

9 **hes**   Accusative form of the personal pronoun. Plural in line 101; possibly also plural here. The geographical distribution of this form is very restricted and scattered: Gloucester, Essex, Middlesex, north Kent and west Norfolk.

10 **haueð**   The unsyncopated form suggests an Anglian origin, but forms of the third-person singular present tense with the syncope and

assimilation associated with Saxon OE are common in the text, e.g. *latt* (10); *forliest* (12). In line 42 *halt* exhibits syncope and assimilation, but the vowel suggests an Anglian form in which breaking has not occurred before *l* + consonant.

15 **wurse**   In this word the reflex of OE *y* is *u* (normally a western feature, but found in London, Middlesex and Essex). It may also be *i/y*: *ʒekynde* (30), *forʒilt* (32) (east Midland); or, most commonly, *e*: *kenne* (17), *euele, hlest* (27), *forʒelt* (30) (south-eastern). Compare the *Proclamation of Henry III* (Excerpt 14).

20 **rihtes** 'by right'   An adverbial may be formed from a noun in OE by the use of the genitive singular inflexion. The idiom continues into later ME. Cf. *his unþankes* (67).

22 **alre manne** 'of all men'   Cf. OE *ealra manna*.

26 **kariteð**   This form represents Anglo-Norman borrowing, perhaps surviving from an earlier version. The central French form, *charite* (10), occurs here in one of its earliest occurrences in English.

30 **after ʒekynde** 'according to nature'   Sinners share human nature with the just man, who must therefore feel compassion, while hating the associated sin.

32 **me bette þin**   *Me* is an indefinite pronoun, *bette* a third-person subjunctive, and *þin* a disjunctive pronoun: 'one should reprove yours'.

35 **hie**   The third-person pronouns all have the *h*-form of OE, but phonetic change has eroded the differences in pronunciation. Here *hie* means 'they'; in line 3 it means 'she'. The masculine singular has its traditional spelling, *he* (29). To appreciate the significance of these spellings, see note to line 1.

43 **hus and ham**   A traditional alliterative phrase in which OE long *ā* shows no sign of rounding (cf. *hali, aʒene*), but traces of rounding are evident in some spellings: *swo* beside *swa*, *more* beside *mare*, *non* (22) and *an* (1), and *na more* (68–69).

69 **heuene riche**   The word *heuene* is a genitive modifier of *riche* 'kingdom'. Although derived from the genitive plural, *heofona*, the number significance is no longer important. See also *nædle eiʒen* (70), *saule hæle* (74), *herte molde* (75). A handful of structures of this type (e.g. *herte rote, lady grace*) survive into late ME.

83–84 **all ðis ʒe mihten hauen**   The author suggests that no harm attaches to earthly possessions, so long as they are secondary to the love of God. For a more sophisticated statement of the Augustinian view that the love of earthly things may lead on to the love of God, see *Ancrene Wisse*.

11 *The* Ancrene Wisse

The *Ancrene Wisse* or 'Guide of Anchorites' vies with the *Peterborough Chronicle* for the title of best-known Early Middle English text. Its importance both to the history of English prose and to the study of language development has often been stressed, but its familiarity is probably due more to the happy chance that such importance can here be found in a document with its own intrinsic appeal. The *Ancrene Wisse* is readable for pleasure and entertainment, for its author's insight and humanity, his wit and his unobtrusive mastery of the presentation of his discourse. His work achieved the distinction of translation into French and Latin, and was copied and adapted throughout the medieval period.

The title *Ancrene Wisse* is given on the first folio of Corpus Christi College, Cambridge MS 402, a text which, although not in the author's hand, is perhaps not much more than a decade later than the date of composition. This version, which is intended for the use of three noble sisters who have forsaken the world to live as recluses, is that normally referred to as *Ancrene Wisse*. Adaptations in other MSS for use by other communities have gained the name *Ancrene Riwle*. Although MS CCCC 402 can be dated at about 1230, nothing is known directly of its origin or the author of its contents. The manuscript was, however, associated with Wigmore Abbey, Herefordshire, by 1300. Evidence has been presented to place the origin of the work in Limebrook Priory, three miles south-west of Wigmore, and the authorship has been more speculatively credited to one Brian of Lingen.

The language of the *Ancrene Wisse* corresponds well with such an origin. Its strikingly consistent spelling system is largely shared with the 'Katherine Group' of texts in MS Bodley 34. Such consistency, involving several texts, implies regulation, and regulation is likely only through scribal training in a major centre. Thus, in the *Ancrene Wisse* we encounter an early and very local example of language standardisation. An instructive comparison might be made between the solutions sought to the problem of writing their local language by these western scribes and by Orm.

The language of the *Ancrene Wisse* is much more conservative than that of northern or eastern texts. OE spelling traditions are maintained (‹þ› tends to be used initially and ‹ð› finally, and ‹ea› and ‹eo› are still written). Moreover, in its writing of short *æ* as ‹e›, *AW* continues the tradition of the Vespasian Psalter. Morphologically, the text is also relatively conservative: *-en* noun plurals are common, the forms of Weak Class 2 verbs are still distinct (*makieð*, 25; *luuien*, 19); past participles preserve their prefix (*ispillet*, 12; *icrunet*, 121); and personal pronouns have *h*-forms. Lexically, there are ample signs of the French influence which reflects the social milieu for which the work was composed, but there are also a few Scandinavian borrowings.

> Seinte Pawel witneð þet alle uttre heardschipes, alle flesches
> pinsunges ant licomliche swinkes, al is ase nawt aȝeines luue,
> þe schireð ant brihteð þe heorte. *Exercitio corporis ad modicum*
> *ualet: pietas autem ualet ad omnia.* Þet is, licomlich bisischipe
> 5 is to lutel wurð, ah swote ant schire heorte is god to alle þinges.
> *Si linguis hominum loquar et angelorum et c.; si tradidero corpus*
> *meum ita ut ardeam etc.; si distribuero omnes facultates meas in*
> *cibos pauperum, caritatem autem non habeam, nichil michi*
> *prodest.* 'Þah ich cuðe,' he seið, 'monne ledene ant englene, þah
> 10 ich dude o mi bodi alle pine ant passiun þet bodi mahte þolien,
> þah ich ȝeue poure al þet ich hefde – ȝef ich nefde luue þerwið to
> Godd, ant to alle men in him ant for him, al were ispillet.'
> For, as þe hali abbat Moyses seide, al þet wa ant al þet heard
> þet we þolieþ o flesch, ant al þet god þet we eauer doð, alle
> 15 swucche þinges ne beoð nawt bute as lomen to tilie wið þe
> heorte. Ȝef þe axe ne kurue, ne spitelsteaf ne dulue, ne þe sulh
> ne erede, hwa kepte ham to halden? Alswa as na mon ne luueð
> lomen for hamseolf, ah deð for þe þinges þet me wurcheð wið
> ham, alswa na flesches derf nis to luuien bute forþi þet Godd te
> 20 reaðere þiderward loki mid his grace, ant makeð þe heorte
> schir ant of briht sihðe, þet nan ne mei habben wið
> monglunge of unþeawes, ne wið eorðlich luue of worltliche
> þinges; for þis mong woreð swa þe ehnen of þe heorte þet ha
> ne mei cnawen Godd ne gleadien of his sihðe. Schir heorte, as
> 25 Seint Bernard seið, makieð twa þinges – þet tu, al þet tu dest,
> do hit oðer for luue ane of Godd, oðer for oþres god ant for
> his biheue. Haue in al þet tu dest an of þes twa ententes, oðer
> ba togederes; for þe leatere falleð into þe earre. Haue eauer
> schir heorte þus, ant do al þet tu wult; haue wori heorte – al
> 30 þe sit uuele. *Omnia munda mundis, coinquinatis uero nichil est*
> *mundum. Apostolus. Item Augustinus: Habe caritatem, et fac*
> *quicquid uis, uoluntate uidelicet rationis.* Forþi, mine leoue
> sustren, ouer alle þing beoð bisie to habben schir heorte. Hwet

Saint Paul bears witness that all external privations, all mortification of the flesh and bodily labour are as nothing compared with love, which purifies and makes the heart bright. *Exercitio corporis ad modicum ualet: pietas autem ualet ad omnia.* That is, bodily exertion counts for little, but a sweet and pure heart is good in all things. *Si linguis hominum loquar et angelorum et c.; si tradero corpus meum ita ut ardeam et c.; si distribuero omnes facultates meas in cibos pauperum, caritatem autem non habeam, nichil michi prodest.* 'Though I knew,' he said, 'the languages of men and of angels, though I inflicted on my body all the pain and suffering that the body might endure, though I gave to the poor all that I had – if I had not love along with it towards God, and towards all people in him and for him, all would be wasted.' For, as the holy abbot Moses said, all the misery and all the harshness that we endure in the flesh, and all the good that we ever do, all such things are as no more than tools with which to cultivate the heart. If the axe did not cut, nor the spade dig, nor the plough plough, who would care to own them? Just as no-one loves tools for themselves, but does so for the things that are achieved with them, so no suffering of the flesh is to be loved except because God more readily may look towards it with his grace, and it makes the heart pure and of clear sight, which none may have with a mixture of vices nor with the earthly love of worldly things; for this mixture troubles the eyes of the heart so that they may not know God nor rejoice in his sight. As St Bernard says, two things make a pure heart: that you do all that you do either solely for the love of God, or for the good and advantage of another. In everything you do, have one of these purposes, or both together; for the latter is included in the former. If you always have a pure heart, thus, you may do all that you wish; have a disturbed heart and everything turns out badly. *Omnia*

is schir heorte? Ich hit habbe iseid ear: þet is, þet ȝe na þing ne
35 wilnin ne ne luuien bute Godd ane, ant te ilke þinges, for Godd,
þe helpeð ow toward him. For Godd, ich segge, luuien ham, ant
nawt for hamseoluen, as is mete, oðer clað, mon oðer wummon
þe ȝe beoð of igodet. For, ase seið Seint Austin, ant spekeð þus
to ure Lauerd: *Minus te amat qui preter te aliquid amat quod non*
40 *propter te amat.* Þet is, 'Lauerd, leasse ha luuieð þe þe luuieð
eawt bute þe, bute ha luuien hit for þe.' Schirnesse of heorte is
Godes luue ane. I þis is al þe strengðe of alle religiuns, þe ende
of alle ordres. *Plenitudo legis est dilectio.* 'Luue fulleð þe lahe,'
seið Seinte Pawel. *Quicquid precipitur, in sola caritate solidatur.*
45 Alle Godes heastes, as Sein Gregoire seið, beoð i luue irotet.
Luue ane schal beon ileid i Seinte Mihales weie. Þeo þe meast
luuieð schulen beo meast iblisset, nawt þeo þe leadeð heardest
lif; for luue hit ouerweieð. Luue is heouene stiward, for hire
muchele freolec. For heo ne edhalt naþing, ah ȝeueð al þet ha
50 haueð, ant ec hireseoluen; elles ne kepte Godd nawt of þet hiren
were.

Godd haueð ofgan ure luue on alle cunne wise: he haueð
muchel idon us, ant mare bihaten. Muchel ȝeoue ofdraheð
luue. Me al þe world he ȝef us in Adam, ure alde-feader; ant
55 al þet is i þe world he weorp under ure fet – beastes ant
fuheles – ear we weren forgulte. *Omnia subiecisti sub pedibus*
eius, oues et boues uniuersas, insuper et pecora campi, volucres
celi, et pisces maris qui perambulant semitas maris. Ant ȝet al
þet is, as is þruppe iseid, serueð þe gode to sawle biheue; ȝet
60 te uuele seruið eorðe, sea, ant sunne. He dude ȝet mare – ȝef
us nawt ane of his, ah dude al himseoluen. Se heh ȝeoue nes
neauer iȝeuen to se lahe wrecches. *Apostolus: Cristus dilexit*
ecclesiam et dedit semet ipsum pro ea. 'Crist,' seið Seinte Pawel,
'luuede swa his leofmon þet he ȝef for hire þe pris of
65 himseoluen. Neomeð nu gode ȝeme, mine leoue sustren, for
hwi me ah him to luuien. Earst, as a mon þe woheð – as a king
þet luuede a gentil poure leafdi of feorrene londe – he sende his
sonden biuoren (þet weren þe patriarches ant te prophetes of þe
Alde Testament) wið leattres isealet. On ende he com him-
70 seoluen, ant brohte þe Godspel as leattres i-openet, ant wrat wið
his ahne blod saluz to his leofmon, luue-gretunge forte wohin
hire wið ant hire luue wealden. Herto falleð a tale, a wrihe
forbisne.

A leafdi wes mid hire fan biset al abuten, hire lond al
75 destruet, ant heo al poure, inwið an eorðene castel. A mihti
kinges luue wes þah biturnd upon hire swa unimete swiðe þet
he for wohlech sende hire his sonden, an efter oðer, ofte somet

munda mundis, coinquinatis uero nichil est mundum.
Apostolus. Item Augustinus: Habe caritatem, et fac quicquid
uis, uoluntate uidelicet rationis.

Therefore, my dear sisters, above all things be diligent to
have a pure heart. What is a pure heart? I have said it before:
it is that you neither love nor desire anything except God
alone, and those very things, for God's sake, that help you
towards him. For God, I say, love them, and not for
themselves, such as food, or clothing, or man or woman that
you are benefited by. For, as St Augustine says, and speaks
thus concerning our Lord: *Minus te amat qui preter te aliquid*
amat quod non propter te amat. That is, 'Lord they love you
less who love anything but you unless they love it for your
sake.' Pureness of heart is simply the love of God. In this is
the entire force of all sects, the purpose of all religious
orders. *Plenitudo legis est dilectio.* 'Love fulfils the law,' says
St Paul. *Quicquid precipitur, in sola caritate solidatur.* All
God's commandments, as St Gregory says, are rooted in
love. Love alone shall be laid in St Michael's balance. Those
who love most greatly shall be most blessed, not those who
lead the hardest life, for love outweighs it. Love is the
steward of heaven, because of her great generosity. For she
withholds nothing, but gives all that she has, and also her
very self; otherwise God would not care for what was hers.

God has earned our love in all manner of ways: he has
done much for us, and promised more. A great gift attracts
love. But he gave us, or our ancestor Adam, the whole
world; and he cast everything in the world beneath our feet –
the animals and birds – before we were convicted of sin.
Omnia subiecisti sub pedibus eius, oues et boues uniuersas,
insuper et pecora campi, volucres celi, et pisces maris qui
perambulant semitas maris. And yet all that exists, as is said
above, the good man uses for the benefit of his soul; yet the
earth, sea and sun serve the evil man. He did yet more: gave
us not only from his possessions, but gave himself entirely. So
noble a gift was never given to such base wretches.
Apostolus: Christus dilexit ecclesiam et dedit semet ipsum pro
ea. Christ, says St Paul, so loved his love that he gave for her
the value of himself. Now take good heed, my dear sisters,
why he ought to be loved. First like a man who goes wooing –
like a king who loved a noble lady from a distant land – he
sent his messengers in advance (who were the patriarchs and
prophets of the Old Testament) with private letters. At last
he came himself, and brought the Gospel as open letters, and

monie; sende hire beawbelez baðe feole ant feire, sucurs of
liueneð, help of his hehe hird to halden hire castel. Heo under-
80 feng al as on unrecheles, ant swa wes heard-iheortet þet hire
luue ne mahte he neauer beo þe neorre. Hwet wult tu mare?
He com himseolf on ende; schawde hire his feire neb, as þe þe
wes of alle men feherest to bihalden; spec se swiðe swoteliche,
ant wordes se murie, þet ha mahten deade arearen to liue;
85 wrahte feole wundres ant dude muchele meistries biuoren hire
ehsihðe; schawde hire his mihte; talde hire of his kinedom;
bead to makien hire cwen of al þet he ahte.
    Al þis ne heold nawt. Nes þis hoker wunder? For heo nes
neauer wurðe forte beon his þuften. Ah swa, þurh his de-
90 boneirte, luue hefde ouercumen him þet he seide on ende:
'Dame, þu art iweorret, ant þine van beoð se stronge þet tu
ne maht nanesweis wiðute mi sucurs edfleon hare honden, þet
ha ne don þe to scheome deað efter al þi weane. Ich chulle,
for þe luue of þe, neome þet feht upo me ant arudde þe of
95 ham þe þi deað secheð. Ich wat þah to soðe þet ich schal
bituhen ham neomen deaðes wunde; ant ich hit wulle
heorteliche, forte ofgan þin heorte. Nu þenne bische ich þe,
for þe luue þet ich cuðe þe, þet tu luuie me, lanhure efter þe
ilke dede dead hwen þu naldest liues.' Þes king dude al þus:
100 arudde hire of alle hire van, ant wes himseolf to wundre
ituket and islein on ende, þurh miracle aras þah from deaðe
to liue. Nere þeos ilke leafdi of uueles cunnes kunde, ȝef ha
ouer alle þing ne luuede him herefter?
    Þes king is Iesu, Godes sune, þet al o þise wise wohede ure
105 sawle þe deoflen hefden biset. Ant he, as noble wohere, efter
monie messagers ant feole goddeden, com to pruuien his luue,
ant schawde þurh cnihtschipe þet he wes luuewurðe; as weren
sumhwile cnihtes iwunet to donne; dude him i turneiment ant
hefde for his leoues luue his scheld i feht as kene cniht on euche
110 half iþurlet. His scheld þe wreah his goddhead wes his leoue
licome þet wes ispread o rode – brad as scheld buuen in his
istrahte earmes, nearow bineoðen as þe an fot (efter monies
wene, set upo þe oðer). Þet þis scheld naueð siden, is for
bitacnunge þet his deciples, þe schulden stonden bi him ant
115 habben ibeon his siden, fluhen alle from him ant leafden him
as fremede, as þe Godspel seið: *Relicto eo omnes fugerunt.* Þis
scheld is iȝeuen us aȝein alle temptatiuns, as Ieremie witneð:
Dabis scutum cordis laborem tuum. Nawt ane þis scheld ne
schilt us from alle uueles, ah deð ȝet mare – cruneð us in
120 heouene *scuto bone uoluntatis.* 'Lauerd,' he seið, Dauið, 'wið
þe scheld of þi gode wil þu hauest us icrunet' – scheld, he

wrote a salutation to his beloved, a love-greeting to woo her with and to possess her love. A tale belongs to this, an example with hidden meaning.

A lady was besieged all around by her enemies, her land laid waste, and she impoverished, within a castle of earth. The love of a great king was however directed towards her, so immeasurably greatly that he sent her in courtship his messengers, one after another, often many together; he sent her precious gifts both many and fine, help with provisions, and aid from his noble court to hold her castle. She received all [this] as one uncaring, and was so hard-hearted that he could never be the closer to her love. What more could you wish? At last he came himself, showed her his handsome face, he who was the fairest of all to look upon. He spoke so very sweetly, and in words so cheering that they might raise the dead to life. He performed many marvels and did great feats in her sight, showed her his power, told her about his kingdom, and offered to make her queen of all he possessed.

All this amounted to nothing. Was not this scorn a marvel? For she was never worthy to be his handmaiden. But, through his graciousness, love had so overcome him that in the end he said: 'Lady, you are attacked, and your foes are so strong that, without my help, you could in no way escape their hands, so that they should not put you to a shameful death after all your miseries. For your love, I will take the fight upon myself and rescue you from those who seek your death. However, I know for sure that I shall receive a mortal wound among them; and I cordially desire it in order to win your heart. Now I beseech you, for the love that I have revealed to you, that you may love me at least after that deed, when I am dead, when you would not when I was alive.' This king did it all: rescued her from all her enemies, and was himself atrociously ill-treated and slain in the end; however, by a miracle, he arose from death to life. Would not this same lady be of a very base nature if she did not love him above all things after that?

This king is Jesus, God's son, who in all these ways wooed our soul that devils had besieged. And, like a noble lover, after many messengers and generous deeds, he came to prove his love, and showed her by deeds of valour that he was worthy of love, as knights were once accustomed to do. He entered a tournament and, for his beloved's love, like a bold knight had his shield pierced on each side. His shield, which covered his deity, was his precious body that was spread out seið, of god wil, for willes he þolede al þet he þolede. *Ysaias: Oblatus est quia uoluit.*

Notes

9 **monne ledene ant englene**   This text preserves genitives descended from both the *-a* genitive plural of the Strong masculine nouns and the *-ena* genitive plural of Weak nouns. The rounding of short *a* before a nasal is found west of a line from Morecambe Bay, following the Pennine chain to the Severn estuary.

13 **hali**   *AW* does not exhibit the southern rounding of OE *ā*. By 1230, however, rounding had extended to Hereford, so this spelling is to be taken as evidence of conservative spelling practice.

15 **lomen**   OE Weak nouns and Strong feminine nouns have plurals in *-en*. Masculine and neuter nouns (and feminines ending in *-ung*) have *-es* plurals.

18 **wurcheð**   OE *wyrcan*. The spelling ‹u› for WS *y* is found in western areas: *lutel* (5), *dude* (10). It originates as an attempt by French-trained scribes to write the OE sound [y], which coincided with the French sound spelt ‹u›.

20 **loki**   Long-stemmed Weak Class 2 verbs lose final *-n* in the infinitive.

23 **ha** 'they'   *AW* possesses a complete system of plural third-person pronouns with medial *a*, and also a nominative singular feminine, *ha*. These forms are almost restricted to Gloucestershire, Worcestershire and Herefordshire. A parallel with the genitive plural *hare* is found in the OE of the Vespasian Psalter gloss, *heara*. The latter probably developed analogically from the demonstrative *þeara* found in VP.

25 **makieð twa þinges**   The sense depends not on word order, but on recognising that *makieð* has a plural inflexion in concord with the plural *þinges*.

32–33 **leoue sustren**   In western areas the reflex of the OE diphthong continued to be written ‹eo› into the fourteenth century (cf. *South English Legendary*).

43 **lahe**   One of a few Scandinavian borrowings in the piece. Most

on the cross, broad like a shield above with his outstretched arms, narrow beneath like the one foot – according to the opinion of many – set upon the other. That this shield has no sides is to signify that his disciples, who should have stood by him and been its sides, all fled from him and left him like a stranger, as the Gospel says: *Relicto eo omnes fugerunt*. This shield is given to us against all temptations, as Jeremiah witnesses: *Dabis scutum cordis laborem tuum*. Not only does this shield shield us from all evils, but it does yet more: it crowns us in heaven *scuto bone uoluntatis*. 'Lord,' he says, David, 'with the shield of your good will you have crowned us' – shield, he says, of good will, because willingly he suffered all that he suffered. *Ysaias: Oblatus est quia uoluit*.

are of widespread use (*lahe*, 62; *baðe*, 78) but the abstract noun-forming suffix *-lec* in *freolec* (49) is worthy of special notice, as is the use of *þah* (9) in preference to OE-derived *þei*, the form common in the South. This Scandinavian influence can be explained by Danish settlement in Shropshire, Worcestershire and Herefordshire in the reign of Canute.

54 **alde-feader**   Failure of breaking before *l*-groups and retraction to *a* suggests an Anglian OE antecedent.

69 **lettres isealet**   Sealed letters are here contrasted with letters patent, both French phrases based upon earlier Latin ones. Letters patent were those documents containing royal Acts for which the letter served as confirmation, and was therefore intended to be accessible to all concerned. Sealed letters contain private communications. The word *saluz* (71) refers to the opening greeting of the letter (cf. Alfred's Preface to the *Cura Pastoralis* or *Kyng Alisaunder*).

78 **beawbelez**   This is the only known ME context of a word which in OF means a child's plaything.

91 **van** 'foes'   The voicing of initial fricatives is a southern feature. AW comes from close to its northern boundary.

93 **ich chulle**   The southern form of the pronoun, spelt *ich*, with assimilation to a western form of the verb 'will'.

102 **of uueles cunnes kunde**   Literally 'of the nature of an evil race'. A sequence of genitive modifiers possible in Old English, but unidiomatic by the fourteenth century.

111–113 **brad as scheld . . . upo þe oðer**   A long kite-shaped shield seems to be envisaged, narrow at the base. The representation of the crucified Christ with one foot nailed over the other would have been a relatively recent iconographic development at the time *AW* was composed.

12 A Kentish Sermon: The Marriage at Cana

The following excerpt is taken from one of five sermons translated into English and included in MS Bodleian Laud Misc. 471 in the latter half of the thirteenth century. All five, and also Anglo-Norman and Latin examples in the same manuscript, are from originals composed between 1168 and 1175 by Maurice de Sully, Bishop of Paris, for use by the priests of his diocese. The popularity of Maurice's sermons in France is attested by the large number of surviving manuscripts; it is a popularity which must have derived in part from the simplicity in structural plan and language, which is evident also in English translation. Like the example given below, Maurice's sermons fall into three parts: the presentation in literal terms of a scriptural event, followed by an exposition of its allegorical and spiritual significance, the whole completed by the application of the teaching to everyday morality.

The translator is unknown, but by comparison with both the language of the OE Kentish glosses and that of the precisely localisable *Ayenbite of Inwit*, he must have been writing in Kent. By the standards of these other texts, however, the Kentish in this manuscript is not pure, so that the text may have been copied by a scribe from a more northerly location. Morphologically, the text shows characteristics of southern origin: a few nouns preserve -*en* plurals (*faten*, 14; *deden*, 37); archaic forms of the verb 'to have' persist (*habbeþ*, 24); the past participle still retains its prefix; *h*-forms of the pronouns are used; and the text still retains substantial traces of grammatical gender in its inflexions. Phonologically, the South-East is indicated by the spelling of the reflex of WS *y* as ⟨e⟩ (*bredale*, 4; *uuluelden*, 16) and of *ēo* as ⟨ie⟩. In areas where the reflex of OE *y* and *ēo* were represented in this way, the spelling of WS *ǣ* as ⟨e⟩ ($\bar{æ}^1$: *deden*; $\bar{æ}^2$: *anhet*) may be taken to indicate Kentish, since more northerly texts with this combination include ⟨a⟩ spellings for *ǣ* (cf. *Vices and Virtues*). Finally, and most specifically Kentish, is the spelling of OE *ēa* as ⟨ia⟩ (*beliaue*, 30, and with lengthened diphthong, *ihialde*, 25). The text does not, however, consistently represent WS short *æ* as ⟨e⟩, nor *ēo* as ⟨ie⟩.

Nuptie facte sunt in Chana Galilee, et erat mater Iesu ibi;
vocatus est autem Iesus ad nuptias et discipuli eius. Þet holi
godspel of today us telþ þet a bredale was imaked ine þo londe
of Ierusalem, in ane cite þat was icleped Cane, in þa time þat
Godes sune yede in erþe flesliche. To þa bredale was ure Leuedi
5 Seinte Marie, and ure Louerd Iesus Crist and hise deciples.
So iuel auenture þet wyn failede at þise bredale; þo seide ure
Leuedi Seinte Marie to here sune: 'Hi ne habbet no wyn.' And
ure Louerd answerde and sede to hire: 'Wat belongeth hit to
me oþer to þe, wyman?' Nu ne dorste hi namore sigge, ure
10 Lauedi; hac hye spac to þo serganz þet seruede of þo wyne, and
hem seyde: 'Al þet he hot yu do, so doþ.'
    And ure Louerd clepede þe serganz and seyde to hem:
'Folvellet,' ha seyde, 'þos ydres [þet is to sigge, þos croos, oþer
þos faten] of watere.' For þer were vi ydres of stone þet ware
15 iclepede baþieres, wer þo Gius hem wesse for clenesse and for
religiun, ase þe custome was ine þo time. Þo serganz uuluelden
þo faten of watere, and hasteliche was iwent into wyne, bie
þo wille of ure Louerde. Þo seide ure Lord to þo serganz:
'Moveth togidere and bereth to Architriclin [þat was se þet
20 ferst was iserued].' And also hedde idrunke of þise wyne þet
ure Louerd hedde imaked of þe watere (ha niste nocht þe
miracle, ac þo serganz wel hit wiste þet hedde þet water
ibrocht), þo seide Architriclin to þo bredgume: 'Oþer men,'
seyde he, 'doþ forþ þet beste wyn þet hi habbeþ ferst at here
25 bredale; and þu hest ido þe contrarie, þet þu hest ihialde þet
beste wyn wath nu!' Þis was þe commencement of þo miracles
of ure Louerde þet he made flesliche in erþe; and þo beleuede
on him his deciples. I ne sigge nacht þet hi ne hedden þerbefore
in him beliaue; ac fore þe miracle þet hi seghe was here
30 beliaue þe more istrengþed.
    Nu ye habbeþ iherd þe miracle; nu ihereþ þe signefiance.
Þet water bitockned se euele Cristeneman. For also þet water
is natureliche schald, and akelþ alle þo þet hit drinkeþ, so is
se euele Cristeman chald of þo luue of Gode, for þo euele
35 werkes þet hi doþ; ase so is lecherie, spusbreche, roberie,
manslechtes, husberners, bakbiteres, and alle oþre euele
deden, þurch wyche þinkes man ofserueth þet fer of helle, ase
Godes oghe mudh hit seid. And alle þo signefied þet water, þet
þurch yemere werkes oþer þurch yemer iwil liesed þo blisce
40 of heuene. Þet wyn, þat is naturelliche hot ine himselue, and
anhet alle þo þet hit drinked, betokned alle þo þet bied anheet
of þe luue of ure Lorde.
    Nu, lordinges, ure Lord God Almichti, þat hwylem in one

The holy Gospel for today tells us that a marriage was arranged in the land of Jerusalem, in a city that was called Cana, in the time that God's son went on earth incarnate. Our Lady Saint Mary, and our Lord Jesus Christ and his disciples had all gone to the wedding. The chance so befell that the wine ran out at this wedding; then our Lady Saint Mary said to her son: 'They have no wine.' And our Lord answered and said to her: 'What concern is that of mine or yours, woman?' Now she dare say no more, our Lady; but she spoke to the servants who had served the wine, and said to them: 'All that he bids you to do, do it.'

And our Lord called the servants and said to them: 'Fill up,' he said, 'those water-vessels [that is to say those water-pots, or those vats] with water.' For there were six stone vessels that were called 'bath-tubs', where the Jews washed themselves for purification and for religious purposes, as the custom was in that time. The servants filled up the vessels with water, and quickly it was turned into wine by the will of our Lord. Then our Lord said to the servants: 'Go together and carry them to the master of the feast [that was he who was served first].' And as soon as he had drunk some of this wine that our Lord had made from the water (he did not know of the miracle, but the servants knew it well who had brought the water), then the master of the feast said to the bridegroom: 'Other men,' he said, 'have the best wine that they have served first at their wedding, and you have done the reverse, in that you have kept the best wine until now!' This was the beginning of the miracles of our Lord that he performed here incarnate on earth; and then his disciples had faith in him. I do not say that they did not have faith in him before that; but because of the miracle that they saw their faith was more strengthened.

Now you have heard the miracle; now hear the meaning. That water signifies the bad Christian. For, as water is cold by nature, and cools all those who drink it, so is the bad Christian cold in the love of God, on account of the wicked deeds that they do: such as lechery, adultery, robbery, murders, arsonists, slanderers, and all other wicked deeds, through which things are deserved the fire of hell, as God's own mouth put it. And the water signifies all those who through wretched deeds or wretched intent have failed to attain the bliss of heaven. The wine, which has the natural property of heat, and which heats all those who drink it, symbolises all those who are warmed by the love of our Lord.

stede and ine one time flesliche makede of watere wyn, yet
45 ha deþ mani time maked of watere wyn gostliche, wanne
þurch his grace maked of þo euele manne good man, of þe
orgeilus umble, of þe lechur chaste, of þe niþinge large; and
of alle oþre folies, so ha maket of þo watere wyn. Þis his si
signefiance of þe miracle. Nu loke euerich man toward
50 himseluen yef he is win: þet is to siggen, yef he is anheet of
þo luue of Gode; oþer yef he is water: þet is, yef þu art chold
of Godes luue. Yef þu art euel man, besech ure Lorde þet he
do ine þe his uertu, þet ha þe wende of euele into gode, and
þet he do þe do swiche werkes þet þu mote habbe þo blisce
55 of heuene. *Quod uobis prestare dignetur.*

Notes

2 **londe**   This form is derived from OE *land* by lengthening before
nd followed by the southern rounding of long *ā* to *o*. Rounding of
OE long *ā* is usual in this passage: *holi* (1), *stone* (14), *gostliche* (45),
one (44), but see also *ane* (3).

4 **flesliche**   The spellings ‹s› and ‹ss› (*wesse*) for [ʃ] are probably due
to the influence of French scribal attempts to render unfamiliar
English sounds, as also are ‹t› (*habbet*), ‹d› (*signified*), and ‹dh›
(*mudh*), written to represent /θ/.

6 **iuel** 'befell'   This preterite form preserves a prefix, but also
exhibits southern voicing of an initial fricative. This voicing is found
south of a line roughly from the Thames estuary to north
Worcestershire. See also *Folvellet* (13) – which also has south-eastern
‹e› for WS *y*.

8 **sede**   WS *sægde*. The loss of the palatal before *d* occurs in Kent
and in Saxon areas, and is accompanied by lengthening of the vowel.
The resulting *ǣ* generally develops to *e* in ME, except in Essex,
where *a*-forms are found. See *Vices and Virtues* (Excerpt 10).

13 **ha**   The *a*-form of the masculine third-person singular pronoun is
found mostly in the same area as the initial voicing of fricatives
mentioned above (note to line 6). Together they became associated
in the Early Modern period with countryfolk, viewed from a London
perspective.

14 **faten**   With *deden* (37), exemplifies the southern use of *-en* noun
plurals.

26 **wath** 'until'   An unusual form, restricted to the language of the
South-East.

Now, lords, our Lord God Almighty, who once, while incarnate, at a particular place and time made wine from water, still he does it many times, makes wine of water spiritually, when through his grace he makes a good man from an evil man, the humble from the proud, the chaste from the lecher, the generous from the miser; and so from all other follies, he makes wine from water. This is the meaning of the miracle. Now let every man consider himself, whether he is wine, that is to say whether he is warmed by the love of God, or whether he is water, that is if you are cold in God's love. If you are a wicked man, beg our Lord that he may put in you his power, so that he may change you from evil to good, and that he may cause you to perform such actions that you may have the bliss of heaven.

32 **se euele Cristeneman**   The south-eastern *e* for WS *y* is frequent in the passage. A conservative – and therefore southern or western – form of ME is indicated by the preservation of different inflexional forms of the definite article. Cf. *þet water* (32), and the use of *þa/þo* for the plural.

33 **schald**   Also *chald* (34). The spelling of the initial consonant of these forms indicates palatalisation caused by a following *ea*, derived from breaking before *ld* at an earlier stage. The antecedent of this form was therefore not Anglian. That the *a* has not been rounded to *o*, as is usual in this text, suggests that it was not lengthened, but see also *chold* (51).

47 **orgeilus**   Of the vices and virtues mentioned here, and the misdemeanours in line 35, a relatively limited number are indicated by words of French origin: *roberie, umble, lechur, chaste, large*. The persistence of OE words in this domain is evidence for the early date of the text. The word *niþinge* is an OE borrowing from Scandinavian.

13 A Proclamation of Henry III (1258)

Although the languages of all official business from the twelfth century until the early fifteenth century were Latin and French, two documents survive which give us a glimpse of the use of English in this domain. The first is a brief charter of 1155 in which Henry II confirms the rights and privileges of the monastery of Christ Church, Canterbury, and whose linguistic forms are strikingly more conservative than the nearly contemporary Final Continuation of the *Peterborough Chronicle*. The second is the following excerpt, an open letter proclaiming the determination of King Henry III to uphold the terms of the agreement reached with the barons in the Provisions of Oxford.

The proclamation was issued in both French and English, the use of English perhaps being dictated by its political importance, since competence in English was seen as a distinguishing characteristic between the settled Anglo-Norman barony and the continental French incomers favoured by the king. The English text survives in two manuscripts, one in the Public Records Office and the other among the city records now in the Bodleian Library, Oxford, and printed with facsimile and translation in O. Ogle, *Royal Letters Addressed to Oxford* (Oxford, 1892). As mentioned in the proclamation, copies were sent to each county in England, and the copy surviving in the Public Records Office, although designated as that for Huntingdonshire, may have been the exemplar upon which other copies were based. The text printed here is that of the Public Records Office version. The language of the proclamation is that of London in the mid thirteenth century, and exhibits many of the southern and linguistically conservative features which may be expected in a city which had originally been the capital of the East Saxons and had remained outside the direct influence of Scandinavian settlement. The diphthongs *ea* and *eo* are still written, and *æ* is written for both long and short vowels. Pronouns still have the OE *h*-forms and Weak Class 2 verbs are still distinguishable from other weak verbs. Verbs also retain the prefix in the past participles, and the southern form of the present participle, *ilestinde* (9–10) is found. The third-person plural, present tense, of the verb 'to have' preserves its earlier OE form *habbeþ* (7). The spelling ‹oa› is used freely to represent a sound developed from OE *ā* and for the long *ā* produced before late OE lengthening groups, *loande, foangen* (but see also *amanges*, 22). The passage is of stylistic interest in that it represents the earliest English example of curial style, a ceremonious official style imitated from Latin and French and marked by the use of legal phrasing both to ensure clarity of reference and to convey a sense of importance. Some features are marked in the notes.

Henri, þur3 Godes fultume King on Engleneloande, Lhoauerd
on Yrloande, Duk on Normandi, on Aquitaine, and Eorl on
Aniow, send igretinge to alle hise holde, ilærde and ileawede,
on Huntendoneschire. Þæt witen 3e wel alle þæt we willen and
5 vnnen þæt, þæt vre rædesmen alle, oþer þe moare dæl of heom,
þæt beoþ ichosen þur3 us and þur3 þæt loandes folk on vre
kuneriche, habbeþ idon and shullen don in þe worþnesse of
Gode and on vre treowþe, for þe freme of þe loande þur3 þe
besi3te of þan toforeniseide redesmen, beo stedefæst and ile-
10 stinde in alle þinge a buten ænde. And we hoaten alle vre
treowe, in þe treowþe þæt heo vs o3en, þæt heo stedefæstliche
healden and swerien to healden and to werien þo isetnesses þæt
beon imakede and beon to makien, þur3 þan toforeniseide
rædesmen, oþer þur3 þe moare dæl of heom, alswo alse hit is
15 biforen iseid; and þæt æhc oþer helpe þæt for to done bi þan
ilche oþe a3enes alle men ri3t for to done and to foangen. And
noan ne nime of loande ne of e3te wherþur3 þis besi3te mu3e
beon ilet oþer iwersed on onie wise. And 3if oni oþer onie
cumen her on3enes, we willen and hoaten þæt alle vre treowe
20 heom healden deadliche ifoan. And for þæt we willen þæt þis
beo stedefæst and lestinde, we senden 3ew þis writ open, iseined
wiþ vre seel, to halden amanges 3ew ine hord. Witnesse
vsseluen æt Lundene þane e3tetenþe day on þe monþe of
Octobre, in þe two and fowerti3þe 3eare of vre cruninge. And
25 þis wes idon ætforen vre isworene redesmen, Boneface Arche-
bischop on Kanterburi, Walter of Cantelow, Bischop on
Wirechestre, Simon of Muntfort, Eorl of Leirchestre, Richard
of Clare, Eorl on Glowchestre and on Hurtford, Roger Bigod,
Eorl on Northfolke and Marescal on Engleneloande, Perres of
30 Sauueye, Willelm of Fort, Eorl on Aubemarle, Iohan of
Plesseiz, Eorl on Warewik, Iohan Geffrees sune, Perres of
Muntfort, Richard of Grey, Roger of Mortemer, Iames of
Aldithele, and ætforen oþre ino3e.

And al on þo ilche worden is isend into æurihce oþre shcire
35 ouer al þære kuneriche on Engleneloande, and ek in-tel
Irelonde.

Henry, through the grace of God King of England, Lord of
Ireland, Duke of Normandy, of Aquitaine, and Earl of
Anjou, sends greeting to all his loyal [subjects], clerical and
lay, in Huntingdonshire. That you may all know well that we
desire and are pleased that that which all our counsellers, or
the greater part of them, who have been chosen by us and by
the common people of our kingdom, have done and shall do
to the glory of God and in loyalty to us, for the country's
benefit through the provisions of the aforesaid counsellers,
should be forever firm and enduring. And we order all our
faithful [subjects] by the loyalty that they owe us, that they
should steadfastly maintain, and swear to maintain and to
defend those agreements that are made and may be made by
the aforementioned counsellers, or by the greater part of
them, as is before stated; and that each should help the other,
by the same oath, to act towards all men so as to give and
receive justice. And no one may seize land or property as a
result of which this provision may be in any way hindered or
impaired. And if any [person] or any [persons] oppose this,
we desire and command that all our loyal [subjects] consider
them deadly enemies. And because we wish that this should
be firm and lasting, we send you this open writ, sealed with
our seal, for you to keep with you in your archives.
Witnessed by ourself in London on the eighteenth day of the
month of October in the forty-second year of our reign. And
this was done before our sworn counsellers, Boniface,
Archbishop of Canterbury; Walter of Cantiloupe, Bishop of
Worcester; Simon de Montfort, Earl of Leicester; Richard of
Clare, Earl of Gloucester and of Hertfordshire; Roger Bigod,
Earl of Northumberland and Marshal of England; Piers of
Savoy; William of Fort, Earl of Albemarle; John of Plessis,
Earl of Warwick; John, Geoffrey's son; Piers of Montfort;
Richard of Grey; Roger of Mortimer; James of Aldithele,
and before many others. And in exactly the same words [this
writ] has been sent to every other county throughout the
kingdom of England, and also into Ireland.

Notes

1–4   **Henry . . . Huntendoneschire**   The *salutatio* of the letter. Compare this, and the connection to the following sentence through a subjunctive, with Alfred's opening of his Preface to the *Pastoral Care*. Alfred does not continue in the plural with the 'royal' *we*.
   King   OE *y* is written ‹i›, but in *kuneriche* (7) is written ‹u›, and in *iwersed* (18), ‹e›. The three different spellings represent three different dialect areas, respectively the east Midlands, west Midlands and the south-east. London texts frequently have all three types.

6   **beoþ ichosen**   The form of the verb 'to be' is identical to that in OE; the past participle retains a phonetically reduced version of the prefix, but the verb (OE *gecoren*) has been remodelled on the infinitive form (*cēosan*).

9   **þan toforeniseide**   Devices to ensure clarity within chains of reference are part of the legal inheritance of curial style. Among these are repetition of words and phrases, as well as identifying phrases such as this and *alse hit is biforen iseid* (14–15).

10   **a buten ænde**   The significance of the spelling with *æ* is not certain, but the failure of Germanic short *a* to develop to *e* when i-mutated before *n* is characteristic of the Essex dialect. See *Vices and Virtues* and *Kyng Alisaunder*. The impressive-sounding phrase is characteristic of documents written in the curial style: *stedefæst and lestinde* (21). Note also the free use of synonymous pairs of words and phrases, and extended qualifications of statements.
   we hoaten   First-person present indicative. In most of the present-tense plural forms of verbs, indicative forms are no longer distinct from subjunctives, as was the case in the east Midlands. Distinct forms are maintained in *habbeþ* (7) and *beoþ* (6).

16   **oþe**   Although the reflex of OE long *ā* is usually distinguished from the reflex of OE *ō* in spelling by the use of ‹oa› for the former, a few spellings suggest that in some words there may have been no distinction in pronunciation: *alswo* (14); *two* (24); *þo* (34).

34   **worden**   There are very few noun plurals in the passage. Although *-en* plurals are normally considered to be associated with the conservative South and West, this OE neuter word occurred very widely either endingless or with the *-en* inflexion for plural. Þinge (10) is an endingless OE neuter; *ifoan* (20) has the original Weak plural ending.

14 The South English Legendary

The *South English Legendary* is the name given by modern scholars to a collection of saints' lives and associated material which was probably compiled in Worcester in the last quarter of the thirteenth century. It was extremely popular from the beginning, flourished in the fourteenth century, and continued to be copied throughout the medieval period. It is anonymous, and its history illustrates graphically the general truth that medieval English texts ceased to be the property of their author, becoming a common heritage adaptable to the purposes of any literate person. The earliest manuscripts contained about seventy lives, but this count had doubled by the end of the fifteenth century.

The excerpt printed here is part of a popular scientific treatise tacked on to the 'Legend of St Michael'. Reference to hell in the legend leads on to an account of the cosmos, meteorology, the human constitution in terms of its composition from the four elements – earth, water, air and fire – and closes with a description of procreation and psychology. The author acknowledges no sources for his eclectic account, and modern scholarship has discovered none; but there are some parallels with the *Secretum Secretorum*, and compare Ælfric's *De Temporibus Anni* (Excerpt 5) above.

The version in Bodleian Library MS Laud Misc. 108, on which this excerpt is based, seems to have been produced in western Oxfordshire about 1300. A southern origin is indicated by the spelling of the reflex of OE *ā* as ‹o›, and rounding is confirmed by the rhymes in lines 40–1, 48–9, 74–5, 98–9. The South is further suggested by the use of *-ene* as a noun plural ending in *steorrene* (9) and *cloudene* (58), the *h*-forms of the personal pronouns, the preservation of the prefix in past participles, and the present participle form in *-inde* (79). The continued use of the spelling ‹eo›, and the writing of WS *y* as ‹u› suggest the West. WS *y* is represented by ‹uy› over a more restricted area, including Worcester, Warwick, Gloucester and west Oxfordshire. The spelling *guod* is found only in the South-East and in west Oxfordshire.

Þe Eorþe nis bote a luytel hurst aȝein þe riȝte heouene, iwis.
Heouene geth al aboute þe eorþe, euene it mot weyȝe;
Amidde riȝt heouene þe eorþe is ase þe streon amidde þe eyȝe.
Muche is þat on þanne more þane þat oþur, for þe leste steorre is
5 In heouene, ase þe bok us tellez, [more] þane al þe eorþe, iwis.
For ho-so were an heiȝ bi an steorre, ȝif it so miȝte beo,
So luyte wolde þe eorþe þinche þat vnneþe he scholde it ouȝt
iseo.
Þe heouene geth ene aboute, þoruȝ daiȝe and þoruȝ nyȝt;
Þe mone and þe steorrene with him heo berth, and þe sonne þat
is so briȝt:
10 For þat is euene aboue þin heued riȝt atþe nones stounde,
Ounder þine fet euene it is at midniȝt onder þe grounde,
And cometh up ȝwane þe sonne arist, and [o]uer þe is at none;
Heo makez euene þus hire cours, and comez aboute wel sone.
Ase an appel þe eorþe is round, so þat eueremo
15 Half þe eorþe þe sonne bischineth, hov-so it euere go,
And noon it is binethen us, ȝwane it is here midniȝt;
Ase man may þe soþe iseo, ho-so hauez guod insiȝt:
Ase ȝif þov heolde ane clere candele biside an appel riȝt,
Euene half þe appel heo wolde ȝiuen hire lijȝt.

20 Eiȝte firmamenz þare beoth, swuche ase we iseoth.
Þe ouemeste is þe riȝtte heouene in ȝwan þe steorrene beoth
For Godes riche is þare aboue þat last withouten ende;
Þarto we beoth imaked – god leue us þudere iwende.
Þare bineoþe beoth seoue firmamenz, þat euerech of heom, iwis,
25 One steorre hath withoute mo, þat planete icleoped is.
Ichulle nemmen heore seoue names, and formest biguynne hext:
Saturnus is al aboue and Iupiter sethþe next,
Þanne Mars bineoþen him, and sethþe þe sonne is,
Venus sethþe, þe clere steorre, Mercurius þanne, iwis,
30 Þat wel selden is of us iseiȝe. Þe Mone is next þe grounde.
Þoruȝ gret wit of clergie heore names weren furst bifounde:
For euerech of þeos seouene mouwen gret wonder on eorþe do,
Boþe of wederes and of fruyt, ase heore power ȝif þareto.
And also man, ȝwane he is ibore onder heore power, iwis,
35 Schullen habbe diuers lijf, euere ase heore vertue is:
Some lechours, some glotones, and some of oþur manere.
And natheles a man of guod inwit of alle he may him skere:
For þe planetes ne doth non oþur but ȝiuez in mannes wille,
To beon luþur oþur guod, ase heore uertue wole to tille,
40 And ȝiuen him also qualite to don so and so;
Ake nouȝt forþan after is inwit; ech wys man may do:

The earth is no more than a little spot compared with the true heaven. Heaven goes all around the earth, steadily it must move. The earth is in the middle of the true heaven like the pupil amid the eye. The one is much larger than the other, for as books tell us the least star in heaven is indeed bigger than the whole earth. For whoever were aloft beside a star (if that could happen) would think the earth to be so small that he should hardly see it at all. The heaven goes steadily round, by day and night, and carries the moon and stars with it, and the sun which is so bright, for what is exactly above your head at noontime, is directly beneath your feet, under the ground, at midnight, and comes up when the sun rises, and is above you at noon; it steadily makes its way thus, and quickly comes around. The earth is round like an apple, so that the sun continously lights up half the earth, wherever it is, and it is noon beneath us when it is midnight here; a truth that anybody can see, who has good perception. It is as if you held a bright candle next to an apple; it would give light to exactly half the apple.

There are eight heavenly spheres. As we can see, the uppermost is the true heaven in which the stars are: for God's kingdom, which lasts without end is above it – we are created for it; God grant us to go there. Seven heavenly spheres are beneath, of which each one has only one star that is called a planet. I shall name their seven names, beginning first from the highest. Saturn is above all, and Jupiter next, then Mars beneath it and afterwards the Sun, the bright star Venus after, then Mercury, that is very rarely seen by us. The Moon is nearest the ground. Their names were first discovered by great skill of learning, for each of those seven may work marvellous effects on earth both with regard to weather and fruit, as their particular virtues extend. And so, according to the force of the planet under which they are born, people have different lives: some lechers, some gluttons, and some have other characteristics. But nevertheless a man of good discrimination can purify himself, because the planets do no more than act upon man's will to be good or grosser, according to what their force extends, and gives him also the disposition to do this or that; but nevertheless there is still conscience, which each wise man may use, for nobody has such a disposition to be a lecher or villain in such a way that he cannot guard against it: but nevertheless, few do so.

For swuch qualite no man ne hath to beon lechor oþur schrewe,
Þat he þarewith ne may him wite – ake natheles so doth fewe.

. . .

Muche is bitwene heouene and eorþe, for þe man þat miȝte go
45 Euereche daye fourty mile, and ȝeot sumdel mo,
He ne scholde nouȝt to hexte heouene, þat ȝe alday iseoth,
Comen in eiȝte þousende ȝer, þere as þe steorrene beoth;
And þei Adam, ore furste fader, hadde bigonne anon
Þo þat he was furst imad, and toward þe heouene igon,
50 And hadde eche daie fourti mile euene opriȝt igo,
He ne hadde nouȝt ȝeot to heuene icome bi a þousende mile
and mo.
Sikere ȝe beon I segge ȝeov soth ileue ho-so ileue –
Hov schulle we þat comiez so late after Adam and Eue?
Ake ȝwane a man is on eorþe ded, and his soule beo guod,
55 Heo nath with hire non heuinesse of flesche ne of blod:
Ȝif heo is þanne withoute sunne, heo hath aungles cuynde,
And mai beo nouþe here and þer, ase quik ase mannes
muynde.
For ase ȝe iseoth þe liȝtengue out of þe cloudene iwende,
Þat comieth of þat on half of þe world and also sone in þe
oþur ende,
60 Wel smartloker scheot ane mannes soule; ȝe, more þane
swuche seuene,
Ȝif heo is oute of sunne, þene riȝte wei into heouene.
Ake wel sonere he may to helle come – þarefore it is isene
Þat wel mo to helle wendez. Ȝe, ich drede swuche tene.

Bineoþe þe loweste heuene, þat þe mone is on ibrouȝt,
65 So beoth þe foure elemenz, of ȝwan we beoth iwrouȝt.
Next þe mone þat fuyr is hext – echone huy beoth rounde –
Þe eir is þanne next bineothe, and tillez riȝt to þe grounde,
Sethþe is watur, and sethþe þe eorþe – þeos beoth foure, iwis,
Of ȝwan man and eche quic þing forsoþe imaked is.
70 Ore louerd in echon of þis foure al dai scheweth is miȝte,
Ase ȝe mowe in þe stude of fuyre iseo a wonder siȝte,
Scheote as þei it a steorre were bi þe lofte an heiȝ,
Ake þe steorrene beoth feorre aboue, for þat is sumdel neiȝ.
Þe sonne may here among us gret strencþe and miȝte do:
75 He drauth up þe kuynde of þe watere, and of the eorþe also;
He drauȝth up of þe eorþe in druye wedere as it were a druye
breth,
So þat þoruȝ hete of þe sonne aboue þe eir it geth,

· · ·

The [distance] between heaven and earth is great, for one could travel forty miles and still a bit more every day and not come to the highest heaven that you see every day, where the stars are, in eight thousand years. And although our first father, Adam, had begun straight away when he was first made, and walked towards heaven forty miles a day directly upwards, he would not yet have come to heaven, by a thousand miles or more. You may be certain I tell you the truth, believe it who may – how shall we who come so late after Adam and Eve? But when a man is dead on earth, and his soul is good, it has with it no heaviness of flesh or blood; if it is then without sin, it has the nature of an angel, and may be now here and now there as quickly as human thought. For as you see the light fall from the skies, that comes from one side of the world and as quickly ends in the other, much quicker shoots a man's soul if he is free from sin, yes, more than seven times as quickly, on the direct route to heaven. But he may come to hell much quicker: therefore it is apparent that far more go to hell – yes, I dread such suffering.

Beneath the lowest heaven, where the moon is lodged, are the four elements from which we are formed. Next to the moon, fire is the highest – each is spherical. Next below that is the air, which extends right to the ground; after that is water, and then the earth. These make four, I think, from which man and every living thing is surely made. In each of these four, Our Lord daily shows his might, as [for example] in the region of fire you may see a wondrous sight: something like a star shoots through the air above; but the stars are farther above, for that is fairly close. The sun can perform great [feats] of strength and power here among us: it draws up the essence from the water and from the earth too. In dry weather it draws up from the earth a kind of dry exhalation, so that carried by the heat of the sun, it goes up above the air, and when it comes among the fire it begins to ignite and shoots forth all burning until it is all burned up. Thus, such things are not seen except when it is hot. Lightning also comes from this source, when it reaches moisture; for that same dry exhalation, when it is drawn aloft by previous heat, and there is a cloud nearby, at once as it is on fire, it shoots through the cloud and while it is in the water, it makes a very loud rumbling, as if a man took an iron ingot that was glowing with fire and thrust it in water, it would rumble

And ȝwane it comez among þe fuyre, sone it bigynnez forto
tiende
And al berninde it scheot forth, þat hit beo ibarnd to ende.
80 Þarefore men ne iseoth no swuch þing bote it beo in hete.
Liȝtingue comez also þare-of ȝwane it comez to wete:
For al þat ilke druye breth þat is so idrawe an heiȝ,
Þoruȝ hete þat was bifore and a cloud þat þare was neiȝ,
Anon so it is afuyre; it scheot þoruȝ þe cloude,
85 And þe ȝwile it is in þe watere, it goþeleth swyþe loude:
Ase ȝif a man nome ane sclabbe of ire, þat glowynde were
afuyre,
And pulte in watere; it wolde goþeli loude, þat men miȝten it
feor ihuyre.
Also þat fuyr up an heiȝ þat bi þe cloude is itend,
Hit goþelez in þe watere loude as it þoruȝout iwent –
90 And þat is þe þondre, iwis, and siker non oþur þing;
And ȝwane þat fuyr scheot þoruȝout, þat is þe liȝting,
And þat scheot abrod þoru al þe world. þat comez aftur þe dunte;
And natheles it þinchez bifore, for it ne may nouȝwere atstunte.
Ȝif here were an heiȝ stepel and a man aboue sete,
95 And men iseiȝen him smiten al an heiȝ guode duntes and grete,
Þou miȝtest him seo wel longue smite þe duntes with þine eiȝe
Are þov scholdest þene dunt iheore, ȝif he were ouȝt heiȝe –
For man mai iseo wel feor a þing anon so it is ido,
Ȝif þare nis noþing bitweone; ake man ne may nouȝt
iheore so.

Notes

1 **hurst**   OE *hyrst*, 'a wooded hill or hillock'. Recorded very rarely
in western ME apparently meaning more generally 'a place'.
5 **tellez**   The third-person singular present-tense inflexion in this
text is normally *-eth*, with numerous examples with the syncopation
of *e* and the subsequent assimilation characteristic of Saxon-derived
forms of ME: *berth* (9), *arist* (12), *last* (22). The fairly frequent *-ez*
forms are best interpreted as arising from spelling confusion.
9 **heo**   Apparently to be interpreted here as 'he', but in line 13 as
'she'.
12 **ȝwane**   The spelling ‹ȝw› for OE ‹hw› is restricted to west
Oxfordshire.
26 **Ichulle**   This contraction of *ich* and *wulle* is of predominantly
southern and western forms of the pronoun and verb.

loudly, so that it could be heard from afar. So that fire up
aloft, that is kindled near the cloud, rumbles loudly in the
water as it passes through; and that, indeed, is thunder, and
certainly nothing else. And when the fire shoots through it,
that is lightning, and that shoots out through the whole
world. That comes after the blow, but nevertheless seems to
be before, because it may nowhere come to an end. If there
were a high steeple and a man seated up above, and people
could see him strike as hard as he could good solid blows, you
would see him strike the blows (with your eye) very long
before you would hear the blow, if he were at all high: for
one can see something from a long way off as soon as it is
done if there is nothing in between, but one cannot hear thus.

53 **comiez**   Also *comieth* (59). The plural inflection proper to Weak
Class 2 verbs has been extended to this Strong verb. Unless the
subject of *comieth* is *cloudene*, the potential distinction offered
between singular and plural is not exploited.

55 **heo nath**   The contracted form of the negative particle *ne* and the
verb 'to have' is commonest in much the same area as the spelling
‹uy›. See introductory notes.

68 **watur**   The spelling of unstressed vowels with ‹u› is predominantly
a western characteristic.

79 **ibarnd**   The retention of the prefix is found broadly in the South,
but the particular form of this verb, with an *-a-* spelling, is south-west
Midland.

85 **goþeleth**   The word has no known etymology, and seems to be
sound echoic. In line 87, the infinitive is formed as a Weak Class 2
infinitive.

86 **sclabbe**   The word *slab* seems to be technical in ME, used only of
a flat mass of iron or steel. The etymology is obscure.

Early Middle English romance should not be confused with the pastoral idylls of later periods any more than with popular modern love stories. Its ethos often has more in common with epic, and although the love between the hero and heroine forms an important thread of the plot in many romances, acts of military heroism, comradeship, repossession of lost domains, and the violent reassertion of justice are more significant themes. Like many early romances, *Kyng Alisaunder* is the adaptation of an Anglo-Norman original, in this case the *Romance of Alexander* by Thomas of Kent. It recounts the Greek hero's exploits and battles, but his love for Candace is no more important to the story than any other episode, and indeed corresponds to a decline in his fortunes shortly preceding his death. This is a narrative of wonders, politics, travel and action, which pauses only briefly to contemplate the deeper significance of the events portrayed.

Like the related romances, *Arthour and Merlin* and *Richard Coer de Lion* (and the less strikingly similar *Seven Sages of Rome*), *Kyng Alisaunder* seems to have been produced in the London area towards the end of the thirteenth century and, like them, was included in the famous Auchinleck MS which was compiled in London in the first third of the fourteenth century. However, only fragments of this version remain, and the poem is nearly complete in two other manuscripts, Lincoln's Inn MS 150 and Bodleian Library MS Laud Misc. 622. The text here is from the latter, a manuscript produced in London in the third quarter of the fourteenth century.

The excerpt contains a scene not unlike that in Shakespeare's *Henry V*, in which a young and inexperienced leader is taunted for his lack of maturity by a more established antagonist. The latter's message is presented as a letter and is marked by stylistic features characteristic of the *ars dictamen* (the art of formal composition of documents and letters in prose) as well as some of the technical language of clerks trained in the art. Linguistically the text belongs to a period in which the London language is showing a tendency towards standardisation: that is, several documents, written by different scribes, employ a similar range of written forms not all directly derived from the native London language. This incipient standard, known as Type II standard

(Samuels, 1972: 165–70), is marked by the use of forms imported as the result of immigration from East Anglia and the south-east Midlands. As may be expected from a translated text, and especially one whose author lays explicit claim to literary sophistication, French borrowings – and even French phrases – are also common.

> Herd ʒee habbeþ, ich wil reherce,
> Hou þe messagers comen from Perce
> For trowage and Philippe ennoyed –
> Hou Alisaunder it hem wiþseide.
> 5 Now atte first þe messagers
> Beeþ ycome to her empirers.
> Hij saluen Darrye her lorde,
> And siggen hym þis worde:
> 'Lorde, we weren in þi message
> 10 Jn Grece after trewage,
> Ac it is wiþseid in al þing,
> Of a ʒonge kniʒth þat þinkeþ be kyng.
> Worþes þee non while he may lyue;
> Oiþer þou most it al forʒyue,
> 15 Oiþer, he þee sent to sigge,
> Dereynen it wiþ swerdes egge.'
> Darrie startleþ for þise tydynges,
> And makeþ anguisshous þretynges.
> He takeþ wiþ hym many a duk
> 20 Þat bileueþ on Belsabuk,
> And gooþ myd hym to on orchard
> And parlement hij haldeþ hard.
> Jch ʒou telle, litel, jwys,
> Of Alisaunder he heldeþ prys,
> 25 And [by] hire aldre radd and want
> A lettre [to] hym is ysant,
> By riche dukes þrittene.
> Bouʒ hi baren of olyue grene.
> Þe duk þere was of Ermynye.
> 30 Of Esclaueyne, and of Sulye,
> Of Pyncenarde, and of Mede.
> Þoo of Nynyue, good at nede,
> Þe duk of Japhes and Taberye,
> Þe duk of Fryse, and of Hungrye,
> 35 Þe duk of Moreb, and Calebyne,
> And þe duk of Palestyne;

You have heard, I will repeat, how the messengers came from Persia for tribute and disturbed Philip; how Alexander denied it to them. Now as soon as possible the messengers are come to their emperor. They greet their lord, Darius, and tell him these words: 'Lord, we were on your errand seeking tribute in Greece but it was utterly denied to us by a young knight who aspires to be king. There will be none for you while he may live. He sent to say to you that either you must forgo it all or claim it with the edge of the sword.' Darius is agitated by this news and utters threats from his dread. He takes with him many a duke who puts faith in Beelzebub, and goes with them to an orchard and they hold earnest council. I tell you they set little store by Alexander, and through the consensus and design of them all a letter is sent to him with thirteen rich dukes. They bear a bough of green olive. The duke of Armenia was there, of Esclaveyne, and of Syria, of Thrace, and of Media. Then of Nineveh, good in a tight corner, the duke of Jaffa and Taberia, the duke of Phrygia, and of Hungary, the duke of Moreb and Calebyne, and the duke of Palestine; they all came hand in hand before Alexander in the land of Tyre, each with an olive branch, that was a sign of peace and accord, and they took him three things, sent to him by Darius as a present: a fine whip and top, a purse full of gold, and a letter in a friendly manner, whose content was this:

'Darius, king of all kings, who has the gods as his ancestors, for his nearest related cousins are Jupiter and Apollo, rulers of all [lit. untaught and educated] who are in this world, sends greeting without esteem to a treacherous young robber. Alexander, you crazy fool, your doomed blood is courting disaster! You have withheld my tribute and committed an outrage against me – burned my towns, slain my men. You deserve to be drawn. However, you have no worth; I blame it all on your young blood. Therefore I have sent you a whip and top as a present, and a little purse with gold, because you are young. Go home and play with them, I

Þai comen alle, honde in honde,
Toforne Alisaundre in Tyre londe,
Vche wiþ bouȝ of olyue,
40 Þat was tokne of pays and of l[o]ue,
And token hym þat Darrye hym sent
Þre þinges to present:
A scourge and a toppe of nobleys,
And ful of golde an haum[u]deys,
45 And a lettre, par amoure,
Of whiche swiche was þe tenure:
'Darrye, kyng of alle kynges,
Þe godes þat he haueþ to eldringes,
For his nexte by-syb cosyn
50 Beeþ Jubiter and Appolyn,
Gouernoures of lewed and lered
Þat beeþ in þis middellerd,
Sendeþ gretyng wiþouten amoure
To a ȝonge fals robboure.
55 Alisaunder, þou conion wood,
Jn þe spilleþ þi faye blood.
Þou hast wiþholde my trowage,
And ydon me more outrage –
Brent myne tounes, myne men yslawe.
60 Þou art worþi to ben ydrawe.
Nere-þe-lees, þou canst no good;
Jch wyte it al þi ȝonge blood.
Þere-fore Ich habbe þee ysent
A top and scourge to present,
65 And wiþ golde a litel punge,
For þou hast ȝeres ȝonge.
Wende þou hom þerewiþ and pleye,
Jch þee rede, ȝonge boye!
Oiþer Ich þee shal doo bete and dynge
70 Wiþ a fewe gadelynge,
And afterwardes quyk þee flen,
And alle þi folk wiþ sorouȝ slen.
Wenestou to be my pere?
Nay, jwys, wrecche pautenere!
75 Jch haue moo kniȝttes to werren
Þan ben in þe walken sterren,
And moo men wiþ stronge bones
Þan ben jn þe cee grauel-stones.
Fleiȝe now swiþe, þat þou ne be yfounde,
80 Oiþer men þee shulle dryue wiþ hounde.'

advise you, young lad! Otherwise I shall have you belaboured and beaten by a few fellows and afterwards skinned alive, and all your people wretchedly put to death. Do you think you are my equal? No, indeed, wretched vagabond! I have more knights to make war than there are stars in the sky, and more strong-boned men than pebbles in the sea. Flee now quickly, so that you may not be found, or you shall be hunted with hounds.'

This was the letter that Darius sent to Alexander as a present; but you shall hear how Alexander made it turn out differently. Alexander sees very well that his knights are disconcerted. He laughs and swears by the sun that he has won Media and Persia, 'Because this whip must signify that I shall win dominion over Darius, and also chastise him and his, the greatest and the least. Also the top, which is round, no doubt signifies that the world, which is round, shall be mine. And by the purse is meant that I shall receive tribute from old and young. Tell Darius this same tale, and that I do not wish to come to agreement with him except by the sword and spear's point.' These messengers hear his speech, and go home by hill and dale. Alexander swiftly disposes of his business with Tyre. He has wrongdoers put to death, and dispenses law and order to the others. (If the governmental law derived from the great lords, Darius is their lord and king.) Alexander established his steward there and went briskly towards Darius.

Þis was þe wrytt þad Darrye sent
To Alisaunder to present,
Ac of Alisaunder ȝee shullen here
Hou he it tourned in oþere manere.

85 Alisaunder wel wele seeþ
Þat his kniȝttes dismaied beeþ.
He leiȝeþ and swereþ by þe sonne
Mede and Perce he haþ ywonne,
'Forþi þis scourge shal signifye

90 Þat J shal wynne þe maistrye
Of Darrye, and also chaste
Hym and hise, þe more and þe laste.
Þe top þat is rounde aboute
Signifieþ also, saunz doute,

95 ðat þe werlde þat rounde is
Shal be myne also, j-wys.
And bitokneþ by þe punge
Þat ich shal of elde and ȝonge
Of þis midlerde tol afonge.

100 Siggeþ Darrye þis ilk songe,
And þat ich nylle myd hym acorde,
Bot wiþ swerd and speres oorde.'
Þise messageres hereþ þis tale,
And wendeþ hom, by doune and dale.

105 Alisaunder alle hise nedes
Aȝeins Tyre swiþe spedes.
Þe mysdoers he dooþ ben yslawe,
And to þe oþere he ȝiueþ lawȝe
(Ȝif lawȝe were of þe grete lordynges

110 Js Darrye her lorde and kyng).
Alisaunder sett þere his baillyf.
To Darrie ward he went blijf . . .

Notes

6 **empirers**   The final -*s*, which enables the rhyme with *messagers*, is preserved from the French nominative case of masculine nouns.

7 **Hij saluen**   The -*en* plural present inflexion is indicative of the east Midlands, but this text also contains the more southerly -*eþ* plural, sometimes in archaic forms like *habbeþ* (1). The third-person plural pronoun is very variable: *he* (24), *þai* (37). This variety is typical of the Type II London standard.

8 **þis worde**   The rhyme confirms that the original had some noun plurals in -*e(n)*. In this case the -*e* plural has been adopted by an OE neuter. See also *sterren* (76), *hounde* (80).

13 **worþes þee**   An impersonal construction with an unexpressed subject. That the -*es* inflexion occurred in the original is proved by the rhyme *nedes–spedes* (105–6). The -*es* inflexion for the third-person singular present tense is generally considered a northern form, but is found in London in the Type II language, where it derives from East Anglian immigration. It still occurs rarely in Chaucer MSS. The more usual inflexion in *KA* is -*eþ*.

25 **radd and want**   The spelling ⟨a⟩ of the reflex of WS $\bar{æ}^1$ in *radd* is characteristic of a small area including Essex, London and Middlesex. The rhyme *laste–chaste* (91–2) confirms an *a* pronunciation for $\bar{æ}^2$ also. The Essex–London association is further emphasised by the spelling ⟨an⟩ rhyming on the *i*-mutation of Germanic short *a* before a nasal in *ysant*. But compare lines 41–2, 63–4, 81–2.

46 **tenure**   The word is a semi-technical one used by scribes recording documents to refer to the essential content of what they were entering into the record. The extensive French influence observable in *KA* stems not only from its status as a translation, or from the cultural pretensions of its author, but also from a milieu in which most scribes were employed in administrative work conducted exclusively in either French or Latin.

47–54 **Darrye . . . robboure**   The letter follows prescribed practice, beginning with a salutation formula placing the name of the more important correspondent before that of the lesser. Their inequality is here ludicrously emphasised by the choice of titles.

59 **Brent**   The past participle appears without a prefix, but more commonly is of the southern type with a prefix, and loss of final -*n* in Strong verbs.

68 **ȝonge boye**   The word *boye* is a social slight, an insult like the accusation of falseness. In early ME, *boye* had no necessary implication of age, and rather alleged low birth or employment as a servant.

85–6 **seeþ . . . beeþ**   The rhyme would not be possible in the east Midlands, where third-person singular and plural inflexions were distinct.

Later Middle English (1300–1500)

The period from 1300 to 1500 includes most of the better-known works of English medieval literature: *Piers Plowman*, *Sir Gawain and the Green Knight*, the craft guild and some morality plays, Malory's *Morte d'Arthur*, and the works of Chaucer (*c*. 1343–1400) and his followers. It saw the triumph of English over French in almost every sphere of life, the rapid expansion of the education of laymen in Latin, the beginnings of more extensive popular literacy (further encouraged by the introduction of printing in 1476), and the emergence of more standardised forms of the written language. Throughout the period, however, texts continued to be copied by scribes, and English remained a language marked by great dialectal variety.

The continuing role of French in England is described in the excerpt from Bokenham's translation of Higden's *Polichronicon*. On the one hand it was the language associated with gentle birth and refinement of accomplishments, and on the other it suggested participation in the world of affairs. In the royal court and some major aristocratic houses, literature in French, which had begun in the opening decades of the twelfth century, continued to be written until the middle of the fourteenth. In the worlds of education, law and administration, French was an official language of instruction, pleading and record until the fifteenth century. In the later fourteenth century, however, it was kept active in these roles with some difficulty, and the formulaic Anglo-French of documents differs markedly from the colloquial mother tongue of everyday life across the Channel. Although legal records continued to employ Anglo-French into the reign of Henry VIII, in most other spheres, documents written in English outnumber those in French after about 1430. Nevertheless, in 1450 instruction in French was still thought to be a valuable qualification for a successful career in commerce, and schools existed to teach it for this purpose.

The relative prestige of French was dependent on the varieties used in England. Initially, and for perhaps as much as a hundred and fifty years after the Conquest, French could be learned within the households of the settlers, or through family contact with lands in Normandy. Hence the earlier kind of French used was based on the dialect of Normandy. But with the loss of Norman lands in 1204, that linguistic connection was lost, and from the middle of the thirteenth century the dominant influence on French in England was from the Ile de France. This change is apparent in the dialectal forms of borrowed words, where central French *charité* and *garde* replace earlier Norman French *carité* and *warde*. As French declined further in the fourteenth century, proficiency in native, artificially learned and largely written Anglo-French begins to be scorned by comparison with the fluency of speakers of fashionable continental French. With the decline of French as a technical written language in the early decades of the fifteenth century, many borrowings of technical words were made into written English.

Although the Early Middle English period had witnessed various individual (cf. Orm) and corporate (cf. *Ancrene Wisse*) attempts to write local dialects consistently, none of these was adopted very widely. The Later Middle English period saw the emergence of spelling systems which achieved much more general use. It is upon one of these, Chancery English, that modern standard written English is based. Chancery English, which begins to be written from about 1415, is the form of London English employed by scribes in the early fifteenth-century Chancery, which was situated in the street now known as Chancery Lane. The wider adoption of this spelling system during the century was partly the result of its status as an official language, partly from the volume of documents written in it, and partly from the acceptability of the dialectal mixture from which it was composed.

Unlike the earliest London English, Chancery English, like Chaucer's before it, was not predominantly southern in its dialect forms. Rather, as the beneficiary of spellings developed in preceding London standards, it had a markedly central and east Midland character. Immigration of literate men into London from further north had gradually altered the type of English written in London. In Chancery English the third-person present tense of the verb is still -*eth* in the singular, but -*e(n)* or endingless in the plural; the *h*-forms of the third-person plural pronoun are still found in oblique cases, but the *th*- forms (first noted in the *Ormulum*) are in the majority, and *they/thay* is the exclusive form of the nominative. The present participle of the verb now ends in *yng/ing*. The normal Chancery spellings of large numbers of words – many of a technical Franco-Latin derivation – are those which eventually became the standard forms. Although the spellings Caxton uses are not always exactly equivalent to those of Chancery documents, both he and later printers are influenced by the Chancery standard, and so helped to establish it as the basis of modern English spelling.

The fifteenth century is notable as the first great era in which the founding of grammar schools was viewed as a meritorious act among the wealthy and influential. During the century many grammar schools were founded, and although universities existed in Britain only in Oxford, Cambridge, St Andrews and Glasgow, the proportion of young men who attended them was relatively high, so that proficiency in Latin was more widespread among the lay population than ever before. Familiarity with Latin among a potential audience contributed to the development of later fifteenth-century prose and poetry. An interest in verbal composition is already evident among writers of Chaucer's time, and John Lydgate and later fifteenth-century authors are progressively more affected by the rhetorical ideas emerging from the Italian Renaissance. They are increasingly eager to exhibit their learning and adorn their verses with words culled from Latin or Franco-Latin sources. In prose, too, Franco-Latin influences are evident. Administrative prose based ultimately on Latin but adapted in French became noticeably more lexically ornate in the last two decades of the fourteenth century, and this tendency is echoed by English administrative prose after the 1420s. Lydgate's prose work, the *Serpent of Divisioun* (1422), imitates the administrative prose in both lexical elaboration and some aspects of syntax, and this prose style, which is paralleled by contemporary developments in France, reaches its extreme in the Middle English period in the work of Skelton (see Excerpt 23), but the pursuit of Latinity as the model for English continued to flourish throughout the Early Modern period.

If the fifteenth century saw the appearance of numbers of Latin-derived multisyllabic words, some of which have become part of the vocabulary of Modern English, it also witnessed important syntactical and phonological developments in the story of English. The final -*e*, which was one of the last remaining traces of the Old English inflexional system, disappeared from pronunciation in the London area in the early decades of the century, although it continued to be written in traditional spellings and as an indication of a long root vowel preceding. Manuscripts of Chaucer's poetry written before about 1415, and also the work of Thomas Hoccleve (*c*. 1369–1426), show clear understanding of the role of final -*e* in metre; but some contemporary and all later copyists and authors can no longer distinguish which -*es* are to be sounded and which left silent. During the earlier fifteenth-century, too, the system of long vowels in Middle English commenced a series of interconnected changes which radically affected the pronunciation of English, distancing it from the vowel systems of continental languages. The Great Vowel Shift can best be represented diagrammatically:

```
ij ← i:          u: → əu
      ↑            ↑
      e:           o:
      ↑            ↑
      ɛ:           ɔ:
         ↑
         a:
```

Middle English in the fourteenth-century possessed the seven pure long vowels shown in the diagram, but by 1500 the highest vowels, front and back, had been diphthongised, and /e:/ and /o:/ had been raised to take their places. During the sixteenth-century the remaining long vowels, /ɛ:/, /ɔ:/ and /a:/ were in turn raised so as to occupy the places vacated above them by the raising of the original fourteenth-century vowels.

Syntactical developments emerging in the later ME period include an increase in the use of periphrastic forms of the verb phrase, for example the emergence of the *do* periphrasis (see next section), and the emergence of the use of *who* as a relative pronoun, at first only in the oblique form, *whom*. By the end of the period, too, the order of an unmarked positive declarative clause was settled in the modern SVO (SPC) structure. Double negation became much rarer during the late fourteenth-century with the disappearance of the particle *ne*.

Robert Mannyng is the author of two extant works, his better-known penitential handbook *Handlyng Synne*, which he translated from the AN *Manuel des Pechiez*, and the largely ignored *Chronicle* which he says he made 'not for þe lerid bot for þe lewid' – those who could neither understand Latin or French, nor over-elaborate English composition. Although directed to a popular audience, the *Chronicle* is a close translation from earlier French sources: its first half is heavily dependent on Wace's *Brut*, and its second half is based on Peter of Langtoft's *Chronicle*. The first half therefore deals with the legendary history of Britain until the death of Cadwallader in 689, and the second with what Mannyng punningly called 'English geste', the deeds (stories) of later English history.

What is known of Mannyng's life must be gleaned from references in his works. He came from Bourne in south Lincolnshire (as the author of the *Ormulum* also seems to have done), and was in Cambridge, perhaps in the Gilbertine house of St Edmund's Hall, in 1300. By 1303 he was a canon in the Gilbertine priory of Sempringham near Bourne, where he translated *Handlyng Synne*, and in 1327 he was a chaplain in Lincoln. He mentions also spending some time in Sixhills priory, seventeen miles to the north-west of Lincoln, where he worked on his *Chronicle*, completing it on Friday 25 May 1338.

The *Chronicle* exists in whole or in part in five extant MSS, the earliest of which is Lambeth Palace 131, the basis of the text below. This manuscript is dated *c*. 1350 but is not the author's holograph, and indeed Mannyng's statement that his work was 'written' by a fellow Gilbertine, one Robert of Malton, should be sufficient warning not to expect a work in pure Lincolnshire dialect. Morphologically, northern influence is apparent in the inflexion of the third-person singular, present tense of verbs in *-es* (the ancestor of the modern form), and northern or north-east Midland in the widespread loss of *-n* in infinitives and from the east Midland form of the third-person plural, present tense (*gynne*, 2), personal pronoun forms with *þ-* and the feminine, *sche*, and the scarcity of prefixes in past participles. The vocabulary has a number of Scandinavian borrowings – *þey* (2), *lowe* (3), *take* (29), *reyse* (43), *saught* (75) – but their quality is very different from those in the *Ormulum*, and French influence is much more evident.

De ingratitudine filiarum, et planctu patris eorum, Leyr

Now gynnes Leyr to myslyke;
'Sone,' he seyde, 'þey gynne me swyke;
Fro myn aboue y am put lowe,
And ȝit scha[l] more wyþynne a þrowe.
5 Myn oþer doughter wyl y proue,
Þey scheo be wroþ to my behoue.'
And dight hym wyþ his apparaille
To wende in to Cornewaille.
He dwelt nought fullyk a ȝer,
10 Þat þey ne made hym gret daunger,
And lessede his knyghtes and oþer men:
Of þritty þey abated ten,
And ȝit of twenty abated fyue.
Þen wold Leyr han ben of lyue:
15 'Alas!' he seyde, 'y hider cam!
Fro wycke vntil wors y nam!'
To Gonorille agayn he ȝede,
He wend sche wold heue mended his nede,
Haue gyuen hym als scheo hadde byforn,
20 Sche swor by god þat hure leet be born
Þat scheo ne wolde, day ne nyght,
Halde bot hym and a knyght.

Lamentacio Regis Leyr

Þenne bygan Leyr to sorewe,
And ment his mone euen and morwe;
25 Þe grete richesse he hadde byforn,
Al was aweye and ylorn:
'To longe alyue haue y be,
Þat euere schold y þys day se!
Ensample of me men may take,
30 And warnyng of sibbe for my sake.
Y hadde richesse, now haue y non;
My wyt and al myn help ys gon.
Lady Fortune, þou art chaungable!
O day art þou neuere stable!
35 No man may of þe affye:
Þou turnes hym doun þat er was heye;
Þat now ys doun, vpward þou turnes;
Wyþ þe nys non þat he ne mournes;
Bot þere þou gyuest þy loue-lokyng,
40 He ys worschiped als a kyng;

*Of the ingratitude of daughters and the lament of their father,
Lear*

Now Lear begins to be displeased and said 'They soon begin
to betray me; from my high estate, I am humiliated, and will
be further so within a short time. I will try my other
daughter, even though she may be opposed to my welfare.'
And he prepared himself to go with his trappings to
Cornwall. He remained there for less than a full year before
they became grudging towards him, and reduced his knights
and other men: from thirty they deducted ten, and from
twenty deducted a further five. Then Lear wished to be dead.
'Alas!' he said, 'that I came here; after bad I got worse.' He
went back to Goneril; he thought she would be ready to
improve his plight, allow him what she had before. She swore
by God who caused her to be born that, day or night, she
would not maintain any more than him and a single knight.

The Lament of King Lear

Then Lear began to mourn, and evening and morning he
complained. The great wealth he had had before was all lost
and gone: 'I have been alive too long, that ever I should see
this day! People can take an example from me and a warning
about relations from my case. I had wealth; now I have none.
My counsel and support is gone. Lady Fortune, you are
changeable; you are never steady for a day. No one can trust
in you: you turn him down who before was high; that man
who is down you raise up. There is no one who does not
lament in your presence. But where you look fondly, he is
honoured as a king; and whoever you turn your look away
from is immediately cast down in misery and woe. You will
raise up the ill-natured and put the good-natured in distress.
When you are displeased with a king or earl, you lamentably
dash away their wealth. When I had possessions and plenty of
money, then I found friends who gathered round me; now
poverty is thrust upon me so that I have lost all sight of them.
Those whose love and loyalty should rightfully belong to me
show me no semblance of it. Lady Fortune, you took away
from me your loving glance and good wishes when I
condemned my young daughter, and took no notice of the
teaching of she who openly told me the truth: I was worthy
according to what I possessed, and just so much she loved
me. She spoke better than I could see; I did not understand
her words at all, but got angry. It was foolish of me; I did not

And whom þou turnest þy lokyng fro,
Sone ys he doune yn sorewe and wo.
Þe vnkynde þou wilt vp reyse,
Þe kynde þou puttest to meseyse.
45 Wyþ kyng and erl, when þe myslikes,
Þer welþe awey to wo þou strykes.
When y had god and welþe ynow,
Þen fond y frende þat to me drow;
Now pouerte ys put me byforn,
50 Þat al þer sight fro me ys lorn.
Þer loue schold lange to me þorow ryght,
Þat schewe me of loue semblaunt ne syght.
Dame Fortune, þy louely lok
And þy gode wille fro me þou tok
55 When y blamed my doughter ȝyng,
And gaf no kepe til hure kennyng
Þat seyde me soþ apertely:
Als y had, so was y worthy,
And also mykel scheo loued me.
60 Scheo seide bettere þan y couþ se;
Hure word noþyng y ne vnde[r]stod,
But mad me wroþ. Y couþe no god;
Y parceyued nought what was hure tent,
Bot now fele y wel what scheo ment;
65 Y fele hit wel þe soþe hit endes.
Whyder may y now to seke my frendes?
Ȝyf y seke hure for any frame,
Þey sche me weyue scheo nys to blame,
For y defended hure my lond,
70 Ne nought hure gaf, ne hure ne fond.
Natheles, hure wol y seke;
Y fond hure euere god and meke.
Wisdam sche has me ytaught;
Wysdam schal make hure wiþ me saught.
75 Ȝyf y may nought bryng hure þerto,
Wors þan þe oþere may sche nought do.
Scheo seyde a þyng y scha[l] now proue:
Als hure fader scheo wolde me loue;
And als scheo seyde, proue schal y
80 Hire kyndnesse and hure curtesy.'

see what she intended, but now I well understand what she meant; I understand well that it sums up the truth. Where may I go now to look for friends? If I approach her for any benefit, she is not to be blamed even though she should disown me, for I denied her my land, gave her nothing and did not provide for her. Nevertheless, I will seek her out. I always found her virtuous and forgiving. She has taught me wisdom, and wisdom shall make her be reconciled with me. If I cannot bring her to that, she can do no worse than the others. I will now put to the test something that she said: she would love me as her father; and according to what she said, I shall test her good-nature and kindness.'

Notes

7 **hym** 'himself'   The pronoun is the usual reflexive form in ME. The *himself* type is developed in emphatic contexts.

14 **han**   This contracted form of the infinitive (*habben* > *haven* > *han*) is a widespread northern and Midland type.

17 **agayn**   The spelling of this word with ‹g› and ‹ay› rather than ‹ʒ› is predominantly a Midland one.

20 **leet be born** 'caused to be born'   The causative *leten* is widespread in ME.

22 **Halde**   An Anglian OE antecedent is suggested by the failure of breaking before an *l*-group. A northerly origin is suggested by the fact that the long *ā* produced by the lengthening group *ld* has not subsequently been rounded. This excerpt shows rounding in some spellings (*longe*, 27) but not in others (*lange*, 51).

24 **his mone**   Lear's complaint is translated quite closely from its source in Wace's AN *Brut*, but behind that lies the complaint of Boethius to Fortune in *De Consolatione Philosophiae*. The work of this fifth-century author, which has been translated into English from King Alfred's time onwards, became the model for such laments, and their expression became formulaic. Compare this with Chaucer's translation of Boethius, Bk II and his use of similar material in the *Book of the Duchess*, 598ff. The passage contains some French vocabulary strongly associated with its theme, *chaungable*, *stable*, *Dame Fortune*, as well as a characteristic use of antithesis.

37–8 **turnes . . . mournes**   The rhyme (cf. 45–6) confirms that the original had an *-es* inflexion in both the second- and third-person singular of the present tense. Although the latter extended south to London in the late fourteenth century, the rhyme is more consistent with the north Midland origin of the poem.

50 **þer** 'their'   Although oblique forms of the third-person plural pronoun are found in south Lincolnshire as early as 1180 in the *Ormulum*, they are used in the London language of Chaucer only as an indication of a character's northern origin in the 'Reeve's Tale'.

59-60 **me . . . se** The rhyme on *me* confirms the evidence of spelling that OE *ēo* has been monophthongised, an east Midland development.

62 **couþe no god** This idiom, literally 'did not know any good', means something like 'I was slow or ignorant', and often carries with it implicit condemnation of social behaviour or lack of awareness.

The *Pearl* is one of four works, all with moral and religious themes, which exist in a single manuscript, British Library MS Cotton Nero A. x., and are generally considered to be by the same author. Of these, *Patience* and *Cleanness* are adaptations of scriptural narratives, *Sir Gawain and the Green Knight* is set in the Arthurian past, and *Pearl* is a dream vision in which the author relates his own experience: the vision of a lady (apparently his recently deceased daughter, now in heaven) who instructs him on the doctrine of grace and redemption. All four poems are written in the alliterative metre which flourished in the North and West from the mid fourteenth until the end of the fifteenth century.

The manuscript is not in the hand of its author, but was written not far from his place of origin, and not long after the work's composition. Modern scholarly opinion dates the manuscript at the end of the fourteenth century and its place of origin as an area in the north-west Midlands close to the borders of south-east Lancashire, east Cheshire, north-east Staffordshire and north-west Derbyshire.

Linguistically, *Pearl* exhibits many features proper to its north-west Midland origin. The northern spelling ‹qu› is used for OE ‹hw› (19). OE *ā* is written both ‹a› and ‹o›, and is proved by rhymes to have had both the northern unrounded and southern rounded pronunciations (85, 87, 89 and 118, 120). The third-person plural present tense of the verb is written *-en* (*stonden*, 53) and also *-eȝ* (*bydeȝ*, 15). The former is characteristic of the east Midlands, the latter a variant of the northern *-es*. The present participle ending is the Scandinavian-derived *-ande*, and Scandinavian influence is strong in the lexis also: *keste* (6), *glent* (10), *bolleȝ* (16), *blo* (23), *wyngeȝ* (33), *bonkeȝ* (50), *sterneȝ* (55). Indeed, Scandinavian borrowings occur at a rate of about three per stanza. Several are unobtrusive grammatical words: *fro* (1), *þay* (20), *ay* (41), *þaȝ* (74), *gayn* (78); and in the case of *syluer* (17) the Scandinavian form has been used in preference to the native *seluer*. The lexical richness of the excerpt is especially notable since French and Latin borrowings are also very dense here, and there are several words, too, of uncertain (*byg*, 42) or possibly Middle Dutch (*trylle*, 18; *schore*, 47) origin.

Fro spot my spyryt þer sprang in space;
My body on balke þer bod in sweuen.
My goste is gon in Godeȝ grace
In auenture þer meruayleȝ meuen.
5 I ne wyste in þis worlde quere þat hit wace,
Bot I knew me keste þer klyfeȝ cleuen;
Towarde a foreste I bere þe face,
Where rych rokkeȝ wer to dyscreuen.
Þe lyȝt of hem myȝt no mon leuen,
10 Þe glemande glory þat of hem glent;
For wern neuer webbeȝ þat wyȝeȝ weuen
Of half so dere adubbemente.

Dubbed wern alle þo downeȝ sydeȝ
Wyth crystal klyffeȝ so cler of kynde.
15 Holtewodeȝ bryȝt aboute hem bydeȝ
Of bolleȝ as blwe as ble of Ynde;
As bornyst syluer þe lef on slydeȝ,
Þat þike con trylle on vch a tynde.
Quen glem of glodeȝ agaynȝ hem glydeȝ,
20 Wyth schymeryng schene ful schrylle þay schynde.
Þe grauayl þat on grounde con grynde
Wern precious perleȝ of oryente:
Þe sunnebemeȝ bot blo and blynde
In respecte of þat adubbement.

25 The adubbemente of þo downeȝ dere
Garten my goste al greffe forȝete.
So frech flauoreȝ of fryteȝ were,
As fode hit con me fayre refete.
Fowleȝ þer flowen in fryth in fere,
30 Of flaumbande hweȝ, boþe smale and grete;
Bot sytole-stryng and gyternere
Her reken myrþe moȝt not retrete;
For quen þose bryddeȝ her wyngeȝ bete,
Þay songen wyth a swete asent.
35 So gracios gle couþe no mon gete
As here and se her adubbement.

So al watȝ dubbet on dere asyse
Þat fryth þer fortwne forth me fereȝ.
Þe derþe þerof for to deuyse
40 Nis no wyȝ worþé þat tonge bereȝ
I welke ay forth in wely wyse;
No bonk so byg þat did me dereȝ.

My spirit sprang up from that place; my body remained
asleep on the mound. Through God's grace my spirit went on
a marvellous voyage where wonders exist. I do not know
where in this world it was, but I knew I was set down where
cliffs cleave [the sky]; and I turned my face towards a forest,
where splendid rocks were to be seen. No one could believe
their light, the resplendent glory that shone from them; for
never were fabrics woven by man of half so splendid
decoration. Those hillsides were all adorned with crystal cliffs
of such a brilliant nature. Bright woodlands are set around
them, with trunks as blue as indigo; like burnished silver the
leaves slide and quivered together, thick on every branch.
When the light from clear patches of sky falls on them, they
shone quite dazzlingly with a gleaming brightness. The
pebbles that crunched on the ground were precious Eastern
pearls. Sunbeams were dull and dim compared to that
splendour. The splendour of the rich hills made my spirit
forget all grief, and so refreshing were the fragrances from
the fruits that I was restored as well as if I had eaten food.
Birds flew there together in the wood, both large and small,
and of flaming colours. But neither citole-string nor a player
on the giterne could reproduce their happy music. For when
those birds beat their wings, they sang in sweet harmony.
You could not have such delightful entertainment as to hear
and see their splendour. Thus all adorned in a noble fashion
was that wood where fortune has transported me. No one
who can speak is worthy to describe its glory. I kept walking
forward in pleasure; no slope so rough that it might hinder
me. The further I went into the wood, the fairer grew the
meadow, the shrubs, the scented herbs, the pear trees; and
the hedgerows, the edges of the streams, and the splendid
water meadows with steep banks like pure gold thread. I
came to a stream that ran swiftly past its banks. Lord, its
splendour was rich! The adornments of those precious depths
were pleasant banks of bright beryl. Swirling sweetly, the
water swept along, flowing directly with a murmuring sound.
In the bed there stood bright stones that glowed and gleamed
like a beam of light through glass, like the streaming stars
that shine in the sky on a winter's night when the men of this
earth are sleeping. For every pebble set there in the pool was
an emerald, a sapphire, or other precious stone, so that all
the pool gleamed with light, so glorious was its embellishment.

The precious embellishment of hill and valleys, wood and

Þe fyrre in þe fryth, þe feier con ryse
Þe playn, þe plontteȝ, þe spyse, þe pereȝ;
45 And raweȝ and randeȝ and rych reuereȝ,
As fyldor fyn her bonkes brent.
I wan to a water by schore þat schereȝ –
Lorde, dere watȝ hit adubbement!

The dubbemente of þo derworth depe
50 Wern bonkeȝ bene of beryl bryȝt.
Swangeande swete þe water con swepe,
Wyth a rownande rourde raykande aryȝt.
In þe founce þer stonden stoneȝ stepe,
As glente þurȝ glas þat glowed and glyȝt,
55 As stremande sterneȝ, quen stroþe-men slepe,
Staren in welkyn in wynter nyȝt;
For vche a pobbel in pole þer pyȝt
Watȝ emerad, saffer, oþer gemme gente,
Þat alle þe loȝe lemed of lyȝt,
60 So dere watȝ hit adubbement.

*   *   *   *   *

The dubbement dere of doun and daleȝ,
Of wod and water and wlonk playneȝ,
Bylde in me blys, abated my baleȝ,
Fordidden my stresse, dystryed my payneȝ.
65 Doun after a strem þat dryȝly haleȝ
I bowed in blys, bredful my brayneȝ;
Þe fyrre I folȝed þose floty valeȝ,
Þe more strenghþe of ioye myn herte strayneȝ.
As fortune fares þer as ho frayneȝ,
70 Wheþer solace ho sende oþer elleȝ sore,
Þe wyȝ to wham her wylle ho wayneȝ
Hytteȝ to haue ay more and more.

More of wele watȝ in þat wyse
Þen I cowþe telle þaȝ I tom hade,
75 For vrþely herte myȝt not suffyse
To þe tenþe dole of þo gladneȝ glade:
Forþy i þoȝt þat Paradyse
Watȝ þer ouer gayn þo bonkeȝ brade.
I hoped þe water were a deuyse
80 Bytwene myrþeȝ by mereȝ made;
Byȝonde þe broke, by slente oþer slade,
I hoped þat mote merked wore.

water and noble meadows inspired joy in me, reduced my misery, undid my distress, and ended my sufferings. Down beside a stream that ceaselessly flows I made my way joyfully, my mind brimful; the further I followed those well-watered valleys the stronger joy stirs my heart. Just as fortune acts whenever she puts anyone to the test, whether she bestows delight or sorrow, the man to whom she sends her will chances to have ever more and more. There was more joy of that kind than I could tell even though I had leisure, for an earthly heart would not be sufficient for the tenth part of those happy joys; therefore I thought that Paradise was over opposite those broad banks. I thought the water was an artificial conduit joining pleasure gardens made by the side of pools. Beyond the stream, by hill or valley, I thought the walled city would be situated. But the water was deep, and I dare not wade, and continuously I longed more and more. More and more, and still much more, I desired to see beyond the brook, for if it were beautiful where I was, the far side was much more lovely. I halted and stared about me; I tried hard to find a ford, but the further I walked along the bank, indeed the more dangers there were. And I kept thinking that I should not shrink from danger where there were so many precious delights. Then a new matter came to my attention that stirred my mind more and more. A greater wonder overwhelmed my reason: I saw beyond that fair flood a gleaming crystal cliff; many a noble ray sprang from it. At its foot there sat a child, a courtly and gentle maiden; her mantle was glistening white. I knew her well, I had seen her before. Like shining gold cut [into gold thread], so shone that beautiful [maiden] beneath the cliff. I looked long at her there, and the longer I looked the more I knew her. The more I examined her fair face, when I had perceived her exquisite form, such heartening splendour slipped into me as rarely was accustomed to happen before that. Desire urged me to call her, but amazement gave my heart a stunning blow. I saw her in such a surprising place, such a blow might well make my heart stunned. Then she raises up her fair forehead, her face white as polished ivory: that pierced my heart in stunned bewilderment, and ever longer, more and more.

Bot þe water watȝ depe, I dorst not wade,
And euer me longed ay more and more.

85 More and more, and ȝet wel mare,
Me lyste to se þe broke byȝonde;
For if hit watȝ fayr þer I con fare,
Wel loueloker watȝ þe fyrre londe.
Abowte me con I stote and stare;
90 To fynde a forþe faste con I fonde.
Bot woþeȝ mo iwysse þer ware,
Þe fyrre I stalked by þe stronde.
And euer me þoȝt I schulde not wonde
For wo þer weleȝ so wynne wore.
95 Penne nwe note me com on honde
Þat meued my mynde ay more and more.

More meruayle con my dom adaunt:
I seȝ byȝonde þat myry mere
A crystal clyffe ful relusaunt;
100 Mony ryal ray con fro hit rere.
At þe fote þerof þer sete a faunt,
A mayden of menske, ful debonere;
Blysnande whyt watȝ hyr bleaunt.
I knew hyr wel, I hade sen hyr ere.
105 As glysnande golde þat man con schere,
So schon þat schene an-vnder shore.
On lenghe I loked to hyr þere;
Þe lenger, I knew hyr more and more.

The more I frayste hyr fayre face,
110 Her fygure fyn quen I had fonte,
Suche gladande glory con to me glace
As lyttel byfore þerto watȝ wonte.
To calle hyr lyste con me enchace,
Bot baysment gef myn hert a brunt.
115 I seȝ hyr in so strange a place,
Such a burre myȝt make myn herte blunt.
Penne vereȝ ho vp her fayre frcount,
Hyr vysayge whyt as playn yuore:
Þat stonge myn hert ful stray atount,
120 And euer þe lenger, þe more and more.

Notes

5 **wace**   The very unusual spelling emphasises the rhymes with *space* and *grace*. The normal spelling in this text is *watȝ*.

18 **con trylle**   The auxiliary *con* has a function equivalent to that of *gan* in Chaucer's language, supplying a metrical variant for the simple preterite, and facilitating the positioning of an infinitive in rhyme (see line 21). The rounding of short *a* before a nasal consonant is characteristic of an area west of a line extending from Morecambe Bay via the Pennine chain to the Severn valley. See also *mon* (9), *plontteȝ* (44). The spelling ‹vch› is also western, but does not occur commonly north of the Mersey.

25 **þo**   This text retains a distinct plural form of the definite article.

26 **gartcn**   This causal auxiliary is essentially an east Midland and northern form.

31 **sytole . . . gyternere**   The citole is an instrument related to the zither; the giterne is a guitar-like instrument.

33 **wyngeȝ**   The word was borrowed from Scandinavian, and replaced OE *feðer* in this sense. Two forms existed in ME: the present one, derived from Old Danish or Swedish, and *wenges*, derived from Old Norwegian.

34 **Þay**   Although the Scandinavian-derived form of the third-person plural pronoun is used in the nominative, the OE *h*-forms are used in oblique cases, as in Chaucer: *her* (33) *hem* (19).

35 **gete**   Derived from Scandinavian *geta*. The OE root *-gietan* occurs only in compounds. First recorded in the *Ormulum*, *gete* quickly develops a very wide range of senses. Idiomatic uses with a following preposition (*get out*, *get in*) are frequent at the end of the fourteenth century.

46 **fyldor fyn** 'pure gold thread'   Like the word *debonere* (102), this represents the reinterpretation of a French phrase as a single word: *fil d'or*, 'golden thread'; *de bon aire*, 'of good breeding'.

48 **hit**   The genitive singular of the third-person pronoun. With the loss of grammatical gender, ME pronouns were redistributed to indicate the sex of the referent; the old neuter forms were used to indicate non-animate referents. In the genitive, no distinction was made between genitive masculine and neuter (both were *his*), but the new functions demanded a distinction and various remedies emerged before *its* was widely adopted for non-animate reference in the later sixteenth century. *Hit* is first recorded, as a possessive, in this manuscript.

58 **gemme**   This word had been borrowed from Latin during the pre-OE period, giving OE *gimm*. Its form here is that of Latin or French, suggesting re-formation or renewed borrowing from one of these languages.

69 **fares . . . ho frayneȝ**   The inflexion of the third-person singular present tense as *-es* is predominantly northern and north Midland. This text renders it occasionally as ‹es› but more commonly as ‹eȝ›, where ȝ is the scribe's form for ‹z›. The use of the ‹z› word ending

derives from French spelling practice, and here suggests voiced pronunciation. The form *ho*, 'she', is developed by rounding from an earlier *hā* (see the excerpt from the *Ancrene Wisse*) and is a distinctively west Midland form.

101 **faunt** 'child'   This is an aphetic form of French *enfant*. Aphetic forms (forms in which an initial unstressed syllable is omitted) are common in this excerpt: *dubbet* (<F *aduber*), *stresse* (<F *destresse*), *strayne3* (<F *estreindre*), *baysment* (<F *abaissement*).

Geoffrey Chaucer (?1343–1400), the outstanding poet of the
English Middle Ages, was born and raised in London, the son of
a family who were of East Anglian origins but who had been
established in London merchant society for two generations.
Chaucer himself was perhaps educated at a London school, but
certainly in the household of the Countess of Ulster. He
proceeded to a career in royal service and held the posts of
Controller of Customs in the Port of London and later Clerk of
the King's Works. He was married to the daughter of a French-
speaking knight who had been part of the entourage of Queen
Philippa, wife of Edward III. Thus, in his employment, in his
social contacts, and perhaps also at home, he was in everyday
contact both with the most elevated secular cultural and social
values, and with the French language. His works may have been
written in part for the nobles of the royal court, but are more
arguably for the interest and entertainment of a group of talented
officials who, like himself, were attached to the court.

From what is known of his life we should expect Chaucer's
language to be a slightly conservative and more carefully selected
version of the language of other London texts of his time,
embellished perhaps by French and Latin borrowing derived
from his experience and reading. This is essentially the case, but
such a statement hides its wider variety. An assessment of
Chaucer's language is complicated by the fact that almost all
manuscripts containing his work date from after his death. In the
rapidly changing linguistic conditions of late medieval London,
this means that they need not precisely represent his own usage.

The examples given below are from three different manuscripts: the excerpt from the 'Reeve's Tale' is from the Hengwrt
MS (National Library of Wales, MS Peniarth 392), written in
London about 1403, that from *Troilus and Criseyde* is from
Corpus Christi College, Cambridge MS 61, also written in
London within two decades of Chaucer's death. *The Equatorie of
the Planetis*, found only in Peterhouse College, Cambridge MS
75.I, is not part of the traditional Chaucer canon but appears to
be signed by the poet, and scholarly opinion is increasingly ready
to accept it as his. If this judgement is correct, the *Equatorie*
would be the only Chaucerian work to survive in its author's own
handwriting. The facsimile shows the opening of Book II in the

Corpus manuscript, and illustrates the luxurious nature of this text. It is written in an elaborated form of the *textura* hand and shows evidence of careful planning by a skilled professional copyist who has taken great care in presenting a text of solid and uniform appearance. His ruling lines can clearly be seen. There is no punctuation, but use is made of capitalisation both to mark the beginning of the Book itself and to introduce each verse line. The stanza structure is meticulously preserved. The expense incurred by the decorative nature of the script was matched in the original plan by a scheme of illustration for which many spaces have been left in the text. Taken together with the high quality of the vellum, this testifies to the growing stature of Chaucer's work among those who might be expected to be able to afford such splendid production.

Some general points to note about Chaucer's language are its east Midland character (deriving from east Midland immigration into London and evident in the use of predominantly *-es* noun plurals, *-en* third-person plural present-tense verbal inflexion, loss of the prefix in past participles, nominative *they*) but also traces of earlier south-eastern forms (some *-en* plurals, assimilated third-person present-tense singulars – see notes RT 70, *TC* 36 – use of the prefix in some past participles, and all oblique forms of personal pronouns remain *h*-forms).

Plate 3   Chaucer, *Troilus and Criseyde*, fol. 27r (*opposite*)

wt of thise blake wawes for to saylle
O wynde o wynde the weder gynneth cleir
ffor in this see the bot hath swych traylle
Of my connyng that vnneth I it steire
This see clepe I the tempestous matere
Of disespeir that Troilus was inne
But now of hope the kalendes bygynne

O lady myn that called art Cleo
Thow be my speed fro this forth and my muse
To ryme wel this bok til I haue do
Me nedeth heir noon otheir art to vse
fforwhi to euery louere I me excuse
That of no sentement I this endite
But out of latyn in my tonge it write

Wherfore I nyl haue neither thank ne blame
Of al this werk but prey zow mekely
Disblameth me if any word be lame
ffor as myn auct Seyde so sey I
Ek though I speke of loue vnfelyngly
No wondre is for it no thyng of newe is
A blynd man kan nat juggen wel in hewis

ze knowe ek that in forme of speche is chaunge
With inne a thousand zeer and wordes tho
That hadden pris now wonder nyce and straunge
Us thenketh hem and zet thei spake hem so
And spedde as wel in loue as men now do
Ek for to wynnen loue in sondry ages
In sondry londes sondry ben vsages

And forthi if it happe in any wyse
That here be any louere in this place
That herkneth as the storie wel deuise
How Troilus com to his lady grace
And thenketh so nold I nat loue purchace
Or wondreth on his speche or his doynge
I noot but it is me no wondrynge

A 'The Reeve's Tale', lines 3994–4105

Thanne were ther yonge, poure scolers two
That dwelten in the halle of which I seye.   *King's Hall*
Testyf they were and lusty for to pleye: *headstrong*
And oonly for hir myrthe and reuerye   *amusement*
5 Vpon the wardeyn bisily they crye   *earnestly*
To yeue hem leue but a litel stounde   *space of time*
To go to mille and seen hir corn ygrounde.
And hardily they dorste leye hir nekke   *certainly, bet their life*
The millere sholde noght stelen hem half a pekke
10 Of corn by sleighte ne by force hem reue.   *cunning, rob*
And atte laste the wardeyn yaf hem leue.
Iohn highte that oon and Aleyn highte that oother.   *was called*
Of oon town were they born that highte Strother,
Fer in the north, I kan noght telle where.
15 This Aleyn maketh redy al his gere
And on an hors the sak he caste anon.
Forth gooth Aleyn the clerk and also Iohn
With good swerd and with bokeler by his syde.   *round shield*
Iohn knew the wey hym neded no gyde.
20 And at the mille the sak adoun he layth.
Aleyn spak first: 'Al hayl, Symkyn, in fayth.
How fares thy faire doghter and thy wyf?'
    'Aleyn welcome,' quod Symkyn, 'by my lyf,
And Iohn also. How now, what do ye here?'
25 'By god,' quod Iohn, 'Symond, nede has na peere.   *equal*
Hym bihoues serue hymself that has na swayn   *must, servant*
Or ellis he is a fool, as clerkes sayn.
Oure maunciple, I hope he wol be deed,   *think*
Swa werkes ay the wanges in his heed.   *so ache, eye-teeth*
30 And therfore is I come and eek Alayn
To grynde oure corn and carie it heem agayn.
I pray yow speed vs heythen what ye may.'   *away from here*
    'It shal be doon,' quod Symkyn, 'by my fay.   *faith*
What wol ye doon whil that it is in hande?'
35 'By god, right by the hoper wol I stande,'
Quod Iohn, 'and se how the corn gas in.
Yet saw I neuere by my fader kyn
How that the hoper wagges til and fra.'
    Aleyn answerde: 'Iohn, wiltow swa?
40 Thanne wol I be byneth, by my crown,
And se how that the mele falles down
Into the trogh. That sal be my desport.

For, Iohn, in faith I may been of youre sort:
I is as ille a millere as ar ye.'
45   This millere smyled of hir nycetee   *silliness*
And thoghte: 'Al this nys doon but for a wyle.   *only for a trick*
They wene that no man may hem bigile.   *believe*
But by my thrift yet shal I blere hir iye
For al the sleighte in hir phislophye.   *learning*
50 The moore queynte crekys that they make,   *subtle tricks*
The moore wol I stele whan I take.
In stede of flour yet wol I yeue hem bren.
The grettest clerkes been noght the wisest men,
As whilom to the wolf thus spak the mare.   *once*
55 Of al hir art counte I noght a tare.   *weed*
   Out of the dore he gooth ful pryuely
Whan that he saugh his tyme softely.
He looketh vp and doun til he hath founde
The clerkes hors ther as it stood ybounde
60 Bihynde the mille vnder a leefsel.   *arbour*
And to the hors he gooth hym faire and wel;
He strepeth of the bridel right-anon.
And whan the hors was laus, he gynneth gon
Toward the fen ther wilde mares renne,
65 And forth with 'wehe' thurgh thikke and thenne.
This millere gooth ayein. No word he seyde,
But dooth his note and with the clerkes pleyde   *job*
Til that hir corn was faire and wel ygrounde.
   And whan the mele was sakked and ybounde,
70 This Iohn gooth out and fynt his hors away
And gan to crye 'Harrow and weilaway,   *alas*
Oure hors is lost. Alayn, for goddes banes
Step on thy feet. Com of, man, al atanes.
Allas oure wardeyn has his palfrey lorn.'
75   This Alayn al forgat bothe mele and corn;
Al was out of his mynde his housbondrye.
'What, whilk wey is he gane?' he gan to crye.
   The wyf cam lepyng inward with a ren.
She seyde: 'Allas youre hors gooth to the fen
80 With wilde mares as faste as he may go.
Vnthank come on his hand that boond hym so   *bad luck*
And he that bettre sholde haue knyt the reyne.'
   'Allas,' quod Iohn, 'Aleyn, for Cristes peyne
Lay doun thy swerd and I wol myn alswa.
85 I is ful wight, god waat, as is a ra.   *swift as a roe deer*
By god hert he sal nat scape vs bathe.

Why ne had thow pit the capil in the lathe?   *horse, barn*
Il-hail, by god. Alayn, thow is a fonne.'   *bad luck, fool*
    This sely clerkes haan ful faste yronne
90 Toward the fen, bothe Alayn and eek Iohn.
    And whan the millere seigh that they were gon,
    He half a busshel of hir flour hath take
    And bad his wyf go knede it in a cake.
    He seyde: 'I trowe the clerkes were aferd.   *afraid*
95 Yet kan a millere maken a clerkes berd
    For al his art. Ye, lat hem goon hir weye.
    Lo wher he gooth. Ye, lat the children pleye.
    They gete hym noght so lightly by my croun.'
        Thise sely clerkes rennen vp and doun
100 With 'Keep, keep; stand, stand; iossa, warderere.   *down! behind!*
    Ga whistle thow and I sal kepe hym heere.'
    But shortly, til that it was verray nyght
    They koude noght, thogh they dide al hir myght,
    Hir capyl cacche, he ran alwey so faste,
105 Til in a dych they caughte hym at the laste.
        Wery and weet as beest is in the reyn
    Comth sely Iohn and with hym comth Aleyn.   *poor*
    'Allas,' quod Iohn 'the day that I was born,
    Now ar we dryuen til hethyng and til scorn.   *contempt*
110 Oure corn is stole. Men wil vs foolis calle,
    Bothe the wardeyn and oure felawes alle,
    And namely the millere weilawey.'   *especially, alas*

B Troilus and Criseyde, Prologue to Book II

Owt of thise blake wawes forto saylle,
O wynde, O wynde, the weder gynneth clere,   *begin*
For in this see the boot hath swych trauaylle
Of my connyng that vnneth I it steere: *understanding*
5 This see clepe I the tempestous matere   *call*
Of disespeir that Troilus was inne –
But now of hope the kalendes bygynne.   *early days*

O lady myn, that called art Cleo,
Thow be my speed fro this forth, and my muse,   *help*
10 To ryme wel this book til I haue do;
Me nedeth here noon othere art to vse.
For-whi to euery louere I me excuse
That of no sentement I this endite,   *feeling, compose*
But out of Latyn in my tonge it write.

15 Wherfore I nyl haue neither thank ne blame
    Of al this werk, but prey 3ow mekely,
    Disomblameth me if any word be lame,
    For as myn auctour seyde, so sey I;
    Ek though I speeke of loue vnfelyngly,
20 No wondre is, for it no thyng of newe is:
    A blynd man kan nat iuggen wel in hewis.   *colours*

    3e knowe ek that in fourme of speche is chaunge
    With-inne a thousand 3eer, and wordes tho   *then*
    That hadden pris now wonder nyce and straunge   *value*
25 Us thenketh hem, and 3et thei spake hem so,
    And spedde as wel in loue as men now do,
    Ek forto wynnen loue in sondry ages,
    In sondry londes, sondry ben vsages.   *customs*

    And forthi if it happe in any wyse,   *way*
30 That here be any louere in this place
    That herkneth, as the storie wol deuise,   *relate·*
    How Troilus com to his lady grace,   *favour*
    And thenketh, 'so nold I nat loue purchace,'   *obtain*
    Or wondreth on his speche or his doynge,   *actions*
35 I noot, but it is me no wonderynge.   *I do not know*

    For euery wight which that to Rome wente   *goes*
    Halt nat o path or alwey o manere;
    Ek in som lond were al the game shente   *ruined*
    If that they ferde in loue as men don here,   *behaved*
40 As thus, in opyn doyng or in chere,   *manner*
    In visityng in forme or seyde hire sawes;   *formal, speeches*
    For-thi men seyn, ecche contree hath hise lawes.

    Ek scarsly ben ther in this place thre
    That haue in loue seide like and don in al,
45 For to thi purpos this may liken the,   *may please*
    And the right nought, 3et al is seide, or schal;
    Ek som men graue in tree, som in ston wal,   *carve in wood*
    As it bitit; but syn I haue bigonne,
    Myn auctour shal I folwen if I konne.

Explicit prohemium secundi libri   *The proem of the second book is*
                                                            complete

Incipit liber secundus   *The second book begins*

50 In May, that moder is of monthes glade,

That fresshe floures blew and white and rede
Ben quike agayn, that wynter dede made, *alive*
And ful of bawme is fletyng euery mede; *perfume, meadow*
Whan Phebus doth his bryght bemes sprede
55 Right in the white Bole, it so bitidde, *Taurus*
As I shal synge, on Mayes day the thrydde,

That Pandarus, for al his wise speche,
Felt ek his parte of loues shotes keene, *share*
That koude he neuere so wel of louyng preche,
60 It made his hewe a-day ful ofte greene;
So shop it that hym fil that day a teene *happened, reversal*
In loue, for which in wo to bedde he wente,
And made er it was day ful many a wente. *turning*

The swalowe Proigne with a sorowful lay
65 Whan morwen com gan make hire waymentyng *lament*
Whi she forshapen was, and euere lay *transformed*
Pandare a-bedde half in a slomberyng,
Til she so neigh hym made hire cheteryng,
How Tireux gan forth hire suster take,
70 That with the noyse of hire he gan awake,

And gan to calle, and dresse hym vp to ryse, *prepare*
Remembryng hym his erand was to doone
From Troilus, and ek his grete emprise, *undertaking*
And caste and knewe in good plite was the moone *took omens*
75 To doon viage, and took his way ful soone *journey*
Unto his Neces palays ther biside;
Now Ianus, god of entree, thow hym gyde!

C The Equatorie of the Planetis

In the name of god pitos and merciable. Seide Leyk: the
largere that thow makest this instrument, the largere ben thi
chef deuisiouns; the largere that ben tho deuisiouns, in hem
may ben mo smale fracciouns; and euere the mo of smale
5 fracciouns, the ner the trowthe of thy conclusiouns.
    Tak therfore a plate of metal or elles a bord that be smothe
shaue by leuel and euene polised. Of which, whan it is rownd
(by compas), the hole diametre shal contene 72 large enches or
elles 6 fote of mesure. The whiche rownde bord, for it shal nat
10 werpe ne krooke, the egge of (the) circumference shal be
bownde with a plate of yren in maner of a karte whel. This bord,

yif the likith, may be vernissed or elles glewed with perchemyn
for honestyte.

Tak thanne a cercle of metal that be 2 enche of brede, and
15 that the hole dyametre (with in this cercle shal) contene the
forseyde 68 enches or 5 fote (and 8 enches), and subtili lat this
cercle be nayled vpon the circumference of this bord, or ellis
mak this cercle of glewed perchemyn. This cercle wole I clepe
the 'lymbe' of myn equatorie that was compowned the yer of
20 Crist 1392 complet, the laste meridie of Decembre.

This lymbe shaltow deuyde in 4 quarters by 2 diametral lynes
in maner of the lymbe of a comune astrelabye – and lok thy
croys be trewe proued by geometrical conclusioun. Tak thanne
a large compas that be trewe, and set the fyx point oucr the
25 middel of the bord, (on) which middel shal be nayled a plate of
metal rownd. The hole diametre of this plate shal contiene 16
enches large, for in this plate shollen ben perced alle the centris
of this equatorie. And ek in proces of tyme may this plate be
turned abowte after that auges of planetes ben moeued in the
30 9 spere: thus may thin instrument laste perpetuel.

Tak thanne, as I haue seid byforn, the fix fot of thy compas
and set it in the middel of this plate, and with the moeuable
point of thi compas descriue a cercle in the ferthest circumference of thy lymbe. And *nota* that the middel poynt of this
35 plate, wheras the fix fot of thy compas stondith, wole I calle
'centre aryn'.

Mak thanne a narwer cercle that be descriued vpon the same
centre aryn but litel quantite fro the forthest forseid cercle in
the lymbe, in which space shollen ben deuyde mynutes of the
40 lymbe. Mak thanne a narwere cercle som what ferther distaunt
fro the last seid cercle, in which shal be deuyded the degres of
the same lymbe. Mak yit a narwere cercle somwhat ferthere
distaunt fro this last seid cercle, in which shal ben writen the
nombres of degres. Mak yit a narwere cercle somwhat ferther
45 distaunt fro this laste seide cercle, in which shollen ben writen
the names of 12 signes. And *nota* that this laste seid cercle
wole I calle 'the closere of the signes'.

Now hastow 5 cercles in thy lymbe, and alle ben descriued
vpon centre aryn; and euerich of the 4 quarters in thi lymbe
50 shal ben deuided in 90 degres that is to sein 3 signes; and eueri
eueri degre shal be deuided in 60 *minuta*; and shortly thi lymbe is
deuided in maner of the lymbe in the bak side of an astrelabie.

Deuyde thanne thilke lyne that goth fro centre aryn vnto the
cercle closere of the sygnes (*versus finem geminorum*) in 32
55 parties equales. Whiche parties ben (cleped) 'degres of the

semydiametre'. Marke thise parties dymli (*ut postea deleantur*) and *nota* that this diametral lyne deuided in 32 parties shal be cleped 'lyne alhudda'.

Set thanne the fix point of thy compas vpon the ende of the
60 firste deuysioun fro centre aryn in lyne alhudda, and the moeuable point vpon the end of the 30 deuisioun fro the fix point of thi compas in the same lyne. So dwelleth ther but 1 deuisioun bytwixe thy moeuable and the closere of the signes, and 1 deuysioun bitwixe thy fix poynt and the centre aryn.
65 And descryue thus a cercle of the sonne. Scrape thanne awey the deuysiouns of lyne alhudda.

Notes

The Reeve's Tale

3 **for to pleye**   The various forms of infinitive possible in Chaucer's language (with and without final -*n*, and with *to* or *for to*) are an important metrical resource (cf. 6).

4 **reuerye**   Closely related in sense to *revelrye* but an independent development from French *resverie*.

5 **they crye**   The east Midland type of third-person plural present tense occurs in Chaucer both with and without final -*n*. Both rhyme (as here and 26–7) and metre may depend on the choice (99).

7 **ygrounde**   The southern form of the Strong verb past participle, with prefix and lacking final -*n*, is required by the metre and the rhyme (cf.lines 58–9 and 89–90).

19 **hym neded**   An impersonal construction. *Hym* is originally a dative form.

21 **Aleyn spak**   Throughout, these northern students speak in dialectal forms distinct from Chaucer's ordinary language. The imitation of a dialect distinct from that of the author and the scribe is rare in ME. The word *hayl* (from a Scandinavian source) is a northern greeting. Other words of northern distribution found in the students' speech include: *wanges, heythen, ille, hethyng, fonne*.

22 **fares**   The use of the -*es* inflexion of third-person singular (*bihoues, wagges*, etc.) and plural (*fares, werkes*, etc.) of the present tense is characteristically northern.

26 **na**   The OE form *nā* remains unrounded in the language of the students; see also *swa, gas, banes, atanes, waat, ra*, etc.).

28 **hope**   The sense 'think, expect' is a northern one.

31 **heem**   It might be expected that the form would have been the unrounded *ham*. This form is derived from Scandinavian *heimr*.

38 **til and fra**   A northern version of the expression, closer in form to its Scandinavian origin (*til ok fra*) than southern equivalents.

42 **sal**   The normal spelling in Chaucer MSS is *shal* or *schal*.

Spellings like this are recorded from Kent, but were common in the North.

44 **I is . . . ar ye** The concord of *I* with *is* is simply outlandish, and an exaggeration of northern barbarism. The form *ar* rather than the more common Chaucerian *ben* is consistent with northern origin but found also in London.

48 **blere hir iye** 'blear their eye' A fairly common idiom. Cf. Modern English *pull the wool over their eyes.*

49 **phislophye** Perhaps a deliberately barbarous form used by a scorner of learning, but possibly simply a scribal error.

53 **grettest clerkes**, etc. The proverb is derived from an Æsopian fable in which a wolf is tricked into reading the price of a foal supposedly written on the mare's hoof. Despite his literacy, he pays the price of rashness.

55 **not a tare** One of numerous Chaucerian expressions of worthlessness. They include reference to beans, haws, leeks, rushes, vetch, herbs, motes, mites and rake handles.

70 **fynt** 'finds' The form exhibits the syncope and assimilation characteristic of dialects descended from Saxon OE – here the earlier London language. Forms with *-eth* are, however, common in Chaucer.

72 **goddes banes** Swearing by parts of God's body was very common at the end of the fourteenth century and is condemned in both 'The Pardoner's Prologue' and 'The Parson's Tale'.

77 **whilk** The Scandinavian-influenced northern equivalent of more usual Chaucerian *which*. This form is recorded widely north of a line from the Mersey to the Wash.

86 **god hert** 'God's heart' Genitive modifiers frequently have reduced forms of the genitive inflexion and are not necessarily northern, but the omission of ‹e› in the spellings may be intended to suggest northern loss of final *-e*.

87 **pit** The east Midland and northern form of the verb 'put'.

89 **haan** Usually spelt ‹han›. This is a north-east Midland form of the plural present tense, contracted from *haven*.

95 **berd** The idiom 'to make someone's beard' means 'to make a fool of someone'.

97 **he gooth** This phrase must refer to the horse, since in Chaucer's language these forms are singular.

104 **capyl** This word is used by Chaucer only for working horses and in lower-life settings. In northern England it was more widely used.

Troilus and Criseyde

2 **gynneth** This is originally the plural form of the imperative. Chaucerian imperatives to a single addressee show considerable variation, ending in *-e*, *-eth* or *-∅*.

3–4 **boot . . . Of my connyng** The complexity of the syntax is here resolved by the dependence of the phrase on Dante's *la navicella del* *mio ingegno*. Translate: 'begin to clear away the stormy weather, because the boat of my understanding has such trouble in this sea that I can hardly steer it'.

11 **me nedeth**   An impersonal construction, with no subject expressed.

13–14 **endite . . . write**   The contrast between *write* and *endite* is here made quite strongly. The former means simply to write down (here from translation); the latter to compose from one's own resources (sometimes without the necessity of writing).

15 **nyl**   A contraction of the negative *ne* and *wyl*. The verb still carries the sense 'wish'.

17 **disomblameth**   Most MSS read *desblameth*, which more closely matches the French form from which the borrowing has been made, *desblasmer*. The *dis-* spelling of the prefix represents Latin influence, which gains ground in the fifteenth century. The *-om-* may be inspired by the elevated stylistic associations of the *-en* prefix (usually spelt ‹em› before *b*) which was productive in the later fourteenth and fifteenth centuries and common in technical and elevated language. The fact that it is unmetrical suggests scribal elevation of the language.

19 **though**   The earlier London form of this word was *þei3*. This Chaucerian form is of Scandinavian origin, and forms part of the east Midland influence on the London language which is also evident in the use of the pronoun *they*.

21 **hewis**   The rhyme on *is* suggests that Chaucer's language possessed a raised variant of the plural inflexion.

22 **fourme of speche**   This phrase does not refer to the forms of language as understood in modern linguistic theory. Chaucer is commenting not on linguistic change but on social change: the formulation of polite and acceptable utterance. The words *pris* and *nyce and straunge*, which indicate social and behavioural judgements, confirm this.

32 **lady grace**   The genitive modifier, derived from an OE weak feminine, is endingless in this formulaic phrase.

36 **wente**   This is apparently the present tense of the verb *wenden*, and exhibits syncope and assimilation common in earlier London (cf. *halt* in the next line, *bitit*, 48, and its preterite form, 55). The final *-e* is therefore unpronounced, and a scribal addition. During the fifteenth century, scribes, who could no longer understand the logic governing the occurrence of final *-e* in words where it was no longer pronounced, tended to overcompensate, adding *-e* randomly to words where it had never been pronounced. An example in this passage, which jeopardises the metre, is: *plite* (74).

42 **hise lawes**   Note that no distinct inanimate form of the third-person pronoun has yet emerged in London English. The development of *its* does not take place until the later sixteenth century.

45 **this may liken the**   An impersonal construction with *this* as subject and the dative form of the personal pronoun. The rhyme with *thre* demonstrates the east Midland development of OE *ēo* to *e*.

52 **Ben**   The east Midland form of the plural present tense, derived from the OE subjunctive form.

65 **gan make**   This is often, as here, a periphrastic form of the preterite, supplying an extra syllable required by the metre, and facilitating a rhyme (as in lines 69–70). In some instances the auxiliary may retain the sense 'began'.

72 **to doone**   As in OE, the inflected form of the infinitive is sometimes used when the sense is passive, i.e. 'to be done'.

The Equatorie of the Planetis

1 **In the name of God**   The traditional Islamic dedication at the beginning of a work, Arabic *bismillah*. The suggestion is that an Arabic original may lie at some remove behind this text. The mysterious *Leyk*, erased in the manuscript, may originate in a misunderstanding of Arabic *qīla*, 'it is said'.

2 **thow**   Address by the singular form of the second-person pronoun is characteristic of learned discourse in late fourteenth-century English. It is found both in secular learning and in religious contexts, where it is frequently used by preachers. The opening paragraph is stylistically distinct from what follows, depending for its coherence on the rhetorical balance of clauses (see note to line 9).

8 **(by compas)**   Matter in parenthesis represents the author's additions to his original text.

large enches   Weights and measures were not fully standardised in Chaucer's time. The 'large enche' is the Saxon inch of 1.1 modern inches. The form with ‹e› for WS ‹y› is a trace of south-eastern Middle English.

9 **The whiche rownde bord**   The coherence of the majority of this excerpt depends on devices of repetition. Within a framework of paragraphs beginning with a plain imperative, the author identifies various key items by unvarying 'technical' names. Reference to those items, as the passage develops, is made through exact repetition of the wording, further pointed by various determiners: *the which*, *the seid* or simply *this*. The former two are closely paralleled in contemporary Anglo-French technical writing.

13 **honestyte** 'evenness'   The word had a very broad range of extended senses in late Middle English. Cf. 'straight' and 'true' in Modern English.

20 **1392 complet**, etc.   31 December 1392.

26 **contiene**   This spelling with ‹ie› is of a south-eastern type, more common in Gower than in Chaucer manuscripts.

34 **nota**   These directions and the Latin explanatory notes (see lines 54 and 56) are a reminder that the usual language for serious scientific work at this time is Latin. Chaucer's English *Treatise on the Astrolabe* is addressed to 'litell Lowys my sone'.

55 **parties equales**   The word 'equal' occurs in Chaucer's works in two forms: *egal* (from French) and *equal* (from Latin). The latter

form is restricted to technical contexts. The word order here, with its French plural concord, can be paralleled also in Chaucer's prose works. Both features may be considered characteristic of late fourteenth-century technical prose. Worthy of notice, too, is the mixture of Latinate vocabulary and idiomatic expression in this excerpt.

19 The Preface to a Wycliffite Biblical Concordance

Two translations of the New Testament into English were made in the last quarter of the fourteenth century – the first a very literal rendering of the Vulgate, and the second, or Later Version, much more idiomatic in style. Collectively they are referred to as the Wycliffite Bible since the stimulus for such translation derived from the doctrines of John Wyclif (c. 1330–84). It is no longer thought that Wyclif himself had a hand in the work, and although the names of Nicholas Hereford, John Purvey and John Trevisa have all been associated with it, scholarly consensus about the translators is still lacking. The important point is that at this period there existed a number of scholars, centred upon Oxford, who saw value in producing a Bible in English and were prepared to devote time and effort to the study of the problems raised by such a project.

The Later Version (1395) is preceded by a Preface which discusses some of the problems of translation with a degree of linguistic sophistication. The text reproduced here belongs to a similar milieu.

British Library MS Royal 17.B.1 is an early fifteenth-century concordance based largely on the Early Version of the Wycliffite Bible but making use also of the Later Version. It commences with a preface which explains its compiler's methodology and the difficulties which he encountered in imposing a usable alphabetical order upon a language whose spellings could be so variable. Guidance is offered to the potential user, and this is followed by more than 1200 separate entries for individual words. The purpose of such a concordance was not primarily the study of language but as a tool for preachers, who could bring together distinct but verbally echoic parts of biblical text, which may then be combined into the theme of a sermon. Nevertheless, this preface provides an unusual insight into how an educated late-medieval Englishman viewed his language as a medium of communication. Its interest lies in its patiently analytic statements, strongly contrasting with the evaluative nature of most near-contemporary linguistic commentary.

The language of the piece has been identified as that of north-east Bedfordshire or extreme south Huntingdonshire, but such precision may be misleading since most of the forms would be equally at home anywhere in the south-central Midlands. The language is very similar to that of other Wycliffite writings and is of a type which has been recognised as an early quasi-standard language. The forms *miche* and *ony* are characteristic of this 'Wycliffite' or central Midland standard, but *suche*, *self* and *stede* (rather than *sich*, *silf* and *stide*) are more generally dispersed forms.

Mannes mynde, þat is oft robbid of þe tresour of kunnyng bi þe enemye of science, þat is forȝetyng, is greetly releeued bi tablis maad bi lettre aftir þe ordre of þe A B C. *Ensaumple*: if a man haue mynde oonly of oo word or
5 two of sum long text of þe Newe Lawe and haþ forȝetyn al þe remenaunt, or ellis if he can seie bi herte such an hool text but he haþ forȝeten in what stede it is writen, þis concordaunce wole lede him bi þe fewe wordis þat ben cofrid in his mynde vnto þe ful text, and shewe him in
10 what book and in what chapitre he shal fynde þo textis which him list to haue.

Þis concordaunce sueþ not oonly þe ordre of þe A B C in þe firste lettris of wordis, but also in þe secounde, in þe þridde, in þe fourþe and so forþ; wherfore *Aaron* stondiþ
15 bifore *Abba*, for þe secounde lettre of *Aaron*, which is *a*, stondiþ in þe A B C bifore *b*, which is þe secounde lettre of *Abba*. And *Abba* stondiþ bifore *Abel*, for þe þridde lettre of *Abba*, þat is *b*, stondiþ in the A B C bifore þe þridde lettre of *Abel*, which is *e*. Þus *conferme* stondiþ bifore *confounde*, bi
20 cause þe fifþe lettre of þis word *conferme* stondiþ in the A B C bifore þe fifþe lettre of *confounde*, þat is *o*; for in þe firste foure lettris of þese two, whiche ben *c*, *o*, *n*, and *f*, in no þing þei discorden. Wherfore, if þou fynde ony word in þis werk þat is not set in þis forme, vnkunnyng or neglygence of þe
25 writere is in cause, and liȝtly, bi oon þat can, may it be amendid. If it seme to ony creature þat cotaciouns of summe textis be not spoken off in wordis þere þei shulde be expressid, if þei be duly plauntid yn, so myche is þe bettir, so þat þei be – not set inordinatly – aftir þe maner of þis
30 drawyng.

Whanne a text conteyneþ two wordis and þou can not wel perceyue in wheþer of þo wordis þou shuldist seeke it, þou shalt fynde it quotid in oon of hem at þe leeste and sumtyme in boþe. As, if þee list fynde þis text: *Womman, lo þi sone*; if

35 þou fynde it not in S in þis word *sone*, þou shalt fynde it in V
   in þis word *womman*. If þou fynde not þis text: *Tribulacioun*
   worchiþ pacience in P in þis terme *pacience*, þou shalt fynde it
   in T in þis word *tribulacioun*; and þus of oþire lijk tixtis.

   In Englisch as in Latyn ben wordis synonemus, þat is to
40 seie manie wordis bitokenynge oo þing, as *kirke* and *chirche*,
   accesse and *nyʒcomynge*, *clepe* and *calle*, *ʒyue* and *gyue*, *ʒift*
   and *gift*, *bigyle* and *disceyue* and *defraude*. And sumtyme
   suche wordis varyen or diuersen al oonly in oo lettre, as *flax*
   and *flex*, *invie* and *envie*, *lomb* and *lamb*. And oþorwhile haþ
45 þat oon a lettre more þan þat oother, as *epistle* and *pistle*.
   Now it may be so þat in sum Newe Lawe is writen in sum text
   þis word *kirke* and in þe same text and in a noþir book is
   writen þis word *chirche*, and þus of oþire wordis bifore
   rehersid, and of manye mo lyk hem. If þou þanne seke a text
50 in ony of suche synonemus, and if þou fynde it not in oon of
   hem, loke in a noþir of hem; ʒhe, loke in alle suche
   synonemus, þouʒ þer be þre or mo of hem, til þou fynde þe
   text wiþ which þe liste mete. Remissioun is ofte maad in þis
   concordaunce fro such a synoneme til a noþir. Sumtyme þe
55 formere remittiþ to þe lattere and sumtyme þe lattere
   remittiþ to þe formere.

   Sumtyme þe same word and þe self þat is writen of sum
   man in oo manere is writen of a noþir man in anoþir manere.
   As wher summe writen þese wordis *thyng* and *theef* with *th*,
60 oþire vsen to writen þoo same wordis with þis figure þ.
   Wherfore alle þe wordis of þis concordaunce of which þe
   firste carecte is þis figure þ bigynnen in þis table with *th* and
   in T þei stonden aftir here ordre axiþ. Summe writen *gh* in
   summe wordis, whiche wordis ben writen of summe oþire
65 with a yogh þat is figured þus ʒ – as sum man writeþ þus þese
   termes: *doughter*, *thought*, where a noþir writeþ hem þus:
   douʒter, *thouʒt*. But for as miche as þe carect yogh, þat is to
   seie ʒ, is figurid lijk a zed, þerfore alle þe wordis of þis table
   þat biginnen wiþ þat carect ben set in Zed, which is the last
70 lettre of þe A B C. Also sum man writeþ sum word wiþ an *h*,
   which saame word anoþer man writiþ wiþouten an *h*; as is of
   þe Englisch word which þis Latyn word *heres* signyfieþ, which
   terme summe writen with *h* þus, *here*, and summe þus, *eir*,
   wiþouten *h*.
75 Þese diuerse maneris of writyng ben to be considerid in þis
   concordaunce. For perchaunce, aftir my manere of writyng,

sum word stondiþ in sum place, which same word aftir þi maner of writyng shulde stonde in anoþer place. If it plese to ony man to write þis concordaunce and him þenkiþ þat
80 summe wordis ben not set in ordre aftir his conseit and his manere of writyng, it is not hard if he take keep wiþ good avisement in his owne writyng to sette such wordis in such an ordre as his owne conseit acordiþ to.

In Englisch also as in Latyn ben wordis equiuouse, þat is
85 whanne oon word haþ manye significaciouns or bitokenyngis: as þis word *kynde* bitokeneþ 'nature', and also such a man clepen we *kynde* which is a free-hertid man and þat gladly wole rewarde what þat men don for hym. An instrument wherwiþ we hewen clepen we an *axe*, and I *axe* God mercy of
90 synnes þat I haue don. Suche wordis in þis concordaunce ben maad knowen bi sum word addid to hem wherby it may be wist whanne þei ben taken in oon significacioun and whanne in a noþir. Textis in whiche ben wordis of plural noumbre ben quotid in þe wordis of singuler noumbre. A word is singuler
95 noumbre þat bitokneþ but oo þing, as *womman, man, foot*; a word of plurel noumbre bitokneþ mo þingis þan oon, as *men, wymmen, feet*. Loke þanne þe textis in whiche ben þese termes *men, wymmen, feet* in her synguleris: *man, womman, foot*. Loke also suche *wordis wakyng, wepyng, fadirheed,*
100 *wickidnesse*, in wordis þat þei comen of – as *wakyng* in *wake, wepyng* in *wepe, fadirheed* in *fadir* and *wickidnesse* in *wickid*, and þus of oþire lyk hem – but if it be so þat boþe þe wordis of whiche oþire wordis comen and also þe wordis þat comen of hem ben expresly sett out in þis table as cheef wordis of þis
105 concordaunce, as is of þese wordis: *seruaunt, serue*, and *seruyce*, for ech of þese þree is expressid bi hemself. And þus it is of oþire wordis: *kyng* and *kyngdom* and of sum oþire, as þou may conceyue liȝtly in þis table if þou take good heede.

Where a chapiter spekiþ miche of a mater, þanne is
110 sumtyme shortly quotyd þe sentence and not þe wordis as in þis word *bischop* is quotyd how – þe firste pistle to Tymothe, þe þridde *cap.*, and Titum þe firste *cap.* – ben specified þe condiciouns of a bischop. And in this word *charite* is quotyd how, in þe firste pistle to Corintheis, þrittenþe *cap.*, Poul
115 spekiþ of þe condicions of charite. Whanne þe cheef wordis of þis concordaunce ben þe firste wordis of þe firste textis þat ben qyotyd in hem, þanne ben þo wordis not rehersyd aȝen in þe same firste textis, forwhi þei ben parties of þe same firste

textis as þou may persyue liʒtli in þese termes: *absent,*
120 *abstene, Acaie, accepcioun,* and in manye oþire. And whanne
suche cheef wordis ben not þe firste wordis of suche firste
textis, þanne stonden þei absolutely and ben sett by hemself
oon, to shewe redyly where þo textis þat suen whiche
perteynen to such wordis may be liʒtly founden, as þou mai
125 se in þese wordis: *Aaron, Abba, Abel,* and in many mo. Þe
cheef wordis of þis concordaunce I clepe alle þo wordis þat
goen bi lettre aftir þe ordre of þe A B C in þis present table.

If ony fruyt come of þis concordaunce, to God be onour
and doynge of þankyngis now and euere. Amen.

Notes

12 **Þis concordaunce sueþ . . . þe ordre of þe A B C**   Reference works
in alphabetical order are today the norm, but medieval glossaries
were frequently arranged in order of topics and themes. Alphabetical
ordering is often very approximate before the seventeenth century.

25 **oon þat can** 'one who knows how'   The verb is still being used as
a full lexical verb, as in OE.

26 **ony creature**   The use of the word *creature* as an indefinite
pronoun ('one, person') is common in Wycliffite writings but is also
more widely spread in later medieval pious texts.

28–30 **so þat . . . drawyng**   The word *drawyng* may refer to a missing
diagram but could have the sense 'arrangement'. In either case, this
would be the earliest occurrence of such a sense. The manuscript
reading is 'so þat þei be not set in ordinatly'. Good sense requires
either the deletion of *not* or the understanding of *but* before *aftir.*

32 **wheþer** 'which [of two]'   The OE sense, etymologically related
to *other.*

35 **þou shalt fynde it in V**   The letter ‹V› is normally used for initial
‹U›, and ‹U› is considered equivalent to ‹W›. In fact only one page
from thirty-one pages of ‹W› entries in the concordance is headed
with ‹V›.

39 **wordis synonemus**   From the modern point of view, many of these
'synonyms' are mere dialectal variants of the same word: *kirke* and
chirche; gyue and *ʒyue; gift* and *ʒift; lamb* and *lomb; flax* and *flex* are
respectively northerly and southerly dialect forms, and *invie*
represents Latin influence on spelling practice. The author is
unconcerned with etymology, however, concentrating rather on
synchronic practicalities.

67–68 **þe carect yogh . . . lijk a zed** 'the symbol "yogh" '   The word
carect tends to be used for written symbols which do not form part of
the normal Latin alphabet (sometimes magical symbols). The Irish
Latin form of ‹g›, *yogh*, is confused in ME with the final *-z* written
by French-influenced scribes to represent /z/ and /s/ (see Excerpt 17).

Although the two symbols had different origins and represented a quite distinct range of sounds, the compiler classes them together purely on their similarity of form in the written language.

84 **wordes equiuouse** 'ambiguous' Not previously recorded. Formed by adding the French derivative suffix *-ous* to Latin *equivoc*. The compiler does not make a distinction parallel to that between homonyms (words with identical form but different senses and different histories) and polysemous words (wordforms in which historical development has produced multiple significance in a single historical form).

87 **free-hertid** 'generous-hearted' Compounds such as this, consisting of an adjective and a denominalised verb past participle, are a fourteenth-century development, but the type is more fully productive in the sixteenth century.

104 **cheef wordis** *Cheef* is to be understood in its French sense – thus 'head words'.

110 **sentence** 'import, content' In ME the word *sentence* refers primarily to meaning or content of an utterance rather than its formal structure. The grammatical conception of a sentence is often denoted by the word *resoun* in late fourteenth-century technical contexts.

122 **absolutly** 'in isolation' Used in the technical grammatical sense of a word standing outside the syntactical relations of text.

128 **fruyt** 'benefit' The word *fruyt* (Latin *fructus*) is commonly used as a figure of the benefit to be derived from any literary activity. Cf. Chaucer's use of the terms *fruyt* and *chaf*.

20   Osbern Bokenham's Mappula Angliae

Osbern Bokenham (1393–?1447) was from a family associated with Old Buckenham, Norfolk, but spent most of his life as an Augustinian friar in the convent of Stoke Clare near the Suffolk–Essex border. In earlier life, however, he spent five years in Venice, and subsequently visited Rome and other parts of Italy on pilgrimage, where he gathered material for his best-known work, a collection of the lives of twelve women saints. In his 'Life of St Agnes' he tells us that he will write simply according to 'þe language of Suthfolk speche'. BL MS Harley 4011, which contains Bokenham's *Mappula Angliae*, was copied by two scribes near the middle of the fifteenth century, and is located by the *Linguistic Atlas of Late Mediaeval English* in Suffolk.

Bokenham confirmed his authorship of the *Mappula* by an acrostic by which the first letter in each chapter serves to spell out his name. His work, he says, is an adaptation of Ranulph Higden's Latin *Polychronicon* (*c.* 1327), and the passage on the diversity of the English people and their language printed here has become well known to students of the history of English from an earlier translation of it made in about 1385 by John Trevisa. Bokenham's version dates from about 1440 and differs in some respects from that of Trevisa. His distrust of the Scots is evident, and they are identified as the foreigners who have contributed to the mangling of English. His conception of linguistic change as corruption emerges more clearly and is more firmly related to Latin concepts of purity and barbarism.

Linguistically Bokenham's work is also influenced by Latin literacy, and the mannerism of fifteenth-century learned prose is already apparent in Latinate sentence constructions, the use of learned forms (*rurales, oryentalis, collaterall, artyke*) carried over from the Latin original, and word-pairs (*commodious and . . . profitable, congresse and conflicte*). Some of this vocabulary is not good Latin but is ostentatiously derived from that source and thus regarded as elevated. Despite Bokenham's statement about his Suffolk dialect, this excerpt shows no forms restricted to the East Anglian area: it is rather the *combination* of certain forms which testifies to East Anglian origin (*hit, here, syche, yche, byn, han(e), schuln*, 96, *yovyn*, 129). Most of the forms in this passage could, however, be found widely in the southern and eastern half of the Midlands at this period.

As towchynge þe firste parte of þis chapiture, hit is to been vndirstondyn that, as mony dyuerys peeples as hit haþe dwellers, so many hit haþe dyuersites of toungis and languagis. Nerþelees they been not all pure, but sum ben mixte and medlid
5 on sundry wysys. Scottis and Walsshmen, þe which ben the Brytouns propirly, as peeple moste ynpermyxt and leste medlyd with oþer, kepyn moste puerly hire firste propir speche or language. Nerþelees Scottys, of grete famulearyte and commvnycacyoun with þe Pyctis, sumwhat hane drawyn an
10 medyllynge in hur toungis. The Flemmynges, þe which as hit is seide beforn, dwellyn yn þe weste marche of Walis, hane left here rude barbarye and spekyn more Saxoonly or Englysshly. Angli, all be hit þat from the firste begynnynge, after þe thre dyuersytees of peeplis of Germayne þe whiche
15 they comyn of, hadyn thre dyuersites of sowndyngis yn hure language and yn þe thre dyuerys places, as Sowþe, Norþe, and Mydlonde, yet of commyxtioun dyuers, firste Danys and sethe with Normannys, they haue corrupte her first natif toungis and vsyn now I ne wot what straunge and pilgryms
20 blaberyng and cheteryng, noþyng acordynge onto here firste speche.
And þis corrupcioūn of Englysshe men yn þer modre-tounge, begunne as I seyde with famylyar commixtion of Danys firste and of Normannys aftir, toke grete augmenta-
25 cioun and encrees aftir þe commyng of William conquerour by two thyngis. The firste was: by decre and ordynaunce of þe seide William conquerour children in gramer-scolis ageyns þe consuetude and þe custom of all oþer nacyons, here owne modre-tonge lafte and forsakyn, lernyd here Donet on
30 Frenssh and to construyn yn Frenssh and to maken here Latyns on þe same wyse. The secounde cause was þat by þe same decre lordis sonys and all nobyll and worthy mennys children were fyrste set to lyrnyn and speken Frenssh, or þan þey cowde spekyn Ynglyssh, and þat all wrytyngis and
35 endentyngis and all maner plees and contrauercyes in courtis of the lawe, and all maner reknyngis and countis yn howsoolde schulle be doon yn the same. And þis seeynge, þe rurales, þat þey myghte semyn þe more worschipfull and honorable and þe redyliere comyn to þe famyliarite of þe
40 worthy and þe grete, leftyn hure modre tounge and labouryd to kunne spekyn Frenssh; and thus by processe of tyme barbariȝid thei in bothyn and spokyn neythyr good Frenssh nor good Englyssh.
And yet yn þe Saxoyne or Englyssh tounge, þe whiche is

45 remaynyd but in a fewe vplondyssh peeple, þe oryentalis, þat
is to sayne þe Est-ynglyssh men with þe men of þe west
acordyn more yn soundynge and spekynge, as men þat ben
vndir oone lyneal climat of hevene, þan don þe northen [with
þe sowthern] men. Also the Meerces, þe which byn clepid
50 mydlonde ynglyssh, as collaterall parteners of bothyn extre-
mytes, bettir vndirstondyn þe collaterall tounges, bothe the
artyke, þe which is þe Northe, and þe antartyke, þe which is
þe Sowthe, þan þe two extremal toungis vndirstondyn
hemself togedir or þan eyþer vndyrstondith other. For, as
55 William pontyficis seith *libro tertio*, the norþehumbirlonde
pepelis tonge, specially yn Yorke, stradelith soo brode and so
vnsavorly is wyde, þat þe sowtherne peple vnnethe can
vndirstondyn hit. And þat is, as he supposith, for oone of þe
two causis, þat [is] or for þe nygheness onto the Scottis or for
60 þe grete distaunce of kyngis of þe londe from þo marchis; the
whiche byn more wone to be conuersaunte yn þe sowþe place
of Ynglond þan yn þe norþe, for comynly þey drawe not
norþe-warde butt yn strong hand, or ageyns the Scottis or for
to reforme and redresse ryot and mysrewle of the same
65 countre. The cause why þat kyngis be more expectant and
abydynge yn the sowþe þan in the norþe, may well be þus:
for þere, þat is to say by sowþe, þe erþe is more plentyvous,
and þe peple more copious, þe cytees and townys more worþi
and honorable, and þe portis or the hauenys more commo-
70 dious and more profitable . . . . Þe peple of þe sowþe place is
more quyete yn þemself and more softe þan is þe norþe place
peple, þe which is euermore inquiete, more mevable and
more cruell. The mydlonde peple is betwix þe norþyn and þe
sowþirne, as is a participle beetwix nowne and verbe, þat is to
75 sey hit is a partyner with bothyn.
    Also, quod he, þe Ynglysshe peeple amonge all oþur
nacyouns is syngulerly yevyn to gloteny and dronkynship, and
moste sumpteous and wastefull yn mete and drynke and
cloþus. This vyce hit is supposid þat þis londe drowh firste of
80 Hardeknut the Dane, þe whiche was þe firste kynge yn þis
londe þat commaundid messe of mete to be sette on his
tablee at sowpeer. This peeple, quod he, is delyvyr and
swyfte boþe on foote and allso on horsbacke, apt and promte
to all maner kynde of armys, and yn euery congresse and
85 conflicte yn batylle is commynly wone, lesse þen tresoun or
fraude and gyle goo vndir, to haue þe ouyr honde and þe
victorye. Thes peeple – and principally of þe norþe place – is
wondur coryous and besy to knowyn and to tellyn tydyngis

and noveltees and merveylles syche as þey hane herde or
90 seyen, prompt to sekyn oþur cuntres, seldoun ryche yn hure
propir soyle, more happe in ferre and foreyn cuntrees þan yn
hure owne cuntree, and kunne bettur purchasyn new þyngis
owtewarde þen kepyn here owne hereditable þyngis at hoom;
for þe which cause þey lyghtly wyllyn be disperbylde yn to
95 straunge cuntrees. This peeple is also apt and redy to euery
dede and manhode; and aforne þat þey schuln ought doo,
inportune þey byn and fulle hardy, but aftir þe dede bettir
avysid and more avesy; and therfore þey lyghtly willyn
forsake þat þey hane begunne. And for þis cause hit is þat
100 pope Eugenye seide Ynglyssh peeple to been apte and able to
euery thynge what so euyr they wolde, and worþi to be
preferryd beforn all othur peeplys, ne were þe lyghtnesse of
hur hertis and the hasty changeablenesse of hur wylle; and
lyke as Hannybal seyde Romaynes myght nevir been
105 ouyrcomyn but yn hure owne cuntre, ryght so þe Englyssh
peeple, quod he, the whiche yn straunge and foreyn
countrees been ynvyncible, in hur owne seetes ben moste esy
to ouercomyn. This peple sone lothith and lakkith hur owne
þyngis and prey[sy]th and commendyth oþur mennys þyngis,
110 vnnethe ony tyme content with þe degre of hure owne estate,
and suche þyngis as longithe to oþur men þey gladly wyllyn
transfyguryn yn hemself. For a yeman wyll takyn vpon hym
þat longith to a squyeer, a squyeer that longith to a knyght, a
knyght that longith to an erle, and an erle þat longith to a
115 duke, a duke þat longyþe to a kynge. And this þey serclyn
abowten euery kynde and þey byn yn no kynde, but þey
attamyn and assayen euery ordir and þey byn yn non ordyr.
For yn hur apporte of araye they byn dysgysid as treiectours
or mynstrals. In commynycacioun and talkyng þey byn
120 Cicerones, þat is to say as eloquent and as gay yn speche as
was þat grete rethoryan Marcus Tullius Cicero . . . . And
vniversaly in all Englyssh men so moche is growyn and
customyd þe variable and þe vnstable chaunge of cloþingis
and þe monyfolde dyuersitees of aray, þat yche of hem as
125 now-adayes semyth for to been newtur gendur, þat is to say
of yche oþer nacyoun þen of his owne. Of þe which thynge
prophecied onys an holy recluse or an anchorite þe tyme of
kynge Egilredus, as seiþ Henricus *libro* 6, seying on þis wyse:
for as moche as Ynglyssh men been yovyn to prodicioun, to
130 drounkynshipe, and to neclygence of goddis howse, they
schull be thries conquerid and born downe and put vndir:
firste, quod he, by Danys, the secounde tyme by Normaundus,

and þe þryde tyme by Scottis, whom they haue yn leste
reputacioun; and yn so moche schall than þe worlde be
135 variant and vnstabull þat þe variaunce and þe vnstablenes of
mennys hertis and soulys schall mone be notid and markyd by
þe monyfolde variaunce and dyuersitees of mennys cloþis.

Notes

6 **ynpermyxt** 'unmingled'   The earliest recorded use of a rare
word, adopted from the Latin original, *impermixti*.

7 **propir**   The word has the Latin sense 'own, characteristic'.

10 **Flemmynges**   Repeated Flemish settlements were made in southern
Pembrokeshire during the course of the twelfth century, commencing
in 1105. These were encouraged by successive English kings as a
means of controlling the native Welsh.

19 **pilgryms** 'foreign, outlandish' (Latin text *peregrinos*)   This sense
of the word is otherwise recorded only in the Wycliffite translation of
the Bible. *Blaberyng* and *cheteryng* are relatively common fourteenth-
century words of onomatopoeic formation.

26 **decre and ordynaunce**   The document to which Bokenham refers
was in fact a fourteenth-century forgery, but this does not invalidate
the sociolinguistic significance of his observations about usage. In his
translation, Trevisa notes that the teaching of Latin through English
had been introduced in Oxford by John of Cornwall in 1349. *Donet*
refers to the fourth-century grammar of Aelius Donatus, the most
widely used introductory Latin grammar in medieval schools.

28–29 **here owne modre-tonge . . . forsakyn**   The syntax parallels the
Latin ablative absolute construction (*derelicto proprio vulgari*). See
also line 37 (*And þis seeynge . . .*), which contains the type of
construction exemplified by the author of the Preface to the Later
Version of the Wycliffite Bible as an unidiomatic English rendering
of the ablative absolute (Latin text *Quibus profecto . . .*).

42 **barbariȝid**   This is the earliest recorded use of the word in English
in its technical Latin sense, that is, the introduction of words and
phrasing of foreign origin into a 'pure' language, resulting in the
corrupcioun of the original. See also line 12, a related but somewhat
different sense, with an implied value judgement. Bokenham's use is
independent of his original.

48 **lyneal climat** (*climate lineati*)   The technical sense of *climat*, 'belt
under the same latitude', appears in the fourteenth century. The
adjective *lyneal* serves to disambiguate the technical term. Adjectives with the Franco-Latin suffix *-al* (cf. *collaterall*, 50; *extremal*, 53)
become much more common in the fifteenth century. Although
lyneal and *collaterall* have counterparts in classical Latin, *extremal* is
a medieval learned formation.

60–61 **the whiche**   This form of connective, modelled on French *liquels*,
is frequent in technical and administrative prose from the fourteenth

century onwards. Its purpose was that of text cohesion, and it was thus often followed by a noun repeating an earlier reference. Here the omission of the noun and the distant remove from its reference (*kyngis*) mean that it does not function effectively as a cohesive device and is best regarded as a mannerism connected with the author's aspiration to learned style.

61   **wone to be conuersaunte** 'accustomed to be habitually living'   The sense is once more close to that of the Latin, *converso*, but the word does not occur in the Latin text.

69–70   **commodious** 'convenient'   (Latin text   *accommodatiores*) Bokenham's form is from Med. Latin *commodiosus*.

78   **sumpteous** 'lavish, extravagant' (Latin text *sumptuosa*)   The first recorded use of this Franco-Latin borrowing in this sense.

84–85   **congresse and conflicte**   These Franco-Latin borrowings, both with the sense 'hostile encounter', are used earlier than Bokenham only in the ME translation of Vegetius's technical work on the art of war. The Latin text supplies only *congressus*.

93   **hereditable** 'able to be inherited, inherited' (Latin text *haereditaria*) The earliest recorded use in English of the Franco-Latin legal term.

118   **treiectours** 'jugglers'   The borrowing took place from French before 1300, and the usual form is *tregetour*. The form here partially restores a supposed Latin form *trans-iactor*. A similar creation of an erroneous Latin form is seen in the development of the familiar *adventure* from earlier French *aventure*.

125   **newtur gendur** 'neuter gender, no clear type'   Bokenham enjoys grammatical comparisons, and in discussing Midlanders (74) he says that they share some of the qualities of both Northerners and Southerners, as a participle (a verbal adjective) shares the qualities of a verb and an adjective, but it is not certain that the allusion here is grammatical. Rather, he is using the vocabulary of Aristotelian classification to emphasise the variety and disorder of the English people.

21 A Paston letter

The letter printed here was sent, probably from Norwich, by Margaret Paston to her husband John, who was on business in London. The date is about 19 May 1448. It is a particularly lively example from a series of family and business letters which commences in 1425 and spans four generations.

John Paston belonged to a family in the ascendant. They originated in the village of Paston, eight miles south of Cromer, and by the seventeenth century had risen to be one of the most important families in East Anglia. John's father, William (1378–1444), had been sent to school and founded the family fortunes by a career in the law. John himself (1421–1466) was educated at Cambridge and the Inner Temple before entering his father's profession. He added to his inheritance by his marriage in about 1440 to Margaret Mautby, through whom he secured more land in Norfolk and Suffolk, and he was forced by lengthy absences in London to leave its administration in her extremely capable hands.

She is not, however, the writer of this letter. She was not literate so she dictated it to a clerk, James Gresham, who came from Holt in north Norfolk and had been a trusted employee of her father-in-law. The postscript, however, is in a different hand, employing a different orthographic system with far more marked East Anglian peculiarities (see Notes). Nothing is known of this clerk except that Margaret employed him more than any other.

Ryght worshipfull husbond, I recomaund me to yow, and
prey yow to wete þat on Friday last passed before noon, þe
parson of Oxened beyng at messe in our parossh chirche,
euyn atte leuacioun of þe sakeryng, Jamys Gloys hadde ben
5 in þe tovne and come homward by Wymondams gate. And
Wymondam stod in his gate and John Norwode his man stod
by hym, and Thomas Hawys his othir man stod in þe strete by
þe canell side. And Jamys Gloys come with his hatte on his
hede betwen bothe his men, as he was wont of custome to do.
10 And whanne Gloys was ayenst Wymondham, he seid þus,
'Couere thy heed!' And Gloys seid ageyn, 'So I shall for the.'
And whanne Gloys was forther passed by þe space of iij or
iiij strede, Wymondham drew owt his dagger and and seid,
'Shalt þow so, knave?' And þerwith Gloys turned hym and

15 drewe owt his dagger and defendet hym, fleyng into my
moderis place; and Wymondham and his man Hawys kest
stonys and dreve Gloys into my moderis place. And Hawys
folwyd into my moderis place and kest a ston as meche as a
forthyng lof into þe halle after Gloys; and þan ran owt of þe
20 place ageyn. And Gloys folwyd owt and stod withowt þe
gate, and þanne Wymondham called Gloys thef and seid he
shuld dye, and Gloys seid he lyed and called hym charl, and
bad hym come hymself or ell þe best man he hadde, and
Gloys wold answere hym on for on. And þanne Haweys ran
25 into Wymondhams place and feched a spere and a swerd, and
toke his maister his swerd. And with þe noise of þis asaut and
affray my modir and I come owt of þe chirche from þe
sakeryng; and I bad Gloys go in to my moderis place ageyn,
and so he dede. And thanne Wymondham called my moder
30 and me strong hores, and seid þe Pastons and alle her kyn
were — e seid he lyed, knave and charl as he was. And he
had meche large langage, as ye shall knowe herafter by
mowthe.

After non my modir and I yede to þe Priour of Norwich
35 and told hym al þis cas, and þe Priour sent for Wymondham
and þerwhyle we yede hom ageyn and Pagraue come with vs
hom. And whil Wymondham was with þe Priour, and we
were at hom in our places, Gloys stod in þe strete at my
moderis gate and Hawys aspyed hym þere as he stod on þe
40 Lady Hastyngis chambre. Anon he come doun with a tohand
swerd and assauted ageyn þe seid Gloys and Thomas my
moderis man, and lete flye a strok at Thomas with þe sword
and rippled his hand with his sword. And as for þe latter
assaut þe parson of Oxened sygh it and wole avowe it. And
45 moche more thyng was do, as Gloys can tell yow by mouthe.
And for þe perilx of þat myght happe by þese premysses and
þe circumstances þerof to be eschewed, by þ'aduyse of my
modir and oþer I send yow Gloys to attend upon yow for a
seson, for ease of myn owen hert; for in good feyth I wolde
50 not for xl li. haue suyche anoþer trouble.

As touchyng my Lady Morlé, she seith þat she atte hire
wille wol haue þe benyfyce of hire obligacion, for hir
counseyll telleth hir, as she seith, þat it is forfayt. And she
wole not haue the relif til she hath your homage, etc.
55 The Lord Moleyns man gaderyth up þe rent at Gresham a
gret pace, and Jamys Gresham shall telle yow more pleynly
þerof at his comyng.

Nomore at þis tyme, but Almyghty God haue yow in his
kepyng. Wretyn in hast on Trynyté Sunday at euyn.

60   Yours, MARGARET PASTON

As touchyng Roger Foke, Gloys shall telle yow all, etc.
Qwhan Wymdham seyd þat Jamys xuld dy I seyd to hym þat I
soposyd þat he xuld repent hym jf he schlow hym or dede to
hym any bodyly harm; and he seyd nay, he xuld never repent
65 hym ner have a ferdyng wurth of harm þow he kelyd ȝw and
hym bothe. And I seyd ȝys, and he sclow þe lest chylde þat
longyth to ȝwr kechyn, and jf he dede he were lyke, I sopose,
to dy for hym. It js told me þat he xall kom to London jn
hast. I pray ȝw be ware hw ȝe walkyn jf he be þere, for he js
70 ful cursyd-hertyd and lwmysch. I wot wel he wyl not set vpon
ȝw manly, but I beleve he wyl styrt vpon ȝw or on sum of ȝwr
men leke a thef. I pray ȝw hertyly þat ȝe late not Jamys kom
hom aȝen in non wyse tyl ȝe kom home, for myn hertys ese;
for be my trwth I wold not þat he were hurt, ner non man þat
75 longyth to ȝw jn ȝwr absens for xx pwnd. And in gode feyth
he js sore hatyd both of Wymdam [sic] and sum of hys men,
and of oþer þat Wymdam tellyth to hys tale as hym lyst, for
þer as Wymdam tellyth hys tale he makyth hem belevyn þat
Jamys js gylty and he no þyng gylty.
80   I pray ȝw hertyly here masse and oþer servys þat ȝe arn
bwn to here wyth a devwt hert, and I hope veryly þat ȝe xal
spede ryth wele in all ȝwr materys, be grase of God. Trust
veryly in God and leve hym and serve hym, and he wyl not
deseve ȝw. Of all oþer materys I xall sent ȝw wurd jn hast.

Notes

1 **Ryght worshipfull husbond ...**   The letter begins with a formal
salutatio or address followed by a *commendatio* and a formula *prey
yow to wete* to introduce the substance or *narratio* of the letter. Cf.
Alfred's Preface to the *Pastoral Care*.
4 **atte leuacioun of þe sakeryng** 'elevation of the host'   The
moment in the mass when the priest officiating raises the consecrated
elements before the congregation. The form *atte* is a contraction of *at
þe*.
8 **Jamys Gloys**   The Paston family chaplain, and frequently also the
clerk who wrote Margaret Paston's letters.
10 **ayeynst Wymondham**   The sense is 'opposite' or 'face to face
with'. Wymondham was a gentleman from Felbrigg near Cromer.
His words 'protect your head!' are to be interpreted as a threat to

which Gloys replies with a calculated insult, since fifteenth-century politeness required a hat to be removed at meeting in token of respect. According to Caxton (*Knight of the Tower*, pp. 24–5) this gesture was observed also by women.

22   **charl**   Like *thef*, *knave* and *stronge hore*, the accusation of being a 'churl' was a frequent insult in the fourteenth and fifteenth centuries. Such abusive language was frequently the cause of legal action and fines being imposed. In fourteenth-century texts, including Chaucer, the Scandinavian-derived form *carl* is used as an insult. The OE-derived form *cherle* is more often used as the description of a social estate. The form here is probably a blend, since the spellings representing the late ME change from *er* to *ar* are not found in other work by Gresham.

40   **Lady Hastyngis**   Wymondham's wife.

50   **suyche**   This form of the word 'such' is predominantly a west Norfolk one. Gresham's language is not strongly dialectal. Most of the forms he uses were widespread in the south-east Midlands, but against this background there occur a number of less distinctively East Anglian forms: *wete*, 'know', *meche*, 'much', *folwyd* (in which the vowel between *l* and *w* has been elided), *wretyn*.

51   **As touchyng**   A favourite connective in clerkly and administrative writing, as also is the use of the cohesive *þe seid* (41). These suggest some freedom of composition within Margaret's dictation. But the coherence of the letter is not dependent on the curial style, since here clauses are connected by a succession of simple additive conjunctions which obscure the more complex causal and temporal connections (contrast with ?Chaucer, *The Equatorie of the Planetis*, or Skelton's dedication of his translation of Diodorus Siculus).

62   **Qwhan**   This northern spelling of 'when' is more or less restricted, south of the Wash, to East Anglia, although occurring sporadically elsewhere. The spellings ⟨xuld⟩ and ⟨xal⟩ are, however, very markedly East Anglian and occur nowhere else. Other, less distinctively East Anglian forms in this postscript are: *schlow/sclow*, *kechyn*, *dede*, *leke*, *hem*, *arn*.

70   **lwmysch** 'contentious'   *MED* (s.v. *loumish*) records the word only from the East Anglian *Promptorium Parvulorum*.

22   Malory, 'The Giant of St Michael's Mount'

On 31 July 1485 England's first printer, William Caxton, published a volume of the adventures of King Arthur, which he called (borrowing the title of the final book) *Le Morte Darthur*. In Caxton's text, the author identifies himself as 'syr Thomas Maleore, knyght', asks for his readers' prayers, and fixes the completion of his task during the year following 4 March 1469. Until 1934, when a manuscript was discovered at Winchester College, Caxton's print was all that was known of Malory's work. The discovery of the manuscript initiated a major reassessment, since not only did it demonstrate that Caxton had made significant changes to his copy, but it provided further details of its author which Caxton had suppressed, notably that the work had been finished in prison.

Attempts to identify this prisoner–knight have been beset by controversy, but the most generally-accepted candidate is an individual from Newbold Revell, Warwickshire, who died on 12 March 1471. His reconstructed career is strikingly eccentric, encompassing origins in an established local family, status as a landowner, service as an MP, and accusations of a list of crimes ranging from rape and attempted murder to cattle-raiding and extortion. He spent numerous periods in prison, making two successful escapes, and it is conjectured that the completion of his Arthurian compilation took place during his imprisonment as a result of unsuccessful political manoeuvring.

Caxton represented Malory's work as translated from French, which suited the prejudices of his intended audience, but this is only partly true, since Book V, from which the following excerpt is taken, is in fact an adaptation of the north Midland ME alliterative *Morte Arthur*. Many of the alliterative phrases and some of the characteristic lexical items of the original remain. The contrast with Caxton is striking: alliterative patterns are discarded; unfamiliar words are replaced by more generally used ones; French-derived lexical items are preferred; there is considerable condensation, turning the dramatic impact of the original into smooth narration. This contrast has recently been given sharper focus by the discovery of ink marks from printer's type in the Winchester manuscript, which prove that it must have been in Caxton's workshop throughout the 1480s.

As well as aspects of lexical style, Caxton also altered the grammatical forms of the original: the north Midland forms of the third-person singular in -ys and -is are replaced by the more southerly form in -eth and northern present participles in -ande are replaced by the more general -ynge.

Caxton had spent many years as a merchant in Bruges, and he imported the new technology of moveable type from sources in Belgium and Germany. Its manufacturers naturally attempted to imitate the writing practices of the skilled copyists who had hitherto been the producers of all books. The facsimile of the epilogue of the *Faytes of Armes* (published 14 July, 1489) is set in Caxton's Type 6, a Flemish *bâtarde* type, which he prefered for the production of books of courtly entertainment and instruction. It emulates a prestigious Flemish style of handwriting of the period. The insular letters, ȝ and þ, are no longer used, but ligatures common in scribal practice are still found: the crossed *ll* and *th*, *he*, *ho*, *be*, *bo*, and *re* among others. Long *s* is used initially and medially, but continental *s* is used finally. Abbreviations marks, especially where a vowel is followed by a nasal, are common, and the Christian Chi-Rho symbol is used in rendering Christine de Pizan's name. Spellings follow scribal practice in showing the elision of the vowel of the definite article before a word beginning with a vowel: *therle*, *tharbre*. Apostrophes are not yet used in English. Punctuation is rather haphazard. The virgule (/) marks off the items in a list and sets off numerals from the text, as well as certain clauses. Capitalisation is used for proper nouns.

Plate 4   Caxton, *The Fayt of Arms and of Chyvalrye*, fols. 141r & 141v (*following two pages*)

Whether it be in Bataylles sieges/rescowse/& all other faytes
subtylees & remedyes for meschieues/Whiche translacyon
was finysshed the/viij/day of Juyll the sayd yere & enpryn
ted the/viiij/day of Juyll next folowyng & ful fynysshyd/ the
ne syth I haue obeyed his most dredeful comaundement/I hu
bly bysecle his most exellent & bountcuous hyeues to pardo;
ne me of this symple & rude translacion Where in be no cury
ous ne gaye termes of rethoryk/But I hope to almighti god
that it shal be entendyble & Understanden to euery man/& al
so that it shal not mocke Uarye in setence fro the coppe recey
ued of my said souerayn lord/And Where as I haue erryd
or made defaulte I besecle them that fynde suche to correcte it
& so doyng I shal praye for them/& yf ther be ony thing ther
in to his pleasir/I am glad & thinke my labour Wel enplo;
yed for to haue the name to be one of the litel seruantes to the
hiest & most cristen kyng & prince of the World/Whom I by
secle almyghty god to preserue/kepe/& contynue in his noble
& most redoubted enterpryses as Wel in Bretayn/flaundres &
other placis that he may haue Uictorie honour/& renomee to
his perpetual glorye/ffor I haue not herd ne rede that ony
prynce hath subdued his subgettis With lasse hurte & c and
also holpen his neighbours & frendis out of this londe/In
Whyche hye enterprises I bysecle almyghty god that he may
remayne alleway Uyctoryous/And dayly encreace fro Uer
tu to Uertue & fro better to better to his laude & honour in this
present lyf/that after thys short & transitorye lyf he may at;
teyne to euerlastyng lyf in heuen/ Whiche god graunte to
hym and to alle his lyege peple   AMEN/

Per Caxton

of the foure elementꝭ it shuld be taken for the lasse noble / ꝯ
of thees seuen colours are dyfferenced all manere of armes
penoncelles and baners by dyuerse deuyses taken by haultnesse fro the tyme ryght auncyent /

℣ Explicit

℣ Thus endeth this boke whiche xppne of ppse made ꝯ drewe out of the boke named Vegecius de re militari ꝯ out of tharbre of batailles wyth many other thynges sett in to the same requisite to werre ꝯ batailles whiche boke beyng in fre she was delyuered to me Willm Caxton by the most crysten kynge ꝯ redoubted prynce my naturel ꝯ soueayn lord kyng henry the / Vij / kyng of englond ꝯ of fraūce in his palais of westmestre the / xxiij / day of Januere the / iiij / yere of his regne ꝯ desired ꝯ wylled me to translate this said boke ꝯ reduce it in to our english ꝯ natural tonge / ꝯ to put it in enprynte to thende that euery gentylman born to armes ꝯ all manere men of werre captayns / souldiours / ꝯ taplers ꝯ all other shold haue knowlege how they ought to behaue theym in the faytes of warre ꝯ of batailles / and so delyuered me the said boke thēne my lord therle of Oxenford awaytig on his said grace / whiche volume conteynyng four bokes / I receyued of his said grace ꝯ accordig to his desire whiche to me I repute a comandemēt / ꝯ verili glad to obeye / ꝯ after the lityl conyng that god hath lente me I haue endeuoyred me to the vttermst of my power to fulfylle ꝯ accoplisshe his desire ꝯ comaundement / as wel to reduce it in to englysshe / as to put it in enprite / to thende that it may come to the sight ꝯ knowlege of euery gentylman ꝯ man of warre / ꝯ for certayn in myn oppiny on it is as necessary a boke ꝯ as requysite / as ony may be for euery estate hye ꝯ lowe that entende to the faytes of werre

B   The Winchester text

Than the kynge yode up to the creste of the cragge, and than he comforted hymself with the colde wynde; and than he yode forth by two welle-stremys, and there he fyndys two fyres flamand full hyghe. And at that one fyre he founde a carefull
5 wydow wryngande hire handys, syttande on a grave that was new marked. Than Arthure salued hir and she hym agayne, and asked hir why she sate sorowyng.

'Alas,' she seyde, 'carefull knyght! Thou carpys over lowde! Yon is a werlow woll destroy us bothe. I holde the
10 unhappy. What doste thou on this mountayne? Thoughe here were suche fyffty, ye were to feyble for to macche hym all at onys. Whereto berys thou armoure? Hit may the lytyll avayle, for he nedys none other wepyn but his bare fyste. Here is a douches dede, the fayryst that lyved; he hath murthered that
15 mylde withoute ony mercy; he forced hir by fylth of hymself, and so aftir slytte hir unto the navyll.'

'Dame,' seyde the kynge, 'I com fro the noble conquerrour, sir Arthure, for to trete with the tirraunte for his lyege peple.'

'Fy on suche tretyse,' she seyde than, 'for he settys nought
20 by the kynge nother by no man ellys. But and thou have brought Arthurs wyff dame Gwenyvere he woll be more blyther of hir than thou haddyste geffyn hym halfendele Fraunce. And but yf thou have brought hir prese hym nat to nyghe. Loke what he hath done unto fyftene kynges: he hath made hym a coote full of
25 precious stonys, and the bordoures thereof is the berdis of fyftene kynges, and they were of the grettyst blood that dured on erthe. Othir farme had he none of fyftene realmys. This presente was sente hym to this laste Crystemasse; they sente hym in faythe for savyng of their peple. And for Arthurs wyffe
30 he lodgys hym here, for he hath more tresoure than ever had Arthure or ony of his elders. And now thou shalt fynde hym at souper with syx knave chyldirne, and there he hath made pykyll and powder with many precious wynes, and three fayre maydens that turnys the broche that bydis to go to his bed, for
35 they three shall be dede within four oures or the fylth is fulfylled that his fleyshe askys.'

'Well,' seyde Arthure, 'I woll fulfylle my message for alle your grym wordis.'

'Than fare thou to yondir fyre that flamys so hyghe, and there
40 thou shalt fynde hym sykerly for sothe.'

Than he paste forth to the creste of the hylle and syghe where he sate at his soupere alone gnawyng on a lymme of a

large man, and there he beekys his brode lendys by the bryght
fyre and brekelys hym semys. And three damesels turned three
45 brochis, and thereon was twelve chyldir but late borne, and they
were broched in maner lyke birdis. Whan the kynge behylde
that syght his herte was nyghe bledyng for sorow. Than he
haylesed hym with angirfull wordys:
'Now He that all weldys geff the sorow, theeff, there thou
50 syttes! For thou art the fowlyste freyke that ever was fourmed,
and fendly thou fedyst the, the devill have thy soule! And by
what cause, thou carle, hast thou kylled thes Crysten chyldern?
Thou haste made many martyrs by mourtheryng of this londis.
Therefore thou shalt have thy mede thorow Mychael that owyth
55 this mounte. And also, why haste thou slayne this fayre
douches? Therefore dresse the, doggys son, for thou shalt dye
this day thorow the dynte of my hondis.'
      Than the gloton gloored and grevid full foule. He had teeth
lyke a grayhounde, he was the foulyst wyghte that ever man sye,
60 and there was never suche one fourmed on erthe, for there was
never devil in helle more horryblyer made: for he was fro the
hede to the foote fyve fadom longe and large. And therewith
sturdely he sterte uppon his leggis and caughte a clubbe in his
honde all of clene iron. Than he swappis at the kynge with that
65 kyd wepyn. He cruysshed downe with the club the coronal
doune to the cold erthe. The kynge coverede hym with his
shylde and rechis a boxe evyn infourmede in the myddis of his
forehede, that the slypped blade unto the brayne rechis. Yet he
shappis at sir Arthure, but the kynge shuntys a lytyll and rechis
70 hym a dynte hyghe uppon the haunche, and there he swappis his
genytrottys in sondir.
      Than he rored and brayed and yet angurly he strykes, and
fayled of sir Arthure and the erthe hittis, that he kutte into the
swarffe a large swerde-length and more. Than the kynge sterte
75 up unto hym and raught hym a buffette and kut his baly in
sundir, that oute wente the gore, that the grasse and the
grounde all foule was begone.
      Than he kaste away the clubbe and caughte the kynge in his
armys and handeled the kynge so harde that he crusshed his
80 rybbes. Than the balefull maydyns wronge hir hondis and
kneled on the grounde and to Cryste called for helpe and
comforte of Arthur. With that the warlow wrath Arthure
undir, and so they waltyrde and tumbylde over the craggis and
busshys, and eythir cleyght other full faste in their armys. And
85 other whyles Arthure was aboven and other whyle undir, and so
weltryng and walowynge they rolled doune the hylle, and they

never leffte tyll they fylle thereas the floode marked. But ever in
the walterynge Arthure smyttes and hittis hym with a short
dagger up to the hyltys, and in his fallynge there braste of the
90   gyauntes rybbys three evyn at onys.

And by fortune they felle thereas the two knyghtes aboode
with theire horsis. Whan sir Kay saw the kynge and the gyaunt
so icleyght togyder,

'Alas,' sayd sir Kay, 'we ar forfete for ever! Yondir is our
95   lorde overfallen with a fende.'

'Hit is nat so,' seyde the kynge, 'but helpe me, sir Kay, for
this corseynte have I clegged oute of the yondir clowys.'

'In fayth,' seyde sir Bedwere, this is a foule carle,' and
caughte the corseynte oute of the kynges armys and there he
100 seyde, 'I have mykyll wondir, and Mychael be of suche a
makyng, that ever God wolde suffir hym to abyde in hevyn.
And if seyntis be suche that servys Jesu, I woll never seke for
none, be the fayth of my body!'

The kynge than lough at Bedwers wordis and seyde,
105 'This seynte have I sought nyghe unto my grete daunger.
But stryke of his hede and sette hit on a trouncheoune of a
speare, and geff hit to thy servaunte that is swyffte-horsed,
and bere hit unto sir Howell that is in harde bondis, and
bydde hym be mery, for his enemy is destroyed. And aftir in
110 Barflete lette brace hit on a barbycan, that all the comyns of
this contrey may hit beholde.

B   Caxton's text

And soo he ascended vp in to that hylle tyl he came to a grete
fyre, and there he fonde a careful wydowe wryngynge her
handes and makyng grete sorowe syttynge by a graue newe
115 made. And thenne kynge Arthur salewed her and demaunded
of her wherfore she made suche lamentacion. To whome she
answerd and sayd,

'Syre knyghte, speke softe for yonder is a deuyll. Yf he
here the speke he wylle come and destroye the. I holde the
120 vnhappy. What dost thow here in this mountayne? For yf ye
were suche fyfty as ye be ye were not able to make resystence
ageynst this deuyll. Here lyeth a duchesse deede, the whiche
was the fayrest of alle the world, wyf to syre Howel, duc of
Bretayne. He hath murthred her in forcynge her and hath
125 slytte her vnto the nauyl.'

'Dame,' sayd the kynge, 'I come fro the noble conqueroure

kynge Arthur for to treate with that tyraunt for his lyege
peple.'

'Fy on suche treatys,' sayd she, 'he setteth not by the kynge
130 ne by no man els. But and yf thou haue broughte Arthurs wyf
dame Gweneuer he shalle be gladder than thow haddest
gyuen to hym half Fraunce. Beware! Approche hym not to
nygh, for he hath vaynquysshed xv kynges and hath maade
hym a cote ful of precious stones enbrowdred with theyre
135 berdes, which they sente hym to haue his loue for sauacion of
theyr peple at this laste Crystemasse. And yf thow wylt speke
with hym at yonder grete fyre at souper.'

'Wel,' sayd Arthur, 'I wyll accomplysshe my message for al
your ferdful wordes.' And wente forth by the creast of that
140 hylle and sawe where he satte atte souper gnawynge on a
lymme of a man, bekynge his brode lymmes by the fyre, and
bercheles, and thre fayr damoysels tornynge thre broches
wheron were broched twelue yonge children, late borne, lyke
yonge byrdes.

145 Whanne kynge Arthur beheld that pyteous syȝte he had
grete compassion on them, so that his hert bledde for sorowe;
and hayled hym, sayeng in this wyse:

'He that alle the world weldeth gyue the shorte lyf and
shameful dethe! And the deuyl haue thy soule! Why hast
150 thow murthred this duchesse? Therfore aryse and dresse the,
thow gloton, for this day shall thou dye of my hand.'

Thenne the gloton anone starte vp and tooke a grete
clubbe in his hand and smote at the kynge that his coronal
fylle to the erthe. And the kynge hytte hym ageyn that he
155 carf his bely and cutte of his genytours that his guttes and his
entraylles fylle doune to the ground. Thenne the gyaunt
threwe awey his clubbe and caught the kynge in his armes
that crusshyd his rybbes. Thenne the thre maydens knelyd
doune and callyd to Cryst for helpe and comforte of Arthur.
160 And thenne Arthur weltred and wrong that he was other
whyle vnder and another tyme aboue. And so weltryng and
walowynge they rolled doune the hylle tyl they came to the
see marke, and euer as they soo weltred Arthur smote hym
with his daggar. And it fortuned they came to the place
165 where as the two knyghtes were and kept Arthurs hors.
Thenne when they sawe the kynge fast in the gyaunts armes
they came and losed hym.

And thenne the kynge commaunded syr Kaye to smyte of
the gyaunts hede and to sette it vpon a truncheon of a spere
170 and bere it to syre Howel and telle hym that his enemy was

slayne, 'and after late this hede be bounden to a barbycan that alle the peple may see and behold hit'.

Notes

8 **Thou carpys** 'you speak' (from OSc *karpa*]   Second-person singular forms with *-ys* and *-is* inflections belong to the north Midlands and the North (elsewhere *-est*). The verb *carpen* is common in (but not restricted to) alliterative verse.

9 **werlow** 'devil' (from OE *wærloga*, cf. *warlock*)   Commoner in northern ME and in alliterative verse.

10 **unhappy** 'unfortunate' (OSc *happ*).

15 **that mylde**   The class shift (conversion) of adjectives to fulfil nominal functions is common in alliterative verse.

21 **more blyther**   Double comparatives of this kind arise in Early Middle English. The modern rules, by which monosyllabic adjectives show comparison by the use of an inflection (except in special stylistic choices), developed in the seventeenth century.

32 **knave chyldirne** 'boy children'   The OE *cild* had both an endingless neuter plural and the nominative plural form *cilderu*. From the latter, with the centralisation of the final vowel, alternative forms developed: *childer* (with loss of final *-e*) and *childeren* (with the adoption of the Weak noun plural inflection). The above form, like the modern standard one, therefore represents a historically double plural.

34 **that turnys**   Present-tense plural inflexions in *-ys* or *-is* are most frequent to the north of an approximate line from the Mersey to the Wash.

44 **brekelys hym semys** 'he seems not to be wearing breeches'   The impersonal is grammatically unusual and may have arisen from confusion about the nature of the construction. Ordinarily the dative pronoun (*hym*, *me*, etc.) would refer to the person experiencing the appearance of something. Here it acts as subject of the verb. Impersonal constructions continued to be formed in the Early ME period, but had ceased to be productive in the fifteenth century.

48 **angirfull wordys** 'hostile words' (cf. OSc *angr* and Lat. *angor*)   The insults used (*theeff* and *carl* especially) were frequent in the fourteenth and fifteenth centuries (see Excerpt 21).

50 **freyke** 'creature'   Derived from the OE poetic word *freca*, 'warrior, hero'. It is most frequent in (although not restricted to) alliterative verse.

59 **sye** 'saw'   This is essentially a south Midland form, occurring most frequently south of the Wash.

66 **colde erthe**   For the poetic use of the adjective *colde* with its associations with fatality and death, see Excerpt 7.

80 **balefull**   Cf. *carefull* (4). According to *OED*, *baleful* was essentially a poetic word before the nineteenth century. Subjective

reference, where the sense is 'full of pain or suffering', is almost restricted to consciously literary contexts, and is extremely rare after the sixteenth century.

93   **icleyght** 'clasped'   Past participle of *clechen*. See also *clegged* (97), 'seized, captured' (OE*clēcen).

94   **ar**   This endingless form is recorded mostly in a belt bounded by a line from Morecambe Bay to the Humber in the North, and from the Mersey to the Wash in the South, but occurs also in London.

97   **corseynte** 'relic' (OF *cors saint*, 'holy body (of a saint))   St Michael's Mount was a place of pilgrimage.
        clowys 'rocky bluffs' (OE *clōh)   Like its modern form, *clough*, the word has a northerly distribution.

114   **makyng grete sorwe**   Caxton makes considerable use of verbal phrases modelled on French constructions with *faire* or *avoir*. See also *made . . . lamentacion* (116), *make resystence* (121), *had . . . compassion* (145–46).

122   **the whiche**   This connective is characteristic of bureaucratic English in the early fifteenth century, where its use is modelled on that of French *liquels*. It occurs already in Chaucer, and becomes very frequent among fifteenth-century writers. Note also the use of *to whome* in line 116, well separated from its antecedent. Both these connective devices have their ultimate origins in administrative Latin.

135   **haue his loue . . .**   This awkward construction again betrays the nature of the administrative prose that Caxton took as his model. The word *loue* is used with diplomatic significance only. Note also Caxton's selection of an abstract nominal phrase in preference to the more obvious verbal one.

145–46   **that pyteous sy3te . . . compassion**   Caxton's addition is a cliché of the kind of courtly narrative into which he is transforming Malory's work.

164   **fortuned**   The verb was used in the late fourteenth century to mean 'pre-destine'. In the fifteenth century it seems to have been adopted, often in legal and administrative language, as a more dignified alternative to *fallen* or *happen*.

23 John Skelton, translation of the Bibliotheca Historica of Diodorus Siculus

Skelton's translation of Diodorus Siculus, made from the Latin version of Poggio, is included as an extreme example of 'aureation' in prose. The description of style as 'aureate' originated early in the fifteenth century with John Lydgate, who used it of his own stylistic aspirations in verse. It implies a careful consciousness in verbal choice based on rhetorical ideals, and more particularly a choice which will lend to the discourse both euphony in sound and dignity through the associations of the words selected. This generally results in the employment of vocabulary and sentence constructions with strong Latin associations. The second sentence here is of lengthy periodic structure, participular clauses are frequent, and the Latin ablative absolute construction can be seen to underlie lines 37–38, 47 and 49. The practice – though not the theory – of aureation is already evident in the bureaucratic and administrative English of some early fifteenth-century letters, and lexical elaboration increases throughout the century. By Skelton's time the practice was a fully conscious and deliberate literary technique expressed in lexical doublets, and heavy modification and qualification. Looking back in his poem *Phyllyp Sparowe* to the time of Chaucer, Skelton found his English attractively simple and clear; but the praise is ambiguous, also implying some lack of distinction. In his own translation of Diodorus Siculus, Skelton was concerned to draw attention to himself as a learned practitioner in the artifice of rhetoric.

Details of Skelton's early life are lacking, although his family probably came from Yorkshire, and he himself was born in the early 1460s. He is best known for his vigorous and often polemical English verse, but three universities (Oxford, Louvain and Cambridge) between 1488 and 1493 honoured his skills in Latin rhetoric, and his translation of Diodorus Siculus is praised by Caxton in his prologue to *Eneydos* (1490). By 1488 he had joined the royal household, later becoming tutor to Prince Henry, and in 1496 he was described by Erasmus as the 'light and glory' of English letters. Although his career was not without reversals, he was closely associated with the court and acted as a kind of 'poet laureate' to Henry VIII, producing a poem to celebrate the Scottish defeat at Flodden in 1513. He died on 21 June 1529.

The precise date at which Skelton translated Diodorus Siculus is unknown, but the text survives in a single manuscript (Corpus Christi College, Cambridge 357) whose paper was probably manufactured in 1486–87.

For the difficulte of the processe, it briefly can not be expowned what the pagans, other-wise called paynyms, supposed of their goddis, and what they were that first gaaue enformacion to haue theyr goddes in reuerence and worshipp, and what oppynyon
5 they hadde of their inmortalite. But, as touchynge those thynges whiche vnto thistorye apperteyne, so as they may be more open and manyfeste vnto theym that shall it here and rede, distributynge theym in-to certayn chapitres so as that nothynge notable of memory shal be lefte behynde and not
10 recounted, takynge our pryncyple of those yeris and seasons passed of olde, as moche as may be done in maters so remotyue, we shal wryte of mannes generacion and of alle the thynges whiche were doon in auncyente dayes by alle the world enuyron. By the iudicial oppynyon of clerkis and noble
15 connynge men whiche brought vnto remembraunce the nature of thynges and mater historyous, it is said hou the first generacion of man was by two maner wayes: somme iudged that the world was without begynnynge and incorruptyble, and that mankynde was without orygynal; somme estemyd
20 how the world had a bygynnynge and that it was corruptible, and how men had the begynnynge of theyr generacion by chaunce.
For they had this opynyon that from the first premordial of thynges, heuen and erthe had one ideal inmyxte with their
25 nature; of whens, by distyncte bodyes to-gydre, this world toke this maner of ordre as we see. The aier for his parte toke his contynuel motyf; the fyre for his parte by reson of his lightnes atteyned vnto suppreme regyons of the ayer. Of the same consideracion, the sonne and the sterris toke their
30 courses for theyr parte. And that mater engrosed that was slymy and pounderous by commyxtion of humours, by resons of his grosenes compacte, stode stylle and in his place remayned. The see hou it was of moysture qualyfyed. The erthe hou it was cloddy and clayye by qualitees endurate, and
35 so euermore remayneth soddy and softe. This erthe, whan it was first condensyd and somwhat enthycked with the sonnes radyant hete, his superficyal or vppermost parte by force of hete enbolned in many placis, ther were many humours

coagulate in whiche were exorted putryfactions couerd ouer
40 wyth a frotthy rayne as we see in fennys, plasshes, and
stondynge waters whan the feruencye of the ayer sodenly
chauffeth the cold ground. Whan it is soo that ony
engendrure is made in thyngis of moisture by hete therto
annexed, and where-as by nyghte the ayer [that] extendith
45 enuyron mynystrith moisture, whiche humour by dayetyme
thurgh hete of the sonne is engrossyd, thenne at the laste tho
putrefactions vnto an hepe to-gyder ensommed, in maner as
it were the tyme of delyueraunce faste approchynge nygh,
and thoo frotthy raynes dissoluyd, they brynge forth formes
50 and facions of alle maner thynge vegetal and sensible lyf. Of
whome, those thyngis whiche hadde more hete than other,
for theyr parte were made byrdys and flewe vpp in-to the
supreme region of the ayer; and those that contenyd in
theym moste of the erthe, they were made crepynge wormes
55 and other lyuynge bestes. Those that toke for theyr parte
moisture naturall, were brought vnto the elemente of theyr
kynde and callyd by name fysshes of the water. The erthe fro
thens forth endreyed from day to day with thardaunt hete of
the sonne bemes, as wel as by the blastys of wynde, it lefte
60 alle engendrynge of more vegetal bestes of sensible lyf; but
those that alle-redy were engendryd, by commyxtion eche of
other they engendryd by procreacion other creatures.

This oppynyon had Euripules, Anoxagoras that philosopher's
discyple, that where-as the heuen and the erthe were first
65 myxte to-gydre by inperfection; after, they were separated.
And thenne they brought forth euery thynge after theyr
nature, as trees, byrdes, wylde bestes, and alle maner of
kyndely thynge.

How-be-it vnto dyuerse persones the first generacion of the
70 erthe be incredible; yet, not-withstondynge, thynges whiche a
dayes be done inferre a trew testymonye of the premysses.
Not fer fro Thebas of the contrey of Egipte, after that the
grete deluge of the flode of Nylus was ceased, the feruente
hete of the sonne chafynge the wosy myre and fylthe whiche
75 of the water remayned, grete multitude of myse out of
syssures and ruptures of the erthe in many places was
engendrid: whiche in maner is an euydence approuyd that of
the prymordiall begynnynge of the world in lyke wyse alle
maner of lyuynge creatures was engendrid. And semblably,
80 they saye, at the begynnynge men were engendryd; and that
they sought their sustenaunce in the wylde felde, nakedly
lyuynge in the busshy wyldernesse; vnto whome herbes and

fruytes of the tre of their owne natural growynge mynystred
their dayly fode and repaste; and how wylde bestes and
85 rauenous were toward this people, of cruelte moeued,
passynge noyous; whome to resiste and withstonde, they
accompanyed theym-self to-gydre for drede and wele
encomyne, eche of theym dyde other assiste and supporte,
ordeyned places for theym-self to enhabyte; and where-as
90 claterynge and noyse whiche they made in maner was but
confuse, afterward it grewe vnto a parfyght voys and
language intelligyble, and so they aptly applyed vnto euery
thynge the very propre name. But for-as-moche as they were
situated in dyuerce places of the world, men saye, they spack
95 not all after one language. Whereupon appiered varyaunce
of speche and dyuerse carrecters and figures of lettres. And
how the first confluence of men to-gyder encompanyed, they
saye, was the first orygynal of their nacion and people.

Notes

2   **pagans . . . paynyms** (Latin *paganus*; OF *paienime*)   The use of
etymological doublets, such as these, and paired synonyms lends
weight to the expression.

5   **inmortalite**   This form, using the Latin prefix *-in*, is a learned
reconstruction. The two nasals, /n/ and /m/, had been assimilated to
produce *immortalitas* even in classical times. See also *inperfection*
(65).

touchynge   The word is commonly used as a connective device in
formal and official prose. The technique derives from French
administrative prose.

11   **remotyue** 'remote, distant'   The use of the suffix *-yue* (Latin *-
ivus*) is not justified by the existence of a Latin parallel (classical
Latin *remotus*). Moreover, the suffix is normally used to form
adjectives from a verbal base.

14   **iudicial** 'judicious'   The modern sense of pertaining to a judge
or legal matters had been established for more than a century. *OED*
records a very few uses with Skelton's sense in the sixteenth and
seventeenth centuries.

15   **men whiche**   *Which* is still frequently used as a personal relative,
while *whom* may be used with non-personal reference (line 51).

16   **historyous**   The more common medieval form of the adjective is
historial. The Anglo-French suffix *-ous*, although a very common
formative with Romance bases, is recorded with this base only in the
works of Skelton.

19   **orygynal** 'source, cause'.

estemyd   Latin *aestimare* has the sense 'to judge worth'. Skelton
uses this verb for lexical variation from *iudged* in an earlier clause.

The word is unusual but is recorded from *c*. 1430.

24 **ideal**   The Platonic 'idea' underlying the undifferentiated and intermingled elements prior to creation.

27 **his . . . motyf** 'motion'   This sense is not recorded by *OED*. The form derives from OF. The form *his* should not be interpreted as personification, since no distinction is made between masculine and non-animate reference.

30 **mater engrosed** 'condensed or solid matter'   The *en-* prefix is derived from French and frequently carries the significance 'to commence, to bring about'. Many formations are on Romance bases, but native bases began to appear from the middle of the fifteenth century: see *enthycked* (36), *enbolned*, 'swelled up' (38), and *endreyed* (58). The *em-* variant develops before labial consonants. In many words there is variation in the fifteenth and sixteenth centuries with the Latin equivalents, *in-* and *-im*.

33 **qualyfyed** 'provided with the qualities of'.

34 **endurate** 'hardened'   The more frequent form of this word has the prefix *in-*. The *-ate* suffix is derived from the Latin passive participle in *-atus* and is used only with Romance bases throughout the ME period.

39 **exorted** 'brought about' (Latin *exortum*, past participle of *exoriri*) Recorded elsewhere only in the *Ludus Coventriae* (*c.* 1475).

50 **vegetal** 'vegetable' (Med. Latin *vegetalis*)   Has the technical sense of a creature which possesses the power of life, growth and reproduction but not of sense or movement.

53 **suppreme** 'uppermost' (Latin *supremus*)   Skelton is the earliest recorded user in this sense.

70–71 **a dayes** 'daily, ?nowadays'   An adverbial phrase formed by a blend of the OE dative (*on dæge*) with the genitive (*dæges*).

71 **inferre** 'introduce'   Again, Skelton uses this word in the technical Latin sense of bringing up an argument or piece of evidence in discourse.

87 **accompanyed** 'associated'   This reflexive use of the verb is uncommon but is paralleled in other fifteenth-century sources.

87–88 **wele encomyne** 'mutual benefit'   Skelton uses this phrase frequently and intends by it that political concept later called 'common weal' and by Chaucer 'commune profit'. The word order suggests influence by French *bien commun*, but the syntactic structure is not clear.

93 **very propre name**   The idea that named objects had individually appropriate names, and that language change and corruption had led to the transfer of words to refer to things other than those to which they properly and originally belonged, was inherited from Greek and Roman linguistic theory. The notion of aptness underlay medieval concepts of stylistic decorum.

Early Modern English (1500–1800)

The Early Modern English period may be taken to extend from about 1500, when printing was becoming widespread, to 1800, when English had become established as a language of international importance and the subject of academic study. The intervening years saw the emergence of the English language both as the medium of an important literature and the occasion of controversy among its users. During this period the automatic pre-eminence accorded to Latin in the fifteenth century as a means of elevating style was challenged by those purists who, like Sir John Cheke, regarded all foreign influence (not merely that of French or Scandinavian) as barbarism, and those who, like the poet Edmund Spenser, saw merit in the native linguistic resources of the medieval past. The English language, reflecting the growing confidence of the English nation, was reckoned to possess its own creative resources and need owe nothing to either French or Latin. The ensuing disagreement, known as the 'Inkhorn Controversy', consumed much of the sixteenth and early seventeenth centuries. It was a debate carried on essentially among practitioners of the language, the underlying impulse being that of rhetoric, the art of eloquent communication, an aspiration which stimulated the earliest works on English, exemplified in this collection by Thomas Wilson's *Art of Rhetorique* (1553). The aim was frankly functional: to perfect English in its role as a national language and a means of literary and individual expression. There were no ultimate victors in the controversy, for although English lexis was greatly enriched from Latin at this period, the debate waned in the seventeenth century when other aspects of the language seized the attention of literary men. The variety and changeableness of English, which had been linked to foreign influence since the twelfth century, was now compared unfavourably with the supposed fixity of Latin. Rather than quarrel over the rhetorical employment of the lexicon, literary men turned their attention to establishing a stable spelling system, regulated grammar and a defined vocabulary. The first dictionary of English, compiled by Robert Cawdrey, appeared in 1604, and its title page offers to instruct its public in both the 'true writing' and the meanings, as well as the proper contexts in which to use, the many unfamiliar words they might encounter in their reading and in listening to the sermons of classically educated clergy. It commenced a lexicographic tradition which evolved to culminate in the publication in 1755 of Dr Johnson's great dictionary, whose avowed purpose was to fix and stabilise English. Johnson, although he had precursors in Nathaniel Bailey, John Kersey and especially Benjamin Martin, marks a watershed in the lexicographic tradition. His dictionary commences with a history of the language, illustrated by exemplary texts, and he turns for the validation of his definitions to the practice of those authors of the past and present whom he esteemed. The English language had been defined as a historical heritage and the object of scholarly study.

Interest in the historical origins of English emerged in Elizabethan times, as a by-product of antiquarian collecting, which was given impetus by the availability of many original documents after the dissolution of the monasteries in 1536. Archbishop Matthew Parker (1504–1575) and his associates were particularly active in this earlier period in Cambridge, where Abraham Wheloc was appointed to the first Lectureship in Anglo-Saxon in about 1623. During the same period, Sir Robert Cotton (1571–1631) made the important collection to which we owe our texts of *Beowulf*, the *Battle of Maldon*, the Vespasian Psalter and much else. Although academic interest in the historical origins of English faded somewhat after the Restoration, it was restored in Oxford when a new generation of scholars led by George Hickes (1642–1715) and Humfrey Wanley (1672–1726) did much to lay the foundations of the modern study of Old English.

Grammarians, too, contributed to the new status of English. William Bullokar's *A Brief Grammar of English* appeared in 1586, followed by Paul Greaves' *Grammatica Anglicana* in 1594, and Alexander Gil's *Logonomia Anglica* in 1619. Both the pace of the production and the extent of grammars quickened in the seventeenth century.

Standardisation of the written language, based upon the

language used by the clerks of Chancery during the fifteenth century, proceeded further, but considerable variation in spelling persisted throughout the period of Early Modern English. Within the spoken language, the prestige of London speech began to assert itself. Already, in the late fifteenth century, Caxton had acknowledged the provinciality of a Kentish dialect, and in 1580 George Puttenham, in his *Arte of English Poesie*, recommended that would-be authors use 'the usual speach of the Court, and that of London and the shires lying about London within sixty myles and not much above'. Echoing the Latin rhetorical origins of much of the synchronic study of English, opinions on its pronunciation pre-date those on its vocabulary and grammar. John Palsgrave (1530) and Sir Thomas Elyot in his *The Governour* (1531) both agree that English is subject to variation in the perceived worth of pronunciations. The latter applies to sociolinguistic and historical developments in the everyday spoken language those rhetorical ideas of the vices of letter and syllable which Chaucer had thought appropriate only to verse composition 150 years earlier. Such emphasis on English elocution led to the study of phonetics and spelling. John Hart's *An Orthographie* (1569), like Gil's *Logonomia Anglica*, is prescriptive in spirit and somewhat fanciful in its representation of phonetic facts, but by the mid seventeenth century the study of the phonetics of English emerged with a more scientific spirit in the works of John Wallis (*Grammatica Linguae Anglicanae*, 1653) and Charles Cooper (*Grammatica Anglicana*, 1685). The eighteenth century brought popular works on the subject, such as the dictionary of pronunciation by an ex-actor, John Walker, first published in 1791 and repeatedly reprinted.

The most striking linguistic developments during the Early Modern period also concern the pronunciation of the language, and may be viewed as continuing the series of raisings of the Great Vowel Shift. By 1750 the sound system of standard English possessed six long-vowel phonemes – /iː/, /eː/, /uː/, /oː/, /ɛː/, /ɑː/ – and the diphthongs /ʌi/, /au/, /ɔi/, /ju/, /ou/. Changes among the consonants include the loss by 1630 of initial /k/, /g/ and /w/ in words like *knight*, *gnaw* and *write*, and of post-vocalic /l/ in *walk* and *folk*. Post-vocalic /r/ was lost in words like *arm* and *earth* by about 1800.

Morphological changes in the period were much more limited than those which distinguish Middle English from Old English, but there was considerable variation in both morphology and syntax and some important developments in the latter sphere. The loss in Middle English of extensive noun inflexion and the simplification of the pronoun system led to a syntactical rather than morphological perception of the possessive genitive marker: *s* was in effect released from its place in the paradigm. In the sixteenth century it was freely attached to nominal groups, and 'group genitives' such as *the king of England's law* emerged alongside (and then displaced) the older type: *the king's law of England*. Ascham and Lyly frequently substitute an inflected pronoun, *his*, for the apostrophe *s*. The third-person singular possessive in Middle English lacks a form with which to distinguish animate from inanimate reference: *his* or *hire* is used in either case. The distinction was possible in the subject case, where three distinct forms had long existed: *he*, *she*, *(h)it*. *Hit* was used as a possessive in the fourteenth century, and the form *its* developed analogically during the first half of the sixteenth century, although it is still avoided by Shakespeare. The emergence of *you* in place of *ye* as the subject form of the second-person plural pronoun followed a process of case simplification which had affected nouns in the Middle English period. Shakespeare was content to use the new form, retaining *ye* for passages of elevated style, but the translators of the King James Bible (1611) limited their usage to the older form. The Middle English distinction in the use of *ye/you* from *thou*, by which the former implied politeness and the latter familiarity, superiority or contempt for the addressee, continued but was abandoned in the latter half of the seventeenth century. The emergence of *who*, *which* as relative pronouns, commencing in the Middle English period, was followed in the seventeenth century by the modern distinction between personal and non-personal reference. Verbal endings in *-es* of the third-person singular present tense can be found in London texts from the early fourteenth century, but seem to have been avoided by writers before Elizabethan times. They then begin to displace the earlier *-eth* ending. Queen Elizabeth herself used them increasingly in her letters; nevertheless the words *hath* and *doth* are usually written in this form, and may have preserved the pronunciation longer. Appearances may, however, be deceptive, since Richard Hodges comments in his *A Special Help to Orthographie* (1643) that in his time, although *-eth* was written, this was pronounced [əs], at least in multisyllabic words.

Syntactical developments also include the final abandonment of double negation in the standard language and the use of more periphrastic tense forms. Considerable fluctuation is apparent in the use of the periphrastic form with the auxiliary *do*. A simple table illustrates the usage in Shakespeare, Middle English and Modern Standard English. Parentheses indicate those usages which are currently marked or marginal.

	Declarative	*Interrogative*	*Imperative*
Do-peri.	(ME) Sh (ModE)	Sh ModE	Sh (ModE)
Plain	ME Sh ModE	ME (Sh)	ME Sh ModE

The negative is as follows:

Do-peri	(ME) Sh ModE	Sh ModE	Sh ModE
Plain	ME (Sh)	ME (Sh)	ME (Sh)

As in other syntactical matters, the flexibility of usage permissible in Elizabethan English is apparent.

Changes in the lexicon in the Early Modern period consist in part of the continuation of Latin influence noted in Later Middle English and associated with the 'Inkhorn Controversy', but borrowings from Spanish and Italian now join these traditional sources of new vocabulary. Striking, too, is the ease with which words migrate between word-classes. The influence of Latin is strongly apparent in word-formation, where for example Latin derivational affixes are sometimes considered equivalent to those of native origin. Thus Shakespeare uses the native suffix -ed just as if it were the Latin -atus, 'having a': *mouthed wounds*, *stelled fires*. Nor is this restricted to poetic language: in botanical description in Culpeper's *Herbal* the leaves of the agrimony are described as *dented* (i.e. 'with teeth').

24   *Thomas Wilson*, The Arte of Rhetorique

Thomas Wilson (*c.* 1523–1581) was the son of prosperous Lincolnshire farming folk who were in a position to send him to Eton and then to King's College, Cambridge. At the first of these he would have undergone an education including the principles of Latin rhetoric, and in Cambridge he may have attended lectures on Greek given by Sir John Cheke, the chief proponent of pure English in the stylistic debates of the sixteenth century. Wilson's earliest work was completed in Latin while acting as a tutor in Cambridge, but he followed this with the first English handbook on logic, and two years later in 1553 he produced his *Arte of Rhetorique*, the first complete work on rhetoric in the English language. After suffering persecution during the reign of Queen Mary, he studied in Italy, gained legal qualifications and returned to England with the accession of Queen Elizabeth. His *Arte of Rhetorique* was reprinted in 1560. His legal career now began, and with patronage from Archbishop Parker, it flourished. He interested himself in and published on political questions, becoming first a royal ambassador and finally a member of the Privy Council.

Rhetoric is that art which instructs on how to make effective legal and political speeches, and, by extension, how to express one's view effectively in any circumstances. Instruction in rhetoric could therefore be considered a necessary skill for public life. Wilson's *Arte of Rhetorique*, which adapted the traditional Latin treatment of rhetoric to the interests of his own time, proved popular, and went through eight editions. It was divided into six sections: on the selection of subject matter (*inventio*), structure of the speech (*dispositio*), narration (*narratio*), style (*elocutio*), techniques of memorising (*memoria*) and techniques of presentation (*pronunciatio*). The following excerpt is what Wilson has to say about simplicity or plainness, the first and most basic of Ciceronian precepts of good style. Its adaptation to the intellectual world of its time means that much of it is concerned with the debate on the place in English of lexical reinforcement from foreign sources, and especially from learned Latin. Wilson deplores the use of elaborate diction where this is merely a badge of fashion and a substitute for meaning, but acknowledges that certain registers need technical diction, and that in those registers foreign phrases have become naturalised. The supposed letter from Lincolnshire was probably never written in this form, yet almost all the words it contains have occurred in the writings of others.

Emong al other lessons, this should first be learned, that we never affect any straunge ynkehorne termes, but so speake as is commonly received: neither sekyng to be over fine, nor yet livyng over carelesse, usyng our speache as most men do, and
5 ordryng our wittes, as the fewest have doen. Some seke so farre for outlandishe Englishe, that thei forget altogether their mothers language. And I dare swere this, if some of their mothers were alive, thei were not able to tell, what thei say, and yet these fine Englishe clerkes, wil saie thei speake
10 in their mother tongue, if a man should charge them for counterfeityng the kynges English. Some farre jorneid jentlemen at their returne home, like as thei love to go in forrein apparell, so thei wil pouder their talke with oversea language. He that cometh lately out of France, wil talke
15 Frenche English, and never blushe at the matter. Another choppes in with Englishe Italianated, and applieth the Italian phrase, to our Englishe speaking, the whiche is, as if an Oratour that professeth to utter his minde in plaine Latine, would needes speake Poetrie, and farre fetched colours of
20 straunge antiquitie. The lawyer wil store his stomack with the pratyng of Pedlers. The Auditour in makyng his accompt and rekenyng, cometh in with sise sould, and cater denere, for vi.s. iiii.d. The fine Courtier wil talke nothyng but Chaucer. The misticall wise menne, and Poeticall Clerkes, will speake
25 nothyng but quaint proverbes, and blynd allegories, delityng muche in their awne darkenesse, especially, when none can tell what thei dooe saie. The unlearned or foolishe phantasticall, that smelles but of learnyng (suche felowes as have seen learned men in their daies) will so latine their tongues,
30 that the simple cannot but wonder at their talke, and thynke surely thei speake by some Revelacion. I knowe them that thynke Rhetorique, to stande wholy upon darke woordes, and he that can catche an ynke horne terme by the taile, hym thei compt to bee a fine Englishe man, and a good
35 Rhetorician. And the rather to set out this folie, I will adde here suche a letter, as Willyam Sommer himself, could not make a better for that purpose. Somme will thinke and swere it to, that there was never any suche thyng written, well I wil not force any man to beleve it, but I will saie thus muche, and

40 abide by it to, the like have been made heretofore, and praised above the Monne.

A letter divised by a Lincolneshire man, for a voide benefice, to a gentilman that then waited upon the lorde Chauncellour, for the tyme beyng.

45 Ponderyng, expendyng, and revolutyng with my self your ingent affabilitee, and ingenious capacitee, for mundane affaires: I cannot but celebrate and extolle your magnificall dexteritee, above all other. For how could you have adepted suche illustrate prerogative, and dominicall
50 superioritee, if the fecunditee of your ingenie had not been so fertile, and wounderfull pregnaunt. Now therfore beeyng accersited, to suche splendent renoume, and dignitee splendidious: I doubt not but you will adivuate suche poore adnichilate orphanes, as whilome ware condis-
55 ciples with you, and of antique familiaritie in Lincolne shire. Emong whom I beeyng a Scholasticall panion, obtestate your sublimitee to extoll myne infirmitee. There is a sacerdotall dignitee in my native countrey, contiguate to me, where I now contemplate: whiche your worshipfull
60 benignitee, could sone impetrate for me, if it would like you to extend your scedules, and collaude me in them to the right honorable lorde Chauncellor, or rather Archi- grammacion of Englande. You knowe my literature, you knowe the pastorall promocion, I obtestate your clemencie,
65 to invigilate thus muche for me, accordyng to my confidence, and as you know my condigne merites, for suche a compendious livyng. But now I relinquishe to fatigate your intelligence with any more frivolous verbositie, and therfore he that rules the climates be evermore your
70 beautreux, your fortresse, and your bulwarke. Amen.

Dated at my Dome, or rather Mansion place, in Lincolnshire, the penulte of the moneth sextile. *Anno Millimo, quillimo, trillimo. Per me Johannes Octo.*
What wise man readyng this letter, will not take him for a
75 very Caulfe, that made it in good earnest, and thought by his ynkepot termes, to get a good personage. Doeth wit reste in straunge wordes, or els standeth it in wholsome matter, and apt declaryng of a mannes mynd? Do we not speake, because we would have other to understand us, or is not the tongue
80 geven for this ende, that one might know what another meaneth? And what unlearned man can tell, what half this letter signifieth? Therfore, either we must make a difference of Englishe, and saie some is learned Englishe, and other

some is rude Englishe, or the one is courte talke, the other is
85 countrey speache, or els we must of necessitee, banishe al
suche affected Rhetorique, and use altogether one maner of
language. When I was in Cambrige, and student in the kynges
College, there came a man out of the toune, with a pinte of
wine in a pottle pot, to welcome the provost of that house,
90 that lately came from the court. And because he would
bestow his present like a clerke, dwellyng emong the
schoolers: he made humbly his thre curtesies, and said in this
maner. Cha good even my good lorde, and well might your
lordship vare: Understandyng that your lordeship was come,
95 and knowyng that you are a worshipfull Pilate, and kepes a
bominable house: I thought it my duetic to come incanti-
vantee, and bryng you a pottell a wine, the whiche I beseche
your lordeship take in good worthe. Here the simple man
beyng desirous to amende his mothers tongue, shewed
100 hymself not to bee the wisest manne, that ever spake with
tongue.

Another good felowe in the countrey, beyng an officer, and
Maiour of a toune, and desirous to speake like a fine learned
man, havyng just occasion to rebuke a runnegate felow, said
105 after this wise in a greate heate. Thou yngram and vacacion
knave, if I take thee any more within the circumcision of my
dampnacion: I will so corrupte thee, that all vacacion knaves
shall take ilsample by thee.

Notes

2 **ynkehorne termes**   'Inkhorn' or 'Inkpot' were the epithets used by
opponents of the practice to castigate the use of learned foreign
borrowings. The earliest use of this kind in *OED* is in 1543.

7 **mothers**   The possessive has lost the unstressed *e* of the ME
inflexion *-es*, but the *s* is still written as though perceived as an
inflexion. No apostrophe is printed.

9 **clerkes**   Wilson conservatively writes ‹er› in most occurrences, but
see the spelling *farre* (ME *ferre*) in line 11.

11 **counterfeityng**   The image comparing language with coinage is
traditional in the rhetorical tradition. Cf. Horace, *Ars Poetica*, 58–59.

farre jorneid   Although this phrase is not hyphenated in the text,
its function as a modifier and its syntactic pattern parallel to that of
many contemporary exocentric compounds suggest that it would be
understood as a compound. Cf. *farre fetched* (19).

13 **oversea**   This is not a new compound but rather a case of
conversion from an adverb to adjectival function. The adverbial
phrase goes back to Old English, but the adjectival function belongs
to the sixteenth century.

16 **Italianated**   The two derivational suffixes (-*ate* and -*ed*) here perform the same function, converting the adjective to a quasi-passive participle. Their sense is something like 'caused to have the qualities of'. The former is from the Latin passive participle ending in -*atus*, and its use is restricted to Franco-Latin bases in Middle English. It becomes more widely productive in the sixteenth century, and with the native past participle inflexion -*ed* is used to create adjectives from nouns as well as verbs.

19 **needes**   Historically an adverb formed by the addition of the -*es* inflexion to a noun base: 'of need'.

23 **Chaucer**   Presumably a reference to the opinions of the archaisers who contended that English style could be improved by the readoption of words and phrases from earlier times. The poet Spenser was later influenced by such views.

28 **smelles**   Wilson usually uses the -*eth* inflexion of the third-person singular in his more earnest discourse, but in his illustration of comic failures in the art of *pronunciatio* he produces a racy list in which all the third-person verbs, singular and plural, end in -*es*. See also *kepes* (95). Despite this distinction, there is little doubt that, except in formal situations, it would have been natural for Wilson the use the -*es* type.

32 **thynke . . . to stande**   This clause imitates closely the Latin accusative and infinitive construction.

34 **compt**   In the French of the fifteenth century, and subsequently in English, the *p* of Latin *computare* was restored to the spelling of a word which had previously existed as ME *counte*.

36 **Sommer**   The court fool to Henry VIII from 1525 to 1547.

45 **expendyng**   Latin *expendere*, 'to weigh'.

46 **ingent affabilitee**   'enormous approachability'   Both words previously recorded in the late fifteenth century. As with all the words in this letter, the senses are those of the Latin forms from which they are derived.
mundane   'of the world'.

49 **adepted**   'achieved'   From Lat. *adeptus* 'having attained'. The earliest recorded use of a rare word.
illustrate . . . dominicall   'illustrious . . . lordly'   The letter is well sprinkled with words exhibiting the Latin-derived suffixes -*ate* and -*all*.

52 **accersited**   'summoned'   Latin *accersitus*, past participle of *accersere*.

54 **adnichilate**   'reduced to nothing'.

56 **panion**   An aphetic (that is, with loss of initial unstressed vowel) form of *companion*.
obtestate   Latin *obtestare*, 'call to witness'.

57 **extoll**   Latin *extollere*, 'raise up'.

60 **impetrate**   Latin *impetrare*, 'obtain by request'.

61 **scedules**   'letters'   Medieval Latin *scedula*, 'a slip or roll of parchment containing writing'.

66 **condigne** 'wholly worthy'   Perhaps through French from Latin *condignus*. The word was popular in late fifteenth-century aureate verse.

67 **compendious** 'advantageous'   Latin *compendiosus*. The *-ous* suffix is associated with stylistic elevation since, before the sixteenth century, it derived adjectives only from French or Latin bases.

71 **Dome** 'house'   Latin *domus*.

75 **Caulfe** 'idiot'   The ⟨au⟩ spelling testifies to diphthongisation of ME /ɑ/ before /lf/. This was followed during the sixteenth century by the loss of /l/, but this development is not apparent from the spelling.

76 **Doeth**   In Middle English interrogatives were formed by subject–verb inversion. The use of auxiliary *do* for this purpose and in negatives developed rapidly during the earlier sixteenth century.

82 **a difference**   Wilson is proposing that English may be stylistically variable. The opposite assumption is the untenable one that English consists of a single style (*maner*).

93 **Cha**   A reduced form of a phrase with the south-eastern dialect form of the pronoun *I* (*ich*). Usually means 'I have'. Used by Elizabethan writers as an index of rural unsophistication. The grammar seems strange here, and the symbolic associations of the phrase may be paramount.

94 **vare**   Illustrates the initial voicing of /f/ found in Middle English throughout the South and south-west Midlands.

97 **the whiche**   This type of connective, although originally part of an elevated written style, was evidently well enough known by this time to be selected by this kind of speaker.

104 **runnegate** 'renegade'   But a popular form in the sixteenth and seventeenth centuries as a more general term of abuse. This form derives through Middle English and French from Latin *renegatus*. The modern form is derived from Spanish.

105 **yngram** 'ignorant'   The variant is recorded from Wilson's time until the nineteenth century.

107 **vacacioun**   Derived from the past participle of Latin *vacare*, 'to be empty'.

25 The Diary of Henry Machyn

The diary kept between 1550 and 1563 by Henry Machyn, a member of the Guild of Merchant Taylors of the City of London, is of linguistic importance because it gives us access to a milieu which is generally closed to later investigations. He was not an important author, a graduate of the universities or a member of the court, but a relatively successful tradesman and an ordinary Londoner. Although it would be naïve to assume that the written language of his diary is a mirror reflection of his everyday speech, unaffected by cultural values more common in sophisticated circles, it has been shown that his diary exhibits features peculiar to his usage, especially in the frequency of occurrence, for example, of the spelling ‹ar› for earlier ‹er› and the confusion of initial ‹v› with initial ‹w›.

The value of the diary is limited somewhat by the limitations of interests displayed. Machyn's business was the supply of trappings for elaborate funerals, and his descriptions of these ceremonies occupy the greater part of his writings. However, although his diary begins as a catalogue of funeral pomp, he quickly begins to include records of other great occasions and lesser happenings such as the burning of a neighbour's house, or the escape of a bear at a bear-baiting.

The manuscript of Machyn's diary (BL MS Cotton Vitellius F. v) was, like that of the Anglo-Saxon *Battle of Maldon* and *Beowulf*, one of those damaged in the Cottonian library fire of 1731. A transcript of parts of it had, however, been made ten years earlier, and the portions in modern spelling in parentheses [] in the following excerpts derive from this source.

[The xx day of March the earl of Bedford, lord privy-seal, who died at his house beside the Savoy, was carried to his burying-place in the country, called Chenies, with three hundred horse all in black. He was carried with three crosses,] with mony
5 clerkes and prestes, [till they came to the hill] a-boyffe sant James, and ther returnyd [certain of them] home; and thay had torchys and armes and money gyven them. And after evere man sett in aray on horrsebake. First on red in blake bayryng a crosse of sylver, and serten prestes on horsebake
10 wayryng ther surples; then cam the standard, and then all the gentyllmen and hed officers; and then cam haroldes, on

beyryng ys elmet, and the mantylls, and the crest, and anodur
ys baner of armes, and anodur ys target with the garter, and
anodur ys cott armur; and anodur ys sword: and then master
15 Garter in ys ryche cott armur and then cam the charett with
vj banars rolles of armes, and a-bowt the charett iiij banars of
ymages, and after the charet a gret horsse trapyd in cloth of
gold with the sadyll of the sam; and then cam mornars, the
cheyffe (of whom) my lord Russell ys sune, and after my lord
20 trayssorer, and the master of the horse, and dyver odur
nobull men all in blake; and evere towne that he whent
thrughe the clarkes and prestes mett ym with crosses; and
thay had in evere parryche iiij nobuls to gyffe to the pore,
and the prest and clarke of evere parryche x^s., tyll he cam to
25 ys plasse at Cheynes; and the morowe after was he bered,
and a grett doll of money; and ther the deyn of Powlles mad a
godly sermon; and after a grett dener, and gret plenty to all
the contrey a-bowt that wold com thether.

The xxv day of Marche, the wyche was owre lade [day,]
30 ther was as gret justes as youe have sene at the tylt at
Vestmynster; the chalyngers was a Spaneard and ser Gorge
Haward; and all ther men, and ther horsses trymmyd in whyt,
and then cam the Kyng and a gret mene all in bluw, and
trymmyd with yelow, and ther elmets with gret tuyffes of blue
35 and yelow fether, and all ther veffelers and ther fotemen, and
ther armorers, and a compene lyke Turkes red in cremesun
saten gownes and capes, and with fachyons, and gret targets;
and sum in gren, and mony of dyvers colers; and ther was
broken ij hondred stayffes and a-boyff. . . .

40 The xvij day of Aprell was a commandment [from the bishop
of London that every] parryche in London shuld have the
sam day, and the morowe, durge and masse and ryngyng for
pope Jully [the third] of that name, and for all crystyn solles.

The xiiij day of Aprell, the wyche was [Ester day,] at sant
45 Margatt parryche at Westmynster, af[ter masse] was done,
one of the menysters a prest of the ab[bay] dyd helpe hym
that was the menyster [to] the pepull who wher reseyvyng of
the blessyd sacrement of [the lord] Jhesus Cryst, ther cam into the chyrche a man that was a monke of Elly, the wyche
50 was marryed to a wyff; the sam day ther that same man sayd
to the menyster, What doyst thow gyff them? and as sone as
he had spokyn he druw his wod-knyffe, and hyt the prest on
the hed and struck hym a grett blowe, and after ran after hym
and struck hym on the hand, and cloyffe ys hand a grett way,
55 and after on the harme a grett wond; and ther was syche a cry

and showtt as has not byne; and after he was taken and cared
to presun, and after examynyd wher-for he dyd ytt.

The xx day of Aprell was raynyd at Powlles a-for the
bysshope of London and many odur and my lord cheyffe
60 justys and my lord mayre and the shreyffes; ys name was
(master Fowler, alias Branch); he was a monke of Ely; and
ther was a goodly sermon, and after he was cast and
condemnyd to have ys hand that hurt the prest cut off or he
shuld suffer, and after dysgracyd, and after cared to Nuwgatt.

65 The xxj day of Aprell ther was wypyd at a cart-hors iij, j
man and ij women, and anodur man a-lone, ij old men with
whyt berdes, and on was for carehyng . . . .

[The xxiijd day of April, being saint George's day, at
Hampton Court, the King, with other lords and knights of the
70 garter, went in their robes on procession, with three] crosses,
and clarkes and prestes, and my lord chancellor, the cheyff
menyster, metered, and all thay in copes of cloth of tyssue
and gold, syngyng *Salva fasta dyes* as thay whent a-bowt; the
Quen('s) grace lokyd owt of a cassement, that hundereds dyd
75 se her grace after she had taken her chambur; and arolds
gohyng a-bowt the Kyng('s) grace.

The xxiij day of Aprell was the sam man cared to
Westmynster that dyd hurt the prest, and had ys hand stryken
of at the post, and after he was bornyd aganst sant Margett
80 chyrche with-owt the cherche-yerde.

Notes

7 **armes**   Read 'alms'. If this misspelling suggests the homophony of
the two words, it pre-dates the accepted homophony by at least a
century. ME [ɑlm] developed through [ɑum] to [ɑ:] by the later
seventeenth century, and [ar] to [a:] not much before 1800.

8 **evere** 'every'   Machyn uses final -*e* to represent a final unstressed
vowel in several words where Modern English would have final -*y*.
See also *cared* (64).

on red 'one rode'   The unhistorical final -*e* is frequently not
written as the word 'one' [OE *ān*]. The preterite *red* is not easily
explicable.

12 **ys elmet**   The pronunciation of initial *h-* is markedly unstable in
Machyn's language. He spells such words both with and without *h-*.
Compare *harme* (55), *haroldes* (11), *arolds* (75).

19 **my lord Russell ys sune**   The genitive inflexion -*ys* [OE -*es*] has
become a syntactical marker of possession which may be attached to
groups. It is sometimes erroneously interpreted as the genitive third-
person pronoun.

22 **clarkes**   The standard spelling was *clerkes* (5), but Machyn often writes ‹er› as ‹ar›, reflecting a pronunciation which had developed in the fifteenth century but which was resisted by many authors, since it seems to have lacked prestige.

25 **bered** 'buried' (OE *byrgian*)   The *e*-spelling suggests the survival of a pronunciation descending from the south-eastern origins of the London language, where WS *y* was written *e*.

29 **the wyche**   This form of the relative, dependent as it is on the usage of administrative French prose, implies some familiarity with the official written English of the period.

31 **Vestmynster**   Machyn frequently writes initial *w-* as ‹v› (cf. *veffelers*, 35, 'one . . . employed to keep the way clear at a procession', *OED* s.v. 'whiffler').

47 **who**   The use of the pronoun *who* as a personal relative is still comparatively unusual at this period. In OE and in Chaucer, *who* occurs only as an interrogative or with indefinite reference. During the fourteenth century it begins to be used as a relative in the North and it is found in its inflected forms, *whose* and *whom*, in the South during the fifteenth century.

58 **raynyd**   An aphetic (see page 150 note 101) form of *arraynyd*, also used by Machyn.

62–63 **cast and condemnyd**   Possibly a tautological pair, but *cast* probably means 'found guilty'.

63–64 **or he shuld suffer** 'before he should suffer death'.

65 **cart-hors**   Elsewhere *cart-ars*, 'the cart-tail', or back of a cart.

74–75 **hundereds dyd se**   The use of the periphrastic construction with the verb 'to do', distinct from the causal construction, is rare before the mid fifteenth century but common during the sixteenth.

26   John Lyly, Euphues or The Anatomy of Wit

John Lyly (?1554–1606) was intimately associated with the secular humanistic Latin learning which emerged in the fifteenth century and flourished in the sixteenth. He was the grandson of a significant literary figure, William Lily, a noted grammarian, and represented the third generation of his family to profit from an education at Magdalen College, Oxford. Little is known of his early life, but he probably attended the Cathedral School in Canterbury where his father was an ecclesiastical official. He received his MA from Oxford in 1575 and moved to London, where he received patronage from the Earl of Oxford. In 1578 he published his *Euphues*, which was an immediate success and was followed in 1580 by *Euphues and his England*. By 1630 the two separate works had gone through twenty-six editions. Lyly's characteristic style became temporarily so fashionable that the royal court is reported to have sought to speak in Euphuisms.

The excitement generated at court by the style of *Euphues* is understandable, since artificial prose deriving from the earlier 'curial style', with its elaborate Latinisms and endless sentences, had been developed specifically within the written medium. Here, in *Euphues*, was an artistic style affiliated with the spoken language. It was one founded on the patterns of Latin rhetoric and seems to have had distant connections with both the Latin of the Church Fathers and Cicero, but to have been created by Lyly by anglicising some of the features of Latin lectures he had encountered in Oxford. The major feature of the style is the use of clauses of moderate length brought into relationship by the exploitation of certain formal features of the language. Two or more clauses of the same syntactic structure are related by some semantic (opposition or synonymy), phonetic (rhyme, assonance or alliteration) or lexical (verbal repetition) device so as to achieve an effect of balance or parallelism. Extended similes derived from handbooks of natural history abound and, like the use of proverbs, they may be arranged into lists. Rhetorical questions are also frequent. The narrative is heavily sententious and didactic, recounting the emotional adventures of a young 'Athenian', Euphues, his infatuation with and then rejection of the faithless Lucilla. The passage occurs when Euphues first finds himself alone with his lady.

Despite its enormous impact, Lyly's fashionable success was

inevitably temporary. Already by 1598, Shakespeare, in *Henry IV* Part 1 II. iv, is satirising Euphuistic style in the speeches of Falstaff imitating King Henry, and by the time of Lyly's death in 1606 his Euphuistic style was beginning to be considered ludicrous in more advanced quarters.

Euphues was surprised with such increadible ioye at this straunge euent, that hee had almost sounded, for seeing his coryuall to be departed, and *Ferardo* to gyue him so friendly entertainment, doubted not in time to get the good wyll of
5 *Lucilla*: Whome findinge in place conuenient without company, with a bolde courage and comely gesture, he began to assay hir in this sort.
  Gentlewoman, my acquaintaunce beeing so little, I am afraide my credite will bee lesse, for that they commonly are
10 soonest beleeued, that are best beloued, and they liked best, whome we haue knowne longest, neuerthelesse the noble minde suspecteth no guile wythout cause, neither condemneth any wight wythout proofe, hauing therefore notise of your heroycall heart, I am the better perswaded of my good hap.
15 So it is *Lucilla*, that cõming to *Naples* but to fetch fire, as the by word is, not to make my place of abode, I haue founde such flames that I can neither quench them wyth the water of free will, neyther coole them wyth wisedome. For as the Hoppe the poale beeing neuer so hye groweth to the ende, or
20 as the drye Beeche kindled at the roote, neuer leaueth vntill it come to the toppe, or as one droppe of poyson disperseth it selfe into euerye vaine, so affection hauinge caughte holde of my hearte, and the sparkles of loue kindled my liuer, wyll sodeinely, thoughe secretlye flame vp into my heade, and
25 spreade it selfe into euerye sinewe. It is your beautie (pardon my abrupte boldenesse) Ladye that hath taken euery part of mee prisoner, and brought me to this deepe distresse, but seeinge women when one praiseth them for their desertes, deeme that hee flattereth them to obteine his desire, I am
30 heere present to yelde my selfe to such tryall, as your courtesie in this behalfe shall require: Yet will you cõmonly obiect this to such as serue you and sterue to winne your good wil, that hot loue is soone colde, that the Bauin though it bourne bright, is but a blaze, that scaldinge water if it
35 stande a while tourneth almost to yse, that pepper though it be hot in the mouth is colde in the mawe, that the faith of men though it frye in their woordes, it freeseth in theire

works: Which things (*Lucilla*) albeit they be sufficient to reproue the lightnesse of some one, yet can it not conuince
40 euery one of lewdenes, neither ought the constancie of all, to be brought in question through the subtiltie of a fewe. For although the worme entereth almost into euery woode, yet he eateth not the *Ceder* tree: Though the stone *Cylindrus* at euery thunder clappe, rowle from the hill, yet the pure sleeke
45 stone mounteth at the noyse, though the rust fret the hardest steele, yet doth it not eate into the Emeraulde, though *Polypus* chaunge his hew, yet yᵉ *Salamander* keepeth his coulour, though *Proteus* transforme himselfe into euery shape, yet *Pygmalion* retaineth his olde forme, though
50 *Aeneas* were to fickle to *Dido*, yet *Troylys* was to faithfull to *Cræssida*, thoughe others seeme counterfaite in their deedes, yet *Lucilla* perswade your selfe that *Euphues* will bee alwayes curraunt in his dealinges. But as the true golde is tryed by the touch, the pure flinte by the stroke of the yron, so the loyall
55 heart of the faithfull louer, is knowen by the tryall of his Lady: of the which tryall (*Lucilla*) if you shall accompte *Euphues* worthy, assure your selfe, hee wyll bee as readie to offer himselfe a sacrifice for your sweet sake, as your selfe shall bee willinge to employe hym in your seruice. Neyther
60 doth hee desire to bee trusted any way, vntill he shall be tried euery way, neither doth hee craue credite at the first, but a good countenaunce til time his desire shall be made manifest by hys desertes. Thus not blynded by lyght affection, but dazeled with your rare perfection, and boldened by your
65 exceeding courtesie, I haue vnfolded mine entire loue, desiring you hauing so good leasure, to giue so friendly an aunswere, as I may receiue comforte, and you commendacion.

Lucilla although she were contented to heare this desired discourse, yet did shee seeme to bee somewhat displeased:
70 And truely I know not whether it bee peculyar to that sex to dissemble with those, whome they most desire, or whether by craft they haue learned outwardely to loath that, which inwardely they most loue: yet wisely did she cast this in hir head, that if she should yeelde at the first assault he woulde
75 thinke hir a lyght huswife, if she should reiect him scornefully a very haggard, minding therefore that he shoulde neyther take holde of hir promise, neyther vnkindenesse of hir precisenesse, she fedde him indifferently, with hope and dispayre, reason and affection, lyfe and death. Yet in the
80 ende arguing wittilly vpon certeine questions, they fell to suche agreement as poore *Philautus* woulde not haue agreed

vnto if hee had bene present, yet alwayes keepinge the body
vndefiled. And thus shee replyed.

85 Gentleman as you may suspecte me of Idelnesse in giuing
eare to your talke, so may you conuince me of lyghtenesse in
answering such toyes, certes as you haue made mine eares
glowe at the rehearsall of your loue, so haue you galled my
hart with the remembrance of your folly. Though you came
to *Naples* as a straunger, yet were you welcome to my fathers

90 house as a friend. And can you then so much transgresse y^e
bounds of honour (I will not say of honestie) as to solicite a
sute more sharpe to me then deathe? I haue hetherto God
bethancked, liued wythout suspition of lewdenesse, and shall
I nowe incurre the daunger of sensuall lybertie? What hope

95 can you haue to obtayne my loue, seeing yet I coulde neuer
affoord you a good looke? Doe you therefore thinke me
easely entised to the bent of your bow, bicause I was easely
entreated to lysten to your late discourse? Or seeing mee (as
finely you glose) to excell all other in beautie, did you deeme

100 that I would exceed all other in beastlynesse? But yet I am
not angry *Eupheus* but in an agony, for who is shee that will
frette or fume with one that loueth hir, if this loue to delude
mee bee not dissembled. It is that which causeth me most to
feare, not that my beautie is vnknown to my selfe but that

105 commonly we poore wenches are deluded through lyght
beliefe, and ye men are naturally enclined craftely to leade
your lyfe. When the Foxe preacheth the Geese perishe. The
Crocodile shrowdeth greatest treason vnder most pitifull
teares: in a kissing mouth there lyeth a gallyng minde. You

110 haue made so large proffer of your seruice, and so fayre
promises of fidelytie, that were I not ouer charie of mine
honestie, you would inueigle me to shake handes with
chastitie. But certes I will eyther leade a Uirgins lyfe in earth
(though I leade Apes in hell) or els follow thee rather then

115 thy giftes: yet am I neither so precise to refuse thy proffer,
neither so peeuish to disdain thy good will: So excellent
alwayes are ye giftes which are made acceptable by the vertue
of the giuer. I did at the firste entraunce discerne thy loue but
yet dissemble it. Thy wanton glaunces, they scalding sighes,

120 thy louing signes, caused me to blush for shame, and to looke
wanne for feare, least they should be perceiued of any. These
subtill shiftes, these paynted practises (if I were to be wonne)
woulde soone weane mee from the teate of *Vesta*, to the
toyes of *Venus*. Besides this thy comly grace, thy rare

125 quallyties, thy exquisite perfection, were able to moue a

minde halfe mortified to transgresse the bondes of maydenly modestie. But God shielde *Lucilla*, that thou shouldest be so carelesse of thine honour as to commit the state thereoff to a stranger. Learne thou by me *Euphues* to dispise things that
130 be amiable, to forgoe delightfull practises, beleeue mee it is pietie to abstayne from pleasure.

Notes

1 **surprised** 'seized'   The use of the verb *surprised* (OF *surprendre*) to express emotional experience has a very long history in romance writing. The idiom is found in twelfth-century French romance.

2 **sounded** 'swooned'   A variant of 'swoon' recorded from the fourteenth century but surviving only in dialect use.

3 **coryuall**   The earliest recorded use of this adoption from a rare Latin form *corrivalis*. The prefix *co-* serves to intensify the relationship expressed by the base. In the sense 'rival in love', it was obsolete by the end of the seventeenth century.

12 **suspecteth**   Lyly avoids the use of the *-es* inflexion of the third-person singular, present tense, which was by this time common in speech and used by contemporary writers (see Queen Elizabeth's letter and Machyn's diary). It is likely that Lyly's background encouraged him to believe that *-eth* was the established and correct form.

14 **hap** 'fortune' (ON *happ*)   Although Euphuistic style readily employs Latinate vocabulary, such vocabulary is less overwhelming than in fifteenth-century aureate style. Lyly draws on a much wider range of sources, bringing his rarer words into more striking relief.

26 **abrupte** 'unannounced, hasty' (Lat. *abruptus*, past participle of *abrumpere*)   This occurrence pre-dates *OED*'s example in Shakespeare's *Henry IV* Part 1.

32 **sterue** 'die'   Still retains the OE sense 'to die' rather than the narrowed sense 'to die of hunger'. Lyly very rarely writes ‹ar› for earlier ‹er› (cf. *hart*, 88), perhaps regarding it as incorrect, much as he did *-es* for *-eth*.

39 **some one**   The phrase still retains the sense of the OE adjective *sum*, 'a particular (one)'.
conuince 'convict'   Latin *convincere* had the sense in legal contexts of 'to convict of a crime'.

45 **fret** 'eat, consume, corrode' (OE *fretan*)   The senses 'corrode' and 'worry' were figurative extensions of the earlier sense. The former of these was discontinued during the eighteenth century.

53 **curraunt**   This is the earliest recorded occurrence in the sense 'genuine' (obsolete by the mid eighteenth century). It is used of currency in figurative opposition to 'counterfeit'.

56 **of the which tryall**   Lyly employs as a feature of formal expression a type of connection developed in French administrative prose and

first encountered in English in the late fourteenth century.

65 **entire** 'whole and perfect'   The French and Latin antecedents had strong moral associations of purity and perfection, which seem to be implied here.

69 **did shee seeme**   The use of periphrastic *do* serves to place sentence stress on *seeme*, while allowing a verb–subject inversion after the adverb *yet*. Negation is found both with (46) and without (43 and 70) the use of periphrastic *do*.

75 **a lyght huswife**   In early ME this had much the same sense as modern 'housewife' but it developed a pejorative sense by 1546. *OED* records this sense last in 1705. From the mid seventeenth century the pejorative sense had begun to be adopted by the phonetically reduced form *hussy*. The development occurred first in collocations like that found here, where *lyght* means 'foolish and unchaste'.

76 **haggard**   Earlier sense, 'a wild hawk caught in her adult plumage', but here the earliest example of a figurative use also favoured by Shakespeare: 'a wild and intractable person [difficult to catch or retain]'.

86 **toyes** 'trifling speeches'   The history of this word is mysterious. It is recorded once in ME but not again until it becomes very frequent in a range of senses from about 1530. The senses have in common a dismissive attitude to the thing referred to, associations with amusement, and frequently eroticism. It seems to have rapidly become an Elizabethan vogue word, but its origins are obscure.

105 **wenches**   The choice of this word is intended to be endearingly self-deprecating. The word is a shortened form of ME *wenchel*, which meant a young person of either sex. The restriction to females developed early, and two connected pejorative senses developed alongside it from the mid fourteenth century: 'serving girl' and 'wanton woman'. Although the sense 'young girl' continued, it was not unprejudiced by the socially and morally pejorative senses. Therefore, the word is inevitably dismissive.

114 **follow thee**   To this point, Lucilla has studiously used *you* as her address form; she now switches to *thou*. *You* (originally accusative and dative) has replaced *ye* as the ordinary subject form, and this plural form had been used in polite society for formal address since the mid thirteenth century. The switch to the familiar *thou* marks the admission of Lucilla's warm feelings for Euphues.

27   Letters of Queen Elizabeth I and King James VI of Scotland

The Renaissance achieved what in the Middle Ages had very often been merely a pious wish – that the occupant of the national throne should exhibit a respect for learning and an interest in literary culture. Although Queen Elizabeth was by no means the financier of literature that might have been desired, and although she encouraged writers such as John Lyly only to prove reluctant to recompense them, yet her interest and encouragement made patronage available from other sources and ensured the fashionable acceptance of literary production and learning. She herself claims notice as the only monarch other than King Alfred to attempt a translation of Boethius's *De Consolatione Philosophiae*.

She employed her literacy also in writing her own letters, of which many survive including a series written to James VI of Scotland, through which she sought to manipulate diplomatic relations between the two countries. These letters are especially interesting because James's replies often survive also, and these make a striking contrast in both attitude and style as well as in language. Elizabeth's letters are written in the London standard of the day, with one or two peculiarities characteristic of her, such as the tendency to write *the* for both 'they' and the definite article; James's are in the contemporary Scots which had developed from the earlier northern Middle English into a quasi-standard. In the following excerpt, written in 1587, perhaps a week before the execution of Mary, Queen of Scots, Elizabeth seeks to justify her decision to have James's mother put to death. Perhaps reflecting the nature of the circumstances, the style is unusually tortuous, and the first sentence becomes almost unintelligible as the result of a sequence of digressive qualifications. James's letter, which like Elizabeth's is in his own hand, is a draft which may never have been sent but is a well-turned piece of diplomatic correspondence, in effect a letter of credit for its bearer.

A Queen Elizabeth's letter

To my deare brother and cousin,
    the kinge of Skotz.

Be not caried away, my deare brother, with the lewd
perswations of suche, as insteade of infowrming you of my to
nideful and helpeles cause of defending the brethe that God
hath given me, to be better spent than spilt by the bloudy
5 invention of traitors handz, may perhaps make you belive,
that ether the offense was not so great, or if that cannot serue
them, for the over-manifest triall wiche in publik and by the
greatest and most in this land hathe bine manifestly proved,
yet the wyl make that her life may be saved and myne safe,
10 wiche wold God wer true, for whan you make vewe of my
long danger indured thes fowre – wel ny fiue – moneths time
to make a tast of, the greatest witz amongs my owne, and
than of French, and last of you, wyl graunt with me, that if
nide wer not mor than my malice she shuld not have her
15 merite.

    And now for a good conclusion of my long-taried-for
answer. Your commissionars telz me, that I may trust her in
the hande of some indifferent prince, and have all her cousins
and allies promis she wil no more seake my ruine. Deare
20 brother and cousin, way in true and equal balance wither the
lak not muche good ground whan suche stuf serves for ther
bilding. Suppose you I am so mad to truste my life in
anothers hand and send hit out of my owne? If the young
master of Gray, for curring faueur with you, might fortune
25 say hit, yet old master Mylvin hath yeres ynough to teache
him more wisdome than tel a prince of any jugement suche a
contrarious frivolous maimed reason. Let your councelors,
for your honour, discharge ther duty so muche to you as to
declaire the absurditie of such an offer; and, for my part, I do
30 assure myselfe to muche of your wisdome, as, thogh like a
most naturall good son you charged them to seake all meanes
the could deuis with wit or jugement to save her life, yet I
can not, nor do not, allege any fault to you of thes
persuations, for I take hit that you wil remember, that advis
35 or desiars aught ever agree with the surtye of the party sent
to and honor of the sendar, wiche whan bothe you way, I
doute not but your wisdome wil excuse my nide, and waite
my necessitie, and not accuse me ether of malice or of hate.

    And now to conclude. Make account, I pray you, of my

40 firme frindeship loue and care, of which you may make sure
accownt, as one that never mindz to faile from my worde, nor
swarve from our league, but wyl increase, by all good
meanes, any action that may make true shewe of my stable
amitie; from wiche, my deare brother, let no sinistar
45 whisperars, nor busy troblars of princis states, persuade to
leave your surest, and stike to vnstable staies. Suppose them
to be but the ecchos to suche whos stipendaries the be, and
wyl do more for ther gaine than your good. And so, God
hold you ever in his blessed kiping, and make you see your
50 tru frinds. Excuse my not writing sonar, for paine in one of
my yees was only the cause.

Your most assured lovinge sistar and cousin,

ELIZABETH R.

B King James's letter

Madame and dearest sister, Quhairas by your lettir and
bearare, Robert Carey youre seruand and ambassadoure, ye
purge youre self of yone unhappy fact. As, on the one pairt,
consiidering your rank and sex, consanguinitie and longe
5 professed good will to the defunct, together with youre many
and solemne attestationis of youre innocentie, I darr not
wronge you so farre as not to iudge honorablie of youre
unspotted pairt thairin, so, on the other syde, I uishe that
youre honorable behauioure in all tymes heirafter may fully
10 persuaide the quhole uorlde of the same. And, as for my
pairt, I looke that ye will geue me at this tyme suche a full
satisfaction, in all respectis, as sall be a meane to strenthin
and unite this yle, establish and maintaine the treu religion,
and obleig me to be, as of befoire I war, youre most louing.
15
[unsigned]
This bearare hath sumquhat to informe you of in my name,
quhom I neid not desyre you to credit, for ye knou I loue
him.

Notes

Elizabeth

1–2 **lewd perswations**   *lewd* has the OE sense 'ignorant' persuasions.
3 **to nideful and helpeles**   'too necessary and unaided'   The spelling
of *nideful* probably represents the raising of /e:/ to /i:/ which had
taken place during the fifteenth century as part of the Great Vowel
Shift. Cf. *bine* (8).

8 **hathe**   The third-person singular present tense of 'to have' retains the -*th* inflexion long after -*es* has been adopted for other verbs. As late as the eighteenth century this form is found in the written language, although it had vanished from spoken usage.

10 **you**   The use of the plural form of the second-person pronoun is, of course, a normal courtesy in these circles. Note, however, the use of the form *you*. Originally this form was proper to object and oblique functions, but it has now displaced *ye* in use as subject also.

14 **mor than my malice**   *Mor* is used in the sense 'greater' (cf. *most*, 8). Elizabeth argues that necessity is more pressing than her personal feelings in demanding that Mary receive her just deserts. Although this extended sentence breaks down syntactically, various rhetorical devices of balance and repetition help to preserve its sense.

16 **long-taried-for**   Ready productivity in phrasal compounds becomes a striking feature of Elizabethan poetic language also.

17 **telz**   Perhaps simply a slip, since this plural inflexion is understandable only as a feature of northern dialect.

22 **Suppose you**   An interrogative clause is still formed, as in OE and ME, by the reversal of subject–verb order. In less formal contexts, however, the use of the auxiliary *do* is emerging in questions.

24 **curring faueur**   The phrase is first recorded in 1510, but as *curry Favel* from about 1400. The original meaning, used figuratively, was to groom or smooth down the chestnut horse (called Favel). The word *favel* consequently developed associations with flattery and duplicity. Formal resemblance between *favel* and *favor* encouraged the development of the modern phrase.

24–25 **fortune say hit**   'chance to say it'   The plain infinitive is used rather more widely than in Modern English. Cf. *than tel* (26).

29–30 **I do assure**   The use of the *do*- periphrasis seems here to carry some suggestion of a marked assertion: 'I am too confident. . .'.

37 **waite**   'consider'   This sense is archaic. *OED* does not record it after 1430.

42 **swarve**   (OE *sweorfan*). The spelling ‹ar› for earlier ‹er› demonstrates that the associated sound change had penetrated into the highest circles. But the spelling is rarer in Elizabeth's letters than in Machyn's diary.

50 **my not writing**   The creation of nominal from a negated verb illustrates a further facet of Elizabethan freedom in language use.

James

1 **Quhairas**   The northern ME spelling ‹quh› of the reflex of OE ‹hw› is the standard spelling in Scots. In the spelling ‹ai›, as also the spellings ‹ei› (*heirafter*) and ‹oi› (*befoire*), *i* indicates the length of the preceding vowel.

2 **ye**   James uses the earlier form of pronoun in contrast to *you* in Elizabeth's letter.

3 **yone**   Developed from the rare OE adjective *geon*. The word is predominantly, although not exclusively northern in ME.

12 **sall**   Forms with initial *s* in ME are generally found to the north of a line from Morecambe Bay to the Wash.

strenthin   The use of ⟨i⟩ or ⟨y⟩ spellings in the unstressed vowels of inflexions is found from the north Midlands northwards. The loss of velarity in the nasal is widespread.

14 **I war**   (ON *váru*). The form belongs to the areas of heavier Scandinavian settlement.

28 George Puttenham, The Arte of English Poesie

The Arte of English Poesie appeared anonymously in 1589 but is attributed to Puttenham (*c*. 1529–1591) with reasonable certainty. The book is thought to have existed in manuscript for as long as two decades before its appearance. It consists of three parts, the first a review of the history and purpose of poetry in the process of civilisation, in which Puttenham represents Chaucer as a learned associate and beneficiary of Richard II, scorns Skelton as a satirical clown, and praises Sir Philip Sydney and 'that other Gentleman who wrate the late Shepheardes Callender'. Book II is concerned with form and metre, and the third book with the ornaments of style. What he has to say on this last topic is drawn from the Latin rhetorical tradition, but he makes some effort to accommodate it to English practice, and enlivens his teaching with anecdotes; the principle of stylistic decorum is illustrated by the story of an inappropriate ale-house tale delivered as a speech at the opening of Parliament by a Yorkshire MP.

Whether or not the anecdote is apocryphal is irrelevant to its purpose of demonstrating provincial ineptitude in eloquence. The underlying suggestion is taken up overtly in the discussion of the language most suited to poetry, which is printed below. The passage presents evidence that the earlier medieval assumption of the equality of English varieties – already being questioned in the fourteenth century – was approaching its end. English was divisible geographically and socially as well as according to technical domain (cf. Excerpt 24). It was divided up along lines already laid down in the treatment by Latin rhetoric of the subject of verbal choice, where the poet was urged to avoid words characteristic of the provinces, the lower classes of Roman society, extreme archaisms, inappropriate domains and genres.

Of language

Speach is not naturall to man sauing for his onely habilitie to speake, and that he is by kinde apt to vtter all his conceits with sounds and voyces diuersified many maner of wayes, by meanes of the many and fit instruments he hath by nature to
5 that purpose, as a broad and voluble tong, thinne and mouable lippes, teeth euē and not shagged, thick ranged, a

223

round vaulted pallate, and a long throte, besides an excellent
capacitie of wit that maketh him more disciplinable and
imitatiue then any other creature: then as to the forme and
10 action of his speach, it commeth to him by arte and teaching,
and by vse or exercise. But after a speach is fully fashioned to
the common vnderstanding, and accepted by consent of a
whole countrey and natiō, it is called a language, and
receaueth none allowed alteration, but by extraordinary
15 occasions by little and little, as it were insensibly bringing in
of many corruptiōs that creepe along with the time; of all
which matters, we haue more largely spoken in our bookes of
the originals and pedigree of the English tong. Then when I
say language, I meane the speach wherein the Poet or maker
20 writeth be it Greek or Latine, or as our case is the vulgar
English, and when it is peculiar vnto a countrey it is called
the mother speach of that people: the Greekes terme it
Idioma: so is ours at this day the Norman English. Before the
Conquest of the Normans it was the Anglesaxon, and before
25 that the British, which as some will, is at this day, the Walsh,
or as others affirme the Cornish: I for my part thinke neither
of both, as they be now spoken and pronounced. This part in
our maker or Poet must be heedyly looked vnto, that it be
naturall, pure, and the most vsuall of all his countrey: and for
30 the same purpose rather that which is spoken in the kings
Court, or in the good townes and Cities within the land, then
in the marches and frontiers, or in port townes, where
straungers haunt for traffike sake, or yet in Vniuersities
where Schollers vse much peeuish affectation of words out of
35 the primatiue languages, or finally, in any vplandish village or
corner of a Realme, where is no resort but of poore rusticall
or vnciuill people: neither shall he follow the speach of a
craftes man or carter, or other of the inferiour sort, though
he be inhabitant or bred in the best towne and Citie in this
40 Realme, for such persons doe abuse good speaches by strange
accents or ill shapen soundes, and false ortographie. But he
shall follow generally the better brought vp sort, such as the
Greekes call [charientes] men ciuill and graciously behauoured
and bred. Our maker therfore at these dayes shall not follow
45 Piers plowman nor Gower nor Lydgate nor yet Chaucer, for
their language is now out of vse with vs: neither shall he take
the termes of Northern-men, such as they vse in dayly talke,
whether they be noble men or gentlemen, or of their best
clarkes all is a matter: nor in effect any speach vsed beyond
50 the riuer of Trent, though no man can deny but that theirs is

the purer English Saxon at this day, yet it is not so Courtly
nor so currant as our Southerne English is, no more is the far
Westerne mãs speach: ye shall therfore take the vsuall speach
of the Court, and that of London and the shires lying about
55 London within lx. myles, and not much aboue. I say not this
but that in euery shyre of England there be gentlemen and
others that speake but specially write as good Southerne as
we of Middlesex or Surrey do, but not the common people of
euery shire, to whom the gentlemen, and also their learned
60 clarkes do for the most part condescend, but herein we are
already ruled by th'English Dictionaries and other bookes
written by learned men, and therefore it needeth none other
direction in that behalfe. Albeit peraduenture some small
admonition be not impertinent, for we finde in our English
65 writers many wordes and speaches amendable, and ye shall
see in some many inkhorne termes so ill affected brought in
by men of learning as preachers and schoolemasters: and
many straunge termes of other languages by Secretaries and
Marchaunts and trauailours, and many darke wordes and not
70 vsuall nor well sounding, though they be dayly spoken in
Court. Wherefore great heed must be taken by our maker in
this point that his choise be good. And peraduenture the
writer hereof be in that behalfe no lesse faultie then any
other, vsing many straunge and vnaccustomed wordes and
75 borrowed from other languages: and in that respect him selfe
no meete Magistrate to reforme the same errours in any other
person, but since he is not vnwilling to acknowledge his owne
fault, and can the better tell how to amend it, he may seeme
a more excusable correctour of other mens: he intendeth
80 therefore for an indifferent way and vniuersall benefite to
taxe him selfe first and before any others.
　These be words vsed by th'author in this present treatise,
sciētificke, but with some reason, for it aūswereth the word
mechanicall, which no other word could haue done so properly,
85 for when hee spake of all artificers which rest either in
science or in handy craft, it followed necessarilie that
scientifique should be coupled with *mechanicall*: or els neither
of both to haue bene allowed, but in their places: a man of
science liberall, and a handicrafts man, which had not bene so
90 cleanly a speech as the other *Maior-domo*: in truth this word
is borrowed of the *Spaniard* and *Italian*, and therefore new
and not vsuall, but to them that are acquainted with the
affaires of Court: and so for his iolly magnificence (as this
case is) may be accepted among Courtiers, for whom this is

95 specially written. A man might haue said in steade of *Maior-domo*, the French word (*maistre d'hostell*) but ilfauouredly, or the right English word (*Lord Steward*). But me thinks for my owne opinion this word *Maior-domo* though he be borrowed, is more acceptable thā any of the rest, other men may iudge
100 otherwise. *Politien*, this word also is receiued from the Frenchmen, but at this day vsuall in Court and with all good Secretaries: and cannot finde an English word to match him, for to haue said a man politique, had not bene so wel: bicause in trueth that had bene no more than to haue said a ciuil
105 person. *Politien* is rather a surueyour of ciuilitie than ciuil, and a publique minister or Counseller in the state. Ye haue also this worde *Conduict*, a French word, but well allowed of vs, and long since vsuall, it soundes somewhat more than this word (leading) for it is applied onely to the leading of a
110 Captaine, and not as a little boy should leade a blinde man, therefore more proper to the case when he saide, *conduict* of whole armies: ye finde also this word *Idiome*, taken from the Greekes, yet seruing aptly, when a man wanteth to expresse so much vnles it be in two words, which surplussage to
115 auoide, we are allowed to draw in other words single, and asmuch significatiue: this word *significatiue* is borrowed of the Latine and French, but to vs brought in first by some Noble-mans Secretarie, as I thinke, yet doth so well serue the turne, as it could not now be spared: and many more like vsurped
120 Latine and French words: as, *Methode, methodicall, placation, function, assubtiling, refining, compendious, prolixe, figuratiue, inueigle.* A terme borrowed of our common Lawyers. *impression*, also a new terme, but well expressing the matter, and more than our English word. These words, *Numerous,*
125 *numerositee, metricall, harmonicall*, but they cannot be refused, specially in this place for description of the arte. Also ye finde these words, *penetrate, penetrable, indignitie*, which I cannot see how we may spare them, whatsoeuer fault wee finde with Ink-horne termes: for our speach
130 wanteth wordes to such sence so well to be vsed: yet in steade of *indignitie*, yee haue vnworthinesse: and for *penetrate*, we may say *peerce*, and that a French terme also, or *broche*, or enter into with violence, but not so well sounding as *penetrate*. Item, *sauage*, for wilde: *obscure*, for darke. Item
135 these words, *declination, delineation, dimention*, are scholasticall termes in deede, and yet very proper. But peraduenture (and I could bring a reason for it) many other like words borrowed out of the Latin and French, were not so well to be

allowed by vs, as these words, *audacious*, for bold: *facunditie*,
140 for eloquence: *egregious*, for great or notable: *implete*, for
replenished: *attemptat*, for attempt: *compatible*, for agreeable
in nature, and many more. But herein the noble Poet *Horace*
hath said inough to satisfie vs all in these few verses.

> *Multa renascentur quæ iam cecidere cadentque,*
145 > *Quæ nunc sunt in honore vocabula si volet vsus*
> *Quem penes arbitrium est & vis & norma loquendi.*

Which I haue thus englished, but nothing with so good grace,
nor so briefly as the Poet wrote.

> *Many a word yfalne shall eft arise*
150 > *And such as now bene held in hiest prise*
> *Will fall as fast, when vse and custome will*
> *Onely vmpiers of speach, for force and skill.*

Notes

1 **onely** 'unique'   The suffix *-līc* forms both adjectives and adverbs
in OE. A few *-ly* adjectives (*comely, costly, ghostly*) survive in
modern English.

5 **voluble** 'moving easily and quickly'   The earliest record of this
sense.

6 **shagged** 'jagged'   Again the earliest record of this sense.

8–9 **disciplinable and imitatiue** 'amenable to teaching and capable of
imitating'   Both are Franco-Latin types. The suffix *-able* was
perceived to be stylistically marked, since it was used only with
Romance bases in ME. The suffix *-ative* was not productive in ME
except in the word *talkative*, first recorded in 1420. The sense of
imitative here is not recorded by *OED* before the mid eighteenth
century.

13 **whole countrey . . .**   Puttenham is defining, in this distinction
between *language* and *speach*, much what modern linguists would
call 'standard language' and 'speech'.

14 **none allowed**   The form of negative with retention of final *-n* (OE
nān) occurs before a following vowel.

19 **maker**   The word is used as a synonym of *poete*, as Puttenham
explains in his opening sentence. The word *poete* is derived from the
Greek *poiein* 'to make'.

26–27 **neither of both** 'neither of the two'.

28 **heedly** 'with attention'   Obsolete by the mid seventeenth century.

34 **peeuish affectation**   The word *peeuish* is of unknown etymology; it
appears first before 1400 but becomes common only in the sixteenth
century. Puttenham regards the learned love of recondite archaisms
as perverse.

36–37 **rusticall . . . vnciuill** 'country . . . unrefined'   The use of these words echoes a Latin contrast between coarse country-dwellers (cf. *rustici*) and urbane and sophisticated city-dwellers (*cives*, *civilis*). The form *rusticall* is derived from French or medieval Latin.

41 **ortographie**   Used in the sixteenth century of both pronunciation and spelling.

42 **brought vp**   First used in the sense 'to raise (a child)' about 1400.

52 **currant** 'universally acceptable'   The image is of coinage or currency.

53 **ye**   Puttenham uses the earlier form of the second-person plural pronoun. Contemporaries frequently use *you*, a form derived from the OE dative and accusative.

57 **specially write as good Southerne**   The ability to write the London language was apparent already among outsiders in the fourteenth century. Immigrants tended to modify their spellings towards those acceptable in the city. The claim that outsiders adopted the southern pronunciation should be regarded sceptically. Sir Walter Raleigh, a favourite at the royal court, spoke with a broad Devonshire accent. Nevertheless, this passage is of great importance, since it is an early statement of the association of dialect speech with social status.

61 **English Dictionaries**   The first true English dictionary was Robert Cawdrey's *Table Alphabeticall* (1604). Puttenham is referring to dictionaries as guides not to word meaning but to spelling and pronunciation. Such works were produced by Sir Thomas Smith, *De recta et emendata Linguae Graecae* (1568), and John Hart, *An Orthographie* (1569), at about the time Puttenham was writing.

68 **straunge termes** 'foreign words or phrases'.

69 **darke wordes** 'words whose meaning is unclear'.

83 **scientificke** 'concerned with the liberal arts' (as opposed to crafts) (Latin and French)   The earliest recorded occurrence of the word. The word *mechanicall* is recorded from 1432.

90 **Maior-domo**   The first recorded occurrence of the word.

93 **iolly**   Used from the early decades of the sixteenth century as a vaguely approving epithet. Cf. modern 'jolly good'. Puttenham is here making the point that certain foreign and unusual terms are appropriate to and unremarkable in certain domains and contexts.

97 **me thinks**   An impersonal construction. The third-person singular is here written -*s* (*soundes*, 108). Puttenham usually has -*eth*.

98–102 **he . . . him**   No personification is intended. Puttenham tends to use *he* and *him* in preference to *it* when the pronoun refers anaphorically (backwards) to the topic of the sentence.

100 **Politien**   A common word in Elizabethan texts, but first recorded only in 1588. *Surueyour* here means 'supervisor' and *ciuilitie* means 'government, political system'.

107 **Conduict** 'command (of an army)'   The word was used in the later fifteenth century in this sense. Earlier ME *conduite* was derived from French, but in both French and English the *c* of Latin *conductus* was restored in the fifteenth century. The form here

derives from Latinised French; the modern form *conduct* is direct from Latin, and the modern *conduit* through ME from earlier French.

119–20 **vsurped Latine and French**   All these words were clearly recognisable to Puttenham as of foreign origin, but not all are recent borrowings: *compendious, prolixe, figuratiue, metricall, penetrable, inueigle* are all learned fourteenth- or fifteenth-century borrowings. *Impression*, said to be a new term, is recorded from the late fourteenth century. *Numerositee*, 'rhythmical quality', and *assubtiling*, 'making subtle', are first recorded here.

126 **arte**   The art of poetical composition. These are technical terms.

149 **yfalne**   Puttenham's verse makes liberal use of archaisms. This past participle has the southern ME prefix *y-*. Both *eft* and *held in . . . prise* are by now poetic (?Chaucerian) archaisms.

29   Thomas Nashe

Thomas Nashe (1567–1601) was born in Lowestoft, attended St
John's College, Cambridge, where, as 'a little ape', he says, he
thought Lyly's *Euphues* was the last word; but he entered
London literary society in 1588, and by 1592 had learned to scorn
Euphuism, seeking his own mode of expression. His career was a
stormy one since many of his writings were polemic or satirical in
tone. He was involved in the Marprelate Controversy on the side
of the bishops, but more notable is his continuing feud with
Gabriel Harvey which expressed itself in a heated debate on
literary style and mutual accusations of the use of Inkhorn terms
(see Excerpt 24). In *The Unfortunate Traveller* (1594) he presents
a caricature of inflated oratory in the person of a 'bursten belly
inkhorne orator called *Vanderhulke*', a luminary of the University of Wittenberg (McKerrow 247–9). Nashe denies, in his
introductory address to readers of the second edition of his
Christs Teares over Jerusalem (1594), that this has any connection
with any English university man save perhaps Harvey, and goes
on to discuss the accusations which have been levelled against his
own style in that work, which is particularly free in lexical
creativity. That defence forms the first excerpt. The second
excerpt is an illustration of his descriptive style in *The
Unfortunate Traveller*, in which he relates the picaresque
adventures of one Jack Wilton, an adventurer living on his wits.
The passage forms part of his account of the seductive luxury of
life among the wealthy inhabitants of contemporary Rome.

A   From the Preface to **Christs Teares over Jerusalem**

The ploddinger sort of vnlearned Zoilists about London
exclaim that it is a puft-vp stile, and full of prophane
eloquence: others obiect vnto me the multitude of my
boystrous compound wordes, and the often coyning of
5 Italionate verbes which end all in Ize, as mummianize,
tympanize, tirannize. To the first array of my clumperton
Antigonists this I answer, that my stile is no otherwise puft
up, then any mãs should be which writes with any Spirite; and
whom would not such a deuine subiect put a high rauishte
10 Spirite into? For the prophanesse of my eloquence, so they

may tearme the eloquence of Saint *Austen, Ierome, Chrysostome,* prophane, since none of them but takes vnto him farre more liberty of Tropes, Figures, and Metaphors, and alleadging Heathen examples and Histories.

15   To the second rancke of reprehenders that complain of my boystrous compound wordes, and ending my Italionate coyned verbs all in Ize, thus I replie: That no winde that blowes strong but is boystrous, no speech or wordes of any power or force to confute or perswade but mustbee swelling

20   and boystrous. For the compounding of my wordes, therein I imitate rich men who, hauing gathered store of white single money together, conuert a number of those small little scutes into great peeces of gold, such as double Pistols and Portugues. Our English tongue of all languages most

25   swarmeth with the single money of monasillables, which are the onely scandall of it. Bookes written in them and no other seeme like Shop-keepers boxes, that containe nothing else saue halfe-pence, three-farthings, and two-pences. Therefore what did me I, but hauing a huge heape of those worthlesse

30   shreds of small English in my *Pia maters* purse, to make the royaller shew with them to mens eyes, had thē to the compounders immediately, and exchanged them foure into one, and others into more, according to the Greek, French, Spanish, and Italian?

35   Come, my maisters, inure your mouths to it, and neuer trust me but when you haue tride the commodity of carrying much in a small roome, you will, like the Apothecaries, vse more compounds then simples, and graft wordes as men do their trees to make them more fruitfull. My vbraided

40   Italionate verbes are the least crime of a thousand, since they are growne in generall request with euery good Poet.

Besides, they carrie farre more state with them then any other, and are not halfe so harsh in their desinence as the old hobling English verbes ending in R; they expresse more then

45   any other verbes whatsoeuer, and their substantiues would be quite barraine of verbs but for that ending. This word Mummianizd in the beginning of my first Epistle is shrewdly called in question; for no other reason that I can conceiue, but that his true deriuatiue, which is Mummy, is somewhat

50   obscure also: To Phisitions and their confectioners it is as familiar as Mumchaunce amongest Pages, being nothing else but mans flesh long buried and broyled in the burning sands of Arabia. Hereupon I haue taken vp this phrase of Ierusalems Mummianized earth, (as much to say as Ierusalems

55 earth manured with mans flesh.) Expresse who can the same
substance so briefly in any other word but that. A man may
murder any thing if hee list in the mouthing, and grinde it to
powder extempore betwixt a huge paire of iawes: but let a
quest of calme censors goe vpon it twixt the houres of sixe
60 and seauen in the morning, and they will in their graue
wisdoms subscribe to it as tollerable and significant.

B   From **The Unfortunate Traveller**

To tell you of the rare pleasures of their gardens, theyr
bathes, theyr vineyardes, theyr galleries, were to write a
seconde part of the gorgeous Gallerie of gallant deuices.
Why, you should not come into anie mannes house of
5 account, but hee hadde fish-pondes and little orchardes on
the toppe of his leads. If by raine or any other meanes those
ponds were so full they need to be slust or let out, euen of
their superfluities they made melodious vse, for they had
great winde instruments in stead of leaden spoutes, that went
10 duly on consort, onely with this waters rumbling discent. I
sawe a summer banketting house belonging to a merchaunt,
that was the meruaile of the world, and could not be matcht
except God should make another paradise. It was builte
round of greene marble like a Theater with-out: within there
15 was a heauen and earth comprehended both vnder one roofe;
the heauen was a cleere ouerhanging vault of christall,
wherein the Sunne and Moone and each visible Starre had
his true similitude, shine, scituation, and motion, and, by
what enwrapped arte I cannot conceiue, these spheares in
20 their proper orbes obserued their circular wheelinges and
turnings, making a certaine kinde of soft angelical murmering
musicke in their often windings and going about; which
musick the philosophers say in the true heauen, by reason of
the grosenes of our senses, we are not capable of. For the
25 earth, it was counterfeited in that liknes that Adam lorded
out it before his fall. A wide vast spacious roome it was, such
as we would conceit prince Arthurs hall to be, where he
feasted all his knights of the round table together euerie
penticost. The flore was painted with the beautifullest flouers
30 that euer mans eie admired; which so linealy were delineated
that he that viewd them a farre off, and had not directly stood
poaringly ouer them, would haue sworne they had liued in
deede. The wals round about were hedgde with Oliues and

palme trees, and all other odoriferous fruit-bearing plants;
35 which at anie solemne intertainment dropt mirrhe and
frankensense. Other trees, that bare no fruit, were set in iust
order one against another, and diuided the roome into a
number of shadie lanes, leauing but one ouerspreading pine
tree arbor, where wee sate and banketted. On the wel
40 clothed boughs of this conspiracie of pine trees against the
resembled Sun beames, were pearcht as many sortes of shrill
breasted birdes as the Summer hath allowed for singing men
in hir siluane chappels. Who though there were bodies
without soules, and sweete resembled substances without
45 sense, yet by the mathemeticall experimentes of long siluer
pipes secretlye inrinded in the intrailes of the boughs
whereon they sate, and vndiscerneablie conuaid vnder their
bellies into their small throats sloaping, they whistled and
freely carold theyr naturall field note. Neyther went those
50 siluer pipes straight, but, by many edged vnsundred writhings
and crankled wanderinges a side, strayed from bough to
bough into an hundred throats. But into this siluer pipe so
writhed and wandering aside, if anie demand how the wind
was breathed; Forsoth ye tail of the siluer pipe stretcht it selfe
55 into the mouth of a great paire of belowes, where it was close
soldered, and bailde about with yron, it coulde not stirre or
haue anie vent betwixt. Those bellowes with the rising and
falling of leaden plummets wounde vp on a wheele, dyd beate
vp and downe vncessantly, and so gathered in wind, seruing
60 with one blast all the snarled pipes to and fro of one tree at
once. But so closely were all those organizing implements
obscured in the corpulent trunks of the trees, that euerie man
there present renounst coniectures of art, and sayd it was
done by inchantment.
65 One tree for his fruit bare nothing but inchained chirping
birdes, whose throates beeing conduit pipt with squared
narrowe shels, and charged siring-wise with searching sweet
water driuen in by a little wheele for the nonce, that fed it a
farre of, made a spirting sound, such as chirping is, in bubling
70 vpwards through the rough crannies of their closed bills.
Vnder tuition of the shade of euerie tree that I haue
signified to be in this round hedge, on delightful leuie
cloisters, lay a wylde tyranous beast asleepe all prostrate;
vnder some, two together, as the Dogge nusling his nose
75 vnder the necke of the Deare, the Wolfe glad to let the
Lambe lye vpon hym to keepe him warme, the Lyon suffering
the Asse to cast hys legge ouer him, preferring one honest

vnmannerly friende before a number of croutching picke-
thankes. No poysonous beast there reposed, (poyson was not
80 before our parent *Adam* transgressed.) There were no
sweete-breathing Panthers that would hyde their terrifying
heads to betray; no men-imitating *Hyænaes* that chaunged
their sexe to seeke after bloud. Wolues as now when they are
hungrie eate earth, so then did they feed on earth only, and
85 abstained from innocent flesh. The Vnicorne did not put his
horne into the streame to chase awaye venome before hee
dronke, for then there was no suche thing extant in the water
or on the earth. Serpents were as harmlesse to mankinde as
they are still one to another: the rose had no cankers, the
90 leues no caterpillers, the sea no *Syrens*, the earth no vsurers.
Goats then bare wooll, as it is recorded in *Sicily* they doo yet.
The torride Zone was habitable: only Iayes loued to steale
gold and siluer to build their nests withall, and none cared for
couetous clientrie, or runing to the Indies. As the Elephant
95 vnderstands his countrey speach, so euerie beast vnderstood
what man spoke. The ant did not hoord vp against winter, for
there was no winter, but a perpetuall spring, as *Ouid* sayth.
No frosts to make the greene almound tree counted rash and
improuident, in budding soonest of all other; or the mulberie
100 tree a strange polititian, in blooming late and ripening early.
The peach tree at the first planting was fruitfull and
wholsome, whereas now, till it be transplanted, it is
poisonous and hatefull: young plants for their sap had balme,
for their yeolow gumme glistering amber. The euening deawd
105 not water on flowers, but honnie. Such a golden age, such a
good age, such an honest age was set forth in this banketting
house.

Notes

Christs Teares over Jerusalem

1 **Zoilists**   Zoilus was a Greek grammarian and critic of the fourth
century BC, who was famous for his harsh criticism of Homer. In
Elizabethan times the name came to mean an ill-disposed critic.
4 **boystrous compound wordes**   Compounding and derivation of a
wide variety of kinds are characteristic of Elizabethan usage. The
word *boystrous*, 'rough, coarse', is more than anything else a value
judgement on compounds found unpleasing.
5 **Ize**   This verb-forming suffix was familiar enough in English from
French sources, from which it is adopted in the form *-ise*. The *-ize*
spelling derives from Latin more commonly than Italian. Of the

words cited, *tirannize* existed in the French form and Nashe had been anticipated in the Latin form by both Spenser and Shakespeare. The other two ('connected with a mummy' and 'to puff up') seem to be Nashe's coinages.

6 **clumperton** 'clownish'   Recorded from 1534.

8 **which writes**   Nashe uses *which* and *whom* consecutively as personal relatives. In the next clause the preposition *into* goes with *whom*. Except for *hath* and *doth*, he normally uses the *-es* form of the third-person singular, present tense.

22 **scutes** 'a coin of small value'   But earlier used for the French *écu*, so called because of the shield stamped on it. The word derives from Anglo-French *scute* and Med. Lat. *scutum*.

30 **Pia maters purse** 'brain'   The *pia mater* is the membrane surrounding the brain. A Latinisation of an originally Arabic phrase meaning 'tender mother'. Recorded in technical contexts from 1400.

39 **vbraided**   The spelling represents a common assimilation.

43 **desinence**   A technical grammatical term for the ending or suffix of a word. This is the earliest recorded occurrence in English.

47 **shrewdly** 'disagreeably'   The ME sense.

51 **mumchance**   Originally a game of dice (MLG *mummenschanze*), but had already come to mean a dumb show or mumming, and by extension, to 'play mumchance' meant to keep silent.

57 **if hee list** 'if it pleases him'   The grammar of impersonal constructions is no longer fully understood, so the nominative equivalent of *he* has replaced the dative *him*.

58 **extempore** 'on the spot' (Lat. *ex tempore*, 'arising out of the time or moment')   The word had been in use in English for about fifty years.

The Unfortunate Traveller

4 **anie mannes**, etc.   The syntax remains that of OE rather than that of the modern group genitive 'any man of account's house'.

7 **slust** 'sluiced'   The spelling with a final *-t* of the past participles (and also preterites) of Weak verbs whose stem ends in a voiceless consonant is common in Nashe. This habit was still in use in some circles in the nineteenth century.

18 **his**   Not personification, but the use of the common masculine and neuter form of the genitive third-person pronoun.

29 **beautifullest**   The modern English rule by which adjectives of more than two syllables form comparatives and superlatives by the use of *more* and *most* has not yet become established.

35 **intertainment**   The distribution of the *in-* and *en-* forms of the prefix is variable. See also *intrailes* (46), *inchantment* (64).

40 **conspiracie** 'collection, combination'   The sense is extended here a little beyond what is usual.

41–42 **shrill breasted**   Although here printed as two words, the pattern is that of a very common type of compound which was highly productive in the sixteenth century. Such compounds are interpreted as extensions into adjectival use (by the suffix -ed) of earlier nominal compounds of the type *redcoat*. Nashe's conscious creativity follows an established pattern of the time.

44 **resembled** 'simulated'   The use of the native suffix -ed in a function similar to that of the Latin passive participle ending -atus leads to the formation of numerous -ed modifiers from both verbs and nouns in Elizabethan English.

46 **inrinded** 'placed within the bark'   The OE word *rind* has been gradually replaced by the Scandinavian borrowing, *bark*, when referring to trees. The word was coined by Nashe.

51 **crankled** 'zig-zag'   The earliest occurrence of a rare word, etymologically related to both 'crank' and 'crinkled'.

71 **tuition** 'protection'   Once again the sense is extended from the usual contemporary senses by the non-personal agent.

78–79 **picke-thankes** 'flatterers'   The compound is recorded from 1412.

81 **sweete-breathing**   This type of adjectival compound, in which the present participle follows an adverb or adjective, has been common since the sixteenth century.

82 **men-imitating**   As with the previous type, compound adjectives with a noun followed by the present participle are found in OE and ME, but the major productivity of the type is from the sixteenth century.

30 Shakespeare, *Love's Labour's Lost*, Act V, scene i

The earliest surviving text of *Love's Labour's Lost* is the quarto dated 1598, which is claimed to be an edition 'newly corrected and augmented' of one apparently lost. Shakespeare's plays were produced for performance and the history of their texts is often complex. In many cases they first appeared in what have become known as 'bad' quartos – carelessly produced copies pirated from productions of the play or from the memory of actors. Such editions were then often followed by corrected, authorised versions, the 'good' quartos; and finally, after Shakespeare's death, his works were collected by his associates into the First Folio of 1623. The 'good' quarto of 1598 was probably assembled from Shakespeare's own papers, but although it may therefore be expected to represent his spelling as closely as any of the plays, this does not mean that it is an exact replica of what Shakespeare wrote. Compositors in Elizabethan times felt free to impose their own practices upon the author's text, so that although the text printed here corrects obvious compositor's errors in typesetting (which are particularly common in this play), it is impossible to determine which among acceptable variants are the spellings of the author's manuscript.

William Shakespeare (1564–1616) was the son of a prosperous glover and wool dealer and received an education at the King's New School in his home town of Stratford-upon-Avon. There is no evidence that he proceeded to any form of higher education. As a grammar-school boy he would have been instructed in the classics of Latin literature, trained in Latin grammar, and grounded in rhetoric. In the later stages he would have been expected to put this theory into practice, composing orations and formal letters based upon the rules of Latin literacy. Both analysis and practice in composition must have awakened him to the discrepancies between Latin and English, and to the debates about the status and improvement of English which occupied the attention of others with similar, and more extended, training. The question of Inkhorn terms and the refurbishment of English from Latin lies behind this scene in *Love's Labour's Lost*. Indeed, it has been suggested that the character Boy (Moth in the Folio) is an allusion to Nashe, and, less persuasively, that Armado and Pedant (Holofernes) may be related to Harvey.

Enter Holofernes the Pedant, Nathaniel the Curat, and Anthony Dull

PEDANT *Satis quid sufficit.*

NATHANIEL I prayse God for you sir, your reasons at Dinner haue been sharpe and sententious: pleasant without scurillitie, wittie without affection, audatious without
5 impudencie, learned without opinion, and strange without heresie: I did conuerse this quondam day with a companion of the kings, who is intituled, nominated, or called, *Don Adriano de Armatho.*

PEDANT *Noui hominum tanquam te,* His humour is loftie, his
10 discourse peremptorie: his tongue fyled, his eye ambitious, his gate maiesticall, and his generall behauiour vaine, rediculous, and thrasonicall. He is too picked, to spruce, too affected, to od as it were, too peregrinat as I may call it.

15 NATHANIEL A most singuler and choyce Epithat,
Draw-out his Table-booke

PEDANT He draweth out the thred of his verbositie, finer then the staple of his argument. I abhorre such phanatticall phantasims, such insociable and poynt deuise companions, such rackers of ortagriphie, as to speake dout *sine* b, when
20 he should say doubt; det, when he shold pronounce debt; d e b t, not d e t: he clepeth a Calfe, Caufe: halfe, haufe: neighbour *vocatur* nebour; neigh abreuiated ne: this is abhominable, which he would call abbominable, it insinuateth me of *insanire: ne intelligis domine,* to make
25 frantique lunatique?

NATHANIEL *Laus deo, bone intelligo.*

PEDANT *Bone? Boon for boon prescian,* a little scratcht, twil serue.

Enter Armado the Bragart, Moth his Boy, and Costard the Clowne

NATHANIEL *Videsne quis venit?*
30 PEDANT *Video, et gaudio.*

ARMADO (*to Moth*) Chirra.

PEDANT (*to Nathaniel*) *Quare* Chirra, not Sirra?

ARMADO Men of peace well incontred.

PEDANT Most millitarie sir salutation.

35 BOY (*aside to Costard*) They haue been at a great feast of Languages, and stolne the scraps.

CLOWNE (*aside to Moth*) O they haue lyud long on the almsbasket of wordes. I maruaile thy M. hath not eaten thee for a worde, for thou art not so long by the head as

40   *honorificabilitudinitatibus*: Thou art easier swallowed then
a flapdragon.
BOY (*aside to Costard*) Peace, the peale begins.
ARMADO (*to Holofernes*) Mounsier, are you not lettred?
BOY Yes yes, he teaches boyes the Horne-booke: What is Ab
45   speld backward with the horne on his head?
PEDANT Ba, *puericia* with a horne added.
BOY Ba most seely Sheepe, with a horne: you heare his
learning.
PEDANT *Quis quis* thou Consonant?
50   BOY The last of the fiue Vowels if You repeate them, or the
fift if I.
PEDANT I will repeate them: a e I.
BOY The Sheepe, the other two concludes it o u.
ARMADO Now by the sault waue of the meditaranium, a
55   sweete tutch, a quicke venewe of wit, snip snap, quicke and
home, it reioiceth my intellect, true wit.
BOY Offerd by a childe to an old man: which it wit-old.
PEDANT What is the figure? What is the figure?
BOY Hornes.
60   PEDANT Thou disputes like an Infant: goe whip thy Gigg.
BOY Lende me your Horne to make one, and I will whip
about your Infamie *circum circa* a gigge of a Cuckolds
horne.
CLOWNE And I had but one peny in the world thou shouldst
65   haue it to buy Ginger bread: (*Giuing money*) Holde, there
is the verie Remuneration I had of thy Maister, thou
halfepennie purse of wit, thou Pidgin-egge of discretion. O
and the heauens were so pleased, that thou wart but my
Bastard; What a ioyfull father wouldest thou make me? Go
70   to, thou hast it *ad dungil* at the fingers ends, as they say.
PEDANT Oh I smell false Latine, *dunghel* for *vnguem*.
ARMADO Arts-man *preambulat*, we will be singuled from the
barbarous. Do you not educate youth at the Charg-house
on the top of the Mountaine?
75   PEDANT Or *Mons* the hill.
ARMADO At your sweete pleasure, for the Mountaine.
PEDANT I do *sans question*.
ARMADO Sir, it is the Kings most sweete pleasur and
affection, to congratulate the Princesse at her Pauilion, in
80   the *posteriors* of this day, which the rude multitude call the
after-noone.
PEDANT The *posterior* of the day, most generous sir, is liable,
congruent, and measurable for the after noone: the worde

is well culd, choise, sweete, and apt I do assure you sir, I
85 do assure.

ARMADO Sir, the King is a noble Gentleman, and my familier,
I do assure ye very good friende: for what is inwarde
betweene vs, let it passe. I do beseech thee remember thy
curtesie. I beseech thee apparrell thy head: and among
90 other important and most serious designes, and of great
import in deede too: but let that passe, for I must tell thee
it will please his Grace (by the worlde) sometime to leane
vpon my poore shoulder, and with his royall finger thus
dallie with my excrement, with my mustachio: but sweete
95 hart let that passe. By the world I recount no fable, some
certaine special honours it pleaseth his greatnes to impart
to *Armado* a Souldier, a man of trauayle, that hath seene
the worlde: but let that passe; the very all of all is: but
sweet hart, I do implore secrecie, that the King would haue
100 me present the Princesse (sweete chuck) with some
delightfull ostentation, or show, or pageant, or antique, or
fierworke: Now vnderstanding that the Curate and your
sweete selfe, are good at such eruptions, and sodaine
breaking out of myrth (as it were) I haue acquainted you
105 withall, to the ende to craue your assistance.

PEDANT Sir, you shall present before her the Nine Worthies,
Sir *Nathaniel*, as concerning some entertainement of time,
some show in the posterior of this day, to be rendred by
our assistance the Kinges commaund, and this most gallant
110 illustrate and learned Gentleman, before the Princesse: I
say none so fit as to present the nine Worthies.

NATHANIEL Where will you finde men worthie enough to
present them?

PEDANT *Iosua*, your selfe, my selfe, *Iudas Machabeus*, and
115 this gallant Gentleman, *Hector*; this Swaine (because of his
great lim or ioynt) shall passe *Pompey* the great, the Page
Hercules.

ARMADO Pardon sir, error: He is not quantitie enough for that
worthies thumbe, he is not so big as the end of his Club.
120 PEDANT Shall I haue audience? He shall present *Hercules* in
minoritie: his enter and exit shalbe strangling a Snake; and
I will haue an Apologie for that purpose.

BOY An excellent deuice: so if any of the audience hisse, you
may cry, Well done *Hercules*, now thou crusshest the
125 Snake; that is the way to make an offence gracious, though
few haue the grace to do it.

ARMADO For the rest of the Worthies?

PEDANT I will play three my selfe.

BOY Thrice worthie Gentleman.

130 ARMADO Shall I tell you a thing?

PEDANT We attende.

ARMADO We will haue, if this fadge not, an Antique. I beseech you follow.

PEDANT *Via* good-man *Dull*, thou hast spoken no worde all

135 this while.

DULL Nor vnderstoode none neither sir.

PEDANT Alone, we will employ thee.

DULL Ile make one in a daunce, or so: or I will play on the Taber to the worthies, and let them dance the hey.

140 PEDANT Most *Dull*, honest *Dull*, to our sport: away.

Exeunt

Notes

1 **Satis** ... 'enough is enough'   In the upper classes of the Elizabethan grammar school, pupils were expected to converse in Latin.

2 **reasons** 'phrases'   The word was used in ME to distinguish the grammatical conception of a sentence from that of its content, which was implied by the word *sentence*. Here the word is being used simply as a technical term suited to the characters.

3 **sententious** 'full of significance'   Adjective formed from the noun *sentence* in the sense above.

5 **opinion** 'arrogance'   This sense recorded by *OED* 5c only from Shakespeare. The word tended to have bad associations from its earlier sense, 'belief not founded upon adequate grounds'.

6 **quondam** 'past' (Latin, 'formerly, once, at one time').

7 **of the kings**   The apostrophe, with its origins in Greek, is a learned introduction towards the end of the sixteenth century and is not employed in this text, but it is frequently used in the Folio to mark the omission of letters unpronounced in delivery, although not for the possessive.

8 **Armatho**   The alternation in spelling with *Armado* reflects confusion brought about by two ME sound changes: (1) in which /ð/ > /d/ when immediately followed by *m*, *n*, *r* or *l* (OE *byrðen*, *morðrian* > ME *burden*, *murdren*); and (2) a fifteenth-century change in which /d/ followed by syllabic *r* > /ð/ (OE *fæder*, *mōder* > late ME *father*, *mother*). Variants in pronunciation arose and confused the spellings.

9 **Noui** ... 'I know the man as well as I know you'   The phrase may have been drawn from Lily's 1549 Latin grammar, where it appears as an example of the use of *tanquam*.

10 **fyled** 'polished'   A word often collocated with *eloquence*. See

also *picked* (12), which is frequently collocated with *terms* in describing eloquence.

12 **rediculous, and thrasonicall** 'laughable and boastful'   Note the ‹e› for ‹i›, which represents a lowered variant in pronunciation common in London English of Elizabeth's time (cf. Excerpt 25). *Thrasonicall* is an adjective derived from 'Thraso', the name of the braggart soldier in Terence's *Eunuchus*. The word had been in use among literary men for over twenty years.

13 **peregrinat** 'having the air of a foreigner'   Shakespeare's is the first and only independent use of the word, but it is an etymological parallel with the use of *pilgrim* as an adjective in the Wycliffite Bible and in Excerpt 20.

17–18 **phanatticall phantasims** 'extravagant fantasists'   *Phantasims* is recorded only in this play, but Florio records the Italian word *fantasima* in 1611. The ‹ph› spellings represent the revived interest in Greek during the Renaissance.

18 **point deuise** 'precise'   Used by Chaucer in adverbial phrases.

19 **ortagriphie**   The word refers to the contemporary arts of pronunciation and correct writing (e.g. John Hart's *An Orthographie*, 1569) which sought Latin or, less usually, Greek etymologies to frame their rules. The words *doubt* and *debt* existed in ME as French borrowings, *doute* and *dette*, and the *b* is restored from the Latin etymology. The spellings *caufe* and *haufe* represent a stage in the phonetic development of the sequence [ɑl] > [ɑul] > [ɑu] > [ɔ:] (cf. *sault*, 54). The final stage was reached in the early seventeenth century. *Neighbour* and *neigh* are given spellings which reflect the loss of the fricative consonant represented by *gh*. This occurred during the fifteenth century. The spelling *abhominable*, preferred by Pedant, derives mistakenly from a supposed Latin phrase *ab homine, 'away from man' (suggesting revulsion), rather than the correct *abominari*, 'to deprecate as an ill omen'.

24 **insinuateth**   The sense of this is not certain. It seems that Pedant is using the word *insinuateth* to mean 'drive mad' and deriving it from an unrecorded Latin verb *insanire, 'to go mad'. He then suggests in Latin that Nathaniel doesn't follow this, and glosses it 'to make frantic or lunatic'. At which Nathaniel praises God for the enlightenment. Pedant picks up his *bone*, used in error for *bene*.

27 **prescian**   Priscian (sixth century) was the author of the advanced Latin grammar most widely used in the Middle Ages and Renaissance.

31 **Chirra**   The form of address to a page from his master would be *sirrah*. This pronunciation may, however, derive from a greeting, *chaere*, in Erasmus's *Familiaria Colloquia*, used as a contemporary schoolbook.

38 **almsbasket**   The basket of scraps left over from a feast and distributed to the poor.

40 **honorificabilitudinitatibus**   Notorious in medieval and Renaissance Latinity as the longest word known.

41 **flapdragon**   A burning raisin or plum floating in punch (or similar) and snapped up by the participants in a Christmas game.

44 **Horne-booke**   A simple alphabet book, perhaps also containing numbers, elements of spelling and the Lord's Prayer, so called because it was mounted on a tablet of wood and protected by a thin sheet of horn. *OED* gives this as the earliest occurrence of the word.

49 **Consonant**   Possibly an expression related to that cited by *OED* in which a fool is paralleled with a consonant and contrasted with a mute (an unvoiced sound). Speaking when silence might have been the better policy is a traditional indicator of folly.

53 **Sheepe**   The Spanish word for 'sheep', *oueia*, was used in Vives' *Exercitatio Linguae Latinae* as a mnemonic for the vowels.
concludes   Both 'finishes' the list of vowels and 'proves' the proposition. The *-es* inflexion is singular and is in concord with *the other*. But see the use of *-es* with the second-person singular in line 60. The loss of final *-t* is especially common in verbs whose base ends in *-t*.

55 **venewe**   In fencing, the attack leading to a hit.

57 **wit-old**   This is a pun on the word *wittol*, 'a contented cuckold'. Apparently formed in late ME by blending the verb *witen*, 'to know', with *cokewold*.

71 **dunghel . . . vnguem**   The Latin tag referred to is *ad . . . unguem*, 'to the nail' – that is, 'exactly'.

79 **congratulate** 'greet, salute'   The word is first recorded in 1548, but this rare sense is recorded only between 1578 and 1611.

82 **liable** 'suitable, apt'   A sense recorded only during the last three decades of the sixteenth century. *Congrue* is used in the fourteenth century to refer to grammatical concord and harmonious composition, and, with the other associated epithets, is a statement of the stylistic ideal of decorum.

87 **I do assure ye**   The spelling of the second-person plural pronoun here indicates unstressed pronunciation with a centralised vowel. It should not be confused with the stressed *ye* of formal discourse.

94 **excrement** 'that which grows out or forth' (Latin *excrescere*, *excrementum*)   First recorded in the sixteenth century, the word was obsolete by the beginning of the eighteenth, perhaps inhibited in use by its homonym.

101 **ostentation**   This is the sole use given by *OED* with the sense 'spectacular show'.

106 **Nine Worthies**   A frequent constituent of popular entertainment in Tudor London. Machyn (Excerpt 25) repeatedly mentions them as part of May games. They were Joshua, David, Judas Maccabeus, Hector, Alexander, Julius Caesar, King Arthur, Charlemagne and either Godfrey of Bouillon or Guy of Warwick. Shakespeare does not follow this traditional list, and includes Hercules and Pompey.

132 **fadge** 'succeed, turn out well'   The etymology of the word is unknown. It first occurs in 1578 and is rare after 1700.

31 Thomas Dekker, The Guls Horne-booke

Although relatively well known for his comedy *The Shoemaker's Holiday*, Thomas Dekker could scarcely have considered himself one of the literary successes of Elizabethan London. Instead, he eked out a precarious living as a popular author, in and out of debtors' prison, writing brief works and pamphlets, collaborating with others on plays, but never achieving lasting personal success. The date of his birth is uncertain but appears to have been about 1572. A Londoner, he first came to prominence as a playwright in the early 1590s, and after 1598 he participated in the composition of more than sixty plays. He was at this time employed by the impresario Philip Henslowe. In 1612 he was committed to the King's Bench Prison for debt and remained there for seven harsh years. Critical opinion of Dekker's personality has been somewhat divided, viewing him both as a man of unfailing good humour and as one who suffered from the discrepancy between his own aspirations as author and gentleman and his humiliating experience as hackwriter and prisoner. His *Guls Horne-booke* (1609) may hold beneath its superficial humour an ironic tone of indignation at the irresponsibility of the privileged young man-about-town. Its form is indeed an ironic inversion of the courtesy books produced for the guidance of those seeking entrance to fashionable society.

The Guls Horne-booke draws its title from elementary Elizabethan schoolbooks bound between plates of horn, and the word *gull* is significantly ambiguous, meaning both 'fop' and 'dupe or fool'. The pamphlet does not seem to have been popular in its own day, since it was not reprinted, but it has more recently been valued as a store of information on the street life of Elizabethan London. Linguistically it is interesting for its cosmopolitan style, mixing recent borrowings and derivational forms (*dedicated, tripos*) of an elevated kind with technical theatrical vocabulary (*properties, hangings*), fashionable Spanish- and Italianisms (*bastinado, zany*) and colloquial and slang usage (*cockatrice, punck*). The printed text preserves some of the phrasings and assimilations of racy speech (*your Inne-a-court-man, one ath Scullery*). Dekker is inventive too in extending the senses of words for verbal play, and creative in coining disparaging compounds to refer to the common people. Also noticeable is his use of words of sound-echoic origin: *flirt, blare, mew, whew.*

244

The text here expands a few abbreviations but otherwise retains the original spelling and punctuation, including the abbreviation *y^e* used by the printer to fit his copy into the line.

How a Gallant should behaue himselfe in a Play-house

Mary let this obseruation go hand in hand with the rest: or rather like a country-seruingman, some fiue yards before them. Present not your selfe on the Stage (especially at a new play) vntill the quaking prologue hath (by rubbing) got cullor into his
5 cheekes, and is ready to giue the trumpets their Cue that hees vpon point to enter: for then it is time, as though you were one of the *Properties*, or that you dropt out of y^e *Hangings* to creepe from behind the Arras with your *Tripos* or three-footed stoole in one hand, and a teston mounted betweene a forefinger and
10 a thumbe in the other: for if you should bestow your person vpon the vulgar, when the belly of the house is but halfe full, your apparell is quite eaten vp, the fashion lost, and the proportion of your body in more danger to be deuoured, then if it were serud vp in the Counter amongst the Powltry: auoid
15 that as you would the Bastome. It shall crowne you with rich commendation to laugh alowd in the middest of the most serious and saddest scene of the terriblest Tragedy: and to let that clapper (your tongue) be tost so high that all the house may ring of it: your Lords vse it; your Knights are Apes to
20 the Lords, and do so too: your Inne-a-court-man is Zany to the Knights, and (many very scuruily) comes likewise limping after it: bee thou a beagle to them all, and neuer lin snuffing till you haue sented them: for by talking and laughing (like a Plough-man in a Morris) you heape *Pelion* vpon *Ossa*, glory
25 vpon glory: As first, all the eyes in the galleries will leaue walking after the Players, and onely follow you: the simplest dolt in the house snatches vp your name, and when he meetes you in the streetes, or that you fall into his hands in the middle of a Watch, his word shall be taken for you, heele cry,
30 *Hees such a Gallant*, and you passe. Secondly, you publish your temperance to the world, in that you seeme not to resort thither to taste vaine pleasures with a hungrie appetite; but onely as a Gentleman, to spend a foolish houre or two, because you can doe nothing else. Thirdly you mightily
35 disrelish the Audience, and disgrace the Author: mary you take vp (though it be at the worst hand) a strong opinion of your owne iudgement and inforce the Poet to take pitty of

your weakenesse, and by some dedicated sonnet to bring you
into a better paradice, onely to stop your mouth.
40   If you can (either for loue or money) prouide yourself a
lodging by the water side: for aboue the conueniencie it brings,
to shun Shoulder-clapping, and to ship away your Cockatrice
betimes in the morning it addes a kind of state vnto you, to
be carried from thence to the staires of your Play-house: hate
45 a Sculler (remember that) more then to be acquainted with
one ath Scullery. No, your Oares are your onely Sea-crabs,
boord them and take heed you neuer go twice together with
one paire: often shifting is a great credit to Gentlemen: and
that diuiding of your Fare wil make ye poore watersnaks be
50 ready to pul you in peeces to enioy your custome: No matter
whether vpon landing you haue money or no, you may swim
in twentie of their boates over the riuer, upon *Ticket*: mary
when siluer comes in, remember to pay trebble their fare,
and it will make your Flounder-catchers to send more thankes
55 after you, when you doe not draw, then when you doe: for
they know, It will be their owne another daie.
  Before the Play begins, fall to cardes, you may win or loose
(as *Fencers* doe in a prize) and beate one another by con-
federacie, yet share the money when you meete at supper:
60 notwithstanding, to gul the *Ragga-muffins* that stand a loofe
gaping at you, throw the cards (hauing first torne foure or
fiue of them) round about the Stage, iust vpon the third
sound, as though you had lost: it skils not if the foure knaues
ly on their backs, and outface the Audience, theres none such
65 fooles as dare take exceptions at them, because ere the play
go off, better knaues then they will fall into the company.
  Now sir if the writer be a fellow that hath epigramd you, or
hath had a flirt at your mistris, or hath brought either your
feather or your red beard, or your little legs etc. on the stage,
70 you shall disgrace him worse then by tossing him in a
blancket, or giuing him the bastinado in a Tauerne, if in the
middle of his play, (bee it Pastorall or Comedy, Morall or
Tragedie) you rise with a skreud and discontented face from
your stoole to be gone: no matter whether the Scenes be
75 good or no, the better they are, the more doe you distast
them: and beeing on your feete, sneake not away like a
coward, but salute all your gentle acquaintance, that are
spred either on the rushes, or on stooles about you, and draw
what troope you can from the stage after you: the *Mimicks*
80 are beholden to you, for allowing them elbow roome: their
Poet cries perhaps a pox go with you, but care not you for

that, theres no musick without frets.

Mary if either the company, or indisposition of the weather
binde you to sit it out, my counsell is then that you turne
85 plain Ape, take vp a rush and tickle the earnest eares of your
fellow gallants, to make other fooles fall a laughing: mewe at
passionate speeches, blare at merrie, finde fault with the
musicke, whew at the childrens Action, whistle at the songs:
and aboue all, curse the sharers, that whereas the same day
90 you had bestowed forty shillings on an embrodered Felt and
Feather, (scotch-fashion) for your mistres in the Court, or
your punck in the Cittie, within two houres after, you
encounter with the very same block on the stage, when the
haberdasher swore to you the impression was extant but that
95 morning.

To conclude, hoord vp the finest play-scraps you can get,
vpon which your leane wit may most sauourly feede for want
of other stuffe, when the *Arcadian* and *Euphuisd* gentle-
women haue their tongues sharpened to set vpon you: that
100 qualitie (next to your shittlecocke) is the onely furniture to a
Courtier thats but a new beginner, and is but in his *A B C* of
complement.

Notes

8 **Tripos**   Formed on the Latin *tripus* but given a Greek-looking
ending. Greek carried greater prestige than Latin in the sixteenth
and seventeenth centuries, being less widely known.

9 **teston**   A silver sixpenny piece. Originally the French name of a
fifteenth-century Milanese coin which bore the head of the Duke
Galeazzo Maria Sforza. Italian *testone* from *testa*, 'head'.

11 **the vulgar**   'the common people' (Lat. *vulgaris*, 'common, ordinary')
This nominal usage was first recorded in 1590.

14 **Counter . . . Powltry**   Dekker here indulges in wordplay on the
name of a debtors' prison. The Counter in the district of the Poultry
was the Sheriff's prison from which Henslowe discharged Dekker on
4 February 1598 with a loan of 40 shillings.

15 **Bastome**   Perhaps a cudgel (Fr. *baston*), but in the context
perhaps also the officer whose function it was to escort prisoners
from the court to the Fleet prison on committal, and thereafter
accompany them on any excursions from the gaol. So called from the
red staff which he carried.

17 **terriblest**   The rule by which the superlative of a multisyllabic
adjective is formed by the use of *most* is not yet fully established.

19 **your Lordes**   The use of the second-person plural pronoun as a
quasi-demonstrative develops in Elizabethan English in informal
contexts and is particularly common in dramatic works in the first
decade of the seventeenth century.

20 **Zany** 'ludicrous imitator' (Italian and French *zani*)   The word is from regional Italian forms of Gianni, and is given to those servants who play the clown's role in the *Commedia dell'arte*.

23 **sented**   (Fr. *sentir*). The modern spelling with ‹sc› does not appear until the seventeenth century.

24 **Pelion . . . Ossa**   In Greek mythology, in order to reach the gods, the giants heaped Mount Pelion upon Mount Ossa and Ossa on Olympus to form a ladder.

42 **Shoulder-clapping** 'arrest, tap on the shoulder'.
Cockatrice 'whore'   This slang sense is recorded only between 1599 and the mid eighteenth century. The word has a complex sense history (see *OED*), and more usually in English from the fourteenth century refers to the mythological basilisk whose gaze could turn an onlooker to stone.

46 **Oares** 'oarsmen'   These work in pairs, as opposed to the sculler, who works alone.

52 **upon Ticket** 'on credit' (Fr. *étiquette*)   Originally referred to a brief note or label attached to something. Develops the sense of 'a promissory note, IOU' from about 1600, and the phrase 'on tick' is recorded from 1642.

58 **prize**   A fencing prize fight or public test undergone by fencers to qualify as masters of defence.

60 **Ragga-muffins** 'the common people' (OE *raggig*, 'rough, shaggy' + MDu *muffe*)   First recorded as a name in 1344, and later as the name of a devil in Langland.

62–63 **third sound**   Trumpets were sounded three times as a warning that the play was about to begin.
it skils not 'it doesn't matter' (ON *skilja*, 'divide, distinguish') This impersonal construction is particularly common from about 1525 to 1670.

68 **flirt** 'jest, jeer'   A sense recorded between 1549 and 1726. The modern sense is not recorded before the mid eighteenth century.

71 **bastinado** 'beating, cudgelling' (Sp. *bastonada*)   The form used here seems to have been borrowed from French *bastonade* and mistakenly re-hispanised on the analogy of the pair *renegade–renegado*.

86 **a laughing**   Derived from OE expressions with a verbal noun (*on huntunge*). Common in the sixteenth and seventeenth centuries, this types declines in modern times.
mewe   The sound-echoic verb is recorded from the fourteenth century but the use as a derisive sound (cf. modern *hoot*) is found only in the works of Dekker.

89 **sharers** 'producers'   Properly, those who were shareholders in the theatre company.

93 **block** 'style, model'   Derived from the block of wood on which hats were formed.

98 **Arcadian and Euphuisd**   (Text reads *Euphuird*.) Affected by imitating the styles of Sir Philip Sidney's *Arcadia* (1590) and John Lyly's *Euphues* (1578). Both were passé in smart circles by this time.

32 John Donne

The excerpts from the works of Donne given here are distinct in textual history. His *Devotions*, composed during a serious illness in 1623, was published in the following year. The two poems from the collection 'Songs and Sonnets' were published in a volume edited by his son in 1633 but may have been written thirty or more years earlier.

Donne was born in 1572 in the same London street as John Milton a generation later. His father was a substantial member of the Ironmongers' Company who claimed gentle descent from a family of Welsh origin, and his mother was related to Sir Thomas More. His father died when Donne was only four, and his mother was remarried to the physician Dr John Syminges. The family were devout Catholics, and Donne received his education at the hands of private tutors who instructed him in Latin and French. He proceeded to Hart Hall (later Hertford College), Oxford, and later may have spent some time in Cambridge, but his Catholicism disqualified him from taking a degree in either university. He was admitted to Lincoln's Inn in May 1592. At some point in the middle 1590s he seems to have renounced his Catholicism and, after military expeditions in which he sailed with Raleigh, begun to pursue a career on the fringes of court society. In 1597 he became secretary to Sir Thomas Egerton, Lord Keeper of the Great Seal, but he ruined his career in 1601 by his clandestine marriage to Ann More, a niece of Sir Thomas's wife. Fourteen uncertain years followed during which he relied on friends and minor patrons, until, at the instigation of King James, he was ordained in 1615 and made Doctor of Divinity by Cambridge University. His career in the Church prospered and he became Dean of St Paul's in 1621, holding this post until his death in March 1631.

The text of the seventeenth Meditation given below is that of the third edition of the *Devotions*, which appeared in 1627. The spelling, although not quite consistent, is relatively modern, but ‹in› and ‹im› are preferred to ‹en› and ‹em› initially, and no apostrophe *s* is used. Morphologically, the *-th* termination is preferred in *doth* and *hath* to the otherwise general *-es* in the third-person present tense, and distinct forms of *my* and *thy* persist before vowels (*mine own*, *thine own*). The use of periphrastic *do* is distinct from that of modern practice. The rhetorical conception of the style, preferring parallel, balanced short clauses, ensures that the syntax echoes the patterns of simple speech.

The verse examples illustrate the use of the apostrophe in order to aid the reader in scanning the lines, where it indicates the elision of *e* in the inflexional endings *-ed* and *-est*. The implication that, at least in verse, *e* might still be pronounced in such contexts is confirmed by the appearance of spellings like *findst* and *mixt* as an alternative means of indicating elision. Further details of Donne's pronunciation can be deduced from the rhymes (see Notes).

A Seventeenth Meditation

Perchance hee for whom this *Bell* tols, may bee so ill, as that he knowes not it tolls for him; And perchance I may thinke my selfe so much better than I am, as that they who are about mee, and see my state, may haue caused it to toll for mee, and
5 I know not that. The *Church* is *Catholike*, *vniuersal*, so are all her *Actions*; *All* that shee does belongs to *all*. When she *baptizes* a *child*, that action concernes me; for that childe is thereby connected to that *Head* which is my *Head* too, and ingraffed into that *body*, whereof I am a *member*. And when
10 she *buries a Man*, that action concernes me; All *mankinde* is of one *Author*, and is one *volume*; when one Man dies, one *Chapter* is not *torne* out of the *booke*, but *translated* into a better *language*; and euery *Chapter* must be so *translated*; *God* imploies seuerall *translators; * some peeces are translated
15 by *age*, some by *sicknes*, some by *war*, some by *iustice*; but *Gods* hand is in euery *translation*: and his hand shall binde vp all our scattered leaues againe, for that *Library* where euery *booke* shall ly open to one another: As therfore the *Bell* that ringes to a *Sermon*, calls not vpon the *Preacher* onely, but
20 vpon the *Congregation* to come; so this *Bell* calls vs all: but how much more *mee*, who am brought so neer the *doore* by this *sicknesse*. There was a *contention* as farre as a *suite*, (in which both *piety* and *dignity*, *religion* and *estimation*, were mingled) which of the religious *Orders* should ring to prayers
25 first in the *Morning*; and it was *determined*, that *they should ring first that rose earliest*. If we understand a right the *dignity* of this *Bell*, that tolls for our *euening praier*, wee would be glad to make it ours, by rising early, in that *application*, that it might be ours, as wel as his, whose indeed it is. The *Bell*
30 doth toll for him that *thinkes* it doth; and though it *intermit*

againe, yet from that *minute*, that that occasion wrought vpon
him, he is united to God. Who castes not vp his *Eye* to the
Sunne when it rises? but who takes off his *Eye* from a *Comet*,
when that breakes out? who bends not his *eare* to any *bell*,
35 which vpon any occation rings? But who can remoue it
from that *bell*, which is passing a *piece of himselfe* out of this
world? No Man is an *Iland*, intire of it self; euery man is a
piece of the *Continent*, a part of the *maine*; if a *clod* be
washed away by the *Sea*, *Europe* is the lesse, as wel as if a
40 *Promontory* were, as well as if a *Mannor* of thy *friends*, or of
thine owne were; Any mans *death* diminishes *mee*, because I
am inuolued in *mankind*; And therfore neuer send to know
for whom the *bell* tols; It tols for *thee*. Neither can we call this
a *begging* of *misery* or a *borrowing* of *misery*, as thogh we
45 were not miserable enough of our selues, but must fetch in
more from the next house, in taking vpon us the *misery* of
our *neighbors*. Truly it were an excusable *couetousnes* if we
did; for *affliction* is a *treasure*, and scarse any man hath
enough of it. No man hath *affliction* enough; that is not
50 matured, and ripened by it, and made fit for *God* by that
affliction. If a Man carry *treasure* in *bullion*, or in a *wedge* of
gold, and haue none coyned into *currant Monies*, his *treasure*
will not defray him as he trauells. *Tribulation* is *Treasure* in
the *nature* of it, but it is not *currant money* in the vse of it,
55 except we get neerer and neerer our *home*, *heauen*, by it.
Another Man may be *sick* too, and *sick* to *death*, and this
affliction may lie in his *bowels*, as *gold* in a *Mine*, and be of
no vse to him; but this *bell* that tels *mee* of his *affliction*, diggs
out, and applies that *gold* to *me*: if by this consideration of
60 anothers danger, I take mine own into contemplation, and so
secure my selfe, by making my recourse to my *God*, who is
our onely *securitie*.

B 'Song'

Goe, and catche a falling starre,
   Get with child a mandrake roote,
Tell me, where all past yeares are,
   Or who cleft the Divels foot,
5 Teach me to heare Mermaides singing,
   Or to keep off envies stinging,
      And finde
      What winde
Serves to'advance an honest minde.

10 If thou beest borne to strange sights,
     Things invisible to see,
   Ride ten thousand daies and nights,
     Till age snow white haires on thee,
   Thou, when thou retorn'st, wilt tell mee
15 All strange wonders that befell thee,
               And sweare
               No where
   Lives a woman true, and faire.

   If thou findst one, let mee know,
20   Such a Pilgrimage were sweet;
   Yet doe not, I would not goe,
     Though at next doore wee might meet,
   Though shee were true, when you met her,
   And last, till you write your letter,
25   Yet shee
               Will bee
   False, ere I come, to two, or three.

C 'The good-morrow'

   I wonder by my troth, what thou, and I
   Did, till we lov'd? were we not wean'd till then?
   But suck'd on countrey pleasures, childishly?
   Or snorted we i' the seaven sleepers den?
5 T'was so; But this, all pleasures fancies bee.
   If ever any beauty I did see,
   Which I desir'd, and got, t'was but a dreame of thee.

   And now good morrow to our waking soules,
   Which watch not one another out of feare;
10 For love, all love of other sights controules,
   And makes one little roome, an every where.
   Let sea-discoverers to new worlds have gone,
   Let Maps to others, worlds on worlds have showne,
   Let us possesse one world, each hath one, and is one.

15 My face in thine eye, thine in mine appeares,
   And true plaine hearts doe in the faces rest,
   Where can we finde two better hemispheares
   Without sharpe North, without declining West?
   What ever dyes, was not mixt equally;
20 If our two loves be one, or, thou and I
   Love so alike, that none doe slacken, none can die.

Notes

Seventeenth Meditation

12 **translated**   A pun, since a common sense of the word from 1300 onwards was 'to transfer (from one place to another)'.

14 **seuerall** 'various'   The word is borrowed from Fr. *several*, from the same Latin root as *separate*. The sense here is first recorded in 1509.

23 **dignity . . . estimation**   'high office . . . status'.

31 **occasion**   The word is recorded from 1789 in the sense of 'a religious function or ceremonial' *OED* 9 (a).

wrought   The OE preterite and past participle of the verb *wyrcan*, 'to work', had the form *worht-* . The metathesised form used here was common in ME, but during the fifteenth century the analogical form *worked* arose which (except as an adjective) entirely replaced the earlier form during the seventeenth century.

37 **it self**   The genitive form of the pronoun *it* is recorded as *its* (replacing earlier *his*) from the third quarter of the sixteenth century. The form *it* is that used also by Shakespeare.

51 **wedge** 'ingot'   This sense is found from OE until the early eighteenth century.

Song

2–4 **roote: foot**   Donne uses the long [u:] pronunciation of *foot*, which is the normal development from ME /o:/. Shortened variants, which are the ancestors of the Modern English pronunciation, were just emerging at this time.

7–9 **finde: winde: minde**   In the sixteenth and seventeenth centuries the word *wind* was pronounced most commonly with a diphthong derived from ME /i:/, that is [əi]. The modern form is a variant pronunciation with a short vowel which becomes widely current in the eighteenth century.

19 **if thou findst**   Donne does not preserve the distinct form of the subjunctive but adopts an indicative form after *if* (cf. line 10). However, he adopts subjunctive forms (*were, last*) after *though* (23, 24).

The good-morrow

1–3 **I: childishly**   The pronunciation [əi] was common for *-ly* following a secondary stress in the sixteenth and first half of the seventeenth centuries. This and the rhyme *equally : I* (19–20) are therefore probably pure rhymes.

5 **bee**   The use of *be* as an indicative form is becoming an archaism by Donne's time. In *Song* (3) he uses *are*, which had begun to supersede *be* in this function in southern English during the earlier sixteenth century.

9 **watch not**   Periphrastic *do* may still be used in declaratives without any apparent emphasis, and to achieve rhyme (6, 16), but omitted from the negative in a manner parallel to that of Middle English.

9–11 **feare: where**   The word *fear* is recorded from this period with both close and open pronunciation. The rhyme here is with the open [ɛ:].

12–14 **gone: showne: one**   The rhyme is a pure one, probably on [o:], but variants of all these words occur with the pronunciation [ɔ:]

16 **plaine** 'open, guileless'   This sense is recorded from the later fourteenth until the early eighteenth century. The series of semantic shifts undergone by this word is a particularly interesting one. See Rudskoger (1970).

The letters reproduced below belong to a series written by Lady Brilliana Harley mostly from her home at Brompton Castle (modern Brampton Bryan) about twelve miles west of Ludlow. Brilliana Harley was born about 1600 while her father, Sir Edward Conway, was Lieutenant-Governor of the Brill. In 1623 she became the third wife of Sir Robert Harley, who had received a legal education, before entering a career in politics. His religious affiliations were with the Puritans and he supported the Parliamentary cause, but opposed the execution of the king in 1649.

The series of letters extends over a period of eighteen years, but most fall between the dates 1638 to 1643 and are usually addressed to her son, beginning after he leaves home to commence study at Oxford, continuing while he is in London at Lincoln's Inn, and concluding when he is an officer in the Parliamentary army.

Almost all are written in the sender's own hand, and they reveal Lady Harley to have been a woman of intelligence and culture as well as warm family affections. She shows a lively interest in the political and intellectual events of the day, both at home and abroad, but her letters are also full of practical maternal concern for the welfare of her son. Her powerful religious convictions are increasingly evident. The series of letters was written in a tragic setting, for the growing tensions of the Civil War pervade the later ones. By the time of the second letter printed here, Brilliana is facing, in her husband's absence, the prospect of the siege of Brompton by Royalist forces. Although doing much damage, the siege was lifted after six weeks. Brilliana did not live to see it resumed in the next spring. Her last letter, dated 9 October 1643, mentions that she has 'taken a very greate coold, which has made me very ill thees 2 or 3 days, but I hope the Lord will be mercifull to me, in giuing me my health, for it is an ill time to be sike in'.

The letters are written in a deceptively artful plain style, which often imitates familiar spoken language but maintains forceful control of discourse structures, achieving effects of balance and verbal parallelism. Modulations of tone are quite adroit, adopting colloquial phrasing, then rising with the urgency of the subject to more overt rhetorical vehemence. The language is fairly standardised, showing few dialectal peculiarities, but the spelling system is rather inconsistent and idiosyncratic, confusing standard forms with the writer's own phonetic spellings.

Letter A

To my deare husband Sr Robert Harley.

Deare S^r – Your two leters, on from Hearifort and the other from Gloster, weare uery wellcome to me: and if you knwe howe gladly I reseaue your leters, I beleeue you would neeuer let any opertunity pase. I hope your cloche did you
5 saruis betwne Gloster and my brother Brays, for with vs it was a very rainy day, but this day has bine very dry and warme, and so I hope it was with you; and to-morowe I hope you will be well at your journis end, wheare I wisch my self to bide you wellcome home. You see howe my thoughts goo
10 with you: and as you haue many of mine, so let me haue some of yours. Beleeue me, I thinke I neuer miste you more then nowe I doo, or ells I haue forgoot what is past. I thanke God, Ned and Robin are well; and Ned askes every day wheare you are, and he says you will come to-morowe. My
15 father is well, but goos not abrode, becaus of his fiseke. I haue sent you vp a litell hamper, in which is the box with the ryteings and boouckes you bide me send vp, with the other things, sowed up in a clothe, in the botome of the hamper. I haue sent you a partriche pye, which has the two pea chikeins
20 in it, and a litell runlet of meathe, that which I toold you I made for my father. I thinke within this muthe, it will be very good drinke. I sende it vp nowe becaus I thinke carage when it is ready to drincke dous it hurt; thearefore, and please you to let it rest and then taste it; if it be good, I pray you let my
25 father haue it, because he spake to me for such meathe. I will nowe bide you god night, for it is past a leauen a cloke. I pray God presarue you and giue you good sugsess in all your biusnes, and a speady and happy meeting.
  Your most faithfull affectinat wife, Brilliana Harley.

Letter B

For my deare sonne Mr. Edward Harley.

My deare Ned – I longe to see you, but would not haue you come downe, for I cannot thinke this cuntry very safe; by the

papers I haue sent to your father, you will knowe the temper
of it. I hope your father will giue me full derections how I
5 may beest haue my howes gareded, if need be; if he will giue
the derections, I hope, I shall foolow it.

My deare Ned, I thanke God I am not afraide. It is the
Lords caus that we haue stood for, and I trust, though our
iniquitys testify aganst vs, yet the Lord will worke for His
10 owne name sake, and that He will now sheawe the men of the
world that it is hard fighting against heauen. And for our
comforts, I thinke neuer any laide plots to route out all Gods
chillderen at once, but that the Lord did sheawe Himselfe
mighty in saveing His saruants and confounding His enimyes,
15 He did Pharowe, when he thought to haue destroyed all
Israell, and so Haman. Nowe, the intention is, to route out
all that feare God, and surely the Lord will arise to healpe vs:
and in your God let your confidence be, and I am assured it is
so. One meet Samuell and not knoweing wheare he dwelt,
20 Samuell toold him he was a Darbesheare man, and that he
came lately from thence, and so he did in discours; the papis
toold him, that theare was but a feawe puretaines in this
cuntry, and 40 men would cut them all off.

Had I not had this ocation to send to your father, yet I had
25 sent this boy vp to Loundoun; he is such a rogeisch boy that I
dare not keepe him in my howes, and as littell do I dare to let
him goo in this cuntry, least he ioyne with the company of
vollentirs, or some other such crwe. I haue giuen him no
more money then will sarue to beare his charges vpe; and
30 becaus I would haue him make hast and be sure to goo to
Loundoun, I haue toold him, that you will giue him
something for his paines, if he come to you in good time and
doo not loyter; and heare inclosed I haue sent you halfe a
crowne. Giue him what you thinke fitte, and I desire he may
35 not come downe any more, but that he may be perswaded to
goo to seae, or some other imployment. He thinkes he shall
come downe againe. Good Ned, do not tell Martaine that I
send him vp with such an intention. I haue derected theas
letters to you, and I send him to you, becaus I would not
40 haue the cuntry take notis, that I send to your father so
offten; but when such ocations come, I must needs send to
him, for I can rely vpon nobodys counsell but his. I pray God
blles you and presarue you in safety, and the Lord in mercy
giue you a comfortabell meeting with

Your most affectinat mother,   Brilliana Harley.

July 19, 1642.   *Brompton Castell.*

45   My cosen Dauis tells me that none can make shot but thos
whous trade it is, so I haue made the plumer rwite to Woster
for 50 waight of shot. I sent to Woster, becaus I would not
haue it knowne. If your father thinke that is not enoufg, I will
send for more. I pray you tell your father that my cosen
50   Robert Croft is in the cuntry. My cosen Tomkins is as violent
as euer, and many thinke that her very words, is in the
Heariford resolutions. I beleeue it was Mr Masons pening. He
is gone to Yorke, for when he carried the letter from the
gentellmen in this cuntry, he was made the kings chapline.

Notes

Letter A

1   **on** 'one'   Final ‹e› is written or omitted inconsistently, but of
course no longer pronounced.

4   **cloche** 'cloak'   It is probable that the spelling ‹ch› attempts to
capture the faint aspiration after the stop consonant rather than that
‹ch› represents the modern sound /tʃ/.

5   **saruis**   Brilliana Harley normally writes ‹ar› for ME ‹er›.

8   **journis end**   The apostrophe *s* is not in use, and the possessive is
normally indicated by the addition of -*s* to the base.

11 **miste**   The preterites and past participles of verbs whose base
ends in a voiceless consonant are written ‹t› only rarely. Generally
‹ed› is preferred.

15 **fiseke** 'medical treatment'   This ME sense became obsolete in
the eighteenth century.

17 **ryteings**   The spelling acknowledges the loss of initial *w*- which
occurred in pronunciation in the seventeenth century. More usually
the idiosyncratic ‹rw› is used.

   boouckes   This spelling suggests an accommodation between
standardised spelling practice and acknowledgement of the phonetic
facts: the long /o:/ of earlier ME had been raised to /u:/ in the Great
Vowel Shift in the fifteenth century.

20 **runlet** 'a cask or vessel of varying capacity' (*OED*)   Recorded
from 1333 into the later nineteenth century.

   meathe 'mead'   *OED* states that forms with medial /ð/ may be
drawn from ON or from Welsh. Since this letter was written on the
Welsh border, the latter explanation seems attractive.

23 **dous it hurt** 'does it harm'   The third-person singular present-
tense inflexion is -*(e)s*, even with the verb 'to do', but *hath* is still
written.

26 **a leaven a cloke** 'eleven o'clock'.

27 **sugsess**   The spelling illustrates a voicing of /ks/ before a stressed
syllable in EModE.

28 **biusnes**   The ME spelling is normally with ‹i›, and ‹u› spellings indicate western origin. The *u*-form became very frequent during the sixteenth century, so that the spelling here may once again indicate uncertainty in spelling as much as western pronunciation.

Letter B

3 **temper** 'climate, atmosphere'   Used figuratively. Originally referred to the balance of elements or humours, but extended to refer to the weather – here, the political climate.

5 **gareded**   The intrusive vowel in this spelling emphasises that post-vocalic /r/ is still pronounced at this period.

8 **the Lords caus**   Much of the phraseology of this second paragraph is that of the Puritans: *our iniquitys, men of the world* (with associations quite distinct from those of the modern phrase), *Gods childeren.*

10 **name sake** 'out of regard for his name or reputation'.   The word *name* is a possessive. The phrase is first recorded in Tindale's New Testament in 1521 with the *-es* inflexion. The endingless form is therefore more probably a later phonetic development than a survival of an ME phrase with endingless genitive.

13 **did sheawe**   The use of periphrastic *do* is perhaps intended as part of the rhetorical heightening of this passage, but Brilliana Harley uses it occasionally in less elevated contexts also.

16 **Haman**   A Persian enemy of the Jewish people who was overthrown after the intervention of Esther (*Esther* III–VII).

18 **I am assured** 'I am confident'   No agent giving assurance is implied.

21 **and so he did in discours** 'and so he entered into conversation'.

29 **beare his charges vpe** 'cover his expenses'.

32 **if he come**   The subjunctive form follows *if*. Brilliana Harley is careful always to use the correct subjunctive forms.

36 **he shall**   Clearly used with the earlier sense of inevitability.

46 **whous**   The spelling represents the fifteenth-century raising of /o:/ to /u:/.

48 **enoufg**   The *f*-spelling represents a sixteenth-century development by which ME /x/ > /f/. The *g* remains owing to the influence of standard spelling practice.

52–53 **He is gone**   The sequence verb 'to be' + past participle of an intransitive verb of motion was common in OE but has been in decline since the eighteenth century. It has survived most fully with the past participle *gone*. In Modern English, however, its use is usually limited to a statement of the fact of absence (*it's gone* opposed to *it's there*), with no implication of action found in this context. Where such circumstances are given, and with a personal subject, present-day English prefers *have*.

34 John Milton, from Paradise Lost, Book II

John Milton (1608–1674) was born in Bread Street, Cheapside, the son of a well-to-do scrivener and composer, who was determined that his son should receive a thorough education. There are stories of the twelve-year-old Milton working into the early hours of the morning. After attending St Paul's School, whose headmaster was Alexander Gil, the author of the *Logonomia Anglica* (1619), Milton went on to Christ's College, Cambridge, taking his MA in 1632. On leaving university he embarked on a tour of Europe, then settled with his father for a period of private study in Greek, Latin and Italian. In 1641 he published a series of pamphlets against the bishops and went on to support the Parliamentary cause in the Civil War. He was appointed Latin Secretary to the Council of State under the Commonwealth. At the Restoration, he went into hiding, was arrested, fined, and released.

Milton began to write his English verse in 1628 or 1629, and his last work, *Paradise Regained*, was published in 1671. His epic *Paradise Lost* seems to have been in partial existence by the early 1640s, but was mostly composed after his blindness in 1651, and completed by 1667.

Milton was a learned author, composing in Latin and Italian as well as English, and the grand style which he employs in *Paradise Lost* has been the subject of criticism for its unidiomatic and artificial language. Milton is indeed heavily influenced by his familiarity with Latin, and this is evident both in Latin syntactical constructions such as the ablative absolute (28, 49, 77) and in his use of unfamiliar Latin forms and senses. But although he uses unusual wordforms and unfamiliar senses, although he exploits very long sentences with multiply embedded clauses, and although he shifts word classes, Milton's language is less innovative than that of many Elizabethan authors. Very few words in this passage are first recorded in Milton. Most of the unfamiliar forms are of sixteenth-century origin: among his innovations are: *abrupt* (used as a noun only by Milton), *remote* (used as an adverb), *horrent* (apparently his own adoption from Latin *horrentem* 'bristling').

The facsimile shows the beginning of Book IX of *Paradise Lost*. The printing is not elegant and carelessness in proofreading is evident in the use of an exclamation mark (still fairly uncommon in English at this time) for lower case *l* in the word *still* (12). The line is also awkwardly truncated. Letter forms have developed from those used by Caxton, but some earlier practices survive, such as the use of the ligatures *ct* and *st*, the use of long *s* in initial and medial position. Italic script is used for personal names. Milton's own spelling practice is apparent in the careful use of apostrophes to mark vowel elision and the stressed (*hee*, *shee*) and unstressed (*thir*) variants of pronouns.

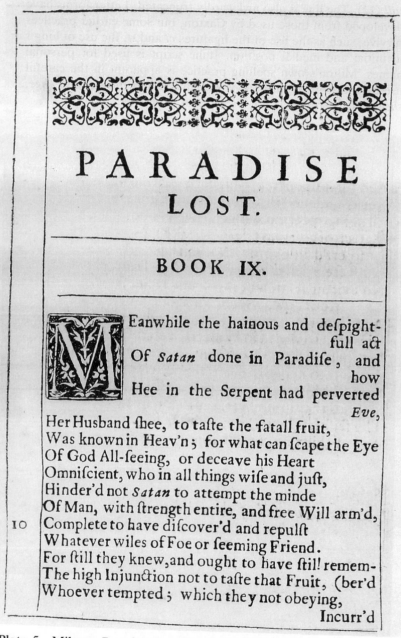

PARADISE
LOST.

BOOK IX.

Eanwhile the hainous and deſpight-
full act
Of *Satan* done in Paradiſe, and
how
Hee in the Serpent had perverted
Eve,
Her Husband ſhee, to taſte the fatall fruit,
Was known in Heav'n; for what can ſcape the Eye
Of God All-ſeeing, or deceave his Heart
Omniſcient, who in all things wiſe and juſt,
Hinder'd not *Satan* to attempt the minde
Of Man, with ſtrength entire, and free Will arm'd,
10 Complete to have diſcover'd and repulſt
Whatever wiles of Foe or ſeeming Friend.
For ſtill they knew, and ought to have ſtil! remem-
The high Injunction not to taſte that Fruit, (ber'd
Whoever tempted; which they not obeying,
Incurr'd

Plate 5   Milton, *Paradise Lost* Book IX (*two pages*)

Paradiſe loſt. Book 9.

Incurr'd, what could they leſs, the penaltie,
And manifold in ſin, deſerv'd to fall.
Up into Heav'n from Paradiſe in haſt
Th' Angelic Guards aſcended, mute and ſad
For Man, for of his ſtate by this they knew,
Much wondring how the ſuttle Fiend had ſtoln   20
Entrance unſeen. Soon as th' unwelcome news
From Earth arriv'd at Heaven Gate, diſpleas'd
All were who heard, dim ſadneſs did not ſpare
That time Celeſtial viſages, yet mixt
With pitie, violated not thir bliſs.
About the new-arriv'd, in multitudes
Th' ethereal People ran, to hear and know
How all befell : they towards the Throne Supream
Accountable made haſte to make appear
With righteous plea, thir utmoſt vigilance,   30
And eaſily approv'd ; when the moſt High
Eternal Father from his ſecret Cloud,
Amidſt in Thunder utter'd thus his voice.
    Aſſembl'd Angels, and ye Powers return'd
From unſucceſsful charge, be not diſmaid,
Nor troubl'd at theſe tidings from the Earth,
Which your ſincereſt care could not prevent;
Foretold ſo lately what would come to paſs,
When firſt this Tempter croſs'd the Gulf from Hell.
I told ye then he ſhould prevail and ſpeed   40
On his bad Errand, Man ſhould be ſeduc't
And flatter'd out of all, believing lies
Againſt his Maker ; no Decree of mine
Concurring to neceſſitate his Fall,
Or touch with lighteſt moment of impulſe
His free Will, to her own inclining left

K k

In

    Well have ye judg'd, well ended long debate,
Synod of Gods, and like to what ye are,
Great things resolv'd; which from the lowest deep
Will once more lift us up, in spite of Fate,
5 Neerer our ancient Seat; perhaps in view
Of those bright confines, whence with neighbouring Arms
And opportune excursion we may chance
Re-enter Heav'n; or else in some milde Zone
Dwell not unvisited of Heav'ns fair Light
10 Secure, and at the brightning Orient beam
Purge off this gloom; the soft delicious Air,
To heal the scarr of these corrosive Fires
Shall breathe her balme. But first whom shall we send
In search of this new World, whom shall we find
15 Sufficient? who shall tempt with wandring feet
The dark unbottomd infinite Abyss,
And through the palpable obscure find out
His uncouth way, or spread his aerie flight
Upborn with indefatigable wings
20 Over the vast abrupt, ere he arrive
The happy Ile; what strength, what art can then
Suffice, or what evasion bear him safe
Through the strict Senteries and Stations thick
Of Angels watching round? Here he had need
25 All circumspection and wee now no less
Choice in our suffrage; for on whom we send,
The weight of all and our last hope relies.
    This said, he sat; and expectation held
His look suspense, awaiting who appeerd
30 To second, or oppose, or undertake
The perilous attempt: but all sat mute,
Pondering the danger with deep thoughts; and each
In others count'nance red his own dismay
Astonisht: none among the choice and prime
35 Of those Heav'n-warring Champions could be found
So hardie as to proffer or accept
Alone the dreadful voyage; till at last
Satan, whom now transcendent glory rais'd
Above his fellows, with Monarchal pride
40 Conscious of highest worth, unmov'd thus spake.
    O Progeny of Heav'n, Empyreal Thrones,
With reason hath deep silence and demurr
Seis'd us, though undismaid: long is the way
And hard, that out of Hell leads up to Light;

45 Our prison strong, thus huge convex of Fire,
   Outrageous to devour, immures us round
   Ninefold, and gates of burning Adamant
   Barrd over us prohibit all egress.
   These past, if any pass, the void profound
50 Of unessential Night receives him next
   Wide gaping, and with utter loss of being
   Threat'ns him, plung'd in that abortive gulf.
   If thence he scape into what ever World,
   Or unknown Region, what remains him less
55 Then unknown dangers and as hard escape?
   But I should ill become this Throne, O Peers,
   And this Imperial Sovranty, adornd
   With splendor, armd with power, if aught propos'd
   And judg'd of public moment, in the shape
60 Of difficulty or danger could deterre
   Mee from attempting. Wherefore do I assume
   These Royalties, and not refuse to Reign,
   Refusing to accept as great a share
   Of hazard as of honour, due alike
65 To him who Reigns, and so much to him due
   Of hazard more, as hee above the rest
   High honourd sits? Go therfore mighty Powers,
   Terror of Heav'n, though fall'n; intend at home,
   While here shall be our home, what best may ease
70 The present misery, and render Hell
   More tollerable; if there be cure or charm
   To respit or deceive, or slack the pain
   Of this ill Mansion: intermit no watch
   Against a wakeful Foe, while I abroad
75 Through all the coasts of dark destruction seek
   Deliverance for us all: this enterprize
   None shall partake with me. Thus saying rose
   The Monarch, and prevented all reply,
   Prudent, least from his resolution rais'd
80 Others among the chief might offer now
   (Certain to be refus'd) what erst they feard;
   And so refus'd might in opinion stand
   His rivals, winning cheap the high repute
   Which hee through hazard huge must earn. But they
85 Dreaded not more th' adventure then his voice
   Forbidding; and at once with him they rose;
   Thir rising all at once was as the sound
   Of Thunder heard remote. Towards him they bend

With awful reverence prone; and as a God
90 Extoll him equal to the highest in Heav'n:
Nor faild they to express how much they prais'd,
That for the general safety he despis'd
His own: for neither do the Spirits damnd
Loose all thir vertue; least bad men should boast
95 Thir specious deeds on earth, which glory excites,
Or close ambition varnisht ore with zeal.
Thus they thir doubtful consultations dark
Ended, rejoycing in thir matchless Chief:
As when from mountain tops the dusky clouds
100 Ascending, while the North wind sleeps, orespread
Heav'ns chearful face, the lowring Element
Scowls ore the dark'nd lantskip Snow, or showre;
If chance the radiant Sun with farewell sweet
Extend his ev'ning beam, the fields revive,
105 The birds thir notes renew, and bleating herds
Attest thir joy, that hill and valley rings.
O shame to men! Devil with Devil damnd
Firm concord holds: men onely disagree
Of Creatures rational, though under hope
110 Of heav'nly Grace; and God proclaiming peace,
Yet live in hatred, enmitie, and strife
Among themselves, and levie cruel warres,
Wasting the Earth, each other to destroy:
As if (which might induce us to accord)
115 Man had not hellish foes anow besides,
That day and night for his destruction waite.
    The *Stygian* Council thus dissolv'd; and forth
In order came the grand infernal Peers:
Midst came thir mighty Paramount, and seemd
120 Alone th' Antagonist of Heav'n, nor less
Then Hells dread Emperour with pomp Supream,
And God-like imitated State; him round
A Globe of fierie Seraphim inclos'd
With bright imblazonrie, and horrent Arms.
125 Then of thir Session ended they bid cry
With Trumpets regal sound the great result:
Toward the four winds four speedy Cherubim
Put to thir mouths the sounding Alchymie
By Haralds voice explaind: the hollow Abyss
130 Heard farr and wide, and all the host of Hell
With deafning shout, returnd them loud acclaim.

Notes

1   **ye**   In his earlier works, Milton uses *you* and *thou*. Here, in epic context, he uses an archaising form of the second-person plural pronoun, which had been in retreat for half a century. The spelling ‹ye› is used when it occurs in unstressed position, and ‹yee› in stressed position. Cf. the forms *wee* (25), *hee* (66).

11   **gloom** 'darkness'   Milton first uses the word in this sense in 1629. It seems to be a back formation from the adjective *gloomy*, first used by Shakespeare. Earlier etymology is uncertain but may be related to Scots *gloaming*.

13   **balme**   A number of words occur which were originally borrowed into ME from French then reformed on the model of Latin: *Abyss* (ME *abisme*), *doubtful* (ME *douteful*), *equal* (ME *egal*). *Balme* may be considered one of these (ME *baume*; Lat. *balsamus*). However, the sound change by which [ɑlm] > [ɑulm] > [ɑum] may have encouraged analogical reformation through an awareness of the relationship between *al* and *au*.

15   **tempt**   Aphetic (see page 150 note 101) form of *attempt*.

19   **indefatigable** 'untiring'   Recorded in 1611 from French, but rare before Milton's use of it.

21   **Ile**   Milton prefers the medieval French and English form to that remodelled on Latin *insula* in French of the fifteenth century and common in English since the mid sixteenth century.

26   **suffrage**   The sense 'intercessionary prayer' belongs to the four-teenth century, but the sense 'election', found here, is contemporary with the poem.

35   **Heav'n-warring**   This type of endocentric adjectival compound consisting of a noun and present participle became common in the sixteenth century and is especially frequent in Shakespeare.

38   **transcendent**   A technical term drawn from medieval Latin philosophy and recorded only in dictionaries before 1611.

40   **Conscious**   This modern sense is not recorded until 1632.

42   **demurr** 'state of irresolution'   Recorded from the sixteenth century.

45   **convex** 'vault (of heaven or hell)' (Lat. *convexum*)   A learned word, but recorded as a noun from 1626.

46   **Outrageous** 'mad, furious'   This sense of the French borrowing was common in Middle English but was obsolete by the mid nineteenth century.

48   **egress** 'right of exit'   A term with legal associations, first recorded in 1538.

50   **unessential** 'insubstantial'   The first recorded occurrence with this sense; the form recorded only from 1656.

57   **Sovranty**   Milton's habitual spelling of *sovereignty* may have been influenced by the Italian *sovrano* but also served to indicate precisely the pronunciation required for the metre.

87   **Thir**   The unstressed form of the pronoun. The stressed form is *their*.

102 **lantskip**   The earlier and colloquial form of the word *landscape*. This was a technical term of artists, borrowed from Dutch *landschap*. First recorded in 1598.

116 **waite** 'keep watch (with hostile intent)'   This Anglo-Norman borrowing was an archaism in Milton's time.

120 **Antagonist**   Borrowed from Greek and first recorded by Ben Jonson in 1599.

121 **Supream**   Milton uses this spelling when he wishes to indicate that the stress is to fall on the second syllable. His spelling for stress on the initial syllable is identical to that of Modern English.

125 **cry** 'proclaim, announce'   Another archaism; common in Middle English.

129 **Abyss**   The ME form, *abisme*, borrowed from OF, is formed colloquially as a superlative of *abyssus*, *abyssimus, 'of profound depth'. The sixteenth-century form *abyss* restores the classical Latin form.

35 *Sir Isaac Newton,* Opticks

The career of Sir Isaac Newton began unpromisingly: his father was dead before Newton's premature birth on Christmas Day 1642, and his mother remarried before he was four, leaving her son to be raised by his grandmother. The child was sickly and not expected to survive, and he grew up during the Civil War in a time of some uncertainty, when Woolsthorpe Manor (six miles south of Grantham) was a Royalist household in a predominantly Parliamentarian countryside. Nothing is known of Newton's early education before he entered the King's School, Grantham at the age of twelve, but legend credits him already with possession of mechanical and experimental aptitude. His schooling was interrupted by the necessity of managing his family's estate, but his outstanding abilities took him to Trinity College, Cambridge in 1661. There his talents were quickly recognised, and the existing Lucasian Professor of Mathematics generously stood down to enable Newton, at the age of twenty-six, to occupy his chair. In 1699 he left Cambridge for London and became Master of the Mint and President of the Royal Society in 1703, holding these two offices until his death in 1727.

Newton's scientific reputation rests on three major achievements: his explanation of the laws of motion, his development of the calculus, and his work in optics. The groundwork for all was laid in a period of extraordinary creativity during his absence from Cambridge during the plague years of 1665–66. His major work, the *Principia*, was published – in Latin as was the custom for important scientific writings – in 1687, and the *Opticks* appeared in English in 1704, with a Latin translation in 1706. A second, augmented edition appeared in 1718, and the present text is based on this, preserving its spelling, capitalisation and punctuation. The language is modern in terms of its spelling and morphology, but not entirely so in syntax and lexis. Some words (*Window-shut*) and senses (*Species* meaning 'image') are obsolete, and periphrastic *do* is both omitted and used in negatives (35, 81) and also in declaratives (14). Newton has a fondness for lengthy sentences with much embedded qualification. His style is formal but not unvaryingly so, and he will use both colloquialisms (*'tis manifest*) and metaphorical or otherwise marked lexical choices: *paint* (9), *lively* (33).

Exper. 8. In Summer when the Sun's Light uses to be strongest, I placed a Prism at the hole of the Window-shut, as in the third Experiment, yet so that its Axis might be parallel to the Axis of the World, and at the opposite Wall in the
5 Sun's refracted Light, I placed an open Book. Then going six Feet and two Inches from the Book, I placed there the above-mentioned Lens, by which the Light reflected from the Book might be made to converge and meet again at the distance of six Feet and two Inches behind the Lens, and there paint the
10 Species of the Book upon a sheet of white Paper much after the manner of the second Experiment. The Book and Lens being made fast, I noted the Place where the Paper was, when the Letters of the Book, illuminated by the fullest red Light of the solar Image falling upon it, did cast their Species
15 on that Paper most distinctly: And then I stay'd till by the Motion of the Sun, and consequent Motion of his Image on the Book, all the Colours from that red to the middle of the blue pass'd over those Letters; and when those Letters were illuminated by that blue, I noted again the place of the Paper
20 when they cast their Species most distinctly upon it: And I found that this last place of the Paper was nearer to the Lens than its former place by about two Inches and an half, or two and three quarters. So much sooner therefore did the Light in the violet end of the Image by a greater Refraction converge
25 and meet, than the Light in the red end. But in trying this the Chamber was as dark as I could make it. For if these Colours be diluted and weakned by the Mixture of any adventitious Light, the distance between the Places of the Paper will not be so great. This distance in the second Experiment where
30 the Colours of natural Bodies were made use of, was but an Inch and an half, by reason of the Imperfection of those Colours. Here in the Colours of the Prism, which are manifestly more full, intense, and lively than those of natural Bodies, the distance is two Inches and three quarters. And
35 were the Colours still more full, I question not but that the distance would be considerably greater. For the coloured Light of the Prism, by the interfering of the Circles described in the second Figure of the fifth Experiment, and also by the Light of the very bright Clouds next the Sun's Body
40 intermixing with these Colours, and by the Light scattered by the inequalities in the Polish of the Prism, was so very much compounded, that the Species which those faint and dark Colours, the indigo and violet, cast upon the Paper were not distinct enough to be well observed.

45   *Exper.* 9. A Prism, whose two Angles at its Base were
equal to one another and half right ones, and the third a right
one, I placed in a beam of the Sun's Light let into a dark
Chamber through a hole in the Window-shut, as in the third
Experiment. And turning the Prism slowly about its Axis
50   until all the Light which went through one of its Angles and
was refracted by it began to be reflected by its Base, at which
till then it went out of the Glass, I observed that those Rays
which had suffered the greatest Refraction were sooner
reflected than the rest. I conceived therefore that those Rays
55   of the reflected Light, which were most refrangible, did first
of all by a total Reflexion become more copious in that Light
than the rest, and that afterwards the rest also, by a total
Reflexion, became as copious as these. To try this, I made
the reflected Light pass through another Prism, and being
60   refracted by it to fall afterwards upon a Sheet of white Paper
placed at some distance behind it, and there by that
Refraction to paint the usual Colours of the Prism. And then
causing the first Prism to be turned about its Axis as above, I
observed that when those Rays which in this Prism had
65   suffered the greatest Refraction and appeared of a blue and
violet Colour began to be totally reflected, the blue and violet
Light on the Paper which was most refracted in the second
Prism received a sensible increase above that of the red and
yellow, which was least refracted; and afterwards when the
70   rest of the Light which was green, yellow and red began to be
totally reflected in the first Prism, the Light of those Colours
on the Paper received as great an increase as the violet and
blue had done before. Whence 'tis manifest, that the beam of
Light reflected by the Base of the Prism, being augmented
75   first by the more refrangible Rays, and afterwards by the less
refrangible ones, is compounded of Rays differently refrangible. And that all such reflected Light is of the same nature
with the Sun's Light before its Incidence on the Base of the
Prism, no Man ever doubted: it being generally allowed, that
80   Light by such Reflexions suffers no alteration in its Modifications and Properties. I do not here take Notice of any
Refractions made in the sides of the first Prism, because the
Light enters it perpendicularly at the first side, and goes out
perpendicularly at the second side, and therefore suffers
85   none. So then, the Sun's incident Light being of the same
Temper and Constitution with his emergent Light, and the
last being compounded of Rays differently refrangible, the
first must be in like manner compounded.

Notes

1   **uses to be**   First recorded during the fourteenth century, this structure becomes rare in the present tense by the mid eighteenth century. In plural uses the distinction between the tenses ·is sometimes lost by the assimilation of *-ed* to the following *t*, and an invariant form *use* is written.

16   **his Image**   Newton's language has the possessive *its* (22), but he chooses to personify the sun, taking its masculine gender from the Latin *sol*.

33   **full . . . lively** 'saturated . . . vivid'   The former is recorded of colour only from 1657; the latter from the fourteenth century. The modern technical term *saturated* dates from 1853 in this use.

37   **the interfering of the Circles**   The overlapping circles of refracted light of different wavelengths found in a spectrum derived from a pin-hole source. The use of the deverbal noun is recorded between the sixteenth and early nineteenth centuries, before it is superseded by *interference*.

55   **refrangible** 'subject to refraction'   First recorded in 1673 from Newton's writings. He seems to have coined the technical term from a supposed Latin adjective *refrangibilis* derived from *refrangere*. The correct Latin form, however, is *refringere*.

Alexander Pope (1688–1744) was born off Lombard Street in London, the son of a linen importer and exporter who was a Roman Catholic. In an age when religious intolerance was rife, the young Alexander's father judged it prudent to move his family to Binfield in Windsor Forest, where the boy grew up and perhaps developed an interest in natural landscape which he indulged in his latter years in Twickenham. As a Catholic, entry to the major educational establishments was out of the question, so that although Pope had two or three years' schooling in Catholic schools, first at Twyford near Winchester and then in Marylebone, he was largely self educated. He seems to have been studious by nature and this inclination was perhaps furthered by a serious illness at the age of twelve which arrested his growth and partially crippled him. He had, however, demonstrated his metrical skills in 'Pastorals', written by the time he was sixteen, and through his friendship with Wycherley he found an entrée into London literary life. Although he wrote some lyric and dramatic verse, his talents lay in narrative and satire. His translations of the works of Homer provided him with the funding with which to develop his literary gifts.

The *Rape of the Lock* is an early work, first published in Lintot's *Miscellaneous Poems and Translations* in 1712, then republished in much-expanded form in 1714, adding the game of Ombre and the mythological machinery of the sylphs. The circumstances were that some time before 1712, Robert, Lord Petre, cut a lock from the hair of Arabella Fermor, to her and her family's indignation. The two families became estranged, and a mutual friend, John Caryll, suggested to Pope that he should heal the rift by composing a comic poem about the incident, to laugh them out of their hostility. This strategy was of limited practical success, since what good had been achieved was afterwards compromised by the poem's publication, but it resulted in the engaging mock-epic from which this excerpt is taken. The text is that of the first edition of 1714. Pope's language was regarded by the Romantics at the end of the century as consciously poetic and artificial, arising partly from his use of archaisms, partly from his Latinism, and partly from the inflation which here plays a comic role. This excerpt, however, is not without colloquialisms which serve comically to deflate the pretensions of the more 'poetic' language.

Close by those Meads for ever crown'd with Flow'rs,
Where *Thames* with Pride surveys his rising Tow'rs,
There stands a Structure of Majestick Frame,
Which from the neighb'ring *Hampton* takes its Name.
5 Here *Britain*'s Statesmen oft the Fall foredoom
Of Foreign Tyrants, and of Nymphs at home;
Here Thou, Great *Anna*! whom three Realms obey,
Dost sometimes Counsel take – and sometimes *Tea.*
Hither the Heroes and the Nymphs resort,
10 To taste awhile the Pleasures of a Court;
In various Talk th' instructive hours they past,
Who gave the *Ball*, or paid the *Visit* last:
One speaks the Glory of the *British Queen*,
And one describes a charming *Indian Screen*;
15 A third interprets Motions, Looks, and Eyes;
At ev'ry Word a Reputation dies.
Snuff, or the *Fan*, supply each Pause of Chat,
With singing, laughing, ogling, and all that.
Mean while declining from the Noon of Day,
20 The Sun obliquely shoots his burning Ray;
The hungry Judges soon the Sentence sign,
And Wretches hang that Jury-men may Dine;
The Merchant from th'*Exchange* returns in Peace,
And the long Labours of the *Toilette* cease –
25 *Belinda* now, whom Thirst of Fame invites,
Burns to encounter two adventrous Knights,
At *Ombre* singly to decide their Doom;
And swells her Breast with Conquests yet to come.
Strait the three Bands prepare in Arms to join,
30 Each Band the number of the Sacred Nine.
Soon as she spreads her Hand, th' Aerial Guard
Descend, and sit on each important Card:
First *Ariel* perch'd upon a *Matadore*,
Then each, according to the Rank they bore;
35 For *Sylphs*, yet mindful of their ancient Race,
Are, as when Women, wondrous fond of Place.
Behold, four *Kings* in Majesty rever'd,
With hoary Whiskers and a forky Beard;
And four fair *Queens* whose hands sustain a Flow'r,
40 Th' expressive Emblem of their softer Pow'r;
Four *Knaves* in Garbs succinct, a trusty Band,
Caps on their heads, and Halberds in their hand;
And Particolour'd Troops, a shining Train,
Draw forth to Combat on the Velvet Plain.

45   The skilful Nymph reviews her Force with Care;
      Let Spades be Trumps! she said, and Trumps they were.
      Now move to War her Sable *Matadores*,
      In Show like Leaders of the swarthy *Moors*.
      Spadillio first, unconquerable Lord!
50   Let off two captive Trumps, and swept the Board.
      As many more *Manillio* forc'd to yield,
      And march'd a Victor from the verdant Field.
      Him *Basto* follow'd, but his Fate more hard
      Gain'd but one Trump and one *Plebeian* Card.
55   With his broad Sabre next, a Chief in Years,
      The hoary Majesty of *Spades* appears;
      Puts forth one manly Leg, to sight reveal'd;
      The rest his many-colour'd Robe conceal'd.
      The Rebel-*Knave*, who dares his Prince engage,
60   Proves the just Victim of his Royal Rage.
      Ev'n mighty *Pam* that Kings and Queens o'erthrew,
      And mow'd down Armies in the Fights of *Lu*,
      Sad Chance of War! now, destitute of Aid,
      Falls undistinguish'd by the Victor *Spade!*
65   Thus far both Armies to *Belinda* yield;
      Now to the *Baron* Fate inclines the Field.
      His warlike *Amazon* her Host invades,
      Th' Imperial Consort of the Crown of *Spades*.
      The *Club*'s black Tyrant first her Victim dy'd,
70   Spite of his haughty Mien, and barb'rous Pride:
      What boots the Regal Circle on his Head,
      His Giant Limbs in State unwieldy spread?
      That long behind he trails his pompous Robe,
      And of all Monarchs only grasps the Globe?
75   The *Baron* now his *Diamonds* pours apace;
      Th' embroider'd *King* who shows but half his Face,
      And his refulgent *Queen*, with Pow'rs combin'd,
      Of broken Troops an easie Conquest find.
      Clubs, *Diamonds*, *Hearts*, in wild Disorder seen,
80   With Throngs promiscuous strow the level Green.
      Thus when dispers'd a routed Army runs,
      Of *Asia*'s Troops, and *Africk*'s Sable Sons,
      With like Confusion different Nations fly,
      Of various Habit and of various Dye,
85   The pierc'd Battalions dis-united fall,
      In Heaps on Heaps; one Fate o'erwhelms them all.
      The *Knave* of *Diamonds* tries his wily Arts,
      And wins (oh shameful Chance!) the *Queen* of *Hearts*.

At this, the Blood the Virgin's Cheek forsook,
90 A livid Paleness spreads o'er all her Look;
She sees, and trembles at th' approaching Ill,
Just in the Jaws of Ruin, and *Codille*.
And now, (as oft in some distemper'd State)
On one nice *Trick* depends the gen'ral Fate.
95 An *Ace* of Hearts steps forth: The *King* unseen
Lurk'd in her Hand, and mourn'd his captive *Queen*.
He springs to Vengeance with an eager pace,
And falls like Thunder on the prostrate *Ace*.
The Nymph exulting fills with Shouts the Sky,
100 The Walls, the Woods, and long Canals reply.
   Oh thoughtless Mortals! ever blind to Fate,
Too soon dejected, and too soon elate!
Sudden these Honours shall be snatch'd away,
And curs'd for ever this Victorious Day.
105   For lo! the Board with Cups and Spoons is crown'd,
The Berries crackle, and the Mill turns round.
On shining Altars of *Japan* they raise
The silver Lamp; the fiery Spirits blaze.
From silver Spouts the grateful Liquors glide,
110 While *China*'s Earth receives the smoking Tyde.
At once they gratify their Scent and Taste,
And frequent Cups prolong the rich Repast.
Strait hover round the Fair her Airy Band;
Some, as she sip'd, the fuming Liquor fann'd,
115 Some o'er her Lap their careful Plumes display'd,
Trembling, and conscious of the rich Brocade.
Coffee, (which makes the Politician wise,
And see thro' all things with his half-shut Eyes)
Sent up in Vapours to the *Baron*'s Brain
120 New Stratagems, the radiant Lock to gain.
Ah cease rash Youth! desist ere 'tis too late,
Fear the just Gods, and think of *Scylla*'s Fate!
Chang'd to a Bird, and sent to flit in Air,
She dearly pays for *Nisus*' injur'd Hair!
125   But when to Mischief Mortals bend their Will,
How soon they find fit Instruments of Ill!
Just then, *Clarissa* drew with tempting Grace
A two-edg'd Weapon from her shining Case;
So Ladies in Romance assist their Knight,
130 Present the Spear, and arm him for the Fight.
He takes the Gift with rev'rence, and extends
The little Engine on his Fingers' Ends,
This just behind *Belinda*'s Neck he spread,

As o'er the fragrant Steams she bends her Head:
135 Swift to the Lock a thousand Sprights repair,
A thousand Wings, by turns, blow back the Hair,
And thrice they twitch'd the Diamond in her Ear,
Thrice she look'd back, and thrice the Foe drew near.
Just in that instant, anxious *Ariel* sought
140 The close Recesses of the Virgin's Thought;
As on the Nosegay in her Breast reclin'd,
He watch'd th' Ideas rising in her Mind,
Sudden he view'd, in spite of all her Art,
An Earthly Lover lurking at her Heart.
145 Amaz'd, confus'd, he found his Pow'r expir'd,
Resign'd to Fate, and with a Sigh retir'd.
   The Peer now spreads the glitt'ring *Forfex* wide,
T'inclose the Lock; now joins it, to divide.
Ev'n then, before the fatal Engine clos'd,
150 A wretched *Sylph* too fondly interpos'd;
Fate urg'd the Sheers, and cut the *Sylph* in twain,
(But Airy Substance soon unites again)
The meeting Points the sacred Hair dissever
From the fair Head, for ever and for ever!
155   Then flash'd the living Lightning from her Eyes,
And Screams of Horror rend th' affrighted Skies.
Not louder Shrieks to pitying Heav'n are cast,
When Husbands or when Lap-dogs breathe their last,
Or when rich *China* Vessels, fal'n from high,
160 In glittring Dust and painted Fragments lie!
   Let Wreaths of Triumph now my Temples twine,
(The Victor cry'd) the glorious Prize is mine!
While fish in Streams, or Birds delight in Air,
Or in a Coach and Six the *British* Fair,
165 As long as *Atalantis* shall be read,
Or the small Pillow grace a Lady's Bed,
While *Visits* shall be paid on solemn Days,
When numerous Wax-lights in bright Order blaze,
While Nymphs take Treats, or Assignations give,
170 So long my Honour, Name, and Praise shall live!
   What Time wou'd spare, from Steel receives its date,
And Monuments, like Men, submit to Fate!
Steel cou'd the Labour of the Gods destroy,
And strike to Dust th' Imperial Tow'rs of *Troy*;
175 Steel cou'd the Works of mortal Pride confound,
And hew Triumphal Arches to the Ground.
What Wonder then, fair Nymph! thy Hairs shou'd feel
The conqu'ring Force of unresisted Steel?

Notes

1 **Meads** The word was used in prose in Middle English but becomes progressively restricted to poetic language after the sixteenth century.

5–6 **foredoom : home** This rhyme, which occurs already in Chaucer, presupposes a raised variant [o:] in *home*, so that the vowels in both words are identical and are raised to /u:/ by the Great Vowel Shift.

7–8 **obey : Tea** The word *tea* made its way to Europe from Chinese by way of Malay and Dutch, *thee*, in the mid seventeenth century. Pronunciations varied between [i:] and [e:] until about 1760, when the modern pronunciation established itself.

17 **Chat** An abbreviated form of *chatter*, which itself seems to have been an onomatopoeic formation often used of birds and implying nonsense. *Chat* is recorded as a noun from 1530 to 1768 with the sense 'frivolous or idle talk', and from 1573 as 'familiar and informal conversation'.

18 **ogling** A slang word, first appearing in the late seventeenth century, probably derived from Dutch *oogheler*, 'to flatter', and Low German *oegeln*, 'to look at'.

29–30 **join : Nine** The word *join* was borrowed into English from two sources: Norman and Central French. The modern pronunciation derives from the latter borrowing, but the former source had a different diphthong ([ui] instead of [oi]) which was smoothed to [i:] in ME and underwent the same development as the ME long vowel. The pronunciation was probably [ʌi].

38 **forky** A rare word closely associated with Pope's literary world; first used by Dryden in 1697 and also by Swift.

40 **expressive** The wordform itself occurs from about 1400 onwards, but the sense 'serving to express, indicate or represent' was new in Pope's time, and is recorded only after 1711.

45–6 **Care : were** The vowel of *were* existed in early ME in both open and close variants, but lowering before /r/ ensured that the former was generalised. OE *eala* in *cearu/caru* was lengthened in an open syllable in early ME and was later progressively fronted and raised to reach [ɛ:] by 1650, when it coincided with the long open [ɛ:] in *were*.

47 **Sable** 'black' Used as a technical term in heraldry from 1352 on. Elsewhere, essentially a poetic word. This adjective is presumed to be derived from the noun, which is a rare medieval borrowing from a Slavic language (Russian *sobol*).

Matadores The principal card in the game of Ombre. One of a number of technical terms to do with the game borrowed from Spanish. All date from the last two decades of the seventeenth century: *Spadillio* (49), the 'ace of spades' (Sp. *espadilla*), *Manillio* (51), the second-best trump (Sp. *malilla*), *Basto* (53), the 'ace of clubs' (Sp. *basto*), *Codille* (92), an expression used in Ombre to describe the circumstances in which the challenger loses (Sp. *codillo*).

48 **swarthy**   The restriction to complexion is relatively recent. The sense 'black' is recorded between 1577 and 1842.

61 **Pam** 'the jack of clubs'   Apparently an abbreviation of French *pamphile*.

62 **Lu**   A card game, Loo or Lanterloo, in which the jack of clubs was the highest card.

70 **Mien** 'bearing'   An aphetic (see page 150 note 101) form of *demean*, but becomes associated in form and sense with French *mine*, 'expression, look'. Recorded from 1513 on, but only in poetic contexts.

80 **strow**   The variant spellings *strew*, *strow* arise from a shift of stress on the diphthong of OE *streowian*.

94 **nice Trick**   The phrase plays on different senses of the two words. The former, derived from Latin *ne scius*, 'ignorant', developed a very extended range of senses but here probably means 'subtle' or perhaps 'trivial'. The word *trick* is recorded in the context of cards from 1599, and often with this play on the older sense, 'deception'.

102 **elate**   This form is recorded from the fourteenth century. The type with the -*ed* suffix does not occur until 1615.

106 **Berries**   Coffee *berries* are mentioned from 1626, but the *OED* has no reference to coffee *beans* before the mid nineteenth century.

109 **grateful** 'pleasing to the senses, agreeable'   This sense recorded between 1553 and 1866.

111–12 **Taste : Repast**   The vowel in *taste* is short. The modern pronunciation developed through ME open-syllable lengthening in the verb form.

117 **Coffee**   Appears more or less simultaneously in all European languages about 1600. Derived from Turkish *kahveh*, probably from an Arabic original.

123 **flit**   (ON *flytja*. 'to move (from one place to another)'). The word had a wide range of senses to do with movement of position, but began to be restricted to the movement of birds from the mid sixteenth century.

37 Daniel Defoe, A Tour through the Whole Island of Great Britain

Defoe's *Tour*, published between 1724 and 1726, was based in part upon literary sources but more significantly on the experiences of an eventful life. Born in London in 1660, the son of a butcher, Defoe was the child of a Presbyterian family and, after initial schooling in Dorking, he was debarred by his religious affiliations from entering a university, instead attending Morton's Academy in Newington Green. There, rather than an education in the classics, he received instruction in English eloquence and composition, modern foreign languages and sciences. By 1680 he was a hose factor (a wholesale haberdasher) trying his hand at a range of other enterprises. His career as a commercial entrepreneur was interrupted when in June 1685 he joined Monmouth's side in an attempted revolution, an indiscretion for which he was pardoned in May 1687. By 1692 he was bankrupt with the enormous debt of £17,000, but he survived in minor government posts and through considerable income from a brick and tile factory near Tilbury which he owned. Following the publication of his first substantial work, the *Essay on Projects* (1697), he became a semi-official apologist for the policies of King William. In 1703, however, he was arrested and placed in the pillory for allegedly publishing a seditious pamphlet, *The Shortest Way with Dissenters*, but he was released and compensated, becoming a political agent for Robert Harley, Speaker of the House of Commons. He subsequently acted as an agent (sometimes a double agent) for both political factions, travelling extensively in Britain collecting information and opinions. Although Defoe was an exceedingly prolific author who is credited with 566 publications, he wrote all his major works between 1715 and his death in April 1731.

The anecdotal interest he shows here in the English language was preceded in his *Essay on Projects* by enthusiasm for standardisation by the foundation of an Academy. Here, however, he is telling entertaining stories rather than pleading a cause. Nevertheless, his account of the contemporary Somerset dialect is in most respects acceptable, even though the *ch*-forms are notoriously stage-rustic. The case of a country boy who reads standard orthography in his own dialect is a reminder that standardised speech had not been universally attained even in the early eighteenth century.

In my return to my western progress, I pass'd some little part
of Somersetshire, as thro' Evil, or Yeovil, upon the river Ivil,
in going to which we go down a long steep hill, which they
call Babylon-Hill; but from what original I could find none of
5 the country people to inform me.

This Yeovil is a market town of good resort, and some clothing is carry'd on, in, and near it, but not much, its main
manufacture at this time is making of gloves.

It cannot pass my observation here, that when we are come
10 this length from London, the dialect of the English tongue, or
the country way of expressing themselves is not easily understood, it is so strangely altered; it is true, that it is so in many
parts of England besides, but in none in so gross a degree as
in this part; This way of boorish country speech, as in Ireland,
15 it is call'd the brogue upon the tongue; so here 'tis call'd
jouring, and 'tis certain, that tho' the tongue be all meer
natural English, yet those that are but a little acquainted with
them, cannot understand one half of what they say: It is not
possible to explain this fully by writing, because the difference
20 is not so much in the orthography of words, as in the tone,
and diction; their abridging the speech, *cham* for *I am*, *chil*
for *I will*, *don*, for *put on*, and *doff*, for put off, and the like.

And I cannot omit a short story here on this subject; coming
to a relations house, who was a school-master at Martock in
25 Somersetshire, I went into his school to beg the boys a play
day, as is usual in such cases; I should have said to beg the
master a play day, but that by the way; coming into the
school, I observ'd one of the lowest scholars was reading his
lesson to the usher, which lesson it seems was a chapter in the
30 Bible, so I sat down by the master, till the boy had read out
his chapter: I observ'd the boy read a little oddly in the tone
of the country, which made me the more attentive, because
on enquiry, I found that the words were the same, and the
orthography the same as in all our Bibles. I observ'd also the
35 boy read it out with his eyes still on the book, and his head
like a meer boy, moving from side to side, as the lines reach'd
cross the columns of the book; his lesson was in the Cant. 5.
3. of which the words are these,

'I have put off my coat, how shall I put it on, I have wash'd
40 my feet, how shall I defile them?'
The boy read thus, with his eyes, as I say, full on the text.

'Chav a doffed my cooat, how shall I don't, chav a wash'd
my veet, how shall I moil'em?'
How the dexterous dunce could form his mouth to express

45 so readily the words, (which stood right printed in the book) in his country jargon, I could not but admire; I shall add to this another peice as diverting, which also happen'd in my knowledge at this very town of Yeovil, tho' some years ago.

50 There liv'd a good substantial family in the town, not far from the Angel Inn, a well known house, which was then, and I suppose is still the chief inn of the town. This family had a dog, which among his other good qualities, for which they kept him (for he was a rare house dog) had this bad one, that he was a most notorious thief; but withal, so cunning a 55 dog, and managed himself so warily, that he preserved a mighty good reputation among the neighbourhood; as the family was well beloved in the town, so was the dog; he was known to be a very useful servant to them, especially in the night, when he was fierce as a lion, but in the day the 60 gentlest, lovingest creature that could be, and as they said, all the neighbours had a good word for this dog.

It happen'd that the good wife, or mistress at the Angel Inn, had frequently missed several peices of meat out of the pail, as they say, or powdering-tub, as we call it; and that 65 some very large peices; 'tis also to be observ'd the dog did not stay to eat (what he took) upon the spot, in which case some peices, or bones, or fragments might be left, and so it might be discover'd to be a dog; but he made cleaner work, and when he fasten'd upon a peice of meat he was sure to 70 carry it away, to such retreats as he knew he could be safe in, and so feast upon it at leisure.

It happen'd at last, as with most thieves it does, that the inn-keeper was too cunning for him, and the poor dog was nabb'd, taken in the fact, and could make no defence.

75 Having found the thief, and got him in custody, the master of the house, a good humour'd fellow, and loth to disoblige the dog's master, by executing the criminal, as the dog-law directs; mitigates his sentence, and handled him as follows; first taking out his knife, he cut off both his ears, and then 80 bringing him to the threshold, he chop'd off his tail; and having thus effectually dishonour'd the poor cur among his neighbours, he tyed a string about his neck, and a peice of paper to the string directed to his master, and with these witty west country verses on it.

85   To my honour'd master – Esq;
        Hail master a cham a' com hoam
        So cut as an ape, and tail have I noan,

For stealing of beef, and pork, out of the pail,
For thease they'v cut my ears, for th' wother my tail;
90   Nea measter, and us tell thee more nor that
And's come there again, my brains will be flat.

I could give many more accounts of the different dialects of
the people of this country, in some of which they are really
not to be understood, but the particulars have little or no
95 diversion in them, they carry it such a length, that we see
their jouring speech even upon their monuments, and grave-
stones; As for example, even in some of the church-yards of
the city of Bristol, I saw this excellent poetry after some other
lines –

100   And when that thou doest hear of thick,
Think of the glass that runneth quick.

But I proceed into Devonshire, from Evil we came to
Crookorn, thence to Chard, and from thence into the same
road I was in before at Honiton.

Notes

8 **making of gloves**   The use of a deverbal noun followed by a
genitive phrase, in which the noun may be understood as object to
the verb underlying the deverbal noun, is common from ME to the
early nineteenth century. This type, where the verbal quality of
making is emphasised by the lack of a determiner, is stigmatised in
the nineteenth century.

15–16 **brogue . . . jouring**   The earlier sense of *brogue* is 'shoe, sandal'
(Irish *brōg*), but the sense 'marked accent' dates from 1705. *Jouring*
(*EDD* 'jower') is quoted as a dialect verb in Shropshire, Somerset
and Devon, meaning 'to grumble, mutter'. Defoe is the only
authority for the sense here.

16–17 **meer natural** 'pure natural' (Lat. *merus*)   Used of speech
commonly between the mid sixteenth and eighteenth centuries, and
later in the phrase 'mere Irish'.

21 **cham**, etc.   These forms of the verbs 'to be' and 'will', arising
originally from *ich am, ich wyl*, had long been conventional
indicators of southern rustic speech. See Wilson's *Arte of Rhetorique*
(Excerpt 24). *Don* and *doff* were widespread in dialect use in the
nineteenth century.

42 **Chav**, etc.   The spelling ‹cooat› represents a non-standard
diphthong; *veet* preserves the voicing of initial fricatives found in the
South and South-West in ME; *moil* is recorded by *EDD* as a verb
with the sense 'defile' from Worcester, Shropshire, Gloucester and
Cornwall. The *a* in the past participles *a doffed* and *a wash'd*

represents the survival of the OE prefix *ge-*. In ME this had survived latest in the South and South-West, spelt ‹y› or ‹i›, but was later lowered and centralised and is here spelt ‹a›.

56 **mighty good**   The use of *mighty* as an intensifier begins in OE, and was felt to belong to informal and colloquial register by the nineteenth century. Something of this colloquialism is already evident in the familiarity of language choice and the irony of this story of the thieving dog. Perhaps in deference to readers' sensibilities, this passage was omitted from the edition of 1778.

60 **lovingest**   The superlative of disyllabic adjectives still permits formation by the suffix *-est*.

62 **good wife**   The phrase had the idiomatic sense 'landlady, lady of the house' as early as the mid thirteenth century, and it is inconsistently written as a compound from the mid fourteenth. *OED* lists its use until the end of the nineteenth century. A reduced form, *goody*, is also recorded from 1589 onwards. Cf. *housewife* and *hussy*.

64 **powdering tub**   'A tub in which the flesh of animals is "powdered" or salted and pickled'.

65 **'tis**   A common abbreviation in this period. Perhaps indicates some relaxation in the formality of the style, but is common also in relatively formal and technical contexts (cf. Newton, Excerpt 35), and should not be regarded as so obvious a colloquialism as its appearance in a modern context would indicate.

74 **nabb'd** 'arrested, taken into custody'   A slang or colloquial expression first recorded in 1686.

78 **mitigates**   The use of the present tense in a predominantly preterite context may be considered a feature of the familiar tone of this narrative. The 'historic present' is recorded from the thirteenth century on. It was probably encouraged by French influence but is found also in other Germanic languages.

81 **effectually** 'effectively'   The noun *effect* gave rise to three derivative adjectives and associated adverbs during the fourteenth century: *effectual*, *effective* and *effectuous*. The first is in retreat, surviving most obviously in *ineffectual*, and the last is not recorded after the seventeenth century.

89 **thease** 'this'   Listed by *EDD* for Hereford, Gloucester, Dorset, Devon and Cornwall.

wother 'other'   Forms with initial *w-* are recorded for Devon and Somerset. Cf. the standard pronunciation of *one*, which developed an initial *w-* by the fifteenth century in the South-West. The *w-* pronunciation began to be acknowledged by orthoepists after 1700. The western pronunciation seems never to have been widely accepted in the case of *other*.

90 **and us** 'if I'   The use of *us* as a first-person singular pronoun is widespread in the West Country.

100 **thick** 'this'   This form is recorded from Worcester, Gloucester, Berkshire, Somerset, Devon and Cornwall.

Samuel Johnson (1709–1784) was born in Lichfield, attended Lichfield Grammar School, and went on to Pembroke College, Oxford. His university career ended after fourteen months when shortage of funds forced his departure without a degree. His struggle for survival saw him successively as an unsuccessful schoolmaster, the proprietor of a private school, and a journalist in Birmingham. In 1737 he moved to London and supported his wife and himself by writing for *The Gentleman's Magazine*. Alongside various hack work, he made time for scholarly and literary production, and in 1747 he announced his 'Plan of a Dictionary' 'by which the pronunciation of our language may be fixed, and its attainment facilitated; by which its purity may be preserved, its use ascertained, and its duration lengthened'. The *Dictionary* was published in 1755, gaining Johnson immediate acclaim, an honorary degree from the University of Oxford, a Crown pension of £300 a year and an honoured place in the contemporary literary world.

As Johnson's remark, quoted from the 'Plan', suggests, the *Dictionary* arose from that concern for the status and function of the English language which had been part of learned debate since the sixteenth century. Men educated in Latin literature had for centuries been concerned by the variety, the expressive limitations and the changes they perceived in English, and as early as 1582 Mulcaster had called for an English dictionary as a remedy. Although English–Latin dictionaries existed in the fifteenth century, and other bilingual dictionaries followed in the sixteenth, there is general agreement that the earliest true dictionary of English is Robert Cawdrey's *A Table Alphabeticall of Hard Words* (1604), whose purpose was to enlighten its readers on the spelling and significance of the many recent borrowings into English. This 'hard word' approach evolved during the sixteenth and earlier seventeenth centuries into the conception of a scholarly dictionary with universal coverage. Johnson's work, which contained 40,000 entries whose senses were established by 114,000 quotations, was the most substantial contribution to the art and stature of lexicography before the publication of the *New English Dictionary* in 1884.

Although the passage quoted below demonstrates Johnson's awareness of the dynamic nature of language, it is clear that he does not view this fact with much satisfaction, and his methodology in compiling the *Dictionary* was more in accord with the statement in the 'Plan', and fundamentally prescriptive. He did not aim to be exhaustive, nor to provide sense histories; much contemporary colloquialism is deliberately excluded, and the senses of words which he establishes by quotation are mostly drawn from authors of an idealised past, from Sidney to the Restoration. Although Johnson exhibits much linguistic common sense, he does not separate himself from the assumption of the age that a regulated and stable language is a desirable, even if doubtfully attainable goal.

Of the event of this work, for which, having laboured it with so much application, I cannot but have some degree of parental fondness, it is natural to form conjectures. Those who have been persuaded to think well of my design, require
5 that it should fix our language, and put a stop to those alterations which time and chance have hitherto been suffered to make in it without opposition. With this consequence I will confess that I flattered myself for a while; but now begin to fear that I have indulged expectation which
10 neither reason nor experience can justify. When we see men grow old and die at a certain time one after another, from century to century, we laugh at the elixir that promises to prolong life to a thousand years; and with equal justice may the lexicographer be derided, who being able to produce no
15 example of a nation that has preserved their words and phrases from mutability, shall imagine that his dictionary can embalm his language, and secure it from corruption and decay, that it is in his power to change sublunary nature, or clear the world at once from folly, vanity, and affectation.
20 With this hope, however, academies have been instituted, to guard the avenues of their languages, to retain fugitives, and repulse intruders; but their vigilance and activity have hitherto been in vain; sounds are too volatile and subtile for legal restraints; to enchain syllables, and to lash the wind, are
25 equally the undertakings of pride, unwilling to measure its desires by its strength. The *French* language has visibly changed under the inspection of the academy; the stile of *Amelot*'s translation of father *Paul* is observed by *Le Courayer* to be *un peu passé*; and no Italian will maintain,
30 that the diction of any modern writer is not perceptibly different from that of *Boccace*, *Machiavel*, or *Caro*.

Total and sudden transformations of a language seldom
happen; conquests and migrations are now very rare: but
there are other causes of change, which, though slow in their
35 operation, and invisible in their progress, are perhaps as
much superiour to human resistance, as the revolutions of the
sky, or intumescence of the tide. Commerce, however
necessary, however lucrative, as it depraves the manners,
corrupts the language; they that have frequent intercourse
40 with strangers, to whom they endeavour to accommodate
themselves, must in time learn a mingled dialect, like the
jargon which serves the traffickers on the *Mediterranean* and
Indian coasts. This will not always be confined to the
exchange, the warehouse or the port, but will be communic
45 ated by degrees to other ranks of the people, and be at last
incorporated with the current speech.

There are likewise internal causes equally forcible. The
language most likely to continue long without alteration,
would be that of a nation raised a little, and but a little,
50 above barbarity, secluded from strangers, and totally
employed in procuring the conveniencies of life; either
without books, or, like some of the *Mahometan* countries,
with very few: men thus busied and unlearned, having only
such words as common use requires, would perhaps long
55 continue to express the same notions by the same signs. But
no such constancy can be expected in a people polished by
arts, and classed by subordination, where one part of the
community is sustained and accommodated by the labour of
the other. Those who have much leisure to think, will always
60 be enlarging the stock of ideas, and every increase of
knowledge, whether real or fancied, will produce new words,
or combinations of words. When the mind is unchained from
necessity, it will range after convenience; when it is left at
large in the fields of speculation, it will shift opinions; as any
65 custom is disused, the words that express it must perish with
it; as any opinion grows popular, it will innovate speech in
the same proportion as it alters practice.

As by the cultivation of various sciences, a language is
amplified, it will be more furnished with words deflected from
70 their original sense; the geometrician will talk of a courtier's
zenith, or the excentrick virtue of a wild hero, and the
physician of sanguine expectations and phlegmatick delays.
Copiousness of speech will give opportunities to capricious
choice, by which some words will be preferred, and others
75 degraded; vicissitudes of fashion will enforce the use of new,

or extend the signification of known terms. The tropes of poetry will make hourly encroachments, and the metaphorical will become the current sense: pronunciation will be varied by levity or ignorance, and the pen must at length
80 comply with the tongue; illiterate writers will at one time or other, by publick infatuation, rise into licentiousness, confound distinction, and forget propriety. As politeness increases, some expressions will be considered as too gross and vulgar for the delicate, others as too formal and ceremonious for the
85 gay and airy; new phrases are therefore adopted, which must, for the same reasons, be in time dismissed. *Swift*, in his petty treatise on the *English* language, allows that new words must sometimes be introduced, but proposes that none should be suffered to become obsolete. But what makes a word
90 obsolete, more than general agreement to forbear it? and how shall it be continued, when it conveys an offensive idea, or recalled again into the mouths of mankind, when it has once by disuse become unfamiliar, and by unfamiliarity unpleasing.
95   There is another cause of alteration more prevalent than any other, which yet in the present state of the world cannot be obviated. A mixture of two languages will produce a third distinct from both; and they will always be mixed, where the chief part of education, and the most conspicuous accom-
100 plishment, is skill in ancient and foreign tongues. He that has long cultivated another language, will find its words and combinations croud upon his memory; and haste and negligence, refinement and affectation, will obtrude borrowed terms and exotick expressions.
105   The great pest of speech is frequency of translation. No book was ever turned from one language into another, without imparting something of its native idiom; this is the most mischievous and comprehensive innovation; single words may enter by thousands, and the fabrick of the tongue
110 continue the same, but new phraseology changes much at once; it alters not the single stones of the building, but the order of the columns. If an academy should be established for the cultivation of our stile, which I, who can never wish to see dependance multiplied, hope the spirit of *English* liberty will
115 hinder or destroy, let them, instead of compiling grammars and dictionaries, endeavour, with all their influence, to stop the licence of translatours, whose idleness and ignorance, if it be suffered to proceed, will reduce us to babble a dialect of *France*.

120 If the changes that we fear be thus irresistible, what
remains but to acquiesce with silence, as in the other
insurmountable distresses of humanity? it remains that we
retard what we cannot repel, that we palliate what we cannot
cure. Life may be lengthened by care, though death cannot
125 be ultimately defeated: tongues, like governments, have a
natural tendency to degeneration; we have long preserved
our constitution, let us make some struggles for our language.

Notes

1 **event** 'outcome'   First recorded 1573. Borrowed from French
with the Latin etymological sense of *evenire*, 'to come out'.

7–8 **with this consequence**   This adverbial is now normally used with
cataphoric (forward) rather than anaphoric (backward) reference.

10 **reason nor experience**   The implied opposition of these two terms
is medieval in origin, relating to deductive and inductive proof. The
words are now no longer felt to be in opposition in ordinary speech.

15 **nation . . . their**   The concord of many corporate nouns is still
uncertain, but *nation* would no longer have plural concord unless
qualified by the name of the nation concerned.

18 **sublunary**   First recorded in 1592. In the sense relevant to this
passage, from 1639. In the Ptolemaic conception of the universe, the
earth was encased in nine concentric spheres, the lowest of which
was that of the moon. All beneath the lunar sphere was subject to
change and decay.

20 **academies**   The Accademia della Crusca had been founded in
1582 and produced an Italian dictionary in 1612, and the French
Academy, founded in 1635, produced its dictionary in 1694.

21 **avenues**   The imagery is military. The word *avenue*, 'approach,
path of entry or exit', was originally a military term borrowed from
French, and was first recorded in 1600.

23 **volatile and subtile**   *Volatile* was borrowed from OF in the
fourteenth century as a noun referring to birds and other flying
creatures. As an adjective it is recorded applied to chemicals from
the early seventeenth century. *Subtile*, with the sense 'fine,
insubstantial', is a fourteenth-century refashioning, on the model of
Latin *subtilis*, of OF and ME *soutil*. Both *subtile* and *subtle* occur as
alternative spellings from the fourteenth to the late nineteenth
century.

28 **Amelot**   Nicolas Amelot de la Houssaye (1634–1706). In 1683 he
published a French translation of the *History of the Council of Trent*
by Paolo Servita.

29 **Le Courayer**   Pierre François Le Courayer published his own
translation of Servita's *History of the Council of Trent* in 1736.

31 **Boccace . . . Caro**   Three Tuscan authors: Giovanni Boccaccio
(1313–1375), Latin encyclopaedist and founder of Italian prose

literature; Niccolo Machiavelli (1469–1527), administrator, literary man and political theorist; Annibale Caro (1507–1566), translator of the *Aeneid* into Italian.

37 **intumescence** 'swelling up'   Recorded as a borrowing from French from 1656.

42 **traffickers**   The word was used from the sixteenth to the nineteenth century to mean 'merchant', not necessarily with pejorative association. But pejorative senses are found throughout that period.

58 **accommodated** 'provided for'   From 1597 onwards. The narrowed sense 'provided with lodging' is recorded only from 1715, but the noun is used in the modern sense, 'suitable lodging', from 1604.

63 **convenience** 'comfort'   This sense recorded from 1703 onwards.

71 **zenith**   Not a very new extension of the meaning of the word, since this figurative use is recorded from 1601.

excentrick   Used of a person or personal attribute from 1685.

72 **sanguine**   Feelings of hopefulness and self-confidence were considered characteristic of the personality of those dominated by sanguine humour. The word was used figuratively to suggest these characteristics from 1673.

phlegmatick   Phlegmatic people were apathetic and not easily enthused. *OED* does not record the sense development foreseen by Johnson for this word, which seems always to be applied to persons.

76 **tropes** 'rhetorical devices' (Lat. *tropus*)   Properly one of those figures of speech that medieval rhetoricians regarded as 'difficult ornament' and which relied on the use of words with modified senses. Metaphor is one such trope.

82 **propriety** 'stylistic decorum, appropriateness'   The suitability of verbal choices to their context, both verbal and situational.

86 **Swift**   Johnson refers to Jonathan Swift's *Proposal for Correcting, Improving, and Ascertaining the English Tongue* (1712), in which he proposes the formation of an English Academy to stabilise English usage.

112 **columns**   The concept of structure belongs to later linguistic thought, but the point Johnson makes about the structural influence of one language upon another is a valid one, evident in phraseology and in modifications to the syntax of sentences.

39 Fanny Burney, a letter from Bath, 8 September 1791

If the desire to write is innate rather than acquired, then Frances (Fanny) Burney (1752–1840) must be an outstanding example of that gift. Her earliest surviving poem, written in a precociously adult style, was composed before her twelfth birthday. When she was fifteen she made a bonfire of her early work, including the first draft of a novel which was to bring her literary recognition when published in revised form as *Evelina* eleven years later. Although she published two other successful novels, a greater and more sustained effort went into her journals which she recommenced after the bonfire and maintained until her sight failed sixty years later. At the same time she kept up a continuous correspondence with members of her family and acquaintances.

Fanny Burney was the daughter of the organist and musical historian Dr Charles Burney. Her father was considered to be the foremost music teacher in the London of his day, and he numbered among his friends Dr Johnson, David Garrick and Sir Joshua Reynolds. Fanny herself was appointed Second Keeper of the Robes to Queen Charlotte in 1786 and held the post for five years. In 1793 she married a French émigré, General d'Arblay, and thereafter lived sometimes in France, sometimes in England as political circumstances allowed.

Although she benefited from a culturally privileged environment, Fanny Burney did not receive a formal education outside the home. She was a voracious reader and largely self-educated. Early in life a family friend, Samuel Crisp, advised her never to frame 'studied letters, that are to be correct, nicely grammatical and run in smooth periods'. Her earliest letters have something of the spontaneity of speech, and this can be found in more familiar correspondence later in life; but she harboured also a growing attachment to fine writing, and this found expression in her last years in the extensive revision and even destruction of her earlier works. The letter which follows, addressed to her elder sister, is sufficiently familiar to exploit playful punning and use some careless grammar and colloquialisms, but is nevertheless rhetorically constructed and uses occasionally elevated vocabulary. The text represents the spelling of the original, but punctuation is modernised. Small capitals are used to represent larger, more emphatic writing.

Queen Square,
Bath – Septr 8th

My dearest Esther will I know rejoice to hear how well the Bath Water has agreed with Me. I am recovering apace, though by no means without severe occasional draw-backs. But you will probably have heard of me and my goings on
5 through our Padre: from whom I have had accounts of yourself and co, which though only in *generals*, have satisfied me all essentials went on well.

Saturday the 10th I set forward for Mickelham: – and there, my dearest Esther, in the course of my *Month's confinement*,
10 I shall hope to see you. I think you will never be able to resist a little peep at our Nursery. Heaven send it prosperous! – I think with our dear Susan there is every possible good augur.

I would send you some News – only I know none.

I ought to give you, from this distance, a little flourish –
15 only I have not *de quoi* to compose one. I am certainly of opinion, after deeply thinking over the matter, that the Heliconian spring did not bring forth hot water. Apollo and the nine must have owed their spirit to streams of more bracing qualities. The Hot water which I quaff here has, in
20 this respect, wholly disappointed me, for it rather renders my ideas vapid than bright, notwithstanding the reasonable expectations I had entertained of its WHETTING MY WITS. And if it does not mend that, it has surely no chance to mend my *humour*; for how can what is moist contribute to what is dry?
25 Thus you see, My dear sister, how small a chance you have to be a gainer by my Bath Beverage.

This City is so filled with Workmen, dust, and lime, that you really want two pair of Eyes to walk about in it – one for being put out, and the other to see with afterwards. But as I,
30 however, have only one pair, which are pretty much dedicated to the first purpose, you cannot, in reason, expect from me a very distinct description of it. Bath seems, now, rather a collection of small Towns, or of magnificent Villas, than one City. They are now building as if the World was but
35 just beginning, and this was the only spot on which its Inhabitants could endure to reside. Nothing is secure from their architectural rage. They build upon the pinnacle of Hills that only to look up to breaks ones neck – and they build in the deepest depths below, which only to look down upon
40 makes one giddy. Even the streets round the Pump room are pulling down for new Edifices, and you can only drink from their choice stream, by wading though their chosen mud.

Their plans seem all to be formed without the least reference
to what adjoins or surrounds them, they are therefore high,
45 low, broad, narrow, long, short, in manners the most
unexpected, and by interruptions the most abrupt; – and
some of their Houses are placed so zig-zag, in and out, you
would suppose them built first, and then dropt, to *find* their
own *foundation*. They seem seldom to attempt levelling the
50 Ground for the sake of uniformity, but, very contentedly,
when they have raised one House on the spot where it could
stand most conveniently, they raise the next upon its nearest
and steepest aclivity, so precisely above it, that from the
Garret of one, you *Mount* into the Kitchen of the other. One
55 street, leading out of Laura Place, of a noble width, and with
a broad handsome Pavement, pompously labelled at the
corner JOHNSON STREET, has in it – only one House: – nor can
another be added, for it opens to Spring Gardens, and even
its vis à vis is occupied by the dead wall belonging to a House
60 in Laura Place. Nor can You make a visit from one street to
another, without such an ascent, or such a declivity, that you
must have the wheel of a carriage *locked* to go from
neighbour to neighbour. – You will ask me if I mean to set
you up with materials for making a model of Bath? but I am
65 perfectly content with having given you a *Model* of Confusion.
Certainly, unless you are advised to come hither for
Health, *I* should advise you not to see this place these 2 years,
at least, for *pleasure*; as the avenues to the pump Rooms will
not sooner be finished, and *walking* here in the winter must
70 be next to impracticable. However, when all these works are
compleated, and the Compleaters, with the usual gratitude of
the world, are driven aloof, this City, already the most
splendid of England, will be as noble as can well be
conceived.
75   It is impossible to tell you how kind, good and considerate
is our excellent Mrs. Ord: yet we are Daily upon the point of
a quarrel concerning my leaving her. 6 weeks is the appointed
time for drinking these waters, and I shall just have halved *it*.
However, I go to peace, good air, good Hours, and the best
80 and dearest Society, and all those will more than compensate
for Bath waters, as my worn strength and wasted spirit want
more of time and care and patience and HAPPINESS for recruit,
than medicine. Mrs. ord gives you her most affectionate
Love. I beg mine to Mr. Burney and all around you. Is my
85 sweet little God Child as well and lovely as ever? A good
question to a mama! – but when I want to get at the simple

truth, I always like to apply to impartial persons. Fanny, I
hope, rapidly improves in an honourable mixture of literature
and notability. sophy can do no better than persevere in
90 her maternal studies; and Richard, I doubt not, will emulate
his friend Dussec, till he will aim at his own superior Father.
– Your news is good, I hope, from the sweet Marianne? and
poor Bessy? I shall now beg you to write to me at
Mickleham, which I flatter myself I shall reach next Monday
95 night, or Tuesday noon. I think from *thence* I shall be able to
write You a MORE – a MOST welcome Letter ere long.
Farewell, my ever dear sister – truly y^{rs}

F B.
Remember me kindly to dear James When you see him –
100 and to *his*. –

Notes

3 **draw-backs**   This compound is first recorded in 1618 in a context
where it refers to the behaviour of an individual and is clearly
derived from a verbal phrase. In the sense 'anything which retards
progress or advance' it is recorded from 1720, but the modern sense,
to which it is now restricted and in which it is opposed to an
advantage in reviewing some course of action, dates from the latter
half of the nineteenth century.

4 **goings on**   In the sense 'actions, experiences', this was first
recorded in a letter by Dr Johnson written in July 1775, but the verb
is used by Defoe to mean 'to get on (with someone)'. There is here
no implication of censure.

9 **confinement**   Fanny's younger sister, Susan, gave birth to her
third child shortly after this letter. The word is used punningly,
exploiting its general sense, dating from the mid seventeenth
century, for Fanny's proposed stay at Mickleham, and the more
restricted sense (recorded only from the 1770s) for Susan's time in
childbed.

18 **the nine**   The nine muses, representing the arts, who lived by the
spring on Mount Helicon whose water gave inspiration in Greek
mythology.

21 **vapid** 'dull, insipid' (Lat. *vapidus)*   Originally borrowed as a
semi-technical term to refer to flavour and used of drinks from 1656.
The figurative extension to ideas and speech is first recorded in
Johnson (1758). The word *bracing* (19) is also first recorded in 1750
to describe the effects of a tonic medicine.

34 **as if . . . was**   In more formal letters the writer is careful to use
the subjunctive in similar clauses.

40–41 **are pulling down**   This type of expression (cf. *the house is
building*) has been called the 'passival' and is common from ME until
the end of the nineteenth century, when it is increasingly replaced by

the type 'being built'. The history of the passival form is confused with that of the type *the house is a-building*, descended from OE expressions with *on* followed by the verbal noun in *-unge*. The coexistence of the two types caused some disagreement among contemporary literary men: Dr Johnson preferred *a-building*, but the majority opinion among grammarians was for *building*.

47 **zig-zag**   Of uncertain etymology, although borrowed immediately from French. The word may exploit sound symbolism, the two vowels suggesting movement in two different directions. First recorded as a noun in 1712.

53 **aclivity** 'upward slope'   The *OED* does not admit the existence of this word, which seems to be the writer's own analogical formation on *declivity* (61), 'downward slope'. The Latin adverb and preposition *de* gave rise to a number of French words in which the *de-* prefix has the sense 'down'; but the *a-* prefix has the sense 'up' in only a few words of OE origin – e.g. *arise*, *awake*.

59 **vis à vis** 'opposite'   An eighteenth-century borrowing, recorded first in 1753 with very specific reference to a particular type of carriage in which the occupants sat face to face. Quickly extended to include other 'face to face' contexts.

72 **aloof**   Earlier written as a phrase *a loof* (see Dekker, Excerpt 31), this word has a nautical origin. Sixteenth-century occurrences mean to 'turn to windward' and 'sail close to the wind'. A range of senses involving physical and then metaphorical distance develops. Perhaps borrowed direct from Dutch *loef*, 'windward'.

Modern English (1800–1920)

The history of English takes on an entirely new dimension after about 1800. No longer is it simply one of the varieties of the Germanic language family, nor subsidiary in its own homeland to French and Latin. Neither, for that matter, is it the symbol of English nationalism, whose merits are trumpeted in order to conceal misgivings about its true value in comparison with the classical languages. In the nineteenth century, English becomes largely standardised at home, expands beyond national boundaries, and is as a result more various in its overseas function as a world language.

The transfer of English outside its historical homeland begins with imperial expansion whose roots can be traced back to the settlements in America and the formalisation of trading relations with India at the end of the sixteenth century, but it is not until the nineteenth century that the languages of these ex-colonies, diverging significantly from that of the mother country, begin to return an influence upon the development of English at home. This relatively recent development is outside the scope of this collection.

In England during the nineteenth century, forces for standardisation were strong. Most notable among them was the great expansion of primary education, the purpose of which was to teach children to read and write and, of course, to spell 'correctly'. It has been calculated that, in 1818, about 600,000 out of some 2,000,000 children were attending some kind of school. The earliest national movements for elementary education were the 'National' and 'British' schools sponsored by religious bodies, but from the 1830s the Government gave financial support to the foundation of schools, and in 1870 the Elementary Education Act enabled the provision of schools by local authorities from an education rate. The expansion of popular education was accompanied by the foundation of Mechanics' Institutes in 1823 to bring

297

instruction to working men, and the 1870s and 1880s saw the foundation of a number of university institutions in the larger industrial cities of the North.

As awareness of a correct form of the written language was promoted by increased literacy, the breakdown of old dialect distributions was hastened by easier communication and the mixing of population. The Industrial Revolution created great new cities – Leeds, Sheffield, Birmingham, Manchester, Glasgow – which developed their own urban dialects from the mixture of immigrants attracted to them. Population movement was greatly facilitated by the expansion of the railway system in the 1840s, and the trend to readier mobility and freer mixing of the population was continued by the development of both road and air transport, but above all by radio communications. The rapid development in public broadcasting after about 1920 led in England and abroad to the establishment of BBC English as a *de facto* spoken standard. This standard, alternatively known as Received Pronunciation, is that of a social and educational élite, originally developed from the manner of speech approved by the nineteenth-century public schools, and concurrently by the universities of Oxford and Cambridge.

The establishment towards the end of the nineteenth century of an approved standard for pronunciation and its subsequent promotion by broadcasting ensured that *non*-standard or dialect variants would henceforth be considered *sub*-standard – that is, not simply different, but inferior. The tendency to assess the social status of a speaker from the accidentals of his speech is universal in linguistic history, but becomes oriented in Modern English into an opposition between dialect speech and the use of the standard. Although still current, in very recent times this opposition has been mitigated by a change in political sentiment on the one hand, and by the development of the objective study of language on the other.

The study of English has always incorporated two distinct traditions and purposes. Indisputably the most familiar and widely followed is the pursuit of communicative effectiveness in the use of the language, both written and spoken. Thomas Wilson's *Arte of Rhetorique* is an early textbook in this tradition, the Fowler brothers' *Modern English Usage* a more recent one. The student's purpose within this tradition is to achieve command of a kind of English to which no one can object, and by which the hearer will be both easily informed and readily impressed. It is a tradition which *prescribes* what may be judged as correct in spelling and grammar, and what is acceptable in aspects of style. A second tradition, which can also be traced back to the sixteenth century and antiquarian interest in the early history of English, is concerned less with prescribing the contemporary uses of English than with describing those uses, their historical derivation and the attitudes of speakers to them. Thus, the academic study of English is characteristically *descriptive* in its orientation. This scientific, descriptive spirit inspiring the study of the English language reached maturity in the nineteenth century, and is represented (admittedly to a debatable extent) in the compilation of the *Oxford English Dictionary*. It is true that the *Dictionary* is relatively weak in its coverage of non-literary and non-standard forms, but the expressed attitudes and practices of its editors should be compared with those of nineteenth-century grammars pressed into service in the burgeoning schools. James Beattie, in *The Vulgarities of Speech Corrected* (1826), gives his opinion, regardless of Shakespearian usage, that 'Nothing is more common, nor more offensive than such . . . expressions as *more greater, most beautifullest, more prettier, most commonest.*' Even in the late 1920s, G. H. McKnight, an American scholar, reveals how his early school instruction in grammatical proprieties has irresistibly moulded his responses. Although he, as a scholar, is able to list examples of its use from about 1500 onwards, he still finds that the British use of *their* to refer back to a single individual 'grates on the ear of the American grammatically trained'. McKnight's position demonstrates an important fact: that prescriptive and descriptive approaches to language are not utterly distinct. Not only can the same individual often accommodate both attitudes, but works such as the *OED*, whose original purpose may have been predominantly investigative and descriptive, are inevitably adopted as authoritative, and are re-used to prescribe correctness and acceptability. Finally, it should not be forgotten that during the nineteenth century, and even today, standard language admits some variation both in pronunciation (the stressing of multisyllabic words such as *controversy*, the alternative pronunciations of *either* and *economics*) and in spelling (*paid, payed*; *-ise, -ize*; *focussing, focusing*; *learned, learnt*; *despatch, dispatch*). If frequency of use, rather than the dictionary which supposedly records it, were to be the arbiter, it is even arguable that the seventeenth-century spelling *seperate* should once again be regarded as an alternative to the 'correct' *separate*.

By comparison with earlier periods, the changes in the English language since 1800 have been relatively superficial. There has been no major systematic change in morphology to compare with the loss of inflection in Early Middle English, nor in phonology to compare with the Great Vowel Shift. Changes to the syntax and especially to the lexicon are more notable, but not so striking as those which took place in Early Modern English.

In the phonology, a number of distinctions have been lost. Except in certain Scottish pronunciation, the distinction between /w/ and /ʍ/ (*wight* and *white*), which was the last survivor of a set of initial consonant groups (*hw, hr, hl, hn*) descended from Old English, had been lost by the late eighteenth century. As an initial consonant, [h] has been unstable since Early Middle English, but objections to its omission as 'h-dropping' date only from about 1800 and the continuing struggle for supposed correctness. This attitude may account for the later restoration of the distinction between /w/ and /ʍ/, which is still heard occasionally. The conception of correctness driving both these examples is one dependent on traditional spellings. The same reasoning has restored the [l] in *falcon*, the [w] in *woman*, and the second [i] in *Christian*. The pronunciation [iŋ], considered vulgar in 1801, extended rapidly after the 1820s, so that the [in] pronunciation of *-ing*, widespread in the first decades of the nineteenth century, itself came to be regarded as sub-standard.

Syntactically, the widening use of the prop-word *one(s)* to substitute for repetition of a noun has been noted since the early nineteenth century in expressions with a determiner, such as *this book is the one I want*, or in interrogatives and plurals, such as *which ones are they?* Some further erosion of morphological contrasts has taken place. The demise of the oblique form of the relative pronoun *whom* was predicted by Sapir in 1926, but the process has been slow and it still survives among careful speakers. The distinction between the present indicative and the subjunctive has further declined in use, so that for most people, the latter occurs only in a few fixed expressions (*if I were you*). By contrast, the periphrastic formation of verb tenses has become more extensive and complex from the Early Modern period onwards. From the late nineteenth century the passival construction *the house is building*, whose origins can be traced in Old and Early Middle English, is gradually replaced by the type *the house is being built*, which first appeared in the late eighteenth century. This was extended in the twentieth century to the perfective durative type *it has been being built*. In Early Modern English the perfect of intransitive verbs could be formed freely with the verb *to be* (*the messenger is come from the king*). But in such uses, *have* has been steadily generalised and captured the last surviving main verb, *become*, during the nineteenth century. The use of *get* as an auxiliary followed by the past participle is first recorded in the mid seventeenth century, but during the later nineteenth and twentieth centuries has encroached rapidly on the use of *to be* in forming passive constructions where there is an implication of a state of affairs coming into existence (*he got arrested*; *she got promoted*).

The lexicon of English has expanded greatly during the past two hundred years, partly by borrowing but also extensively by word-formation. Many new compounds have been produced on patterns which go back to the earliest periods of English, and a new type, the reduplicative compound, has added a few examples: *hush-hush*; *fifty-fifty*; *pretty-pretty*. A considerable number of compound verbs has emerged since the nineteenth century by a process of back-formation from nominals: *shoplift* (1820), *housekeep* (1842), *moonlight* (1887) and, more recently, *dryclean*, *doublepark* and *wordprocess*. Although some suffixes have become newly productive (*-ish*, *-ism*, *-ist*) and a few new ones become productive for the first time (*-ette*), prefixes have been more prolific. During the nineteenth century, scientific studies introduced many new prefixes from neo-Latin and Greek and extended the use of others to combine with native bases, among them *micro-*, *ante-*, *intra-*, *meta-*, *mono-*, *hypo-*, *para-*, *tele-*, *multi-*, *retro-* and *semi-*. Words formed by shortening or 'clipping' words and phrases are numerous. Nineteenth-century examples are *bus* (from Latin *omnibus*, 'for all'), *vet*, *van* (from *caravan*), *exam*, *lab*, *photo*, *fan* (from *fanatic*), *express* (from *express train*) and *pants* (from *pantaloons*). Deliberate word-creation also plays a part, through blending, as with *mingy* (1928) or Lewis Carroll's *chortle* and *slithy*, and, less consciously, through the adoption of trade, personal or place names: *colt*, *boycott*, *shrapnel*, *bayonet*.

Borrowing, however, is the most fertile source of additions to the lexicon. French and Latin continue to contribute heavily but are joined by borrowings from other, more distant European languages of words with varying degrees of assimilation into the ordinary English wordstock. The nineteenth century saw the Italian loans *vendetta*, *mafia*, *salami*, *risotto*, *studio*, *replica*, *prima donna* and *inferno*. Spanish loans, often by way of

America, are *guerilla, mustang, bronco, bonanza, patio, cafeteria, rodeo, pueblo.* German contributed *poodle, dachshund, lager, leitmotiv, kindergarten, seminar, hinterland, zeitgeist,* and Russian was the source of *vodka, samovar, tundra* and *polka.* Extended trade and colonial contacts, which began to contribute vocabulary to a significant extent in the final decades of the eighteenth century, continue to be an important source in the nineteenth, too. From contact with Hindustani in India, we have *thug, khaki, cashmere, pyjama, chutney, gymkhana, polo;* from Sanskrit, *nirvana, yoga* and *swastika.* The African colonies contributed few words (*gorilla, ju-ju* and *tsetse* are examples), but a number were borrowed from Afrikaans: *veldt, commando, trek, commandeer* and *spoor.* Australian words in this period include *wombat, boomerang* and *budgerigar. Kiwi* is first recorded in 1835. The opening up of Japan gave the words *tycoon, geisha, hara-kiri* and *ju-jitsu.*

Although this introduction seeks to indicate some of the linguistic developments during the period from 1800 until the date of the latest excerpts in about 1920, it should not be forgotten that linguistic variety and change are always present, affecting the language of today just as they did that of the past. Change today may not seem as dramatic as the major developments of the past, but historical events, scientific discoveries and social movements still influence the language. It is worth considering in the light of past change what may be the effects on the English language of some developments during the last three-quarters of a century: the virtual abandonment of grammar teaching in primary schools, the rise of feminism, immigration into Britain of settlers whose mother tongue is not English, the electronic revolution with (American) English as its mother tongue, the continuing spread of the use of English overseas, and the growing probability of some political unity in Europe. All these may be expected to leave their mark on the English language, and in retrospect may seem to future generations as spectacular in their effect as any of the developments which have been illustrated by the excerpts in this collection.

Thomas Carlyle (1795–1881) was born at Ecclefechan, Dumfries-shire, the son of a stonemason. He attended Annan Academy and went on to Edinburgh University. His family intended him to become a Presbyterian minister, but the intellectual life of Edinburgh dissuaded him from this calling and he instead supported himself by teaching, reviewing and literary work. He studied German literature and published a number of studies, anthologies and translations. In 1826 he married Jane Welsh, the daughter of a doctor, to whom he had acted as tutor in German. She was well equipped intellectually and temperamentally to support her husband's literary career, and later became famous as a literary hostess and correspondent of many of the contemporary literati.

Carlyle and his wife at first found life financially difficult, and they had to withdraw from Edinburgh to Jane's farm at Craigen-puttock. It was here that he wrote *Signs of the Times*, which was first published in the *Edinburgh Review* in 1829. This was followed by *Sartor Resartus*, published in *Fraser's Magazine* (1833–34). The Carlyles then moved to Chelsea, where Thomas's reputation was established first by his *History of the French Revolution* (1837) and then by a series of lectures delivered to a fashionable audience during 1840 on *Heroes, Hero-Worship and the Heroic in History*. From here, Carlyle went on to become an admired pundit on matters social and historical, and his idealising evocations of pre-industrial, pre-capitalist medieval society inspired John Ruskin and William Morris.

Although his reputation in the late nineteenth century was very high, the anti-democratic elitism which accompanied his romanticism caused a decline of his reputation in the twentieth century. Contemporary critics found his style worthy of comment and even ridicule. His love of apostrophe, emphatic use of capitals and italics, eccentric punctuation, archaisms and lexical creativity earned it the title 'Carlylese'. Of the lexical creations recorded in *OED*, many exploit the derivational possibilities of English rather than represent new base forms: thus *abortional*, *absolvable*, *absolvent*, *assassinative*, or the use of *adze* as a verb. Many of these formations achieved no lasting circulation, but Carlyle is the first recorded user of a large number of words now in familiar use, among them *admonitorily*, *affordable*, *alleviatory*, *animalism, anonymity, approvingly, approximately, autobiographical* and *baggy.*

In fact, if we look deeper, we shall find that this faith in Mechanism has now struck its roots down into man's most intimate, primary sources of conviction; and is thence sending up, over his whole life and activity, innumerable stems, – fruit-
5   bearing and poison-bearing. The truth is, men have lost their belief in the Invisible, and believe, and hope, and work only in the Visible; or, to speak it in other words: This is not a Religious age. Only the material, the immediately practical, not the divine and spiritual, is important to us. The infinite, absolute
10   character of Virtue has passed into a finite, conditional one; it is no longer a worship of the Beautiful and Good; but a calculation of the Profitable. Worship, indeed, in any sense, is not recognised among us, or is mechanically explained into Fear of pain, or Hope of pleasure. Our true Deity is Mechanism. It has
15   subdued external Nature for us, and we think it will do all other things. We are Giants in physical power: in a deeper than metaphorical sense, we are Titans, that strive, by heaping mountain on mountain, to conquer Heaven also.
   The strong Mechanical character, so visible in the spiritual
20   pursuits and methods of this age, may be traced much farther into the condition and prevailing disposition of our spiritual nature itself. Consider, for example, the general fashion of Intellect in this era. Intellect, the power man has of knowing and believing, is now nearly synonymous with Logic, or the
25   mere power of arranging and communicating. Its implement is not Meditation, but Argument. 'Cause and effect' is almost the only category under which we look at, and work with, all Nature. Our first question with regard to any object is not, What is it? but, How is it? We are no longer instinctively driven
30   to apprehend, and lay to heart, what is Good and Lovely, but rather to inquire, as on-lookers, how it is produced, whence it comes, whither it goes. Our favourite Philosophers have no love and no hatred; they stand among us not to do, nor to create anything, but as a sort of Logic-mills to grind out the true causes
35   and effects of all that is done and created. To the eye of a Smith, a Hume or a Constant, all is well that works quietly. An Order of Ignatius Loyola, a Presbyterianism of John Knox, a Wickliffe or a Henry the Eighth, are simply so many mechanical phenomena, caused or causing.

40   The *Euphuist* of our day differs much from his pleasant predecessors. An intellectual dapperling of these times boasts
chiefly of his irresistible perspicacity, his 'dwelling in the
daylight of truth,' and so forth; which, on examination, turns
out to be a dwelling in the *rush*-light of 'closet-logic,' and a deep
45   unconsciousness that there is any other light to dwell in or any
other objects to survey with it. Wonder, indeed, is, on all hands,
dying out: it is the sign of uncultivation to wonder. Speak to any
small man of a high, majestic Reformation, of a high majestic
Luther; and forthwith he sets about 'accounting' for it; how the
50   'circumstances of the time' called for such a character, and
found him, we suppose, standing girt and road-ready, to do its
errand; how the 'circumstances of the time' created, fashioned,
floated him quietly along into the result; how, in short, this
small man, had he been there, could have performed the like
55   himself! For it is the 'force of circumstances' that does everything; the force of one man can do nothing. Now all this is
grounded on little more than a metaphor. We figure Society as a
'Machine,' and that mind is opposed to mind, as body is to body;
whereby two, or at most ten, little minds must be stronger than
60   one great mind. Notable absurdity! For the plain truth, very
plain, we think is, that minds are opposed to minds in quite a
different way; and *one* man that has a higher Wisdom, a hitherto
unknown spiritual Truth in him, is stronger, not than ten men
that have it not, or than ten thousand, but than *all* men that have
65   it not; and stands among them with a quite ethereal, angelic
power, as with a sword out of Heaven's own armory, sky-
tempered, which no buckler, and no tower of brass, will finally
withstand.
     But to us, in these times, such considerations rarely occur.
70   We enjoy, we see nothing by direct vision; but only by
reflection, and in anatomical dismemberment. Like Sir
Hudibras, for every Why we must have a Wherefore. We have
our little *theory* on all human and divine things. Poetry, the
workings of genius itself, which in all times, with one or another
75   meaning, has been called Inspiration, and held to be mysterious
and inscrutable, is no longer without its scientific exposition.
The building of the lofty rhyme is like any other masonry or
bricklaying: we have theories of its rise, height, decline and fall,
– which latter, it would seem, is now near, among all people. Of
80   our 'Theories of Taste,' as they are called, wherein the deep,
infinite, unspeakable Love of Wisdom and Beauty, which
dwells in all men, is 'explained,' made mechanically visible,
from 'Association' and the like, why should we say anything?

Hume has written us a 'Natural History of Religion;' in which
85 one Natural History all the rest are included. Strangely too does
the general feeling coincide with Hume's in this wonderful
problem; for whether his 'Natural History' be the right one or
not, that Religion must have a Natural History, all of us, cleric
and laic, seem to be agreed. He indeed regards it as a Disease,
90 we again as Health; so far there is a difference; but in our first
principle we are at one.

Notes

3 **thence** 'from there'   Carlyle also employs *whence*, 'from where',
and *whither*, 'to what place' (31–32). The group of adverbials expressing motion to and from a place – *thence, hence, whence, thither, whither*
and *hither* – is already archaic and consciously literary. The last three
descend from OE forms *þider, hwider* and *hider*. The former three are
thirteenth century formations employing the adverbial-forming
inflexion *-es* (on *thenne, henne* and *whenne*).

35 **Smith**, *et al.*   Adam Smith (1723–1790), Scottish philosopher and
socio-economic theorist, was the author of the *Theory of Moral
Sentiments* (1759) and the *Wealth of Nations* (1776), both developed
as lectures at Glasgow University. He was a friend of the Edinburgh
philosopher David Hume (1711–1776), who was the author of a
Treatise of Human Nature (1740). Benjamin Constant (1767–1830)
was a French-born political philosopher who was also temporarily
resident in Edinburgh, and like the other two was concerned with
questions of human personality and moral and religious feeling.
Carlyle is objecting to a tendency of all three to explain human
personality in terms of environmental experience rather than innate
ability, and the operations of associations rather than reason. By
comparison, Ignatius Loyola, founder of the Jesuit order, and John
Knox, Wickliffe and Henry VIII, jointly seen as instigators of the
Reformation, are considered inspired men of vision.

40 **Euphuist**   Properly, one who imitates the rhetorical style of Lyly's
Euphues (see Excerpt 26), but here used ironically of an author who
affects impressive style without significant substance.

41 **dapperling** 'a little dapper fellow'   The only previously recorded
use of this scornful epithet is in Cotgrave's Anglo-French dictionary
of 1611.

49 **accounting**   *OED* gives 1768 as the earliest occurrence of the
sense 'to explain'. Earlier senses are more closely related to the idea
of arithmetical calculation; therefore Carlyle's dislike of this term
probably arises from a strong awareness of these 'mathematical'
associations, and the implied claim of irrefutable proof made by its
use.

51 **girt and road-ready**   *OED* notes that the verb *gird* is confined

largely to rhetorical (often biblically influenced) contexts throughout its history. The earliest sense of *gird* is to 'surround or encircle (with a belt etc.)', sometimes to confine clothes preparatory to some action. Early sense developments were to 'belt on a sword', to 'saddle a horse', and to 'be prepared for action'. The compound *road-ready* is a nonce creation parallel to the contemporary *roadworthy*. Compound adjectives of this type are found in OE, but many are modern formations.

72 **Hudibras**   The main protagonist of Samuel Butler's *Hudibras* (1662–80), a satirical work in the form of a mock romance, whose narrative development is hidden by the numerous disputations and digressions of which it is largely composed.

83 **Association**   Associations deriving from environmental experience as a factor in forming moral and aesthetic judgements were argued by Hume and David Hartley (1705–1757), popularised by Joseph Priestley, and adopted in Coleridge's early theorising on the role of the imagination in poetry.

84 **Natural History**   Hume was the author of a dissertation on the *Natural History of Religion*, which traced the origin and development of religions in an analytic spirit. His religious works betray a strong scepticism about the 'revealed' nature of religion, and he finds in them an echo of the human mind.

Charles Dickens was born on 7 February 1812. He spent a happy childhood at Chatham, where his father was a clerk, but the boy's world collapsed when his father, whom he greatly admired, was imprisoned for debt. At the age of twelve, Dickens was forced to fend for himself, working for six shillings a week in a blacking factory. The misery of these months is reflected in the early part of *David Copperfield.* But there were also benefits, since it was then that he accumulated that knowledge of London street life which served him well in his later career. He returned to school after his father's release, then, aged fifteen, entered a solicitor's office as an under-clerk. He made strenuous efforts to learn shorthand, and so gained a role as a reporter of parliamentary debates. Entry into newspaper publishing led to a series of contributions to the *Evening Chronicle* and *Monthly Magazine,* which developed into his earliest work, *Sketches by 'Boz'* (1836–37). These were sufficiently popular to encourage the publishers Chapman and Hall to commission him to write a series on the activities of a fictional gentleman's club. *The Posthumous Papers of the Pickwick Club* appeared in episodes from April 1836 onwards, and were published in book form in the following year. The series achieved success with the introduction of Sam Weller into the story, so that, by the end of the year, Dickens had earned two thousand pounds. His literary career was established, and he pursued it through a series of novels, journalistic and editorial work, and in later times through readings of his works. He interested himself in philanthropic and radical causes, travelled extensively, and died unexpectedly of a stroke at his home in Rochester on 9 June 1870.

This excerpt is full of the good spirits of Christmas at Dingley Dell, expressing them in two contrasting styles: the standard English of the narrator, and Sam Weller's pastiche of Cockney dialect features. In both, humour depends in part on verbal inflation. The former exploits mock formality to describe trivial events (*this same branch, the mystic branch, appropriating to his own use*) but emphasises the incongruity by using colloquialisms also (*good long sitting, somewhere about five-and-forty, pretty certain*). The latter mingles the features of sub-standard speech (simplified consonant clusters, omission of unstressed vowels, invariable use of the third-person present tense, non-standard preterites and past participles, and malapropisms) with the same predilection for the elevated word and orotund phrase which once formed part of the eloquence of Dickens' own father.

Long before Mr. Pickwick was weary of dancing, the newly-married couple had retired from the scene. There was a glorious supper down stairs, notwithstanding, and a good long sitting after it; and when Mr. Pickwick awoke, late the next
5 morning, he had a confused recollection of having, severally and confidentially, invited somewhere about five-and-forty people to dine with him at the George and Vulture, the very first time they came to London; which Mr. Pickwick rightly considered a pretty certain indication of his having taken
10 something besides exercise, on the previous night.

'And so your family has games in the kitchen to-night, my dear, has they?' inquired Sam of Emma.

'Yes, Mr. Weller,' replied Emma; 'we always have on Christmas eve. Master wouldn't neglect to keep it up, on any
15 account.'

'Your master's a wery pretty notion of keepin' anythin' up, my dear,' said Mr. Weller; 'I never see such a sensible sort of man as he is, or such a reg'lar gen'l'm'n.'

'Oh, that he is!' said the fat boy, joining in the conversa-
20 tion; 'don't he breed nice pork!' and the fat youth gave a semi-cannibalic leer at Mr. Weller, as he thought of the roast legs and gravy.

'Oh, you've woke up, at last, have you?' said Sam.

The fat boy nodded.

25 'I'll tell you what it is, young boa constructer,' said Mr. Weller, impressively, 'if you don't sleep a little less, and exercise a little more, ven you comes to be a man you'll lay yourself open to the same sort o' personal inconwenience as was inflicted on the old gen'l'm'n as wore the pig-tail.'

30 'What did they do to him?' inquired the fat boy, in a faltering voice.

'I'm a goin' to tell you,' replied Mr. Weller; 'he was one o' the largest patterns as was ever turned out – reg'lar fat man, as hadn't caught a glimpse of his own shoes for five-and-forty
35 years.'

'Lor!' exclaimed Emma.

'No, that he hadn't, my dear,' said Mr. Weller, 'and if you'd put an exact model of his own legs on the dinin' table afore him, he wouldn't ha' known 'em. Well, he always walks

40 to his office with a wery handsome gold watch-chain hanging out, about a foot and a half, and a gold watch in his fob pocket as was worth – I'm afraid to say how much, but as much as a watch can be – a large, heavy, round manafacter, as stout for a watch, as he was for a man, and with a big face 45 in proportion. "You'd better not carry that 'ere watch," says the old gen'l'm'n's friends, "you'll be robbed on it," says they. "Shall I?" says he. "Yes, will you," says they. "Vell," says he, "I should like to see the thief as could get this here watch out, for I'm blessed if *I* ever can; it's such a tight fit," 50 says he, "and venever I vants to know what's o'clock, I'm obliged to stare into the bakers' shops," he says. Well, then he laughs as hearty as if he was a goin' to pieces, and out he walks agin' with his powdered head and pig-tail, and rolls down the Strand vith the chain hangin' out furder than ever, 55 and the great round watch almost bustin' through his grey kersey smalls. There warn't a pickpocket in all London as didn't take a pull at that chain, but the chain 'ud never break, and the watch 'ud never come out, so they soon got tired o' dragging such a heavy old gen'l'm'n along the pavement, and 60 he'd go home and laugh till the pig-tail wibrated like the penderlum of a Dutch clock. At last, one day the old gen'l'm'n was a rollin' along, and he sees a pickpocket as he know'd by sight, a-comin' up, arm in arm vith a little boy vith a wery large head. "Here's a game," says the old gen'l'm'n to 65 himself, "they're a-goin' to have another try, but it won't do." So he begins a chucklin' wery hearty, ven, all of a sudden, the little boy leaves hold of the pickpocket's arm, and rushes headforemost straight into the old gen'l'm'n's stomach, and for a moment doubles him right up vith the 70 pain. "Murder!" says the old gen'l'm'n. "All right, Sir," says the pickpocket, a whisperin' in his ear. And ven he come straight agin', the watch and chain was gone, and what's worse than that, the old gen'l'm'n's digestion was all wrong ever artervards, to the wery last day of his life; so just you 75 look about you, young feller, and take care you don't get too fat.'

As Mr. Weller concluded this moral tale, with which the fat boy appeared much affected, they all three wended their way to the large kitchen, in which the family were by this time 80 assembled, according to annual custom on Christmas eve, observed by old Wardle's forefathers from time immemorial.

From the centre of the ceiling of this kitchen, old Wardle had just suspended with his own hands a huge branch of

misletoe, and this same branch of misletoe instantaneously
85 gave rise to a scene of general and most delightful struggling
and confusion; in the midst of which Mr. Pickwick with a
gallantry which would have done honour to a descendant of
Lady Tollimglower herself, took the old lady by the hand, led
her beneath the mystic branch, and saluted her in all courtesy
90 and decorum. The old lady submitted to this piece of
practical politeness with all the dignity which befitted so
important and serious a solemnity, but the younger ladies not
being so thoroughly imbued with a superstitious veneration of
the custom, or imagining that the value of a salute is very
95 much enhanced if it cost a little trouble to obtain it, screamed
and struggled, and ran into corners, and threatened and
remonstrated, and did every thing but leave the room, until
some of the less adventurous gentlemen were on the point of
desisting, when they all at once found it useless to resist any
100 longer, and submitted to be kissed with a good grace. Mr.
Winkle kissed the young lady with the black eyes, and Mr.
Snodgrass kissed Emily; and Mr. Weller, not being particular
about the form of being under the misletoe, kissed Emma
and the other female servants, just as he caught them. As to
105 the poor relations, they kissed everybody, not even excepting
the plainer portion of the young-lady visiters, who, in their
excessive confusion, ran right under the misletoe, directly it
was hung up, without knowing it! Wardle stood with his back
to the fire, surveying the whole scene, with the utmost
110 satisfaction; and the fat boy took the opportunity of
appropriating to his own use, and summarily devouring, a
particularly fine mince-pie, that had been carefully put by, for
somebody else.

Notes

16 **keepin' anythin'**   The loss of velarity in the pronunciation of *ing*
begins in Late Middle English. Although a characteristic of Sam
Weller's language, it is not necessarily considered lower class at this
period, and is found also in the speech of Wardle. Emily Brontë does
not make it a feature of Joseph's language in *Wuthering Heights*,
although it was probably found in contemporary Haworth.

21 **semi-cannibalic**   The word *cannibal* is a variant of the tribal name
Carib, used of a people who were credited by early travellers to the
West Indies with eating human flesh. The noun is first recorded in
1553 and has several derivative adjectives – *cannibalean* (1602),
cannibalish (1837), *cannibalistic* (1851). Dickens is the first recorded
user of *cannibalic*.

28   **personal inconwenience**   Part of the comic appeal of Sam Weller's speech is in the incongruity of his peculiar pronunciation and relatively elevated diction. The confusion between [v] and [w] in his language is characteristic of Dickens' representation of lower-class London English, and is indeed found in other contemporary literature. A similar confusion was already evident in the sixteenth-century English of Henry Machyn (see Excerpt 25). In fact, this phonetic peculiarity was not restricted to London and could be found also in Essex and East Anglia.

32   **a goin**   This form of the present participle is very common in Sam Weller's speech. Although no longer normal in standard English by the nineteenth century, it was common in Early Modern English. It originates in an OE prepositional phrasal type (*on huntinge*), whose noun became confused in ME with the newly emerging participle in -*ing*.

33   **patterns** 'specimens'   The sense is last recorded by *OED* in 1829.

45   **that 'ere**   Compare *this here* (48). The demonstrative phrase is developed from *that there* by assimilation of the following fricative to the stop [t].

54   **furder**   Examples of the change of the voiced dental fricative [ð] to the voiced alveolar stop [d], when occurring between two vowels, is found also in the language of Sam's father and that of Mrs Gamp in *Martin Chuzzlewit*. Variation of this kind was responsible for the emergence of the forms *father, mother, weather* in the fifteenth century from earlier forms with a stop consonant.

56   **warn't**   This is a dialectally widespread negative form in sub-standard English. The origin of the forms in London and northern English may be different, since in areas of Scandinavian settlement, ME *ware* may be influenced by *várum*, whereas in the south-east Midlands the development of OE /æ/ to /aː/ occurred independently.

74   **artervards**   The ⟨ar⟩ spelling represents the long vowel [aː]. The following [f] has been assimilated to the [t].

106   **visiters**   The modern spelling, *visitor*, derives from fifteenth-century Latinisation of an originally French borrowing. Dickens is among the last authors quoted by *OED* to use the older spelling; he himself changed his practice during his later career. The spelling *misletoe* was also commonly used from the sixteenth to the early nineteenth centuries, when the modern spelling *mistletoe* restored the OE antecedent form, *mistiltān*.

Emily Brontë was born on 30 July 1818, the fifth of the six children of Patrick Brontë, perpetual curate of Haworth. The morbidity which contemporaries found in *Wuthering Heights* is paralleled in the history of the family. Emily was only three when her mother died, and her two eldest sisters were dead by the time she was seven. None of the children attained the age of forty, and she herself died of tuberculosis before Christmas 1848.

Except for a few months at boarding schools, a brief visit to Brussels and some time as a governess near Halifax, her life was spent in Haworth and its neighbourhood. Her education, therefore, was largely at home with her sisters, through her own reading and through collaborating with them in writing poetry and poetic drama. *Wuthering Heights* was written during 1845–46 and appeared in 1847 under the pseudonym Ellis Bell.

In this excerpt, extensive use is made of Haworth dialect forms. These are quite accurately represented, but their purpose is the traditional literary one of indicating social status through language choice. In addition, they emphasise the dissociation between the malevolent old servant, Joseph, and the narrator, an unwelcome interloper into his world. Consequently, most of the dialect forms belong to Joseph, while Catherine speaks a rather literary standard. Their mutual antipathy is focused in Joseph's mockery of the word *parlour* and his scathing use of the hypercorrection *rume* in contrast to his usual pronunciation, *rahm*. Their linguistic division is not, however, quite complete, since the word *thible* (22), 'a smooth stick or spatula', is a dialect form recorded only from north of the Humber–Mersey line, and *cranky* (53), 'rickety', is restricted to Lancashire and Yorkshire. It is possible that Emily was not aware, when she used them, of the dialectal status of these words. Dialect speech is represented by standard spelling except where segments differ from the standard in pronunciation. Here, dialect sounds are indicated by deviant spellings based on an analogy with unambiguous representations of the particular sound in standard spelling practice: thus the sound [a:] is spelt ⟨ah⟩ in words where the standard would have [au], ⟨ou⟩ and [u:], ⟨oo⟩. Shortened vowels are indicated by following double consonants: *brocken* (110). Consistency is high, and variants may represent real variation in the dialect (*ye/yah*) or the existence of unstressed forms (*yuh*, *bud*). A proportion of the words, phrases and pronunciations are archaic from the point of view of the standard (*barn, gang, marred, nave, desarve, froo this*), and although the dialect matches quite well that of the present day, certain words and pronunciations have now become rare or disappeared altogether – thus *ortherings* (13) and *bothom* (29) are now more common in Lancashire.

Joseph was bending over the fire, peering into a large pan that swung above it; and a wooden bowl of oatmeal stood on the settle close by. The contents of the pan began to boil, and he turned to plunge his hand into the bowl; I conjectured that this
5 preparation was probably for our supper, and, being hungry, I resolved it should be eatable – so crying out sharply, '*I'll* make the porridge!' I removed the vessel out of his reach, and proceeded to take off my hat and riding habit. 'Mr. Earnshaw,' I continued, 'directs me to wait on myself – I will – I'm not
10 going to act the lady among you, for fear I should starve.'
    'Gooid Lord!' he muttered, sitting down, and stroking his ribbed stockings from the knee to the ankle. 'If they's tuh be fresh ortherings – just when Aw getten used tuh two maisters, if Aw mun hev a *mistress* set o'er my heead, it's loike time tuh
15 be flitting. Aw niver *did* think tuh say t' day ut Aw mud lave th' owld place – but Aw daht it's nigh at hend!'
    This lamentation drew no notice from me; I went briskly to work, sighing to remember a period when it would have been all merry fun; but compelled speedily to drive off the remem-
20 brance. It racked me to recall past happiness, and the greater peril there was of conjuring up its apparition, the quicker the thible ran round, and the faster the handfuls of meal fell into the water.
    Joseph beheld my style of cookery with growing indignation.
25 'Thear!' he ejaculated. 'Hareton, thah willn't sup thy por-ridge tuh neeght; they'll be nowt bud lumps as big as maw nave. Thear, agean! Aw'd fling in bowl un' all, if Aw wer yah! Thear, pale t' guilp off, un' then yah'll hae done wi't. Bang, bang. It's a marcy t' bothom isn't deaved aht!'
30 It *was* rather a rough mess, I own, when poured into the basins; four had been provided, and a gallon pitcher of new milk was brought from the dairy, which Hareton seized and commenced drinking and spilling from the expansive lip.
    I expostulated, and desired that he should have his in a mug;

35   affirming that I could not taste the liquid treated so dirtily. The
old cynic chose to be vastly offended at this nicety; assuring
me, repeatedly, that 'the barn was every bit as gooid' as I, 'and
every bit as wollsome,' and wondering how I could fashion to
be so conceited; meanwhile, the infant ruffian continued
40   sucking, and glowered up at me defyingly, as he slavered into
the jug.

'I shall have my supper in another room,' I said. 'Have you
no place you call a parlour?'

'*Parlour!*' he echoed, sneeringly, '*parlour*! Nay, we've noa
45   *parlours*. If yah dunnut loike wer company, they's maister's;
un' if yah dunnut loike maister, they's us.'

'Then I shall go upstairs,' I answered; 'shew me a chamber!'
I put my basin on a tray, and went myself to fetch some
more milk.

50   With great grumblings, the fellow rose, and preceded me in
my ascent: we mounted to the garrets; he opening a door, now
and then, to look into the apartments we passed.

'Here's a rahm,' he said, at last, flinging back a cranky board
on hinges. 'It's weel eneugh tuh ate a few porridge in. They's a
55   pack uh corn i' t' corner, thear, meeterly clane; if yah're feared
uh muckying yet grand silk cloes, spread yer hankerchir ut t'
top on't.'

The 'rahm' was a kind of lumber-hole smelling strong of
malt and grain; various sacks of which articles were piled
60   around, leaving a wide, bare space in the middle.

'Why, man!' I exclaimed, facing him angrily, 'this is not a
place to sleep in. I wish to see my bed-room.'

'*Bed-rume!*' he repeated, in a tone of mockery. 'Yah's see all
t' *bed-rumes* thear is – yon's mine.'

65   He pointed into the second garret, only differing from the
first in being more naked about the walls, and having a large,
low, curtainless bed, with an indigo-coloured quilt, at one end.

'What do I want with yours?' I retorted. 'I suppose Mr.
Heathcliff does not lodge at the top of the house, does he?'

70   'Oh! it's Maister *Hathecliff's* yah're wenting?' cried he, as if
making a new discovery. 'Couldn't ye uh said soa, at onst? un'
then, Aw mud uh telled ye, baht all this wark, ut that's just one
yah cannut sea – he allas keeps it locked, un' nob'dy iver mells
on't but hisseln.'

75   'You've a nice house, Joseph,' I could not refrain from
observing, 'and pleasant inmates; and I think the concentrated
essence of all the madness in the world took up its abode in my
brain the day I linked my fate with theirs! However, that is not

to the present purpose – there are other rooms. For heaven's
80 sake, be quick, and let me settle somewhere!'
　　He made no reply to this adjuration; only plodding doggedly
down the wooden steps, and halting before an apartment
which, from that halt, and the superior quality of its furniture,
I conjectured to be the best one.
85　　There was a carpet, a good one, but the pattern was
obliterated by dust; a fire-place hung with cut paper dropping
to pieces; a handsome oak-bedstead with ample crimson
curtains of rather expensive material and modern make. But
they had evidently experienced rough usage: the valances hung
90 in festoons, wrenched from their rings, and the iron rod
supporting them was bent in an arc, on one side, causing the
drapery to trail upon the floor. The chairs were also damaged,
many of them severely; and deep indentations deformed the
panels of the walls.
95　　I was endeavouring to gather resolution for entering, and
taking possession, when my fool of a guide announced –
　　'This here is t' maister's.'
　　My supper by this time was cold, my appetite gone, and my
patience exhausted. I insisted on being provided instantly with
100 a place of refuge, and means of repose.
　　'Whear the divil,' began the religious elder. 'The Lord bless
us! The Lord forgie us! Whear the *hell*, wold ye gang? ye
marred, wearisome nowt! Yah seen all bud Hareton's bit uf a
cham'er. They's nut another hoile tuh lig dahn in i' th' hahse!'
105　　I was so vexed, I flung my tray and its contents on the
ground; and then seated myself at the stairs-head, hid my face
in my hands, and cried.
　　'Ech! ech!' exclaimed Joseph. 'Weel done, Miss Cathy! weel
done, Miss Cathy! Hahsiver, t' maister sall just tum'le o'er
110 them brocken pots; un' then we's hear summut; we's hear hah
it's tuh be. Gooid-fur-nowt madling! yah desarve pining froo
this tuh Churstmas, flinging t' precious gifts uh God under
fooit i' yer flaysome rages! Bud, Aw'm mista'en if yah shew
yer sperrit lang. Will Hathecliff bide sich bonny ways, think
115 ye? Aw nobbut wish he muh cotch ye i' that plisky. Aw nobbut
wish he may.'
　　And so he went scolding to his den beneath, taking the
candle with him, and I remained in the dark.

Notes

11 **gooid**   The spelling represents the pronunciation [ui]. A similar pronunciation for *foot* is implied by the spelling ⟨fooit⟩ (113), but modern Haworth dialect uses the standard form for the latter word.

14 **mun hev** 'must have'   The modal auxiliary *mun* is derived from OSc *munu*. *Mud*, 'might' (15), and the unstressd form *muh*, 'may' (115), are recorded in this area in the nineteenth century, but the latter has not been found by recent dialect workers. There is variation in the form of the verb 'to have'. The form *hae* (28) illustrates a widespread northern loss of medial [v] (*forgie*, 102).

16 **daht** 'fear'   See the introduction for the spelling. The sense is the French one common in ME.

25 **Thear**   Pronounced with the diphthong [iə]. Compare the forms *agean, deaved, whear*.
   thah   Joseph uses the familiar (originally second-person singular) mode of address to the child, but the more distant (hardly *polite* in this passage) form to his social superior.

27 **nave** 'fist'   From OSc *hnefi*. Found in Scotland, Ireland and the northern counties, as far south as Notts, Derby and Lincoln. In ME, south to Worcester.
   in bowl   The reduction of the definite article before a noun beginning with a consonant is usually represented by *t'*. Its omission here is phonetically quite probable, but may be a misprint since the first edition of *Wuthering Heights* was far from perfectly printed.

28 **pale t' guilp off** 'skim the thin liquid off'   The standard English [i:] is in this dialect [e:i] or [ɛ:i]: *ate* (54), *clane* (55); *Hathecliff* (70). Modern Haworth dialect has a reduced number of words with this pronunciation. The word *guilp* is uncertain in both meaning and origin.

29 **marcy**   The text represents a number of standard ⟨er⟩ or ⟨or⟩ spellings by ⟨ar⟩: *desarve, wark*. The fifteenth-century development of ME *er* to *ar* was earliest and most extensive in the North, and is preserved here in words where it had never occurred, or had been replaced, in more southerly localities. The modern standard spelling, *work*, derives from a western form, the pronunciation from the south-east Midlands.
   deaved 'smashed'   This sense is a unique occurrence, but the verb is recorded north of the Humber meaning 'deafen'.

37 **barn** 'child'   The Scandinavian and Anglian OE forms of this word are identical. The spelling *bairn* is Scots.

55 **meeterly** 'moderately' (OE *gemetlīc*).

64 **yon**   Derived from the OE adjectival demonstrative *geon*, and not, as is often implied by the spelling *yon'*, an abbreviation of preposition and adverb *yond* (OE *geond*). Joseph's pronominal use is found from the early fourteenth century onwards but retreats into northern dialect usage after the seventeenth century.

71 **soa**   The evidence of present-day dialect suggests that this spelling represents the diphthong [uə].

73 **mells on't** 'interferes with it'   Widespread in dialectal usage. Derived from OF *meller, mesler*.

103 **marred** 'spoilt' (OE *merran*)   Widely used of spoilt children in nineteenth-century dialects. This represents a narrowing of its usage compared with ME or the language of Shakespeare.

104 **hoile** 'hole'   This pronunciation is still common in south-west Yorkshire.

lig 'lie'   From OSc *liggja*. Found widely north of Staffs and Derbyshire.

109 **sall**   This northern form is recorded from ME onwards.

113 **flaysome** 'fearsome'   Widespread in dialectal usage.

115 **plisky** 'trick, escapade'   Used in Cumbria, Yorkshire and Scotland. Here with ironic implication.

43 Charles Darwin, The Descent of Man

Among scientific authors of the nineteenth century, Charles Darwin has perhaps the strongest claim to have revolutionised the way in which the ordinary man views the world in which he lives. His theory of the evolution of species, which undertook to explain the mechanism by which the diversity of terrestrial life developed, was implicitly opposed to the scriptural account of instantaneous creation. It was very widely read and caused great anguish in the Victorian world by its implied conflict between faith and science. Darwin, a retiring and sensitive man whose health was poor, played no personal role in the controversy, and his cause was fought by the biologist T. H. Huxley.

Darwin (1809–1882) was born in Shrewsbury into a medical family. After attending Shrewsbury school, he studied medicine at Edinburgh University, but, revolted by contemporary surgery, entered Christ's College, Cambridge with the intention of becoming an Anglican priest. Here he came under the influence of John Stevens Henslow, Professor of Botany, and it was he who recommended Darwin as a naturalist to accompany HMS *Beagle* on its round-the-world voyage from 1831 to 1836. Inspired by Lyell's *Principles of Geology* (1830), the observations made on this voyage provided him with the material from which his theories developed. Most of this development took place in a period of intense activity from 1837 to 1839, but his ideas were not widely published until they seemed in danger of pre-emption by Alfred Russel Wallace. The *Origin of Species* (1859) did not, however, emphasise the point that mankind participated in the evolutionary rules governing the rest of the natural world, and it was only in 1871, after preparatory works by Huxley and Lyell, that Darwin published *The Descent of Man and Selection in Relation to Sex*, in which evolutionary principles were applied to the human species.

The excerpt printed here concerns the origins of language, a matter of great importance since Wallace was prepared to accept a clear distinction between the human and other species owing to the enormous gulf in intellectual subtlety, which he believed to be too great to derive from natural selection. Darwin's argument is that mental dexterity is a product of the possession of language. This echoes a traditional distinction between the human and other species going back to Isocrates, but it is here

framed in terms of eighteenth- and nineteenth-century philological speculation on the origins of language.

That which distinguishes man from the lower animals is not
the understanding of articulate sounds, for, as every one
knows, dogs understand many words and sentences. In this
respect they are at the same stage of development as infants,
5 between the ages of ten and twelve months, who understand
many words and short sentences, but cannot yet utter a single
word. It is not the mere articulation which is our distinguishing character, for parrots and other birds possess this power.
Nor is it the mere capacity of connecting definite sounds with
10 definite ideas; for it is certain that some parrots, which have
been taught to speak, connect unerringly words with things,
and persons with events. The lower animals differ from man
solely in his almost infinitely larger power of associating
together the most diversified sounds and ideas; and this
15 obviously depends on the high development of his mental
powers.

As Horne Tooke, one of the founders of the noble science
of philosophy, observes, language is an art, like brewing or
baking; but writing would have been a better simile. It
20 certainly is not a true instinct, for every language has to be
learnt. It differs, however, widely from all ordinary arts, for
man has an instinctive tendency to speak, as we see in the
babble of our young children; whilst no child has an
instinctive tendency to brew, bake, or write. Moreover, no
25 philologist now supposes that any language has been deliberately invented; it has been slowly and unconsciously
developed by many steps. The sounds uttered by birds offer
in several respects the nearest analogy to language, for all the
members of the same species utter the same instinctive cries
30 expressive of their emotions; and all the kinds which sing,
exert their power instinctively; but the actual song, and even
the call-notes, are learnt from their parents or foster-parents.
These sounds, as Daines Barrington has proved, 'are no more
innate than language is in man.' The first attempts to sing
35 may be compared to the 'imperfect endeavour in a child to
babble.' The young males continue practising, or as the bird-
catchers say, 'recording,' for ten or eleven months. Their
first essays show hardly a rudiment of the future song; but as
they grow older we can perceive what they are aiming at; and
40 at last they are said to sing 'their song round.' Nestlings which

have learnt the song of a distinct species, as with the canary-birds educated in the Tyrol, teach and transmit their new song to their offspring. The slight natural differences of song in the same species inhabiting different districts may be
45 appositely compared, as Barrington remarks, 'to provincial dialects;' and the songs of allied, though distinct species may be compared with the languages of distinct races of man. I have given the foregoing details to shew that an instinctive tendency to acquire an art is not peculiar to man.
50   With respect to the origin of articulate language, after having read on the one side the highly interesting works of Mr. Hensleigh Wedgwood, the Rev. F. Farrar, and Prof. Schleicher, and the celebrated lectures of Prof. Max Müller on the other side, I cannot doubt that language owes its
55 origin to the imitation and modification of various natural sounds, the voices of other animals, and man's own instinctive cries, aided by signs and gestures. When we treat of sexual selection we shall see that primeval man, or rather some early progenitor of man, probably first used his voice in
60 producing true musical cadences, that is in singing, as do some of the gibbon-apes at the present day; and we may conclude from a widely-spread analogy, that this power would have been especially exerted during the courtship of the sexes – would have expressed various emotions, such as
65 love, jealousy, triumph, – and would have served as a challenge to rivals. It is, therefore, probable that the imitation of musical cries by articulate sounds may have given rise to words expressive of various complex emotions. The strong tendency in our nearest allies, the monkeys, in
70 microcephalous idiots, and in the barbarous races of mankind to imitate whatever they hear deserves notice, as bearing on the subject of imitation. Since monkeys certainly understand much that is said to them by man, and when wild, utter signal-cries of danger to their fellows; and since fowls give
75 distinct warnings for danger on the ground, or in the sky from hawks (both, as well as a third cry, intelligible to dogs), may not some unusually wise ape-like animal have imitated the growl of a beast of prey, and thus told his fellow-monkeys the nature of the expected danger? This would have been a first
80 step in the formation of a language.

Notes

17 **Horne Tooke**   Horne Tooke, author of the *Diversions of Purley* (1786, 1805), enjoyed a high reputation in England for half a century after its publication but had lost this authority by the time Darwin wrote. His purpose had been to demonstrate by etymology that the entire vocabulary could be reduced to names for physical objects, which had often been modified and abbreviated by use. His etymologies are, however, often fanciful. His mechanical explanation of the origins and evolution of language, and belief that language is the basis of mental activity, suited Darwin's purpose well.

26 **invented**   Rousseau had pointed out that, in order to invent language and agree on its use, early man would have had to have possessed it already.

33 **Daines Barrington**   (1727–1800). Lawyer, antiquary and naturalist, who is credited with inspiring Gilbert White to write *The Natural History of Selborne*.

37 **recording**   An example of the restriction of a word to a technical context. In ME, primary senses are 'to learn by heart' and 'to recite'. In the sixteenth century the sense begins to be restricted to the song of birds.

42 **canary-birds**   Canaries were first imported from the Canary Islands in the sixteenth century. The abbreviated form *canary* is recorded from the mid seventeenth century on but did not become the dominant form until the first quarter of the twentieth century.

47 **distinct races**   Darwin was very careful to point out that all modern men belong to the single species *homo sapiens* and vary only in race, but the association of language with race, and the failure to distinguish this from culture, is strange to modern ears (cf. *barbarous races*, 70).

48 **shew**   The spelling, which was common in the eighteenth and first half of the nineteenth centuries, had become restricted to legal language by the early twentieth century. The variants *shew* and *show* derive from forms of the OE *scēawian* with respectively a falling and a rising diphthong.

52 **Wedgwood**   Wedgwood was Darwin's brother-in-law and the author of a book, *On the Origin of Language* (1866). Schleicher, the prominent German philologist and Indo-European scholar, drew a parallel between evolutionary theory and language development in his book *Die Darwinische Theorie und die Sprachwissenschaft* (1863). Farrar, who became Dean of Canterbury, was the author of the very popular edifying school story *Eric; or Little by Little*, but also wrote essays on the *Origins of Language* (1860) and *Chapters on Language* (1865). Max Müller was Professor of Comparative Philology in the University of Oxford from 1868 to 1900 and the author of two popular lecture series on the 'Science of Language'. The two theories of language origin referred to are that it originated from the imitation of animal cries (the 'bow-wow' theory) and that it was the

extension into sound of physical gesture (the 'pooh-pooh' theory). Responsible linguistic opinion deplored these speculations about language origin, which were considered incapable of proof.

62 **widely-spread**   The addition of *-ly* to an adverbial form which had existed since OE, and in a compound of very well-established use, must be a piece of hypercorrection.

44 From the General Explanations to the New English Dictionary

The first fascicle (A–ANT) of the *New English Dictionary* (after 1895 the *Oxford English Dictionary*) appeared under the editorship of Dr James A. H. Murray in the spring of 1884 (see Excerpt 45). It was the beginning of a series which continued until the final fascicle in spring 1928 and afterwards, in various other forms, until the present day. The origin of the *Dictionary* was recognition by members of the Philological Society that changes to the lexicon had overtaken existing dictionaries. But when an investigatory committee was formed in 1857, it was soon realised that advances in philological scholarship also justified not mere revision but the creation of an entirely new dictionary, planned to trace historical development and aiming at exhaustive coverage of the literary language. Work proceeded slowly at first but was supported by the efforts of hundreds of volunteers, whose task was to read widely, entering interesting words on slips of paper with notes of their context and source. By the time Murray was appointed editor in 1879, substantial collections existed, but much of the credit for ordering and augmenting the materials belongs to him.

His General Explanations, which precede the text, echo the weighty significance of the enterprise. An explicit figurative parallel is drawn between the lexicographical task and the pursuit of science. The whole is framed in very extended sentences, exploiting heavily modified and qualified nominal phrases, lexical pairing, and extended adverbials. The technical language of the appropriate sciences is also used: *nebulous*, *species*, *order*, *nucleus*, *class*, *aberrant forms*. This rhetorical opening is more than mere bravado. The dictionary belongs to the flourishing climate of nineteenth-century science, to a period when enormous strides had been made in etymology and it seemed that sound change could be subject to explanatory laws. In discussing semantic change, Murray again seeks the analogy of evolutionary science: but for inadequacy of sources, the ramifications of sense developments might be set out like the biologists' phylogenetic trees. This conception lies beneath the arrangement of senses in the dictionary itself.

In discussing the lexicon, Murray addresses himself to the uses rather than the meanings of words, noting special appropriateness to particular contexts (an ancient stylistic conception) but also emphasising from experience the impracticality of making sharp distinctions in such classifications. The literary foundations of the *NED* (for which it has been criticised) are frankly acknowledged, but despite occasionally raised objections to its prescriptivism, it is notable that Murray regards the question of 'correctness' quite liberally, and in the light of historical development.

The Vocabulary of a widely-diffused and highly-cultivated living language is not a fixed quantity circumscribed by definite limits. That vast aggregate of words and phrases which constitutes the Vocabulary of English-speaking men
5 presents, to the mind that endeavours to grasp it as a definite whole, the aspect of one of those nebulous masses familiar to the astronomer, in which a clear and unmistakable nucleus shades off on all sides, through zones of decreasing brightness, to a dim marginal film that seems to end nowhere, but
10 to lose itself imperceptibly in the surrounding darkness. In its constitution it may be compared to one of those natural groups of the zoologist or botanist, wherein typical species forming the characteristic nucleus of the order, are linked on every side to other species, in which the typical character is
15 less and less distinctly apparent, till it fades away in an outer fringe of aberrant forms, which merge imperceptibly in various surrounding orders, and whose own position is ambiguous and uncertain. For the convenience of classification, the naturalist may draw the line, which bounds a class or
20 order, outside or inside of a particular form; but Nature has drawn it nowhere. So the English Vocabulary contains a nucleus or central mass of many thousand words whose 'Anglicity' is unquestioned; some of them only literary, some of them only colloquial, the great majority at once literary
25 and colloquial, – they are the *Common Words* of the language. But they are linked on every side with other words which are less and less entitled to this appellation, and which pertain ever more and more distinctly to the domain of local dialect, of the slang and cant of 'sets' and classes, of the
30 peculiar technicalities of trades and processes, of the scientific terminology common to all civilized nations, of the actual languages of other lands and peoples. And there is absolutely no defining line in any direction: the circle of the English language has a well-defined centre but no discernible circum-
35 ference. Yet practical utility has some bounds, and a

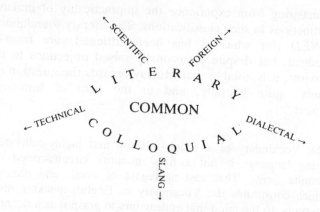

Dictionary has definite limits: the lexicographer must, like the naturalist, 'draw the line somewhere', in each diverging direction. He must include all the 'Common Words' of literature and conversation, and such of the scientific,
40 technical, slang, dialectal, and foreign words as are passing into common use, and approach the position or standing of 'common words', well knowing that the line which he draws will not satisfy all his critics. For to every man the domain of 'common words' widens out in the direction of his own
45 reading, research, business, provincial or foreign residence, and contracts in the direction with which he has no practical connexion: no one man's English is *all* English. The lexicographer must be satisfied to exhibit the greater part of the vocabulary of *each* one, which will be immensely more
50 than the whole vocabulary of *any* one.

In addition to, and behind, the common vocabulary, in all its diverging lines, lies an infinite number of *Proper* or merely *denotative* names, outside the province of lexicography, yet touching it in thousands of points, at which these names, and
55 still more the adjectives and verbs formed upon them, acquire more or less of connotative value. Here also limits more or less arbitrary must be assumed.

The Language presents yet another undefined frontier, when it is viewed in relation to *time*. The living vocabulary is
60 no more permanent in its constitution than definite in its extent. It is not to-day what it was a century ago, still less what it will be a century hence. Its constituent elements are in a state of slow but incessant dissolution and renovation. 'Old words' are ever becoming obsolete and dying out: 'new

65 words' are continually pressing in. And the death of a word is
not an event of which the date can be readily determined. It
is a vanishing process, extending over a lengthened period, of
which contemporaries never see the end. Our own words
never become obsolete: it is always the words of our grand-
70 fathers that have died with them. Even after we cease to use
a word, the memory of it survives, and the word itself
survives as a possibility; it is only when no one is left to whom
its use is still possible, that the word is wholly dead. Hence,
there are many words of which it is doubtful whether they are
75 still to be considered as part of the living language; they are
alive to some speakers, and dead to others. And, on the
other hand, there are many claimants to admission into the
recognized vocabulary (where some of them will certainly one
day be received), that are already current coin with some
80 speakers and writers, and not yet 'good English', or even not
English at all, to others.

   If we treat the division of words into current and obsolete
as a subordinate one, and extend our idea of the Language so
as to include all that has been English from the beginning, or
85 from any particular epoch, we enter upon a department of
the subject, of which, from the nature of the case, our
exhibition must be imperfect. For the vocabulary of past
times is known to us solely from its preservation in written
records; the extent of our knowledge of it depends entirely
90 upon the completeness of the records, and the completeness
of our acquaintance with them. And the farther back we go,
the more imperfect are the records, the smaller is the
fragment of the actual vocabulary that we can recover.

   Subject to the conditions which thus encompass every
95 attempt to construct a complete English Dictionary, the
present work aims at exhibiting the history and signification
of the English words now in use, or known to have been in
use since the middle of the twelfth century. This date has
been adopted as the only natural halting-place, short of going
100 back to the beginning, so as to include the entire Old English
or 'Anglo-Saxon' Vocabulary. To do this would have
involved the inclusion of an immense number of words, not
merely long obsolete but also having obsolete inflexions, and
thus requiring, if dealt with at all, a treatment different from
105 that adapted to the words which survived the twelfth century.
For not only was the stream of English literature then
reduced to the tiniest thread (the slender annals of the Old
English or Anglo-Saxon Chronicle being for nearly a century

its sole representative), but the vast majority of the ancient
words that were destined not to live into modern English,
comprising the entire scientific, philosophical, and poetical
vocabulary of Old English, had already disappeared, and the
old inflexional and grammatical system had been levelled to
one so essentially modern as to require no special treatment
in the Dictionary. Hence we exclude all words that had
become obsolete by 1150. But to words actually included this
date has no application; their history is exhibited from their
first appearance, however early.

Within these chronological limits, it is the aim of the
Dictionary to deal with all the common words of speech and
literature, and with all words which approach these in
character; the limits being extended farther in the domain of
science and philosophy, which naturally passes into that of
literature, than in that of slang or cant, which touches the
colloquial. In scientific and technical terminology, the aim
has been to include *all words English in form*, except those of
which an explanation would be unintelligible to any but the
specialist; and such words, not English in form, as either are
in general use, like *Hippopotamus, Geranium, Aluminium,
Focus, Stratum, Bronchitis*, or belong to the more familiar
language of science, as *Mammalia, Lepidoptera, Invertebrata*.

Down to the Fifteenth Century the language existed only in
dialects, all of which had a literary standing: during this
period, therefore, words and forms of all dialects are
admitted on an equal footing into the Dictionary. Dialectal
words and forms which occur since 1500 are not admitted,
except when they continue the history of a word or sense
once in general use, illustrate the history of a literary word,
or have themselves a certain literary currency, as is the case
with many modern Scottish words. It is true that the dialectal
words are mostly genuine English, and that they are an
essential part of the contents of a *Lexicon totius Anglicitatis*;
but the work of collecting them has not yet been completed;
and, even when they shall have been collected, the phonetic
variety in which they exist in different localities, and the want
of any fixed written forms round which to group the
variations, will require a method of treatment different from
that applicable to the words of the literary language, which
have an accepted uniform spelling and an approximately
uniform pronunciation.

Notes

4 **English-speaking men**   The phrase is perfectly possible in present-day English, but even before such uses of *men* were sensitised by the sexual politics of the 1970s, this would have been a verbose and rather portentous expression, in keeping with the opening sentences of this piece.

16 **aberrant forms**   The word *aberrant* is recorded from 1830, where it is used in Lyell's *Principles of Geology* (see Excerpt 43). *OED* lists its use as characteristic of natural history. The succeeding statement, that nature has drawn the line between species 'nowhere', is relevant to this linguistic context but more audacious with reference to biology than it appears today, since it implicitly accepts the Darwinian dictum of the arbitrary distinction between species, which had been so controversial in 1860.

23 **'Anglicity'**   The quotation marks identify a new formation made on the analogy of Latin *Latinitas*: the stylistic ideal of correct and pure Latin, uncorrupted by errors of grammar or – more relevant here – barbarous foreign borrowings. The Latin form occurs in line 142, where the phrase may be translated as 'a dictionary of the whole of English literacy'.

30 **peculiar** 'characteristic, particular'   The sense 'strange, odd, eccentric' seems to have developed in the later nineteenth century, and was still regarded as colloquial when *OED* was compiled. The development of the senses of this word from Latin *pecus*, 'cattle', is complex and interesting. Compare also *pecuniary*, *fee*, *cattle* and *chattel*.

34 **circumference**   The author here adds the following note: 'The above diagram will explain itself, as an attempt to express to the eye the aspect in which Vocabulary is here presented, and also some of the relations of its elements typical and aberrant. The centre is occupied by the "common" words, in which literary and colloquial usage meet. "Scientific" and "foreign" words enter the common language mainly through literature; "slang" words ascend through colloquial use; the "technical" terms of crafts and processes, and the "dialect" words, blend with the common language both in speech and literature. Slang also touches on one side the technical terminology of trades and occupations, as in "nautical slang", "Public School slang", "the slang of the Stock Exchange", and on another passes into true dialect. Dialects similarly pass into foreign languages. Scientific terminology passes on one side into purely foreign words, on another it blends with the technical vocabulary of art and manufactures. It is not possible to fix the point at which the "English Language" stops, along any of these diverging lines.'

53 **denotative**   The contrast between *denotative* and *connotative* terms reflects a technical distinction in the philosophy of John Stuart Mill, but is here used to distinguish those words which simply 'refer to' particular people or things, and those which have a more general

reference together with associated attributes. Thus, it is often said that proper nouns are merely denotative labels. Murray, however, makes the point that this distinction is not always easy to maintain. Consider, for example, the associative power of names like Ferrari or Jaguar.

64 **ever** 'always' This sense has become rare during the course of the twentieth century. It is now found mostly in phrases and formulae, such as *yours ever, ever-loving*.

85 **department** 'separate division or part of a whole' Although this word was borrowed in the fifteenth century with the sense 'departure', the modern senses date from a separate borrowing in the eighteenth century. Johnson's *Dictionary* considers it a French word. During the last third of the eighteenth century it was used (especially in America) to refer to offices of administration and government. It is this development which, in the twentieth century, has ousted the other senses.

87 **exhibition** 'presentation' Although the sense 'presentation, act of demonstrating' is still occasionally found, such contexts are becoming rarer, and the word seems be be becoming restricted in sense to 'public display, thing exhibited'.

93 **actual** 'contemporary' This sense is recorded from the mid seventeenth century. Although modern dictionaries still list it, the sense which contrasts with 'potential, possible, fictional' is that which has been most familiar for some decades.

108 **Anglo-Saxon Chronicle** The reference is to the *Peterborough Chronicle*, which was continued until 1154 (see Excerpt 8).

45   Henry Bradley, Review of the New English Dictionary

The publication in 1884 of the first volume of the *New English Dictionary* (afterwards, when published by Oxford, called the *Oxford English Dictionary*) was the most significant event in English lexicography since the appearance of Johnson's *Dictionary* in 1755. It represented the central achievement of nineteenth-century philology, both establishing guidelines for the historical study of the lexicon and stimulating, as its own source material, the editing from manuscript of numerous earlier texts. The origin of the Early English Text Society was intimately bound up with the Philological Society's project for a complete and authoritative dictionary of written English sources.

This publication also marked the establishment of the career of the philologist Henry Bradley, a career which is in many ways characteristic of the educational ideals of his time. Bradley was largely self-educated. Although born in Manchester in 1845, he was from a family of farmers and millers in north Derbyshire and Nottinghamshire, and he returned there the following year. He attended Chesterfield Grammar School from 1855 to 1859, where he was an outstanding scholar, but his social background did not encourage his entry to university and, after moving to Sheffield, he instead acted as tutor to the sons of two local physicians until 1863, when he joined a cutlery firm as a corresponding clerk. His studies had been begun in the library of Dr Lennard's house, and his post as a clerk left him the opportunity to broaden them. For twenty years he worked as a clerk, teaching himself modern and classical languages and even some Hebrew in his spare time, and writing a column on place names in the local newspaper. His reviews also began to establish contacts for him within the scholarly world. He had married in 1872, and when the family doctor advised that they should move south for the sake of his wife's health, Bradley was able to rely on his reputation with the editors of literary journals to ensure him some income. It was on the packing cases, unopened in his new home in Fulham, that Bradley wrote the review of the *NED* which is quoted here, and which brought him to the attention of the dictionary's chief editor, leading eventually to his own occupation of that post and a DLitt from the University of Oxford. His work on the dictionary occupied much of his time after 1889 until his death in

1923, but his books on *The Goths* (1888) and *The Making of English* (1904) represent a peculiarly nineteenth-century amalgam of scholarly authority and popular accessibility. The latter has remained in print (in a revised version) until the present day.

It is now nearly twenty-seven years since the Philological Society commenced the collection of materials for its great English Dictionary. The number of persons who have shared in the task amount to thirteen hundred, and this great
5　company of labourers have accumulated a body of three millions of quotations, taken from over five thousand different authors. The first instalment of the work for which these unexampled preparations have been made is at length before the world, and it is now possible to judge whether the
10　new Dictionary will be worthy of the enormous labour which has been expended upon it. Happily for the credit of English scholarship, the present specimen affords every reason to hope that the skill of Dr. Murray and his assistants will prove equal to the arduous task which lies before them. It would be
15　wonderful indeed if, in so vast an undertaking, there should not be many things to which criticism might object; but it may be confidently asserted that, if the level of excellence reached in this opening part be sustained throughout, the completed work will be an achievement without parallel in the
20　lexicography of any living language.

In comparing the Philological Society's English Dictionary with the only works which can claim to be regarded as its peers – the French Dictionary of Littré and the unfinished German Dictionary of Grimm – it must be remembered that
25　the scope of the English work is in several respects far larger than that proposed in either of the others. For one thing, the period of time embraced in the English Dictionary is by several centuries longer than that surveyed by the great French and German lexicographers. The classic French
30　language of Littré begins no earlier than the seventeenth century, and the New High German treated by Grimm goes back only to the middle of the fifteenth century. But the aim of Dr. Murray and his coadjutors is nothing less ambitious than to catalogue and, so far as the materials suffice, to
35　discuss historically every word which has belonged to the standard English vocabulary at any time since the language passed out of the fully inflected stage known as Anglo-Saxon. The epoch of this change is fixed by Dr. Murray at the year

1150. The literary barrenness of the hundred years preceding
40 this date happily obviates much of the inconvenience usually
attending the assignment of a definite year as the commencement of a linguistic period. The compilers of the English
Dictionary have therefore to trace the development of the
language through a period of respectively three or five
45 centuries, rich in literary remains, before arriving at the
chronological points at which the labours of Grimm and
Littré commence. Moreover, the year 1150 is not in the same
sense the beginning of Dr. Murray's work as the dates fixed
by Grimm and Littré are the beginning of theirs. It is true
50 that both the French and the German writers have drawn
largely on the literature of earlier centuries for the philological illustration of the words included in their Dictionaries,
but they have not done so with anything like the fullness
aimed at in the present work. Although Dr. Murray admits
55 no word which became obsolete before his initial date, yet
every word which he does admit is carefully traced from its
earliest appearance in 'Anglo-Saxon' writings, and the
successive variations of sense and form which it underwent in
the oldest period are discussed with the same fullness of
60 detail and illustration as those which took place throughout
the succeeding ages. Again, while in the French and German
Dictionaries there are many words and special senses of
words for which no literary authority is adduced, many of the
illustrative examples being simply sentences framed for the
65 occasion, Dr. Murray in almost every case furnishes a
quotation from an English writer, with minute references to
chapter or page. The authorities quoted range in date from
the Ruthwell Cross (here assigned to A.D. 700) to the *Daily
News* of July 6, 1883.
70 Another point which has added to the arduousness and the
value of Dr. Murray's undertaking is that his standard for the
admission of words to dictionary rank is rightly much less
rigid than those set up by his predecessors. The Teutonic
purism of Grimm led him to reject many words which every
75 German understands, and which are freely used in the
literature of his own and earlier times. No doubt many of the
swarm of foreign words, and of words clumsily adapted from
foreign languages by tacking on the termination *-iren*, never
ought to have become German. But their naturalization has
80 been in fact recognized by the mass of speakers and writers of
the language, and they should find a place in its Dictionary,
although they might be branded with an obelus as philo-

logically infamous. Dr. Murray has wisely gone to the extreme of admitting every word which is used by any English
85 author, provided that the author who employs it himself regards it as standard English, and not as foreign, dialectal, or technical.

One great merit of the new Dictionary is the remarkable manner in which the convenience of readers is consulted in
90 the typographical expedients employed to ensure facility of reference. This advantage is indeed shared to some extent by the other lexicographical publications of the Clarendon Press, and notably by the Etymological Dictionary of Professor Skeat; but it is here carried to a degree of perfection never
95 before aimed at. The size of the page is identical with that adopted in Littré's Dictionary; but a page of Littré is, typographically, a chaos through which the reader must find his way as best he can, while in the English Dictionary the eye is at once directed to the object of which it is in search.
100 Littré, for instance, prints the illustrative examples in the same type, and continuously with the definitions, the only use of strengthened type being in the Arabic figures prefixed to each definition. In the present work, the standard form of each word is printed in large 'Clarendon' type, which stands
105 out boldly from the page, so as to catch the eye at once. The various historical forms are given in 'small Clarendon', and the definitions in ordinary type. Under the definition of each sense of a word are arranged the quoted examples in a smaller letter, each quotation being preceded by its date in
110 heavy figures, so that the chronological range over which a word, or a sense of a word, extends may be measured at a glance. In this way the several definitions of a word are spaced off from each other by an intervening paragraph of smaller type. The value of this arrangement in abridging the
115 labour of consulting the Dictionary can scarcely be over-estimated.

With regard to the definitions, which form the strongest point of Littré's Dictionary, and the weakest point of that of Grimm, the present work may, perhaps, be considered to
120 hold a middle rank between the two. It can scarcely be charged as a fault that Dr. Murray has not imitated the excessive subdivision of significations into which Littré has frequently run. To give twenty-three numbered senses of the word *eau*, for instance, is an over-refinement which is rather
125 confusing than helpful. The definitions of previous lexicographers have frequently been adopted by Dr. Murray, in

many cases with due acknowledgement of their source. Here and there we notice a definition which seems incorrect or inadequate. The modern sense of *ache*, for instance, is not
130 exactly 'a continuous or abiding pain, in contrast to a sharp or sudden one'; and when it is said that this word is 'used of both physical and mental sensation', it should have been noted that the latter use is somewhat forced and rhetorical. We speak quite naturally of a mental *pain*; but when we use
135 *ache* in a similar sense we are consciously employing figurative language. Kingsley's phrase, 'healthy animalism', is certainly out of place as part of the definition of *Animal Spirits*; the expression (at least as Kingsley used it) denotes something quite different.
140   The one portion of the Dictionary which may be charged with incompleteness is what may be termed the phraseological department. Here, as in the definitions, Littré often falls into an excess of copiousness which need not be imitated. Still, a dictionary of this character ought to contain
145 every combination of words which has any fair claim to rank as an idiomatic phrase. Thus, under the word *Acting* we may reasonably look for 'acting edition', 'acting play'; under *Agent* for 'free agent', and other similar expressions; under *Able* for 'able seaman'. None of these are formally noted in
150 this Dictionary, though some of them appear in the quotations. Under *Alive* we miss the familiar phrase 'alive and kicking', for which literary authority could probably be found. Under *Age* the combination 'old age' of course occurs in the examples, but its idiomatic character is not properly
155 pointed out. These deficiencies, however, are probably common to all existing English dictionaries, and the present work certainly contains an abundance of idiomatic phrases which we should fail to find in its predecessors. Among these we note the expression 'adventure school', which we had
160 thought to be a coinage of the last few years, but which is here illustrated by a quotation dated as far back as 1834.
  The most valuable feature of the new Dictionary is of course its wealth of illustrative quotations, and the skill with which these have been arranged so as to exhibit the
165 successive changes of form and meaning which the words have undergone since the time of their earliest appearance in English. The examples, as already stated, are placed under the definition which they severally illustrate, the original sense of the words being first explained, the derivative senses
170 following in the order of their logical descent. In the case of

words of foreign origin, it does not always happen that the original English sense of a word is that indicated by its etymology, as such words were often first introduced in some technical acceptation, which was afterwards extended in
175 accordance with the wider meaning of the Latin or other original. In these cases the editor has varied his mode of treatment according to the circumstances. Under the word *Advent* the ecclesiastical and religious senses of the word are mentioned first, and it is afterwards pointed out that it has
180 been in later times applied to 'any important or epoch-making arrival', and 'poetically or grandi' uently to any arrival'. This order is justified by the fact that the earlier applications of the word have given a colour to its subsequent extension of meaning. In the article *Annunciation* a different
185 course has been followed, the etymological sense of the word being first given, and afterwards its applications to the church festival and to the event which it commemorates, although these technical senses are of earlier occurrence in English.

Exception may perhaps be taken to the frequent introduc-
190 tion of examples from publications of the last two or three years, which may seem to savour too much of 'bringing the work down to the latest date'. It should be remembered, however, that in a few years many words now current will probably have become obsolete or changed in sense; and in
195 such instances these latest examples will be of especial value to students of the history of the language. We have noted one or two cases in which useless or misleading quotations are given, or in which examples are ranged under wrong heads. Under *Advertiser* the title 'Morning Advertiser' is quoted,
200 with the date 1882 (why not still later?). This conveys a wrong impression, as the signification which it is intended to exemplify was obsolete long before the time here indicated. In the article *Amour* the extracts from Chaucer and from R. Burney given under the first definition really belong to the
205 second. It is rather amusing to find that the only authority adduced for *Anamorphose* is a quotation from 'J.A.H. Murray, in *Mill Hill Mag.* iv. 79.' When Part II of the Dictionary appears, we shall see whether Dr. Murray is able to quote any precedent for the (certainly very convenient)
210 word *aphetized*, which he employs frequently in his etymo-logical remarks.

We reserve for a second notice the etymology and phonology. Meanwhile, we may briefly say that in these departments, as in those already discussed, the opening part

215 of the 'Great Dictionary' fully satisfies the high expectations
which have been formed respecting it. It is earnestly to be
hoped that the work will be carried to its conclusion in a
manner worthy of this brilliant commencement.

Academy, Feb. 16, 1884.

Notes

5–6 **three millions of**   This construction, in which *million* is treated as
a quasi-noun, is common from the earliest borrowing (late fourteenth century) onwards. The twentieth-century use as a quasi-
adjective, and thus uninflected after a numeral, dates only from the
mid nineteenth century. Bradley's usage would have been considered
more correct in 1884, but compare Murray's use of the expression
many thousand words in the General Explanations of the *Dictionary*
(see Excerpt 44).

17–18 **if . . . be**   This careful observation of the use of the subjunctive
form following *if* would now seem pedantic even in a scholarly
review.

33 **coadjutors** 'collaborators, helpers'   This very literary word is a
fifteenth-century borrowing from OF.

38 **epoch** 'assigned position in chronological sequence'   The senses
of L. Latin *epocha* which connote a fixed time reference are now
restricted to technical discourse (e.g. astronomy), and the more
frequent senses connote a period of time.

78 **-iren**   Large numbers of verbs with a Latin base, and employing
the derivative suffix *-ieren*, were adopted into German in the course
of the fifteenth and sixteenth centuries.

82 **obelus** 'a symbol ($\div$) used in text to mark inauthenticity'
Through L. Latin from Greek *obelos*, 'spit'.

129 **ache**   It seems doubtful that the compound *heart-ache*, recorded
from Shakespeare on, is felt to be figurative.

199 **Advertiser**   The sense referred to is presumably that of giving
public notice of an event, etc.

210 **aphetized**   Murray included the word and a definition ('to shorten
by aphesis') in the second volume, but did not offer any examples of
its use.

46   Henry Sweet, The Practical Study of Languages

Henry Sweet (1845–1912) was described by an admiring George Bernard Shaw as 'the brainiest Oxford don of his time', and he is best known to the general public through Shaw's supposed transformation of him into the irascible phonetician Professor Higgins in *Pygmalion* and subsequently the musical *My Fair Lady*. The real Sweet was the son of a barrister at the Inner Temple. As a child he was subject to fits and was so short-sighted that he had difficulty in reading. He attended a private school in Tottenham, and then King's College School, London before moving in 1864 to study philology in Heidelberg. He then spent a brief period as a clerk before entering Balliol College, Oxford in 1869. He seems not to have been suited to the study of classical languages and achieved very poor results, although drawing attention to himself by winning the Taylorian prize in German.

Even as an undergraduate, he was engaged in scholarly publication – in 1871 his edition of the Alfredian *Cura Pastoralis*, which established the principles of OE dialectology, and his *History of English Sounds* a year after graduation, in 1874. These were followed by a series of major works on Old English, the history of the language, English grammar and phonetics. His *Anglo-Saxon Reader* and *Anglo-Saxon Primer* formed the mainstay of undergraduate courses in Old English for a century after their publication in 1876 and 1888 respectively. Sweet's stature in the field of English Language studies was acknowledged in his own time, but he waited long for formal recognition. Although resident in Oxford from 1895 onwards, he was repeatedly disappointed in his applications for chairs. The causes for these repeated snubs to so eminent a scholar are not clear, but are not unconnected with the abrasiveness of his personality and a sensitivity to criticism which led him into misunderstandings and feuds with the academic establishment: perhaps, in Shaw's words, 'his Satanic contempt for all academic dignitaries and persons in general who thought more of Greek than of phonetics'.

Sweet belonged to no particular school of philological thought, and much of what he has to say retains its general validity. The practical bias of his work emerges contentiously in *The Practical Study of Languages* (published in 1899 but drafted twenty-two years earlier) where he ridicules the rigidity of the scholarly establishment. 'Living philology', he insists, should be based upon the spoken word, and original fieldwork requires greater gifts than preparing endless editions of old texts. Phonetics is seen as the foundation of both language learning and dialectology, and he challenges 'some real University' to recognise that fact. In 1901 he was at last appointed to an Oxford University Readership in Phonetics.

The second main axiom of living philology is that all study of language, whether theoretical or practical, ought to be based on the spoken language.

5   The distinction between the literary and the colloquial form of the same language has considerably complicated the problem of learning languages. This distinction is not solely the result of the use of writing and printing, for even such unlettered savages as the Andaman islanders have an archaic poetical dialect which differs considerably from their ordinary spoken

10 language; but writing – and, still more, printing – have naturally increased the divergence. In many Oriental languages the divergence is so great that the colloquial is no longer a mere variation of the literary form, but the two practically constitute distinct, mutually unintelligible languages.

15 In European languages, where the difference is much less, most grammarians tacitly assume that the spoken is a mere corruption of the literary language. But the exact contrary is the case: it is the spoken which is the real source of the literary language. We may pick out the most far-fetched

20 literary words and forms we can think of, but we shall always find that they are derived from the colloquial speech of an earlier period. Even such forms as *thou hast, he hath*, were ordinary colloquialisms a few centuries ago, though they now survive only as fossil, dead colloquialisms side by side with

25 the living colloquialisms *you have, he has*. Every literary language is, in fact, a mixture of colloquialisms of different periods.

Every literary language must indeed in its first beginnings be purely colloquial. It is certainly difficult to realize that

30 such a language as the classical Italian of Dante and Petrarch was originally nothing but a rough attempt to write down what were then considered the slovenly colloquialisms of Late Latin; but nevertheless such is the origin not only of Italian, but of all the other Romance languages as well. The tradition

35 of the origin of Italian is still kept up in the word for 'translate', namely *volgarizzare*, literally 'make popular.'

Accordingly, it is now an axiom not only of Romance philology, but of philology generally, that the real life of language is better seen in dialects and colloquial forms of 40 speech than in highly developed literary languages, such as Greek, Latin, and Sanskrit.

Important as this principle is from a scientific point of view, it is still more so from a practical one, and for the following reasons: –

45 If we compare the written and spoken language of a given period, we shall find that the literary language is full of superfluous words and phrases, which the spoken language nearly always gets rid of. Thus in the English spoken language the idea 'sky' is expressed by this word only, while in the literary 50 language it may also be expressed by *heaven, heavens, firmament, welkin*. So also the form *hath* was still used in literary prose in the last century in such phrases as *the author hath* . . ., and it is still used in poetry and in the liturgical language of the Bible and Prayer-book, while in the spoken language the 55 only form used is *has*. Again, nothing is more difficult than to give definite grammatical rules for the use of the subjunctive mood in literary English; in the spoken language the subjunctive is not used at all except in a few perfectly definite constructions, such as *if it were*. So also in spoken French the two 60 most difficult tenses of the verb, the preterite indicative and subjunctive, have been supplanted by the perfect. So completely is the preterite obsolete that Passy, in his translation of the Gospel of Luke into modern French, discards it entirely, as in the beginning of the parable of the vineyard; 65 œn ɔm a plã̄ãte yn viñ, i l a lwe a de viñrō, e il e parti pur lōōtā (20. 9). According to Passy (Elementarbuch, 156), it occurs only in comic imitations of the South French dialect. Even in German the complicated rules for the inflection of proper names – *Luise*, gen. *Luise'ns, Cato, Cato's*, plur. 70 *Cato'ne, Leibnitz*, plur. *Leibnitz'e* – are swept away bodily in the spoken language, which, as a general rule, does not inflect such words at all.

Again, in literature the context is often vague, as in the Homeric *méropes ánthrōpoi*, where *méropes* may mean any 75 quality that can be predicated of men generally. So also in the Sanskrit Vēdas we have whole hymns, which, when epitomized, leave not much more than 'the bright shiner (that is, the sun) shines brightly.' In simple colloquial prose, on the

other hand, the meaning of a word is generally quite clear
80 from the context. The spoken language, too, is far stricter in
its use of epithets: it hardly ever introduces an adjective or
other qualifier except to convey some definite information.
Thus in ordinary speech we do not talk of 'the bright sun' or
'the silver moon,' simply because the epithets convey no
85 information – tell us nothing that is not already implied in the
words *sun* and *moon* themselves. Even such a phrase as 'the
sun shines brightly' has an uncolloquial ring about it,
although it is not exactly anti-colloquial. We could say 'the
moon is bright to-night,' because this really conveys informa-
90 tion. The spoken language also prefers a simple paratactic
arrangement of sentences. The complicated periods of
literary prose would, indeed, often be unintelligible in
speech.
We see, then, that the advantage as regards clearness and
95 definiteness is on the side of the spoken language: by starting
from the spoken language we have less to learn, and we learn
it accurately. Everything therefore points to the conclusion
that in learning foreign languages we should follow the
natural order in which we learn our own language: that is,
100 that we should begin with learning the spoken language
thoroughly, and then go on to the literary language.

Notes

4 **literary and colloquial**   Sweet is at pains to make a distinction of
some complexity. Literary language is mostly written language, and
colloquial language mostly spoken, but the opposed pairs are not
identical. Colloquial language is also defined by its use in everyday
communication; literary language is consciously artful and involved
with various cultural values. Colloquial language is connected with
contextual situations, and is less complex in various ways than
literary language, which may preserve various earlier stages in its set
of expressions, as well as a wider range of registers. Sweet himself
here introduces into a generally learned discourse some familiar,
colloquial elements: *can think of* (20), *gets rid of* (48).

16 **grammarians**   The point is that contemporary grammars, as well
as lexicographical works such as the *OED*, were based upon written,
and indeed largely literary, sources. Spoken variants from the norms
of such sources were therefore likely to be considered ungrammatical
or sub-standard.

32 **slovenly colloquialisms**   Indeed, both Chaucer and a fourteenth-
century Wycliffite commentator refer to Italian as 'corrupt Latin'.

49 **sky**   This group of synonyms forms an interesting example of the

processes of lexical development. The Scandinavian borrowing *sky* replaced the OE *wolcen*, which became restricted to poetic contexts during the sixteenth century. *Firmament* was borrowed from Latin and French in technical contexts in the late thirteenth century, and has been largely restricted to poetic language from the seventeenth century. *Heaven* has become increasingly specialised in sense in religious contexts, and its plural form is now most frequent in written language.

51 **hath** Sweet is referring to earlier eighteenth-century practice. Already in 1643, Richard Hodges had noted that this spelling was pronounced with final -*s*.

62 **Passy** The excerpt from Passy's translation reads 'un homme a planté une vigne, il l'a louée à des vignerons, et il est parti pour longtemps'. P. Passy was the director of the International Phonetics Association, and editor of its journal, *Le Maître phonétique*. Sweet's 'Romic' phonetic notation, in which broad transcription appears in parentheses, narrow in square brackets, and which shows vowel length by doubling the vowel symbol, was the precursor of the International Phonetic Alphabet.

74 **méropes ánthrōpoi** 'men endowed with speech' But the expression is formulaic and means little more than 'human men'.

83 **bright sun** The point is one reintroduced from information science into linguistic theory in the 1950s in the work of, among others, André Martinet: meaning implies choice. If the occurrence of a form is determined by preceding context, then its occurrence contributes no additional meaning to the message. Such redundancy is not characteristic of colloquial communication.

The three letters which make up this excerpt are from front-line troops of very different social and educational backgrounds. The first two were written by Captain Ainslie Douglas Talbot, a regular army officer, the son of a regular army Colonel, who had been educated at Sandhurst. The first of them is addressed to his wife Dorothy, the second to his close friend Lt Col Tom Slingsby, MC, with whom he had served in India with the Lancashire Fusiliers. The third letter was written by Private David John Sweeney of the 2nd Battalion, Lincoln Regiment to his girlfriend Ivy, whom he married at the end of 1917. It was almost certainly written in July 1916. He was the son of a Clerkenwell confectioner and had become a regular soldier after being educated at the local council school. Ivy had been educated at a private school and worked as a solicitor's clerk.

Talbot's letters are written from a hospital ship at Gallipoli, where he had taken part in the ill-fated attempts to seize the Dardanelles, re-supply Russia, and take Turkey out of the war. The landings on 25 April 1915 were fiercely resisted and before the troops were finally evacuated in December there had been 252,000 Allied casualties through illness and disease as well as combat.

The first battle of the Somme (Sweeney's letter), whose purpose was to relieve German pressure on the French at Verdun, commenced on 1 July 1916 on a fifteen-mile front. The assault was on well-prepared German fortifications and casualties were heavy – as high as 60,000 in one day. Although a salient five miles deep was created, further advance proved impossible and the rains of October and November brought the battle to a close.

The letters are printed here with their original spelling and punctuation. Their style reflects both their purpose as letters home and their authors' cultural values: conversational devices (*Well, mind, by Jove* and familiar address-forms) to simulate closeness, formal evocations of religious piety in addressing their ladies, and some awkward gestures in the use of literary phrasing (*they little thought*). Despite these formalities, their style is essentially colloquial, and the coherence of the letters is often jeopardised; omission or confusion of words, errors of grammatical concord, the awkward use of cataphoric reference (reference forward in the discourse) or changes in topic, and failure to recognise sentence boundaries are found in both men. This last is especially noticeable when they are narrating stirring action in which they had been involved, and in Sweeney's letter emotional involvement is also often accompanied by the rhetorical use of capitalisation. A marked distinction between them is in their use of slang words and expressions, and especially in Talbot's fondness for intensifying adverbs (*all*, *frightfully*, *awfully*, *pretty*, *fairly*, *simply*) as well as the literary allusions by which he attempts to express depths of feeling in a way he could approve as manly.

A Two letters from Captain Talbot

30 April 1915

Just a line Dorfie darling to let you know I am all strong. All correspondence has been stopped to an from here and this may never reach you; I am getting a wounded officer to post it at (?) where he is shortly being sent. I have a sprained
5 ankle at present but expect to be back in the firing line soon; I did it falling into a trench on the second night. I do wonder what came out in the papers about this show at home. Well girly thanks to your prayers etc. I have been most frightfully lucky so far. I long to talk a lot about it all but mus'nt. Keep
10 up cheer mind; I know you must be awfully anxious, but worrying wont help either of us; and as I have escaped so far I should be able to escape anything I think. Best love and hope this reaches you fairly soon. I must say I just can't realize that my pals, that have already been killed, are dead.
15 I find myself quoting 'Cathcarts Hill' to myself.
    Your loving Douglas.

2nd May. On Board SS Alaunia

Dear Wang,

I sent you a line yesterday via a wounded oficer; who was going to post it at the base, but as this boat is the out of mail headquarters I drop a line again, as I can censor it myself. I got through the landing without a scratch thanks to my
20 natural instinct to see cover on a flat beach; but strained my ankle badly the second night falling into a trench in the dark. By jove it was pretty hot that Sunday morning. I can hardly

write about it yet. Poor old Porter was killed by a hand
grenade I think climbing up the cliff on my right. I am awfully
25 sick he got knocked over. Tom Mannsell and Tommy were
shot getting out of the boat. Clark was shot through the head
sitting in the boat. I tell you I looked pretty slippy about
getting ashore I jumped overboard into 5 feet of water I dont
think the men realized how hot the fire was they were
30 laughing and joking till the last.
  Of course you know we were under HOB as "Screams"
had been sacked previously. Bishop is d'd good and as cool as
a cucumber under fire. Well I think we fairly made a name
for ourselves as we were the first to establish a hold on the
35 peninsula. I only got about five men ashore alive in my boat
and not one of them could use their rifles owing to sand
jamming the bolt. Seekham did d'd well all day. I believe he
has since been hit through the shoulder. The sniping is simply
awfull here one is more likely to get a bullet in the back than
40 in the front. they hide all over the place. I dont think for the
first 24 hours there was a single second when you could not
hear a bullet overhead hardly.
  I must say I think this kind of fighting is a bit too warm for
words. I had two horse gunner signallers who were with L
45 battery in France with me the first day and they said they had
never seen any thing like that first landing. We spent the
night on HMS *Euryalus* and landed in boats in tows early at
daylight. I can tell you the sight of the peninsula being shelled
by the fleet was grand with the sun rising above it all. We
50 kicked off right outside the supporting ships and went in
fairly fast untill we were right under the canons mouth. the
noise of the 10" etc: were deafening.
  We never got a shot fired at us till the oars were tossed
around and then they started in earnest. The first bullet that
55 struck the water brought up loud jeers from our men, but
poor devils they little thought what they were in for. Brocka
was the runner was in my boat, he has a charmed life as he
left his rifle on board and ran back for it and never got
touched. C. S. Wilson was about the first man I saw hit he got
60 out first from the boat next me and was hit in the stomach at
once I didn't need Kipling's words to stop me from looking
twice at him. Gus was hit just through the head above his
eyes I hope he wont loose his eyesight. Meekins hit his arm
badly shattered I am afraid he will have lost it. Keanly had
65 his arm broken. I dont know how much I am allowed to tell
you of all this, but by the time you get this you will most

likely know all the casualties. I must say I am sorry for the
girls in Nuneaton, if they really cared; but it will show that
part of the country what a soldier does have to go through.
70 Well I expect to be back in the firing line in a day or so but
my foot is still bruised and although I feel an awfull
scrimshanker on this ship when I can see the battle going on
on land. I know if I go too soon my foot will go again. I could
not move my toes for the first day and Pirie thought it was
75 broken. Well best luck old chap. I am d'd glad you are not
here for Mrs Wang's sake, do try and cheer my poor girl up, I
am afraid when she finds out what the fighting is like out here
it will make her feel rather sick. . .

Every yours, Addy.

B Excerpt from a letter by Private Sweeney

Well dearest the 30th June was a verry busy day for us. We
received orders that Greatly supprised all of My Regt, and
this is what it was the Attack was going to be made on the 1st
July and we were in Support. on our way up to the firing line
5 Every man had to Carry something some would get Tools and
Water Cans. I was rather unlucky, I had to carry a box of 4
Stokes Shells which were no light weight. Well the morning
of the 1st July came and I was verry tired as we had not had
much rest but it had to be done no one knew even on the
10 Morning of the 1st what time the attack was being made but
the artillery started at 6.30 and at 7.30 we heard the C.O
shout The Boys are going over and where we was by getting
on the hill near us we could see the Boys going like Mad
across no mans land but we could not look for long as Fritzs
15 artillery Observers mite have spotted us well at 8 o clock we
began to move up but we had to go verry slowley up the
Communication Trenches as Fritz was shelling all of them
well we got our loads and after a very hot time we came into
our owne Fire trench now was the worst part of the Job as we
20 had to get up the Ladders and get across to the German
trench with our loads as quick as we could how I managed it I
shall never be able to say but as soon as we were on top the
Germans started sending big Shrapnell Shells terrible things I
heard when we got in to the German 1st line of trenches that
25 15 of our Boys were killed and wounded coming across. Well
we got into his first line we lost 24 men killed by 1 shell
buried them all I was blown against the Back of the trench

and just Managed to get into a German Dugout before 3
more big Ones came well that night we had to go into the
30   firing line and relive the Boys who had made the charge we
captured 4 lines of trenches that day not so bad. Well we got
into those trenches safe and we were there a few hours when
he started his Counter attack. We mowed them down in
hundreds and he never got within 20 yards of our trench he
35   soon got fed up and did not try again that night.

Well Dear we were in the Fire line all the Night of the 1st
also 2nd and we were Relived on the Night of the 3rd by the
10th Division. Well we all came out by way of a Road and we
were verry [lucky] in not getting one wounded.
40   Well my Darling we are now out of hearing of the Guns as
we have had a 26 mile Train Ride, but I dont think it will be
long befor we are into them again, but at present we are not
strong enough. I told you Dear I was happy Well so I am, but
when I think of My Poor Dear Old Chums who have fallen I
45   could Cry I had to cry in the Trench about one of my Chums
Poor Old Jack Nokes he has been out hear Since the Verry
bigginning of the War and has not received a scratch he has
never been home on Leave because he has had a small Crime
his home is at Wimbleton Poor Lad he died Game with his
50   Mother's Name his last Word. I cryed like a Child, not only
him but a lot more of my poor comrades have gone. Ivy my
Darling I am sure it is You and My Poor Sister Praying for
me that God has spared me. I said my Prayers at lease 1000
times a Day (Please God Spare me to get out of this War
55   safely for my dear Ivy's and my Sisters Sake). O Ivy I cannot
tell you the Horrors of this War, you cannot Realise what it is
like to see Poor Lads Lying about with such terrible Wounds
and we cannot help them.

Notes

Talbot

7   **this show**   *OED* attributes the broadened sense 'event, enterprise'
to American influence, extended from the field of entertainment,
and records it first in 1889. In the military context, however, the use
of the word may be connected with *OED* 1c, 'a demonstration of
military strength', which is recorded between 1548 and 1853.
14   **pals**   Recorded from 1681 onwards, this is an adoption from
Romany, where it means 'brother, mate'. It is first used in lower-life
slang to mean 'accomplice, partner in crime' but is widespread in
colloquial use by 1915. Cf. *chums* and *comrades* (below).

15 **'Cathcarts Hill'**   During the Crimean War, Cathcart's Hill was an observation station overlooking the city of Sebastopol. It was later the site of a cemetery and memorials to the British dead. It derived its name from General Sir George Cathcart, who was killed on 5 November 1854 at the battle of Inkerman while leading his troops up to a ridge, now heavily defended by the Russians, which he had earlier abandoned. His last words are said to have been, 'I fear we are in a mess.' I have not been able to identify the poem to which Talbot refers.

23 **Poor old Porter**   The adjectives *poor* and *old* carry with them a strong emotional charge, and their connotations of pity or affectionate familiarity are frequently exploited in these letters. The former is recorded in this shifted sense as early as the thirteenth century in Laȝamon; the latter from 1588, when it is used by Shakespeare.

27 **looked pretty slippy**   Derived from an imperative clause, an order to move quickly. *Slippy* is recorded in the sense 'quick' in colloquial and dialectal use from the mid nineteenth century.

40 **they**   The Turkish snipers. The reference of the pronoun presupposes the knowledge and involvement of the recipient of the letter. More careful textual construction would have ensured a more specific reference in the preceding clauses. Loose coherence of this kind is typical of situated conversation (cf. Sweeney's use of *he* in line 33).

53 **we never got a shot fired at us**   This structure emphasises the subjective focus as compared with a simple passive (*shots were not fired at us*). The structure would more usually occur with *have* as auxiliary. The verb *get* has greatly extended its uses as an auxiliary in speech in the modern period. Cf. *and never got touched* (58–59). This passive use of *get* as an auxiliary does not appear before the mid seventeenth century but is now common in spoken English, although not yet in writing.

57–58 **as he left his rifle**   The use of *as* with causative or resultative senses is traceable from 1400 but is rare before the twentieth century. H. W. Fowler (*Modern English Usage*, 1926) strongly disapproved of it: 'All good writers instinctively avoid it; but, being common in talk, it is much used in print also by those who have not yet learnt that composition is an art and that sentences require arrangement.' Even in spoken language it is now rare, and may sound old-fashioned, but it is particularly common in the speech-based prose of these letters.

61 **Kipling's words**   The reference is probably to some lines from one of Kipling's *Barrack-Room Ballads* (1892), 'The Young British Soldier':

> When first under fire an' you're wishful to duck
> Don't look nor take 'eed at the man that is struck
> Be thankful you're livin', and trust to your luck
>   And march to your front like a soldier.

72 **scrimshanker** 'shirker, slacker'   Recorded in army slang from 1890. The etymology is unknown.

75 **old chap**   The word *chap* is ultimately derived from *chapman* (OE *cēapman*), 'merchant, trader'. The shortened form occurs rarely in the sixteenth century and is found more widely and contemptuously in the eighteenth. Its development as a term of affection may be compared with such phrases as 'old rascal'.

Sweeney

3 **and this is what it was**   Sweeney apparently breaks the rules of grammatical concord (*orders . . . it*). However, this is perhaps best construed as a rhetorical device in which *it* is not considered to refer back to orders, but operates vaguely and cataphorically, emphasising the important information which follows.

7 **Stokes Shells**   The Stokes gun was a trench mortar, developed during 1915 by an agricultural engineer of that name and considered to be an improvement in convenience and portability when compared with previous such weapons. The word *shrapnel* (23) is also derived from the name of its inventor during the Peninsular War, General Henry Shrapnel. The original sense was that of 'a hollow shell containing bullets which are scattered by an explosive charge'. The word is now more often used to refer to the metal fragments scattered by the explosion of an ordinary high-explosive bomb or shell.

44 **Poor Dear Old Chums**   The pity and affection implied by the concatenation of modifiers is present also in the word *chum*, which is first recorded from the late seventeenth century to denote a friend with whom one shares university lodgings. It seems subsequently to have moved down the social scale, and at the time of the compilation of *OED* was found in young male society: schoolboys, criminals and convicts. It seems, like *pals*, to have been partially rehabilitated in the early years of the twentieth century.

49 **died Game** 'died bravely'   The expression is derived from cock-fighting, in which game-cocks were pitted against each other. Both the sense 'sport' and the sense 'animals used in sport' are derived from the OE *gamen*, 'sport, merriment'. The phrase *to die game* is first recorded in 1727 in *The Beggar's Opera*.

51 **comrades**   Like *chum*, the word originally meant 'that one with whom a lodging is shared, room-mate' (Fr. *camarade*; Sp. *camarada*). It is recorded from 1591 especially in military contexts. The association with left-wing politics is, of course, a later development.

48 D. H. Lawrence, 'Fanny and Annie'

This excerpt is taken from one of Lawrence's second collection of short stories, *England, My England*, published in 1922 although written during 1919. Its setting is the industrial Midlands where Lawrence was born on 11 September 1885, grew up, and located much of his writing about the lives of ordinary people. The son of a Nottinghamshire miner and an ex-schoolteacher, his childhood was uncomfortable owing to the pressure on family finances of four other children, and also to the stormy relationship of his parents. Nevertheless, his mother determined that he should not follow his father into mining, and encouraged him at school. At thirteen he obtained a scholarship to Nottingham High School, but left before his sixteenth birthday to work first as a clerk in a surgical goods factory at thirteen shillings a week, and then a teacher in Eastwood. He entered Nottingham University College in 1906 to study for a teacher's certificate, and was already writing poetry and short stories. In the three years from 1911 to 1913 he published three novels, *The White Peacock*, *The Trespasser* and *Sons and Lovers*, the last of these largely autobiographical.

During this period Lawrence struck up a relationship with the German wife of his old professor in Nottingham. After a spell in Germany, they settled during the war in Cornwall. Although Lawrence was increasingly recognised by contemporary literary circles, the publication of *The Rainbow* in 1915, which was seized as obscene, reinforced a notoriety which persisted until long after his death. After the war, Lawrence and his wife left for Italy and he spent most of the rest of his life abroad, visiting Ceylon, Australia, America and Mexico, and returning to Italy only when chronic tuberculosis was diagnosed. Attempts to find a cure proved fruitless, and Lawrence died in Venice on 2 March 1930.

'Fanny and Annie' tells of the homecoming of a lady's maid to marry the foundry-worker lover of her youth. She is smartly dressed, elegant and bright, 'such a lady' in the eyes of her aunt. He wears no cap or collar, is awkward, and she thinks he 'drags her down'. Her return is capitulation to fate. The division between the outlook of the two is symbolised in their use of language. Her future husband's mother fully appreciates this, and makes dialect speech a weapon against her new daughter-in-law,

turning the knife in the wound. Some of the dialect forms used
are today associated more with Derbyshire than Nottinghamshire
but may well have been found in the western part of the county,
where the story is set.

He stayed till about half past nine. She went to the door with
him.

'When are you coming up?' he said, jerking his head in the
direction, presumably, of his own home.

5 'I'll come tomorrow afternoon,' she said brightly. Between
Fanny and Mrs Goodall, his mother, there was naturally no
love lost.

Again she gave him an awkward little kiss, and said good-
night.

10 'You can't wonder, you know, child, if he doesn't seem so
very keen,' said her aunt. 'It's your own fault.'

'Oh, Aunt, I couldn't stand him when he was keen. I can
do with him a lot better as he is.'

The two women sat and talked far into the night. They
15 understood each other. The aunt, too, had married as Fanny
was marrying: a man who was no companion to her, a violent
man, brother of Fanny's father. He was dead, Fanny's father
was dead.

Poor Aunt Lizzie, she cried woefully over her bright niece,
20 when she had gone to bed.

Fanny paid the promised visit to his people the next afternoon. Mrs Goodall was a large woman with smooth-parted
hair, a common, obstinate woman, who had spoiled her four
lads and her one vixen of a married daughter. She was one of
25 those old-fashioned powerful natures that couldn't do with
looks or education or any form of showing off. She fairly
hated the sound of correct English. She *thee'd* and *tha'd* her
prospective daughter-in-law, and said:

'I'm none as ormin' as I look, seest ta.'

30 Fanny did not think her prospective mother-in-law looked
at all orming, so the speech was unnecessary.

'I towd him mysen,' said Mrs Goodall, ''Er's held back all
this long, let 'er stop as 'er is. 'E'd none ha' had thee for *my*
tellin' – tha hears. No, 'e's a fool, an' I know it. I says to him,
35 "Tha looks a man, doesn't ter, at thy age, goin' an' openin' to
her when ter hears her scrat' at th' gate, after she's done gallivantin' round wherever she'd a mind. That looks rare an'
soft." But it's no use o' any talking: he answered that letter o'
thine and made his own bad bargain.'

40   But in spite of the old woman's anger, she was also flattered at Fanny's coming back to Harry. For Mrs Goodall was impressed by Fanny – a woman of her own match. And more than this, everybody knew that Fanny's Aunt Kate had left her two hundred pounds: this apart from the girl's savings.

45   So there was high tea in Princes Street when Harry came home black from work, and a rather acrid odour of cordiality, the vixen Jinny darting in to say vulgar things. Of course Jinny lived in a house whose garden end joined the paternal garden. They were a clan who stuck together, these Goodalls.

50   It was arranged that Fanny should come to tea again on the Sunday, and the wedding was discussed. It should take place in a fortnight's time at Morley Chapel. Morley was a hamlet on the edge of the real country, and in its little Congregational Chapel Fanny and Harry had first met.

55   What a creature of habit he was! He was still in the choir of Morley Chapel – not very regular. He belonged just because he had a tenor voice, and enjoyed singing. Indeed his solos were only spoilt to local fame because when he sang he handled his aitches so hopelessly.

60   'And I saw 'eaven hopened
     And be'old, a wite 'orse –'

This was one of Harry's classics, only surpassed by the fine outburst of his heaving:

'Hangels – hever bright an' fair –'

65   It was a pity, but it was inalterable. He had a good voice, and he sang with a certain lacerating fire, but his pronunciation made it all funny. And *nothing* could alter him.

So he was never heard save at cheap concerts and in the little, poorer chapels. The others scoffed.

70   Now the month was September, and Sunday was Harvest Festival at Morley Chapel, and Harry was singing solos. So that Fanny was to go to afternoon service, and come home to a grand spread of Sunday tea with him. Poor Fanny! One of the most wonderful afternoons had been a Sunday afternoon

75   service, with her cousin Luther at her side, Harvest Festival in Morley Chapel. Harry had sung solos then – ten years ago. She remembered his pale blue tie, and the purple asters and the great vegetable marrows in which he was framed, and her cousin Luther at her side, young, clever, come down from

80   London, where he was getting on well, learning his Latin and his French and German so brilliantly.

However, once again it was Harvest Festival at Morley
Chapel, and once again, as ten years before, a soft, exquisite
September day, with the last roses pink in the cottage gardens,
the last dahlias crimson, the last sunflowers yellow. And
85 again the little old chapel was a bower, with its famous
sheaves of corn and corn-plaited pillars, its great bunches of
grapes, dangling like tassels from the pulpit corners, its
marrows and potatoes and pears and apples and damsons, its
purple asters and yellow Japanese sunflowers. Just as before,
90 the red dahlias round the pillars were dropping, weak-headed
among the oats. The place was crowded and hot, the plates of
tomatoes seemed balanced perilously on the gallery front, the
Rev. Enderby was weirder than ever to look at, so long and
emaciated and hairless.
95 The Rev. Enderby, probably forewarned, came and shook
hands with her and welcomed her, in his broad northern,
melancholy singsong before he mounted the pulpit. Fanny
was handsome in a gauzy dress and a beautiful lace hat. Being
a little late, she sat in a chair in the side-aisle wedged in, right
100 in front of the chapel. Harry was in the gallery above, and she
could only see him from the eyes upwards. She noticed again
how his eyebrows met, blond and not very marked, over his
nose. He was attractive too: physically lovable, very. If only –
if only her *pride* had not suffered! She felt he dragged her
105 down.

'Come, ye thankful people come,
Raise the song of harvest-home.
All is safely gathered in
Ere the winter storms begin –'

110 Even the hymn was a falsehood, as the season had been
wet, and half the crops were still out, and in a poor way.

Notes

4 **presumably**   The point of the adverb is to draw attention to the
unelaborated nature of Harry Goodall's speech. He relies heavily
upon his interlocutor's familiarity with the circumstances and with
expected etiquette.

12–13 **I can do with him** 'get on with, tolerate'   The expression
meaning 'to be concerned with' goes back to the thirteenth century,
but the modern colloquial sense is first recorded by Jane Austen in
1815.

21 **his people**   Although the use of this phrase to refer to someone's
family is recorded from the fourteenth-century, the *OED* (3c)

remarks that it is especially prevalent as a university and public-school colloquialism. Perhaps the phrase represents usage from Fanny's years of service in Gloucester.

26–27 **fairly hated** The context confirms that *fairly* is here an intensifier. Although this use is now colloquial, and more common in the North, it is recorded more widely in the sixteenth and seventeenth centuries.

27 **thee'd** The *th-* forms of the second-person pronoun are used in familiar and in scornful address in dialects from the counties of Yorkshire, Derbyshire and Cheshire northward, where forms of *thou* are used in subject position. Western Nottinghamshire shares this feature. *Th-* forms with *thee* as subject occur in the south-west Midlands and the West Country.

29 **ormin'** 'awkward' and perhaps 'foolish' Recorded only from Nottinghamshire by *EDD*. A significant contrast is made with Fanny's correction of the form to *orming*.

seest ta The second-person singular inflexion *-st*, rather than *-s*, belongs to the very west of Nottinghamshire and to much of Derbyshire but varies with the *-s* form, which is normal further north.

32 **'er** This subject form of the feminine personal pronoun is not recorded for Nottinghamshire in the *Linguistic Atlas of England* but is found in Derbyshire.

33 **'E'd none** This form of negative is recorded for western Derbyshire and north Staffordshire but no longer in Nottinghamshire at the time of the Survey of English Dialects.

36 **scrat** 'scratch' The verb is not a form of *scratch*, however, but a distinct verb-form recorded from the thirteenth century. Both OF *egrater* and OSw *kratta* have been cited as parallels, but the etymology is uncertain.

36–37 **done gallivantin'** The verb is recorded from 1819 with the sense 'flirting indiscreetly', and may be a humorous development from *gallant*.

51 **It should take place** The more usual choice of auxiliary in this environment is *would*. *Should* here implies inevitability, a significance which goes back to OE but which had been re-established by seventeenth-century grammarians and handed down in the school tradition.

61 **wite** The comic spelling serves to emphasise the lack of aspiration in Harry's pronunciation, which corresponds with his handling 'his aitches so hopelessly'.

Translation of the Bible into English was first attempted in the Old English period, when Ælfric and those associated with him produced a version of the Pentateuch. During the tenth century also, the four Gospels were translated into West Saxon, and in the next century the Psalter was rendered, partly into prose, and partly into verse. Despite King Alfred's apparent interest in the project (see Excerpt 2), no translation of the complete Bible was made. The diminished status of English after the Conquest discouraged further attempts at translation until two versions of the Bible were produced by the Wycliffite reformers in the late fourteenth century. The version reproduced here is the earlier, and more literal, of the two, perhaps prepared as an exercise to facilitate the production of the later. The translator of the next excerpt, William Tyndale, was executed for his religious opinions in 1536. He had been forced by opposition at home to commence publication of his work in Cologne, but may nevertheless be considered the father of the Modern English Bible. The Authorised Version of the Bible, which was produced with official approval by a committee of scholars, owes much to Tyndale and his successors both in its phrasing and in the conscious archaism of some of its forms (e.g. its use of the subject form *ye*, the personal relative *which*, and its almost total avoidance of the genitive pronoun form *its*).

The passages which follow have been selected to give a general outline of developments in a thousand years of English linguistic history. Changes in the language can most readily be recognised if the subject matter dealt with remains constant. However, exact parallelism in the content of these passages is subject to some disruption, both from the source material of the translations, and from the differing intentions of the translators. The Old English and Wycliffite versions were based upon the text of the Latin Vulgate, whereas Tyndale and later scholars consulted Greek and also Hebrew sources. Moreover, earlier translators revered the exact wording of their sources, whereas later translators are more concerned with making accessible to a contemporary audience the full significance of the text before them. In this respect, the New English Bible is a freer rendering than earlier ones, and does not necessarily match them word for word.

In the following passages, punctuation has been modernised in all the versions prior to that of 1611, and in the Old English passages the spelling has been regularised to conform to an Early West Saxon norm. General guidance on the periods of linguistic history represented by the passages may be found in the introductions to the main period sections.

A Mark 6: 18–30

Old English (c. 1000)

18 Ðā sǣde Iohannes Herode: 'Nis þē alȳfed tō hæbenne þīnes brōðer wīf.'

19 Ðā syrwde Herodias ymbe hine, and wolde hine ofslēan, and hēo ne mihte.

20 Sōðlice Herodes ondrǣd Iohannem, and wiste þæt hē wæs rihtwīs and hālig, and hē hēold hine on cwerterne. And hē gehīerde þæt hē fela wundra worhte, and hē lufelice him hīerde.

21 Þā se dæg cōm Herodes gebyrdtīde, hē gegearwode micele feorme his ealdormannum, and þǣm fyrmestum on Galilea.

22 And þā ðā þǣre Herodiadiscan dohtor inn-ēode and tumbode; hit līcode Herode and eallum þǣm ðe him mid sǣton. Se cyning cwæð þā tō ðǣm mǣgdene: 'Bidde mē swā hwæt swā þū wille, and ic þē selle';

23 And hē swōr hire, 'Sōðes ic þē selle swā hwæt swā þū mē bitst, þēah þū wille healf mīn rīce.'

24 Ðā hēo ūt-ēode, hēo cwæð tō hire mēder, 'Hwæs bidde ic?' Þā cwæþ hēo, 'Iohannes hēafod þæs fulluhteres.'

25 Sōna þā hēo mid ofste inn tō þǣm cyninge ēode; hēo bæd and þus cwæð: 'Ic wille þæt ðū mē hrædlīce on ānum disce selle Iohannes hēafod.'

26 Þā wearð se cyning geunrēt for þǣm āðc, and forþǣm ðe him mid sǣton nolde þēah hīe geunrētan,

27 Ac sende ānne cwellere, and bebēad þæt man his hēafod on ānum disce brōhte. And hē hine þā on cwerterne behēafdode,

28 And his hēafod on disce brōhte, and hit sealde þǣm mǣgdene, and þæt mǣgden hit sealde hire mēder.

29 Ða his cnihtas þæt gehīerdon, hīe cōmon, and his līchaman nāmon, and hine on byrgene legdon.

30 Sōðlice þā ðā apostolas tōgædere cōmon, hīe cȳddon þǣm Hǣlende eall þæt hīe didon and hīe lǣrdon.

Wycliffite (c. 1375)

18 Sothly Johne seide to Eroude, 'It is not leefful to thee, for to haue the wyf of thi brother.'

19 Erodias forsothe leide aspies to him, and wolde sle him, and miȝte not.

20 Sothly Eroude drede John, witinge him a iust man and hooly, and kepte him. And him herd, he dide many thingis, and gladly herde hym.

21 And whanne a couenable day hadde fallun, Eroude in his birthe day made soupere to the princis and tribunys and to the firste of Galilee.

22 And whanne the douȝter of thilke Erodias hadde entride yn, and lepte, and pleside to Eroude, and also to men restynge, the kyng seide to the wenche, 'Axe thou of me what thou wolt, and I schal ȝyue to thee';

23 And he swoor to hir: 'For what euere thou schalt axe, I schal ȝyue to thee, thouȝ the half of my kyngdom.'

24 The whiche, whanne sche hadde gon out, seide to hir modir, 'What schal I axe?' And sche seide, 'The heed of John Baptist.'

25 And whanne sche hadde entrid anon with haste to the kyng, she axide, seyinge, 'I wole that anoon thou ȝyue to me in a dische the heed of John Baptist.'

26 And the kyng was sory for the ooth, and for men sittinge to gidere at mete he wolde not hir be maad sory;

27 But a manquellere sent, he comaundide the heed of John Baptist for to be brouȝt. And he bihedide him in the prison,

28 And brouȝte his heed in a dische, and ȝaf it to the wenche, and the wench ȝaf to hir modir.

29 The which thing herd, his disciplis camen, and token his body, and puttiden it in a buriel.

30 And apostlis comynge to gidere to Jhesu, tolden to hym alle thingis that thei hadden don and tauȝt.

Tyndale (1525)

18 Jhon said vnto Herode, 'It is not laufull for the, to have thy brothers wyfe.'

19 Herodias layd waite for him, and wolde have killed him, butt she coulde not;

20 For Herode feared Jhon, knowynge that he was iuste and holy, and gave him reverence. And when he herde him, he did many thinges, and herde him gladly.

21 And when a convenyent daye was come, Herode on hys

birth daye made a supper to the lordes, captayns, and chefe estates of Galile.

22 And the doughter of the same Herodias cam in, and daunsed, and pleased Herode and them that sate att bourde also. Then the kinge sayd vnto the mayden: 'Axe of me what thou wilt, and I will geve it the';

23 And he sware vnto her, 'What soever thou shalt axe of me, I will geve it the, even vnto the one halfe of my kyngdom.'

24 And she went forth, and sayde to her mother, 'What shall I axe?' And she sayde: 'Jhon Baptistes heed.'

25 And she cam in streigth waye with haste vnto the kinge and axed, sayinge: 'I wyll that thou geve me by and by in a charger the heed of Jhon Baptist.'

26 And the kinge was sorye, yet for hys othes sake, and for their sakes which sate att supper also, he wolde not put her besyde her purpost;

27 And immediatly the kynge sent the hangman, and commaunded his heed to be brought in. And he went and beheeded him in the preson,

28 And brought his heedde in a charger, and gave it to the mayden, and the mayden gave it to her mother.

29 When his disciples herde of it, they cam and toke vppe his body, and put it in a toumbe.

30 And the apostles gaddered them selves to geddre to Jesus, and tolde him all thynges, booth what they had done and what they had taught.

The Authorised Version (1611)

18 For John had said unto Herod, 'It is not lawful for thee to have thy brother's wife.'

19 Therefore Herodias had a quarrel against him, and would have killed him; but she could not.

20 For Herod feared John, knowing that he was a just man and an holy, and observed him; and when he heard him, he did many things, and heard him gladly.

21 And when a convenient day was come, that Herod on his birthday made a supper to his lords, high captains, and chief estates of Galilee;

22 And when the daughter of the said Herodias came in, and danced, and pleased Herod and them that sat with him, the king said unto the damsel, 'Ask of me whatsoever thou wilt, and I will give it thee.'

23 And he sware unto her, 'Whatsoever thou shalt ask of me, I will give it thee, unto the half of my kingdom.'

24 And she went forth, and said unto her mother, 'What shall I ask?' And she said, 'The head of John the Baptist.'

25 And she came in straightway with haste unto the king, and asked, saying, 'I will that thou give me by and by in a charger the head of John the Baptist.'

26 And the king was exceeding sorry; yet for his oath's sake, and for their sakes which sat with him, he would not reject her.

27 And immediately the king sent an executioner, and commanded his head to be brought: and he went and beheaded him in the prison,

28 And brought his head in a charger, and gave it to the damsel: and the damsel gave it to her mother.

29 And when his disciples heard of it, they came and took up his corpse, and laid it in a tomb.

30 And the apostles gathered themselves together unto Jesus, and told him all things, both what they had done, and what they had taught.

The New English Bible (1961)

18 John had told Herod, 'You have no right to your brother's wife.'

19 Thus Herodias nursed a grudge against him and would willingly have killed him, but she could not;

20 For Herod went in awe of John, knowing him to be a good and holy man; so he kept him in custody. He liked to listen to him, although the listening left him greatly perplexed.

21 Herodias found her opportunity when Herod on his birthday gave a banquet to his chief officials and commanders and the leading men of Galilee.

22 Her daughter came in and danced, and so delighted Herod and his guests that the king said to the girl, 'Ask what you like and I will give it you.'

23 And he swore an oath to her: 'Whatever you ask I will give you, up to half my kingdom.'

24 She went out and said to her mother, 'What shall I ask for?' She replied, 'The head of John the Baptist.'

25 The girl hastened back at once to the king with her request: 'I want you to give me here and now, on a dish, the head of John the Baptist.'

26 The king was greatly distressed, but out of regard for his oath and for his guests he could not bring himself to refuse her.

27 So the king sent a soldier of the guard with orders to bring John's head. The soldier went off and beheaded him in the prison,

28 Brought the head on a dish, and gave it to the girl; and she gave it to her mother.

29 When John's disciples heard the news, they came and took his body away and laid it in a tomb.

30 The apostles now rejoined Jesus and reported to him all that they had done and taught.

B Matthew 7:13–29

Old English (c. 1000)

13 Gangað inn þurh þæt nearwe geat; forþon þe þæt geat is swīþe wīd, and se weg is swīþe rūm þe to forspillednesse gelæt, and swīþe manega sind þe þurh þone weg farað.

14 Ēalā hū nearu and hū angsum is þæt geat, and se weg þe tō līfe gelæt, and swīþe feawa sind þe þone weg finden.

15 Warniað ēow fram lēasum wītegum, þā cumað tō ēow on scēapa gegyrelum, ac hīe bēoð innane rēafigende wulfas.

16 Fram hiera wæstmum gē hīe undergietað. Cwist þū gaderað man wīn-berian of þornum, oððe fic-æppla of þyrncinum?

17 Swā ælc gōd trēow byrþ gōde wæstmas; and ælc yfel trēow byrþ yfele wæstmas.

18 Ne mæg þæt gōde trēow beran yfle wæstmas, ne þæt yfele trēow gōde wæstmas.

19 Ælc trēow þe ne byrð gōdne wæstm, sīe hit forcorfen, and on fȳr āworpen.

20 Witodlīce be hiera wæstmum gē hīe oncnāwað.

21 Ne gæð ælc þāra on heofena rīce, þe cwyþ tō mē, 'Drihten, Drihten'; ac sē þe wyrcð mīnes fæder willan þe on heofenum is, sē gæð on heofena rīce.

22 Manega cweþað on þæm dæge tō mē, 'Drihten, Drihten, hū ne wītegode wē on þīnum naman, and on þīnum naman wē ūt āwurpon dēoflu, and on þīnum naman wē worhton micle mihta?'

23 Þonne cwæðe ic tō him, Þæt 'ic ēow næfre ne cūðe; gewītað fram mē, gē þe worhton unrihtwīsnesse.'

24 Eornustlīce ælc þāra þe ðās mīne word gehīerð, and þā

wyrcð, bið gelīc þǣm wīsan were, sē his hūs ofer stān getimbrode.

25 Þa cōm þǣr regn and micele flōd, and þǣr blēowon windas, and āhruron on þæt hūs, and hit nā ne fēoll; sōðlice hit wæs ofer stān getimbrod.

26 And ǣlc þāra þe gehīerþ ðās mīne word, and þā ne wyrcð, sē biþ gelīc þǣm dysigan men þe getimbrode his hus* ofer sand-ceosel.

27 Þā rīnde hit, and þǣr cōmon flōd, and blēowon windas, and āhruron on þæt hūs, and þæt hūs fēoll; and his hryre wæs micel.

28 Þā wæs geworden, þā se Hælend þās word geendode, þā wundrode þæt folc his lāre.

29 Sōþlice hē lærde, swilcc hē anweald hæfde, and nā swā swā hiera bōceras and sundor-hālgan.

Wycliffite (c. 1375)

13 Entre ȝe bi the streyt ȝate; for the gate that ledith to perdicioun is brode, and the weye large, and ther ben many that entren bi it.

14 How streit is the ȝate, and narewe the weye, that ledith to lijf, and there ben fewe that fynden it.

15 Perceyue ȝe, and flee fro fals prophetis, the whiche cummen to ȝou in clothingis of sheepis, bot wythynne thei ben rauyshynge wolues.

16 Of her fruytis ȝe shulen knowe hem. Whether men gaderen grapis of thornys, or fijgis of breeris?

17 So euery good tree makith good fruytis; sothely an yuel tree makith yuel fruytis.

18 A good tree may nat make yuel fruytis, nether an yuel tree make good fruytis.

19 Euery tree that makith nat good fruyt, shal be kitte doun, and shal be sent in to the fire.

20 Therfore of her fruytis ȝee shulen knowe hem.

21 Nat eche man that saith to me, 'Lord, Lord', shal entre into the kyngdam of heuenes; but he that doth the wille of my fadir that is in heuenes, he shal entre in to the kyngdam of heuenes.

22 Many shul say to me in that day, 'Lord, Lord, whether we han nat prophecied in thi name, and han cast out deuelis in thi name, and han don many vertues in thi name?'

23 And than Y shal knowliche to hem, 'For I knew ȝou neuer, departe awey fro me, ȝe that worchen wickidnesse.'

24   Therfore eche man that herith these my wordis, and doth hem, shal be maad liche to a wijse man, that hath bildid his hous vpon a stoon.

25   And rayn came doun, and flodis camen, and wyndis blewen, and rusheden in to that hous; and it felle nat doun, for it was foundid on a stoon.

26   And euery man that herith these my wordis, and doth hem nat, is liche to a man fool, that hath bildid his hous on grauel.

27   And rayn came doun, and floodis camen, and wyndis blewen, and thei hurliden in to that hous; and it felle doun, and the fallyng doun therof was grete.

28   And it is maad, when Jhesus hadde eendid these wordis, the cumpanyes wondreden on his techyng;

29   Sothely he was techynge hem, as a man hauynge power, and nat as the scribis of hem and Pharisees.

Tyndale (1525)

13   Enter in at the strayte gate; ffor wyde is the gate, and broade ys the waye thatt leadeth to destruccion, and many there be which goo yn there att.

14   For strayte ys the gate, and narowe is the waye, that leadeth vnto lyfe, and feawe there be that fynde it.

15   Beware off falce prophettes, whiche come to you in shepes clothynge, but inwardly they are ravenynge wolves.

16   Ye shall knowe them by their frutes. Do men gaddre grapes off thornes, or figges of bryres?

17   Even soo evry good tree bryngethe forthe good frute; butt a corrupte tree bryngethe forthe evyll frute.

18   A good tree cannott brynge forthe bad frute, nor yett a bad tree can brynge forthe good frute.

19   Every tree that bryngethe not forthe good frute, shalbe hewne doune, and cast into the fyre.

20   Wherfore by there frutes ye shall knowe them.

21   Not all they thatt say vnto me, 'Master, Master', shall enter into the kyngdome off heven; but he that fulfilleth my fathers will which ys in heven.

22   Many will saye to me yn that daye, 'Master, Master, have we nott in thy name prophesied, and in thy name have we not cast oute devyls, and in thy name have we nott done many miracles?'

23   And then will I knowlege vnto them, That I never knewe them; 'depart from me, ye workers of iniquite'.

24   Whosoever hearethe off me these saynges, and doethe the same, I wyll lyken hyme vnto a wyseman, which byllt his housse on a rocke.

25   And aboundance off rayne descended, and the fluddes cam, and the wynddes blewe, and bett vppon that same housse; and it was not over throwen, because it was grounded on the rocke.

26   And whosoever heareth of me these sainges, and doth not the same, shalbe lykened vnto a folysh man, which bilt his housse apon the sonde.

27   And abundaunce of rayne descended, and the fluddes cam, and the wynddes blewe, and beet vppon that housse; and it was over throwen, and great was the fall off it.

28   And it cam to passe, that when Jesus had ended these saynges, the peple were astonnied at his doctryne;

29   For he taught them, as one havynge power, and not as the scribes.

The Authorised Version (1611)

13   Enter ye in at the strait gate: for wide is the gate, and broad is the way, that leadeth to destruction, and many there be which go in thereat:

14   Because strait is the gate, and narrow is the way, which leadeth unto life, and few there be that find it.

15   Beware of false prophets, which come to you in sheep's clothing, but inwardly they are ravening wolves.

16   Ye shall know them by their fruits. Do men gather grapes of thorns, or figs of thistles?

17   Even so every good tree bringeth forth good fruit; but a corrupt tree bringeth forth evil fruit.

18   A good tree cannot bring forth evil fruit, neither can a corrupt tree bring forth good fruit.

19   Every tree that bringeth not forth good fruit is hewn down, and cast into the fire.

20   Wherefore by their fruits ye shall know them.

21   Not every one that saith unto me, Lord, Lord, shall enter into the kingdom of heaven; but he that doeth the will of my Father which is in heaven.

22   Many will say to me in that day, Lord, Lord, have we not prophesied in thy name? and in thy name have cast out devils? and in thy name done many wonderful works?

23   And then will I profess unto them, I never knew you: depart from me, ye that work iniquity.

24 Therefore whosoever heareth these sayings of mine, and doeth them, I will liken him unto a wise man, which built his house upon a rock:

25 And the rain descended, and the floods came, and the winds blew, and beat upon that house; and it fell not: for it was founded upon a rock.

26 And every one that heareth these sayings of mine, and doeth them not, shall be likened unto a foolish man, which built his house upon the sand:

27 And the rain descended, and the floods came, and the winds blew, and beat upon that house; and it fell: and great was the fall of it.

28 And it came to pass, when Jesus had ended these sayings, the people were astonished at his doctrine:

29 For he taught them as one having authority, and not as the scribes.

The New English Bible (1961)

13 Enter by the narrow gate. The gate is wide that leads to perdition, there is plenty of room on the road, and many go that way;

14 But the gate that leads to life is small and the road is narrow, and those who find it are few.

15 'Beware of false prophets, men who come to you dressed up as sheep while underneath they are savage wolves.

16 You will recognize them by the fruits they bear. Can grapes be picked from from briars or figs from thistles?

17 In the same way, a good tree always yields good fruit, and a poor tree bad fruit.

18 A good tree cannot bear bad fruit, or a poor tree good fruit.

19 And when a tree does not yield good fruit it is cut down and burnt.

20 That is why I say you will recognize them by their fruits.

21 Not everyone who calls me "Lord, Lord" will enter the kingdom of Heaven, but only those who do the will of my heavenly Father.

22 When that day comes, many will say to me, "Lord, Lord, did we not prophesy in your name, cast out devils in your name, and in your name perform many miracles?"

23 Then I will tell them to their face, "I never knew you: out of my sight, you and your wicked ways!"

24 What then of the man who hears these words of mine

and acts upon them? He is like a man who had the sense to build his house on rock.

25   The rain came down, the floods rose, the wind blew, and beat upon that house; but it did not fall, because its foundations were upon rock.

26   But what of the man who hears these words of mine and does not act upon them? He is like a man who was foolish enough to build his house on sand.

27   The rain came down, the floods rose, the wind blew, and beat upon that house; down it fell with a great crash.'

28   When Jesus had finished his discourse the people were astounded at his teaching;

29   Unlike their own teachers he taught with a note of authority.

References and background reading

General

Baugh, A.C. and Thomas Cable, *A History of the English Language*, 3rd edn (London: RKP, 1978).

Blake, N.F., *Non-standard Language in English Literature* (London: Deutsch, 1981).

Fisiak, J., *A Bibliography of Writings for the History of the English Language* (Berlin: Mouton de Gruyter, 1987).

Jones, Charles, *A History of English Phonology* (London: Longman, 1989).

Jones, Richard Foster, *The Triumph of the English Language* (Stanford: Stanford UP, 1953).

Marchand, Hans, *The Categories and Types of Present-Day English Word-Formation*, 2nd edn (Munich: Beck, 1969).

The Oxford English Dictionary, 2nd edn, prepared by J.A. Simpson and E.S.C. Weiner (Oxford: Clarendon, 1989).

Partridge, A.C., *English Biblical Translation* (London: Deutsch, 1973).

Prins, A.A., *A History of English Phonemes* (Leiden: Leiden UP, 1972).

Quirk, Randolph, Sidney Greenbaum, Geoffrey Leech and Jan Svartvik, *A Comprehensive Grammar of the English Language* (London: Longman, 1985).

Samuels, M.L., *Linguistic Evolution with Special Reference to English* (Cambridge: CUP, 1972).

Strang, Barbara M.H., *A History of English* (London: Methuen, 1970).

Tajima, Matsuji, *Old and Middle English Language Studies. A Classified Bibliography 1923–1985* (Amsterdam/Philadelphia: Benjamins, 1988).

Visser, F.Th., *An Historical Syntax of the English Language*, 3 vols (Leiden: Brill, 1970–73).

Wyld, H.C., *A History of Modern Colloquial English* (Oxford: Blackwell, 1936).

Old English

Bright, James Wilson (ed.), *The Gospel of St Mark in West Saxon* (Boston and London: Heath, 1905).

Campbell, A., *Old English Grammar* (Oxford: Clarendon, 1969).

    (ed.) *The Battle of Brunanburh* (London: Heinemann, 1938).

Fowler, David C., *The Bible in Early English Literature* (Seattle and London: University of Washington, 1976).

Gneuss, Helmut, 'The origin of Standard Old English and Æthelwold's school at Winchester' *ASE* 1 (1972), 63–83.

Hall, J.R.C., *A Concise Anglo-Saxon Dictionary*, 4th edn with a Supplement by Herbert Dean Meritt (Cambridge: CUP, 1960).

Kemble, John M. and Charles Hardwick (eds), *The Gospel According to St Matthew in Anglo-Saxon and Northumbrian Versions* (Cambridge: CUP, 1858).

Henel, Heinrich (ed.), *Ælfric's De Temporibus Anni*, EETS OS 213 (London, 1942).

Hurt, James, *Ælfric* (New York: Twayne, 1972).

Ker, N.R. (ed.), *The Pastoral Care*, Early English Manuscripts in Facsimile 6 (Copenhagen: Rosenkilde and Bagger, 1956).

Kuhn, Sherman M. (ed.), *The Vespasian Psalter* (Ann Arbor: University of Michigan, 1965).

Morrell, Minnie Cate, *A Manual of Old English Biblical Materials* (Knoxville: University of Tennessee, 1965).

Oman, C.W.C., *The Art of War in the Middle Ages* (Ithaca and NY: Cornell, 1953).

Salmon, Vivian, 'Some Connotations of Cold in Old and Middle English' *MLN* 74 (1968), 314–22.

Skeat, W.W. (ed.), *The Gospel According to St Mark in Anglo-Saxon and Northumbrian Versions* (Cambridge: CUP, 1871).

Venezky, Richard Lawrence and Antonette diPaolo Healey, *A Microfiche Concordance to Old English* (Toronto: University of Toronto, 1980).

Wright, David H., *The Vespasian Psalter*, Early English Manuscripts in Facsimile 14 (Copenhagen: Rosenkilde and Bagger, 1967).

Middle English

Ancrene Wisse, Parts 6 and 7, edited by Geoffrey Shepherd (London: Nelson, 1959).

Burnley, David, *The Language of Chaucer* (London: Macmillan, 1989).

Dobson, E.J., *The Origins of the Ancrene Wisse* (Oxford: Clarendon, 1976).

Elliott, R.W.V., *Chaucer's English* (London: Deutsch, 1974).

Forshall, Josiah and Frederic Madden (eds), *The Holy Bible containing the Old and New Testaments with the Apocryphal Books . . . by John Wycliffe and his Followers*, 4 vols (Oxford: Clarendon, 1850).

Hellinga, Lotte. 'The Malory Manuscript and Caxton' in Toshiyuki Takamiya and Derek Brewer (eds), *Aspects of Malory* (Cambridge: Brewer, 1981), 127–41.

Horstmann, Carl, 'Mappula Angliae, von Osbern Bokenham', *Englische Studien* 10 (1887), 1–34.

Jordan, Richard, *Handbook of Middle English Grammar: Phonology*, translated and revised by Eugene J. Crook (The Hague: Mouton, 1974).

Kuhn, Sherman M., 'The Preface to a Fifteenth-Century Concordance', *Speculum* 43 (1968), 258–73.

Kurath, Hans, Sherman M. Kuhn, Robert E. Lewis *et al.*, *Middle English Dictionary* (Ann Arbor: University of Michigan, 1954, in progress).

Kyng Alisaunder, edited by G.V. Smithers, 2 vols, EETS OS 227 and 237 (1952 and 1957).

McIntosh, Angus, M.L. Samuels and Michael Benskin, *A Linguistic Atlas of Late Mediaeval English*, 4 vols (Aberdeen University Press, 1986).

McIntosh, Angus, 'Some Linguistic Reflections of a Wycliffite' in Jess B. Bessinger, Jr and Robert P. Creed (eds), *Medieval and Linguistic Studies in Honor of Francis Peabody Magoun, Jr* (London: Allen and Unwin, 1965), 290–93.

Mustanoja, T.F., *Middle English Syntax* (Helsinki, 1960).

Parkes, M.B., 'On the Presumed Date of the Manuscript of the *Orrmulum*: Oxford, Bodleian Library, MS Junius I' in *Five Hundred Years of Words and Sounds: A Festschrift for Eric Dobson*, edited by E.G. Stanley and Douglas Gray (Cambridge: Brewer, 1983), 115–27.

Paston Letters and Papers of the Fifteenth Century, edited by Norman Davis, 2 vols (Oxford: Clarendon, 1971; 1976).

Pearl, edited by E.V. Gordon (Oxford: Clarendon, 1953).

Polychronicon Ranulphi Higden Monachi Cestrensis, edited by Churchill Babington and J.R. Lumby, 9 vols, HMSO Rolls Series (London: Longman, 1865–86).

Price, Derek, *The Equatorie of the Planetis* (Cambridge: CUP, 1955).

Shaw, Sally, 'Caxton and Malory' in J.A.W. Bennett (ed.), *Essays on Malory* (Oxford: Clarendon, 1963), 114–45.

The Bibliotheca Historica of Diodorus Siculus, translated by John Skelton, edited by F.M. Salter and H.L.R. Edwards, EETS OS 233 (1956).

The Early South-English Legendary, edited by Carl Horstmann, EETS OS 87 (1887).

The Ormulum, edited by R.M. White and Robert Holt, 2 vols (Oxford: Clarendon, 1878).

The Peterborough Chronicle 1070–1154, edited by Cecily Clark, 2nd edn (Oxford: Clarendon, 1970).

The Story of England by Robert Mannyng of Brunne, edited by Frederick J. Furnivall, 2 vols, HMSO Rolls Series (1887).

The Works of Sir Thomas Malory, edited by Eugène Vinaver, 2nd edn, 3 vols (Oxford: Clarendon, 1967).

Turville-Petre, Thorlac, 'Politics and Poetry in the Early Fourteenth Century: The Case of Robert Manning's *Chronicle*', *RES* 39 (1988), 1–28.

Vices and Virtues, edited by F. Holthausen, 2 parts, EETS OS 89, 159 (1888, 1921).

Early Modern English

Abbot, E.A., *A Shakespearian Grammar* (London: Macmillan, 1870).

Bald, R.C., *John Donne: A Life* (Oxford: Clarendon, 1970).

Bruce, John (ed.), *Letters of Queen Elizabeth and King James VI of Scotland* (London: Camden Society 46, 1849).

Butterworth, C.C., *The Literary Lineage of the King James Bible 1340–1611* (Philadelphia: University of Pennsylvania, 1941).

Corns, Thomas N., *Milton's Language* (Oxford: Blackwell, 1990).

Defoe, Daniel, *A Tour through England and Wales*, 2 vols (Dent: London, 1928).

Dobson, E.J., *English Pronunciation 1500–1700*, 2 vols, 2nd edn (Oxford: Clarendon, 1968).

Donne, John, *The Elegies and the Songs and Sonnets*, edited by Helen Gardner (Oxford: Clarendon, 1965).

Emma, Ronald David, *Milton's Grammar* (The Hague: Mouton, 1964).

Hulme, Hilda M., *Explorations in Shakespeare's Language* (London: Longman, 1962).

Hunter, G.K., *John Lyly: the Humanist as Courtier* (London: RKP, 1962).

Hussey, S.S., *The Literary Language of Shakespeare* (London: Longman, 1982).

Hutson, Lorna, *Thomas Nashe in Context* (Oxford: Clarendon, 1989).

Lewis, Thomas Taylor (ed.), *Letters of the Lady Brilliana Harley* (London: Camden Society 58, 1854).

Lloyd, Christopher, *Fanny Burney* (London: Longman, 1936).

Mack, Maynard, *Alexander Pope. A Life* (New Haven: Yale, 1985).

McKerrow, Ronald B. (ed.), *The Works of Thomas Nashe*, 5 vols (Bullen/Sidgwick and Jackson: London, 1904–10).

Nichols, John Gough (ed.), *The Diary of Henry Machyn* (London: Camden Society 42, 1858).

Richetti, John J., *Daniel Defoe* (Boston: Twayne, 1987).

Pendry, E.D. (ed.), *Thomas Dekker* (London: Arnold, 1967).

Pope, Alexander, *The Rape of the Lock*, edited by Geoffrey Tillotson (London: Methuen, 1940).

Puttenham, George, *The Arte of English Poesie*, edited by Gladys Doidge Willcock and Alice Walker (Cambridge: CUP, 1936).

Rudskoger, Arne, *Plain: A Study in Co-text and Context* (Stockholm: Almqvist and Wiksell, 1970).

Sledd, James H. and Gwin J. Kolb, *Dr Johnson's Dictionary* (Chicago: University of Chicago, 1955).

The Complete Works of John Lyly, edited by R. Warwick Bond, 3 vols (Oxford: Clarendon, 1902).

The Journals and Letters of Fanny Burney (Madame d'Arblay), edited by Joyce Hemslow with Curtis D. Cecil and Althea Douglas (Oxford: Clarendon, 1972), Vol I, 1791–2.

The Poetical Works of John Milton, edited by Helen Darbishire (London: OUP, 1958).

Wells, Stanley and Gary Taylor (eds), *William Shakespeare: The Complete Works. Original Spelling Edition* (Oxford: Clarendon, 1986).

Wilson, Thomas, *Arte of Rhetorique*, edited by Thomas J. Derrick (New York: Garland, 1982).

Modern English

Bridges, Robert, *The Collected Papers of Henry Bradley* (Oxford: Clarendon, 1928).

Brontë, Emily, *Wuthering Heights*, edited by Hilda Marsden and Ian Jack (Oxford: Clarendon, 1976).

Brook, G.L., *The Language of Charles Dickens* (London: Deutsch, 1970).

Carlyle, Thomas, *Works, The Standard Edition*, 18 vols (London: Chapman and Hall, 1839), Vol. 5: 'Critical and Miscellaneous Essays'.

Chitham, Edward, *A Life of Emily Brontë* (Oxford: Blackwell, 1987).

Darwin, Charles, *The Descent of Man and Selection in Relation to Sex*, 2 vols (London: Murray, 1871).

Dickens, Charles, *The Pickwick Papers*, edited by James Kingsley (Oxford: Clarendon, 1986).

Howard, Jonathan, *Darwin* (Oxford: OUP, 1982).

Petyt, K.M., *Emily Brontë and the Haworth Dialect* (Menston: Yorkshire Dialect Society, 1970).

Sagar, Keith (ed.), *A D.H. Lawrence Handbook* (Manchester: Manchester UP, 1982).

Sørensen, Knud S., 'Dickens on the Use of English', *ES* 70 (1989), 551–9.

Sweet, Henry, *The Practical Study of Languages* (London: Dent, 1899).

Tauber, Abraham (ed.), *George Bernard Shaw on Language* (London: Peter Owen, 1965).

Index

Phonetic, phonological and orthographic features

Anglian smoothing 8,10,15,87
aphesis 150,206,211,267,279,337
assimilation 235
back mutation 11,15
breaking, failure before *l*-groups
8,10,73,96,105,111,141
Great Vowel Shift 136,220,258,
278
h-dropping 210,300,354
i-mutation 8,12,15,53,73,86
i-mutation before a nasal 95,116,
131
loss of final -*e* 15,162,210
loss of final -*n* 12,65,89,131
ME open syllable lengthening 80
Mercian 'second fronting' 8,11
metathesis 253

OE lengthening groups 79–80,
110,113
reflexes of WS $\bar{æ}^1$ and $\bar{æ}^2$ 90,94,
107,110,131
reflexes of WS *ēo* 64,73,86,94,
104,107,117,142
reflexes of WS *y* 64,72,87,90,
96,104,107,116,117,161,211,259
rounding of OE /a:/ 65,87,90,
104,110,111,113,117,141,143,
150,160
variation between initial ‹v› and
‹w› 208,211
variation between ‹er› and ‹ar›
180,205,208,211,216,221,258,317
voicing of initial fricatives 65,
105,110,207

Morphological features

dual number 3,41,87,169

Noun plurals
endingless 76,86,87
in -*en* 65,98,104,110,116,131

Pronouns
adjective agreement 163
adjectives, comparatives and
superlatives 235,247,284
adjectives, double comparatives
and superlatives 189,299
indefinite pronoun 24,61,96,
169

personal pronouns
he 110,122
I, me 16,105,122,283
it(s) 149,162,200,253
she 64,87,96,122,137,150
they, their 11,15,64,66,87,96,
104,131,135,141,149,218,267,
299
you/ye/your 200,228,243,247,267
reflexive pronouns 141
relatives, personal and
non-personal 61,136,175,194,
200,211,235,300

371

Word-Formation

Syntax

Style and Discourse